Plato

Plato's Best Thoughts

Compiled from Prof. Jowett's Translation of the Dialogues of Plato

Plato

Plato's Best Thoughts
Compiled from Prof. Jowett's Translation of the Dialogues of Plato

ISBN/EAN: 9783337189488

Printed in Europe, USA, Canada, Australia, Japan

Cover: Foto ©Thomas Meinert / pixelio.de

More available books at **www.hansebooks.com**

PLATO'S BEST THOUGHTS

COMPILED FROM

PROF. JOWETT'S TRANSLATION

OF THE

DIALOGUES OF PLATO

BY

REV. C. H. A. BULKLEY, A.M.
PROFESSOR IN FAITH TRAINING COLLEGE, BOSTON, MASS.

NEW YORK
SCRIBNER, ARMSTRONG, AND COMPANY
1876

To

PROFESSOR JOWETT,

WHOSE SCHOLARSHIP IS UNEXCELLED IN EITHER HEMISPHERE,

AND WHO PREEMINENTLY MERITS

THE TITLE OF

"PLATO'S INTERPRETER,"

This Volume,

THE GATHERED FRUIT OF HIS TOIL,

IS RESPECTFULLY

DEDICATED.

RALPH WALDO EMERSON, in his Essay on Books, writes thus: "Of Plato I hesitate to speak, lest there should be no end. You find in him that which you have already found in Homer, now ripened to thought,— the poet converted to a philosopher, with loftier strains of musical wisdom than Homer reached; as if Homer were the youth, and Plato the finished man; yet with no less security of bold and perfect song, when he cares to use it, and with some harp-strings fetched from a higher heaven. He contains the future, as he came out of the past. In Plato, you explore modern Europe in its causes and seed,— all that in thought which the history of Europe embodies or has yet to embody. The well-informed man finds himself anticipated,— Plato is up with him too. Nothing has escaped him. Every new crop in the fertile harvest of reform, every fresh suggestion of modern humanity is there. If the student wish to see both sides, and justice done to the man of the world, pitiless exposure of pedants, and the supremacy of truth and the religious sentiment, he shall be contented also. Why should not young men be educated on this book? It would suffice for the tuition of the race, — to test their understanding and to express their reason. Here is that which is so attractive to all men, — the literature of aristocracy shall I call it?— the picture of the best persons, sentiments, and manners, by the first master, in the best times,— portraits of Pericles, Alcibiades, Crito, Prodicus, Protagoras, Anaxagoras, and Socrates, with the lovely background of the Athenian and suburban landscape, — or, who can overestimate the images with which Plato has enriched the minds of men, and which pass like bullion in the currency of all Nations? Read the 'Phædo,' the 'Protagoras,' the 'Phædrus,' the 'Timæus,' the Republic, — and the 'Apology of Socrates.'"

INTRODUCTION.

BY THE COMPILER.

THE late Dr. Nott, who, for so many years, was the efficient President of Union College, is said to have remarked that, " a professional man — especially a clergyman — needed to be familiar with but three books, namely the Bible, Bûtler's Analogy, and Shakespeare." To complete the circle, he might have added Plato. With his dialectic skill, universality of thought, subtle philosophy and purity of style, every scholar and thinker should familiarize himself. Their influence on all one's mental processes cannot fail to be stimulating and strengthening.

Few readers of the Greek, however, in this land, are sufficiently versed in that language to read Plato's original with much freedom and pleasure. Fewer professional men, in our age of active toil, have the time and opportunity even, to peruse throughout, the admirable translation of Prof. Jowett. Nevertheless, every thoughtful man — and even ordinary readers — may desire to reap the benefits of such a work, and become somewhat acquainted with the best thoughts of the great Greek Philosopher. The present volume has been undertaken with this design. It presents, in the most accessible form, the wide range of subjects upon which Plato dwells, and exhibits him in all his varied aspects of philosopher, moralist, socialist, logician, rhetorician, scientist, and critic. The extracts here given have been carefully collated, so as to be unique and integral in thought. A few of the discussions, however, may seem to end somewhat abruptly, as could scarcely be avoided when taken from the midst of a prolonged dialogue.

These quotations are not to be regarded as giving, in every case, the proper views of Plato, or even of Socrates. Other characters, opposed and refuted, are made to speak. Their words are here given to be read and received as germs of thought, and stimulants to inquiry in the reader, even as they were first written by Plato, rather than as expressions of his own opinions.

Many fine passages have been necessarily omitted with regret, because their introduction here would swell this volume beyond the dimensions designed for the ordinary reader. Every theme, therefore, upon which Plato dilates, has not been presented in full. But there has been such a selection as may give the reader a fair idea of his diversity of thought.

While those who are able to purchase, and desirous to peruse the complete translation of Prof. Jowett, will doubtless do this, yet there are many others to whom this volume will be welcome as giving them the finest wheat of Plato in a ready, readable form, at a moderate rate. Even the possessor and reader of the fuller work may be glad to have with him a compendium of Platonic thought so available, — because alphabetical, — for cursory perusal and casual quotation.

It is hoped, at least, by the compiler, that these limited morsels of Plato's Hymettian honey will excite the desire for a fuller feast from the rich banquet which Prof. Jowett has so laboriously and sumptuously provided for those who relish true thought and elegant language, whether coming from ancient or modern thinkers.

The design at first was to interweave the choicest paragraphs of this Translator from his learned and thoughtful Introductions, but it was found that this would have made too large a book. Those who desire to enter Plato's temple of thought with the clearest comprehension of his master-mind, should pass through the grand gateways which this eminent English scholar has erected

These interpretations of the great Greek thinker, are essential to the full understanding of his ideas. Meanwhile, those who cannot yet reach the head-waters of such mental invigoration, may refresh themselves with the limited draughts of Plato's lore, herein bottled up for them, from his perennial springs of thought. C. H. A. B.

PUBLISHER'S NOTE.

This volume was originally prepared from the American edition, to which the references with each extract are made. Every page of it, however, has since then been carefully compared with and corrected by Prof. Jowett's latest and improved issue.

PLATO'S BEST THOUGHTS.

Ability and strength, difference between.
—— Socrates, When you asked me, I certainly did say that the courageous are the confident; but I was not asked whether the confident are the courageous; for if you had asked me that, I should have answered, "Not all of them:" and what I did answer you have not disproved, although you proceed to show that those who have knowledge are more courageous than they were before they had knowledge, and more courageous than others who have no knowledge; and this makes you think that courage is the same as wisdom. But in this way of arguing you might come to imagine that strength is wisdom. You might begin by asking whether the strong are able, and I should say, "Yes:" and then whether those who know how to wrestle are not more able to wrestle than those who do not know how to wrestle, and more able after than before they had learned, and I should assent. And when I had admitted this, you might use my admissions in such a way as to prove that upon my view wisdom is strength; whereas in that case I should not have admitted, any more than in the other, that the able are strong, although I have admitted that the strong are able. For there is a difference between ability and strength; the former is given by knowledge as well as by madness or rage, but strength comes from nature and a healthy state of the body. And in like manner I say of confidence and courage, that they are not the same; and I argue that the courageous are confident, but not all the confident courageous. For confidence may be given to men by art, and also, like ability, by madness and rage; but courage comes to them from nature and the healthy state of the soul.— *Protagoras*, i. 150.

Absolute, the.

—— Simmias: Is there or is there not an absolute justice? Assuredly there is. And an absolute beauty and absolute good? Of course. But did you ever behold any of them with your eyes? Certainly not. Or did you ever reach them with any other bodily sense? (and I speak not of these alone, but of absolute greatness, and health, and strength, and of the essence or true nature of everything). Has the reality of them ever been perceived by you through the bodily organs? or rather, is not the nearest approach to the knowledge of their several natures made by him who so orders his intellectual vision as to have the most exact conception of the essence of that which he considers? Certainly.

And he attains to the purest knowledge of them who goes to each of them with the mind alone, not allowing when in the act of thought the intrusion or introduction of sight or any other sense in the company of reason, but with the very light of the mind in her clearness searches into the very truth of each; he has got rid, as far as he can, of eyes and ears and of the whole body, which he conceives of only as a disturbing element, hindering the soul from the acquisition of truth and knowledge when in company with her — is not this the sort of man who, if any man, is likely to attain to the knowledge of true being? — *Phaedo,* i. 391.

Absolute knowledge in God.

—— Would you, or would you not, say that absolute knowledge, if there is such a thing, must be a far more exact knowledge than our knowledge, and the same of beauty and of all other things? Yes.

And if there be such a thing as participation in absolute knowledge no one is more likely than God to have this most exact knowledge? Certainly.

But then, will God, having absolute knowledge, have a knowledge of human things? Why not?

Because, Socrates, said Parmenides, we have admitted that the ideas are not relative to human things, nor human things to them; the relations of either are in their respective spheres.

Yes, that has been admitted.

And if God has this perfect authority, perfect knowledge, his authority cannot rule us, nor his knowledge know us, or any human thing; just as our authority does not extend to the gods, nor our knowledge know anything which is divine, so by purity of reason they, being gods, are not our masters; neither do they know the things of men.

Yet, surely, said Socrates, to deprive God of knowledge is monstrous.

These, Socrates, said Parmenides, are a few, and only a few, of the difficulties which arise on the hypothesis that there are ideas of things and that each idea is an absolute and determinate unity; they will lead him who is told of them to doubt the very existence of ideas — he will say that even if they do exist they must of necessity be unknown to man; and he will seem to have reason on his side; and as we were remarking just now, will be very difficult to convince; a man must be a man of very considerable ability before he can learn that everything has a class and an absolute essence; and still more remarkable will he be who discovers all these things for himself, and can teach another to understand them thoroughly. *Parmenides*, iii. 252.

Abstract ideas. See *Ideas, abstract.*

Achilles; his self-sacrifice.

—— Now Achilles was quite aware, for he had been told by his mother, that he might avoid death and return home, and live to a good old age, if he abstained from slaying Hector. Nevertheless he gave his life to revenge his friend, and dared to die, not only on his behalf, but after his death. Wherefore the gods honored him even above Alcestis, and sent him to the Islands of the Blest. These are my reasons for affirming that Love is the eldest and noblest and mightiest of the gods, and the chiefest author and giver of virtue, in life and of happiness after death. — *The Symposium*, i. 475.

Achilles; condemned.

—— Neither is Phoenix, the tutor of Achilles, to be approved or regarded as having given his pupil good counsel when he told him that he should take the gifts of the Greeks and assist them; but that without a gift he should not be reconciled to them. Neither will we believe or allow Achilles himself to have been such a lover of money that he took Agamemnon's gifts, or required a price as the ransom of the dead.

Undoubtedly, he said, these are not sentiments which ought to be approved.

Loving Homer as I do, I hardly like to say what I must say, nevertheless, that in speaking thus of Achilles, or in believing these words when spoken of him by others, there is downright impiety. As little can I credit the narrative of his insolence to Apollo, where he says, —

" Thou hast wronged me, O far-darter, most abominable of deities. Verily I would be even with thee, if I had only the power;"

or his insubordination to the river-god, on whose divinity he is ready to lay hands; or the dedication to the dead Patroclus of his own hair, which had been previously dedicated to the other river-god Spercheius; or his dragging Hector round the tomb of Patroclus, and his slaughter of the captives at the pyre; of all this I cannot believe that he was guilty, any more than I can allow our citizens to believe that he, Cheiron's pupil, the son of a goddess and of Peleus who was the gentlest of men and third in descent from Zeus, was in such rare perturbation of mind as to be at one time the slave of two seemingly inconsistent passions, meanness, not untainted by avarice, combined with overwhelming contempt of gods and men. — *The Republic*, ii. 214.

Actual and Ideal. See *State, actual.*
Adulterations. See *Oaths.*
Advocate, Art of the, corrupting the State. See *State*, etc.
Affections; opposing.

—— *Ath.* Each one of us has in his bosom two counselors, both foolish and also antagonistic; of which, the one we call pleasure and the other pain.

Cle. True.

Ath. Also there are opinions about the future, which have the general name of expectations; and the specific name of fear, when the expectation is of pain; and of hope, when of pleasure; and further, there is reflection about the good or evil of them, and this when embodied in a decree by the State, is called Law.

Cle. I am hardly able to follow you; proceed, however, as if I were.

Meg. I am in the like case.

Ath. Let us look at the matter in this way: May we not

regard every living being as a puppet of the gods, either their plaything only, or created with a purpose — which of the two we cannot certainly know? But this we know, that these affections in us are like cords and strings, which pull us different and opposite ways, and to opposite actions; and herein lies the difference between virtue and vice. According to the argument there is one among these cords which every man ought to grasp, and never let go but to pull with it against all the rest; and this is the sacred and golden cord of reason, called by us the common law of the state; there are others which are hard and of iron, but this is soft because golden; and there are several other kinds. Now we ought always to coöperate with the lead of the best, which is law. For inasmuch as reason is beautiful and gentle, and not violent, her rule must needs have ministers in order to help the golden principle in vanquishing the other principles. And thus the moral of the tale about our being puppets will not be lost, and the meaning of the expression "superior or inferior to a man's self" will become clearer; as also that in this matter of pulling the strings of the puppet, cities as well as individuals should live according to reason; which the individual attains in himself, and the city receives from some god, or from the legislator; and makes it her law in her dealings with herself and with other states. In this way virtue and vice will be more clearly distinguished by us. And when they have become clearer, education and other institutions will in like manner become clearer.— *Laws*, iv. 175.

Age; its evil and its good.

—— I find that at my time of life, as the pleasures and delights of the body fade away, the love of discourse grows upon me. I only wish that you would come oftener, and be with your young friends here, and make yourself altogether at home with us.

I replied: There is nothing which I like better, Cephalus, than conversing with aged men like yourself; for I regard them as travelers who have gone a journey which I too may have to go, and of whom I ought to inquire, whether the way is smooth and easy, or rugged and difficult. And this is a question which I should like to ask of you who have arrived at that time which the poets call the "threshold of old age,"— Is life harder towards the end, or what report do you give of it?

I will tell you, Socrates, he said, what my own feeling is.

Old men flock together; they are birds of a feather, as the proverb says; and at our meetings the tale of my acquaintance commonly is — I cannot eat, I cannot drink; the pleasures of youth and love are fled away: there was a good time once, but that is gone, and now life is no longer life. Some of them lament over the slights which are put upon them by relations, and then they tell you plaintively of how many evils their old age is the cause. But to me, Socrates, they seem to blame what is not to blame; for if old age were the cause, I too being old, and every other old man, would have felt the same. Such however is not my experience, nor that of others whom I have known. How well I remember the aged poet Sophocles, when in answer to the question, How does love suit with age, Sophocles, — are you still the man you were? Peace, he replied; most gladly have I escaped that, and I feel as if I had escaped from a mad and furious master. His words have often come into my mind since, and they seem to me still as good as at the time when I first heard them. For certainly old age has a great sense of calm and freedom; when the passions relax their hold, then, as Sophocles says, you have escaped from the control not of one mad master only, but of many. And of these regrets, as well as of the complaint about relations, Socrates, the cause is to be sought, not in men's ages, but in their characters and tempers; for he who is of a calm and happy nature will hardly feel the pressure of age, but he who is of an opposite disposition will find youth and age equally a burden. — *The Republic*, ii. 149.

Age, poverty and riches in. See *Poverty*.
Age, love in old. See *Ibycus*.
Age, as viewing eternity.

—— Let me tell you, Socrates, that when a man thinks himself to be near death he has fears and cares which never entered into his mind before; the tales of a life below and the punishment which is exacted there of deeds done here were a laughing matter to him once, but now he is haunted with the thought that they may be true: either because of the feebleness of age, or from the nearness of the prospect, he seems to have a clearer view of the other world; suspicions and alarms crowd upon him, and he begins to reckon up in his own mind what wrongs he has done to others. And when he finds that the sum of his transgressions is great, he will many a time like a child start up in his sleep for fear, and he is filled with dark forebodings. But to him who is conscious of no sin, sweet hope, as Pindar charmingly says, is the kind nurse of age :

" Hope," as he says, " cherishes the soul of him who lives in holiness and righteousness, and is the nurse of his age and the companion of his journey; — hope, which is mightiest to sway the restless soul of man."

How admirable his words are ! — *The Republic*, ii. 151.

Age, Philosophy in. See *Philosophy*, etc.

Age; learning in.

—— Solon was under a delusion when he said that a man as he is growing older may learn many things — for he can no more learn than he can run ; youth is the time of toil.

Very true.

And, therefore, calculation and geometry, and all the other elements of instruction, which are a preparation for dialectic, should be presented to the mind in childhood ; not, however, under any notion of forcing them. — *The Republic*, ii. 364.

Allegory; not for youth.

—— The narrative of Hephaestus binding Here his mother, or how on another occasion Zeus sent him flying for taking her part when she was being beaten, — such tales must not be admitted into our State, whether they are supposed to have an allegorical meaning or not. For the young man cannot judge what is allegorical and what is literal ; anything that he receives into his mind at that age is apt to become indelible and unalterable; and therefore the tales which they first hear should be models of virtuous thoughts.— *The Republic*, ii. 201.

Ambition, inordinate. See *Inordinate*, etc.

Ambition of money-making.

—— Suppose the representative of timocracy to have a son : at first he begins by emulating his father and walking in his footsteps, but presently he sees him founder in a moment on a sunken reef, and he and' all that he has are lost; he may have been a general or some other high officer who is brought to trial under a prejudice raised by informers, and either put to death, or exiled, or deprived of the privileges of a citizen, and all his property taken from him.

Nothing more likely.

And the son has seen and known all this — he is a ruined man, and his fear has taught him to knock ambition and passion headforemost from his bosom's throne; humbled by poverty he takes to money-making, and by mean and miserly savings and hard work gets a fortune together. Is not such an one likely to seat the concupiscent and covetous elements on the vacant throne? They will play the great king within him, and he will array them with tiara and collar and scimitar.

Most true, he replied.

And when he has made reason and spirit sit on the ground obediently on either side, and taught them to know their place, he compels the one to think only of the method by which lesser sums may be converted into larger ones, and schools the other into the worship and admiration of riches and rich men; and to be ambitious only of wealth, and of the pursuits which lead to it.

Of all conversions, he said there is none so speedy or so sure as when the ambitious youth changes into the avaricious one. — *The Republic*, ii. 381.

Ambitious men.

—— If they cannot be generals, they are willing to be captains; and if they cannot be honored by really great and important persons, they are glad to be honored by inferior people, — but honor of some kind they must have. — *The Republic*, ii. 302.

Ambitious woman.

—— The character of the son begins to develop when he hears his mother grumbling at her husband for not having a seat in the government, of which the consequence is that she loses her precedence among other women. Further, when she sees her husband not very eager about money, and instead of battling and railing in the law courts or assembly, taking whatever happens to him quietly; and when she observes that his thoughts always centre in himself, while he treats her with considerable indifference, she is annoyed, and says to her son that his father is only half a man and far too easy-going; not to mention other similar complaints which women love to utter. *The Republic*, ii. 376.

Amusement; arguing for.

—— Young men, as you may have observed, when they first get the taste in their mouths, argue for amusement, and are always contradicting and refuting others in imitation of those who refute them; like puppy-dogs, they delight to tear and pull at all who come near them.

Yes, he said, there is nothing of which they are fonder.

And when they have made many conquests and received defeats at the hands of many, they violently and speedily get into a way of not believing anything that they believed before, and hence, not only they, but philosophy generally, has a bad name with the rest of the world.

Too true, he said.

But when a man begins to get older, he will no longer be guilty of such insanity; he will imitate the dialectician who is seeking for truth, and not the eristic, who is contradicting for the sake of amusement; and the greater moderation of his character will increase instead of diminishing the honor of the pursuit. — *The Republic*, ii. 367.

Amusement and harmless pleasure.

—— *Ath.* I should say that learning has a certain accompanying charm which is the pleasure; and that the right and the profitable, the good and the noble, are qualities given to it by the truth.

Cle. Exactly.

Ath. And so in the imitative arts, if they succeed in making likenesses, and are accompanied by pleasure, may not their works be said to have a charm?

Cle. Yes.

Ath. But equal proportions, whether of quality or quantity, and not pleasure, speaking generally, would give them truth or rightness.

Cle. Yes.

Ath. Then that only can be rightly judged by the standard of pleasure, which makes or furnishes no utility, or truth, or likeness, nor on the other hand is productive of any hurtful quality, but exists solely for the sake of the accompanying charm; and the term "pleasure" is most appropriately used when these other qualities are absent.

Cle. You are speaking of harmless pleasure, are you not?

Ath. Yes; and this I term amusement, when doing neither harm nor good in any degree worth speaking of. — *Laws*, iv. 197.

Anarchy resulting from freedom.

—— Freedom in a democracy is the glory of the State, and therefore, in a democracy only will the freeman of nature deign to dwell.

Yes; the saying is often enough repeated.

I was going to observe, that the insatiable desire of this and the neglect of other things introduces the change in democracy, which occasions a demand for tyranny.

How so?

When a democracy which is thirsting for freedom has evil cup-bearers presiding over the feast, and has drunk too deeply of the strong wine of freedom, then, unless her rulers are very amenable and give a plentiful draught, she calls them to account and punishes them, and says that they are cursed oligarchs.

Yes, he replied, a very common thing.

Yes, I said; and loyal citizens are insulted by her as lovers of slavery and men of naught; she would have subjects who are like rulers, and rulers who are like subjects: these are men after her own heart, whom she praises and honors both in-private and public. Now, in such a state, can liberty have any limit?

Certainly not.

By degrees the anarchy finds a way into private houses, and ends by getting among the animals and infecting them.

How do you mean?

I mean that the father gets accustomed to descend to the level of his sons and to fear them, and the son to be on a level with his father, he having no shame or fear of either of his parents; and this is his freedom, and the metic is equal with the citizen and the citizen with the metic, and the stranger on a level with either.

Yes, he said, that is true.

That is true; and there are other slight evils such as the following; the master fears and flatters his scholars, and the scholars despise their masters and tutors; and, in general, young and old are alike, and the young man is on a level with the old, and is ready to compete with him in word or deed; and old men condescend to the young, and are full of pleasantry and gayety; they do not like to be thought morose and authoritative, and therefore they adopt the manners of the young.

Quite true, he said.

The last extreme of popular liberty is when the slave bought with money, whether male or female, is just as free as his or her purchaser; nor must I forget to tell of the liberty and equality of the two sexes in relation to each other. — *The Republic,* ii. 391.

Animal, — the world a great and intelligent.

―――― Let me tell you why the creator created and made the universe. He was good, and no goodness can ever have any jealousy of anything. And being free from jealousy, he desired that all things should be as like himself as possible. This is the true beginning of creation and of the world as we shall do well in believing on the testimony of wise men: God desired that all things should be good and nothing bad in so far as this could be accomplished. Wherefore also finding the whole visible sphere not at rest, but moving in an irregular and disorderly manner, out of disorder he brought order, considering that this was far better than the other. Now the deeds of him who is the best can never be or have been other than the fairest, and the creator, reflecting upon the visible works of nature, found that no unintelligent creature taken as a whole was fairer than the intelligent taken as a whole; and that intelligence could not exist in anything which was devoid of soul. For these reasons he put intelligence in soul, and soul in body, and framed the universe to be the best and fairest work in the order of nature. And therefore, using the language of probability, we may say that the world became a living soul and truly rational through the providence of God.

This being supposed, let us proceed to consider the further question, in the likeness of what animal did the Creator make the world? Certainly we cannot suppose that the form was like that of any being which exists in parts only; for nothing can be beautiful which is like any imperfect thing; but we may regard the world as the very likeness of that whole of which all other animals, both individually and in their tribes are portions. For the original of the universe contains in itself all intelligible beings, just as this world comprehends us and all other visible creatures. For the Deity, intending to make this world like the fairest and most perfect of intelligible beings, framed one visible animal comprehending all other animals of a kindred nature. Are we right in saying that there is one heaven, or shall we rather say that there are many and infinite? There is one, if the created heaven accords with the original. For that which includes all other intelligible creatures cannot have a second or companion; in that case there would be need of another living being which would include those two, and of which they would be parts, and the likeness would be more truly said to resemble not those two, but that other which included them. In order then that the world might be like the perfect animal in unity, he who made the worlds made them not two or infinite in number; but there is and ever will be one only-begotten and created heaven.— *Timaeus*, ii. 524.

Animalism.

———— Those who know not wisdom and virtue, and are always busy with gluttony and sensuality, go down and up again as far as the mean; and in this region they move at random throughout life, but they never pass into the true upper world; thither they neither look, nor do they ever find their way, neither are they truly filled with true being, nor do they taste of true and abiding pleasure. Like cattle, with their eyes always looking down and their heads stooping, not indeed to the earth but to the dining-table, they fatten and feed and breed, and, in their excessive love of these delights, they kick and butt at one another with horns and hoofs which are made of iron; and they kill one another by reason of their insatiable lust. For they fill themselves with that which is not substantial, and the part of themselves which they fill is also unsubstantial and incontinent.

Their pleasures are mixed with pains. How can they be otherwise? For they are mere images and pictures of the true, and are colored by contrast, which exaggerates both light and shade, and so they implant in the minds of fools insane desires of themselves; and they are fought about as Stesichorus says that the Greeks fought about the shadow of Helen at Troy in ignorance of the truth.

And must not the like happen with the spirited or passionate element of the soul? Will not the passionate man who carries his passion into action be in a like case whether he is envious and ambitious, or violent and contentious, or angry and discontented, if he be seeking to attain honor and victory and the satisfaction of his anger without reason or sense?— *The Republic*, ii. 417.

Antagonisms; human.

———— There is a story which I remember to have heard, and on which I rely. The story is that Leontius, the son of Aglaion, coming up one day from the Piraeus, under the north wall on the outside, observed some dead bodies lying on the ground by the executioner. He felt a longing desire to see them, and also a disgust and abhorrence of them; for a time he turned away and averted his eyes, and then, suddenly overcome by the impulse, forced them open, and ran up, saying (to his eyes), Take your fill, ye wretches, of the lovely sight.

I have heard the story myself, he said.

The moral is that anger differs from the desires, and is sometimes at war with them.

Yes, that is the meaning, he said.

And are there not many other cases in which we observe that when a man's desires violently prevail over his reason, he reviles himself, and is angry at the violence within him, and that in this struggle, which is like the struggle of factions in a state, his spirit is on the side of his reason; but for the passionate or spirited element to take part with the desires when reason decides that she should not be opposed, is a sort of thing which, I believe, that you never observed occurring in yourself, nor, as I think, in any one else?

Certainly not, he said.

Suppose, I said, that a man thinks he has done a wrong to another, the nobler he is the less able he is to feel indignant; his anger refuses to be excited at the hunger or cold or other suffering, which he deems that the injured person may justly inflict upon him?

True, he said.

But when he thinks that he is the sufferer of the wrong, then he boils and chafes, and is on the side of what he believes to be justice; and because he suffers hunger or cold or other pain he is only the more determined to persevere and conquer; he must do or die, and will not desist, until he hears the voice of the shepherd, that is, reason, bidding his dog bark no more. — *The Republic*, ii. 266.

Antagonisms and counterparts in nature.

—— *Soc.* Whereas the sharp and flat, the swift and the slow are infinite or unlimited, does not the addition of them introduce a limit, and perfect the whole frame of music?

Pro. Yes, certainly.

Soc. Or, again, when cold and heat prevail, does not the introduction of them take away excess and indefiniteness and infuse moderation and harmony?

Pro. Certainly.

Soc. And from a like admixture of the finite and infinite come the seasons, and all the delights of life?

Pro. Most true.

Soc. I omit to speak of ten thousand other things, such as beauty and health and strength, and of the many beauties and high perfections of the soul; methinks, O my fair Philebus, that the goddess saw the universal wantonness and wickedness of all things, having no limit of pleasure or satiety, and she devised the limit of law and order, tormenting, as you say, Philebus, or, as I affirm, saving the soul. — *Philebus*, iii. 161.

Appearance of good.

—— Do we not see that many are willing to appear to have, or to do, or to be the just and honorable without the reality; but no one is satisfied with the appearance of good — the reality is what they seek; in the case of the good, appearance is despised by every one.

Very true, he said.

This, then, which every man pursues and makes his end, having a presentiment that there is such an end, and yet hesitating because neither knowing the nature nor having the same sure proof of this as of other things, and therefore having no profit in other things, — is this, I would ask, a principle about which the best men in our State, to whom everything is to be intrusted, ought to be in darkness? — *The Republic*, ii. 333.

Appetites; natural.

—— I see that among men all things depend upon three wants and desires, of which the end is virtue, if they are rightly led by them, or the opposite, if wrongly. Now these are eating and drinking, which begin at birth; every animal has a natural desire for them, and is violently excited, and rebels against him who says that he must not satisfy all his pleasures and appetites, and get rid of the corresponding pains. And the third and greatest and sharpest want and desire breaks out last, and is the fire of sexual lust, which kindles in men every species of wantonness and madness. And these three disorders we must endeavor to master by the three great principles of fear and law and right reason; turning them away from that which is called pleasantest to the best, using the muses and the Gods who preside over contests to extinguish their increase and influx. — *Laws*, iv. 303.

Argument; the state of mind for.

—— Let us be careful of admitting into our souls the notion that there is no truth or health or soundness in any arguments at all; but let us rather say that there is as yet no health in us, and that we must quit ourselves like men and do our best to gain health, — you and all other men with a view to the whole of your future life, and I myself with a view to death. For at this moment I am sensible that I have not the temper of a philosopher; like the vulgar, I am only a partisan. For the partisan, when he is engaged in a dispute, cares nothing about the rights of the question, but is anxious only to convince his hearers of his own assertions. And the difference between him and me at the present moment is only this, — that whereas he seeks to convince his hearers that what he says is true, I am rather seeking to convince myself; to convince my hearers is a secondary matter with me. And do but see how much I gain by the argument. For if what I say is true, then I do well to be persuaded of the truth; but if there be nothing after death, still, during the short time that remains, I shall not distress my friends with lamentations, and my ignorance will not last, but will die with me and therefore no harm will be done. This is the state of mind, Simmias and Cebes, in which I approach the argument. And I would ask you to be thinking of the truth and not of Socrates; agree with me, if I seem to you to be speaking the truth; or if not, withstand me might and main, that I may not deceive you as well as myself in my enthusiasm, and like the bee, leave my sting in you before I die. — *Phaedo*, i. 419.

Argument, less than character.

—— Let others praise the rewards and appearances of justice; that is a manner of arguing which, coming from them, I am ready to tolerate, but from you who have spent your whole life in thinking about the question, unless I hear the contrary from your own lips, I expect something better. And therefore, I say, not only prove to us that justice is better than injustice, but show what they either of them do to the possessor of them, which makes the one to be a good and the other an evil, whether seen or unseen by gods and men. — *The Republic*, ii. 189.

Argument, not found in numbers.

—— If you have no better argument than numbers, let me have a turn, and do you make trial of the sort of proof which, as I think, ought to be given; for I shall produce one witness only of the truth of my words, and he is the person with whom I am arguing; his suffrage I know how to take; but with the many I have nothing to do, and do not even address myself to them. — *Gòrgias*, iii. 60.

Art, — nature and chance as opposed to. See *Nature,* etc.
Art imitative. See *Likeness-making.*
Art-colors less than words.

—— Our discussion might be compared to a picture of some living being which had been fairly drawn in outline, but had not yet attained the life and clearness which is given by the blending of colors. Now to intelligent persons a living being is more truly delineated by language and discourse than by any painting or work of art; to the duller sort by works of art. — *Statesman,* iii. 561.

Art military, youth instructed in. See *Military.*

Arts; the higher, what they require.

—— All the superior arts require many words and much discussion of the higher truths of nature; hence comes all loftiness of thought and perfectness of execution. And this, as I conceive, was the quality which, in addition to his natural gifts, Pericles acquired from Anaxagoras whom he happened to know. He was thus imbued with the higher philosophy and attained the knowledge of Mind, which was the favorite theme of Anaxagoras and applied what he learned to the art of speaking. — *Phaedrus,* i. 575.

Arts; experimental.

—— O Chaerephon, there are many arts among mankind which are experimental, and have their origin in experience, for experience makes the days of men to proceed according to art, and inexperience according to chance, and different persons in different ways are proficients in different arts, and the best persons in the best arts. — *Gorgias,* iii. 32.

Arts; inquiry ruinous to.

—— *Str.* Yet once more, we shall have to enact, that if any one is detected inquiring into sailing and navigation or health, or into the true nature of medicine, or about the winds, or other conditions of the atmosphere, contrary to the written rules, and has any ingenious notions about such matters, he is not to be called a pilot or physician, but a cloudy talking sophist; also a corrupter of the young, who would persuade them to follow the art of medicine or piloting in an unlawful manner, as the irresponsible masters of the patients or ships; and any one who is qualified by law may inform against him, and indict him in some court, and then if he is found to be corrupting any, whether young or old, he is to be punished with the utmost rigor of the law; for no one should presume to be wiser than the laws; and as touching healing and health and piloting and navigation, the nature of them is known to all, for anybody may learn the written laws and the national customs. If such were the mode of procedure, Socrates, about these sciences and about generalship, and any branch of hunting, or about painting or imitation in general, or carpentry, or any sort of manufacture, or husbandry, or planting, or if we were to see an art of rearing horses, or tending herds, or divination, or any ministerial service, or draught-playing, or any science conversant with number, whether simple or square or cube, or comprising motion, — I say, if all these things were done in this way according to written regulation, and not according to art, what would be the result?

Y. Soc. All the arts would utterly perish, and could never be recovered, because inquiry would be unlawful. And human life, which is bad enough already, would then become utterly unendurable. — *Statesman*, iii. 585.

Artists; what they should be.

—— Are they also to be prohibited from exhibiting the opposite forms of vice and intemperance and meanness and indecency in sculpture and building and the other creative arts; and is he who does not conform to this rule of ours to be prohibited from practicing his art in our State, lest the taste of our citizens be corrupted by him? We would not have our guardians grow up amid images of moral deformity, as in some noxious pasture, and there browse and feed upon many a baneful herb and flower day by day, little by little, until they silently gather a festering mass of corruption in their own soul. Let our artists rather be those who are gifted to discern the true nature of beauty and grace; then will our youth dwell in a land of health, amid fair sights and sounds; and beauty, the effluence of fair works, will visit the eye and ear, like a healthful breeze from a purer region, and insensibly draw the soul even in childhood into harmony with the beauty of reason. — *The Republic*, ii. 225.

Artists; their work.

—— Will not the good man, who says whatever he says with a view to the best, speak with a reference to some standard and not at random; just as all other artists, whether the painter, the builder, the shipwright, or any other, look to their work, and do not select and apply at random what they apply, but keep in view the form of their work? The artist disposes all things in order, and compels the one part to harmonize and accord with the other part, until he has constructed a regular and systematic whole; and this is true of all artists, and in the same way the trainers and physicians, of whom we spoke before, give order and regularity to the body. — *Gorgias*, iii. 94.

Astronomy, how learned. See *Heavenly bodies*.

Authority of the State.

——— "Tell us what complaint you have to make against us which justifies you in attempting to destroy us and the State? In the first place did we not bring you into existence? Your father married your mother by our aid and begat you. Say whether you have any objection to urge against those of us who regulate marriage?" None, I should reply. " Or against those of us who after birth regulate the nurture and education of children in which you also were trained? Were not the laws, which have the charge of education, right in commanding your father to train you in music and gymnastic?" Right, I should reply. " Well then, since you were brought into the world and nurtured and educated by us, can you deny in the first place that you are our child and slave, as your fathers were before you? And if this is true you are not on equal terms with us; nor can you think that you have a right to do to us what we are doing to you. Would you have any right to strike or revile or do any other evil to your father or to your master, if you had one, because you have been struck or reviled by him, or received some other evil at his hands? — you would not say this? And because we think right to destroy you, do you think that you have any right to destroy us in return, and your country as far as in you lies? Will you, O professor of true virtue, pretend that you are justified in this? Has a philosopher like you failed to discover that our country is more to be valued and higher and holier far than mother or father or any ancestor, and more to be regarded in the eyes of the gods and of men of understanding? also to be soothed, and gently and reverently entreated when angry, even more than a father, and if not persuaded, obeyed? And when we are punished by her, whether with imprisonment or stripes, the punishment is to be endured in silence; and if she lead us to wounds or death in battle, thither we follow as is right; neither may any one yield or retreat or leave his rank, but whether in battle or in a court of law, or in any other place, **he must do what his city and his country order him**; or he must change their view of what is just: and if he may do no violence to his father or mother, much less may he do violence to his country." — *Crito*, i. 355.

Authorship; motives to.

—— I see, Parmenides, said Socrates, that Zeno is your second self in his writings too; he puts what you say in another way, and would fain deceive us into believing that he is telling what is new. For you, in your poems, say All is one, and of this you adduce excellent proofs; and he, on the other hand, says There is no many; and on behalf of this he offers overwhelming evidence. To deceive the world, as you have done, by saying the same thing in different ways, one of you affirming the one and the other denying the many, is a strain of art beyond the reach of most of us.

Yes, Socrates, said Zeno. But although you are as keen as a Spartan hound in pursuing the track, you do not quite apprehend the true motive of the composition, which is not really such an ambitious work as you imagine; for what you speak of was an accident; I had no serious intention of deceiving the world. The truth is, that these writings of mine were meant to protect the arguments of Parmenides against those who scoff at him, and show the many ridiculous and contradictory results which they supposed to follow from the affirmation of the one. My answer is an address to the partisans of the many, whose attack I return with interest by retorting upon them that their hypothesis of the being of many, if carried out, appears in a still more ridiculous light than the hypothesis of the being of one. A love of controversy led me to write the book in the days of my youth, and some one stole the copy; and therefore I had no choice of whether it should be published or not; the motive, however, of writing, was not the ambition of an old man, but the pugnacity of a young one. — *Parmenides*, iii. 244.

Avaricious men. See *Miserly men*, etc.

Bachelorhood an impiety. See *Immortality in time*.
Bad man's faults increased by power.

—— He who is the real tyrant, whatever men may think, is the real slave, and is obliged to practice the greatest adulation and servility, and to be the flatterer of the vilest of mankind. He has desires which he is utterly unable to satisfy, and has more wants than any one, and is truly poor, if you know how to inspect the whole soul of him: all his life long he is beset with fear and is full of convulsions and distractions, even as the State which he resembles; and surely the resemblance holds?

True, he said.

Moreover, as we said before, he grows worse from having power: he becomes of necessity more jealous, more faithless, more unjust, more friendless, more impious than he was at first; he entertains and nurtures every evil sentiment, and the consequence is that he is supremely miserable, and he makes everybody else equally miserable. — *The Republic*, ii. 409.

Battle; death in.

—— O Menexenus! death in battle is certainly in many respects a noble thing. The dead man gets a fine and costly funeral, although he may have been poor, and an elaborate speech is made over him by a wise man who has long ago prepared what he has to say, although he who is praised may not have been good for much. The speakers praise him for what he has done and for what he has not done — that is the beauty of them — and they steal away our souls with their embellished words; in every conceivable form they praise the city; and they praise those who died in war, and all our ancestors who went before us; and they praise ourselves also who are still alive. — *Menexenus*, iv. 565.

Beauties tyrannical.

—— *Soc.* A man who was blindfolded has only to hear you talking, and he would know that you are a fair creature and have still many lovers.

Men. Why do you say that?

Soc. Why, because you always speak in imperatives: like all beauties when they are in their prime, you are tyrannical; and also, as I suspect, you have found out that I have a weakness for the fair, and therefore I must humor you and answer. — *Meno*, i. 249.

Beautiful true and good, the.

—— Now, that which imparts truth to the known and the power of knowing to the knower is what I would have you term the idea of good, and that you will regard as the cause of science and of truth, as known by us; beautiful too, as are both truth and knowledge, you will be right in esteeming this other nature as more beautiful than either; and, as in the previous instance, light and sight may be truly said to be like the sun, and yet not to be the sun, so in this other sphere, science and truth may be deemed like the good, but not the good; the good has a place of honor yet higher.

What a wonder of beauty that must be, he said, which is the author of science and truth, and yet surpasses them in beauty. — *The Republic*, ii. 336.

Beauty permeating our souls.

—— Beauty is certainly a soft, smooth, slippery thing, and therefore of a nature which easily slips in and permeates our souls. For I affirm that the good is the beautiful. You will agree to that?

Yes.

This I say from a sort of notion that what is neither good nor evil is the friend of the beautiful and the good, and I will tell you why I am inclined to think so; I assume that there are three principles — the good, the bad, and that which is neither good nor bad. What do you say to that?

I agree.

And neither is the good the friend of the good, nor the evil of the evil, nor the good of the evil, — that the preceding argument will not allow; and therefore the only alternative is — if there be such a thing as friendship or love at all — that what is neither good nor evil must be the friend, either of the good, or of that which is neither good nor evil, for nothing can be the friend of the bad. — *Lysis*, i. 56.

Beauty, absolute.

—— There is nothing new, he said, in what I am about to tell you; but only what I have been always and everywhere repeating in the previous discussion and on other occasions; I want to show you the nature of that cause which has occupied my thoughts, and I shall have to go back to those familiar words which are in the mouth of every one, and first of all assume that there is an absolute beauty and goodness, and greatness, and the like; grant me this, and I hope to be able to show you the nature of the cause, and to prove the immortality of the soul.

Cebes said: You may proceed at once with the proof, for I grant you this.

Well, he said, then I should like to know whether you agree with me in the next step; for I cannot help thinking that if there be anything beautiful other than absolute beauty, that can only be beautiful in as far as it partakes of absolute beauty — and this I should say of everything. Do you agree in this notion of the cause?

Yes, he said, I agree.

He proceeded: I know nothing and can understand nothing of any other of those wise causes which are alleged; and if a person says to me that the bloom of color, or form, or anything else of that sort is a source of beauty, I leave all that, which is only confusing to me, and simply and singly, and perhaps foolishly, hold and am assured in my own mind that nothing makes a thing beautiful but the presence and participation of beauty in whatever way or manner obtained; for as to the manner I am uncertain, but I stoutly contend that by beauty all beautiful things become beautiful. That appears to me to be the only safe answer that I can give, either to myself or to any other, and to that I cling, in the persuasion that I shall never be overthrown. — *Phaedo*, i. 429.

The lovers of sounds and sights, I replied, are, as I conceive, fond of fine tones and colors and forms, and all the artificial products that are made out of them, but their mind is incapable of seeing or loving absolute beauty.

True, he replied.

Few are they who are able to attain the sight of this.

Very true.

And he who, having a sense of beautiful things, has no sense of absolute beauty, or who, if another lead him to a knowledge of that beauty is unable to follow — of such an one I ask, Is he awake or in a dream only? Reflect: is not the dreamer, sleeping or waking, one who puts the resemblance in the place of the real object?

I should certainly say that such an one was dreaming.

But take the case of the other, who recognizes the existence of absolute beauty and is able to distinguish the idea from the objects which participate in the idea, neither putting the objects in the place of the idea nor the idea in the place of the objects — is he a dreamer, or is he awake?

He is wide awake. — *The Republic*, ii. 304.

Beauty, one and everlasting.

—— " These are the lesser mysteries of love, into which even you, Socrates, may enter; to the greater and more hidden ones which are the crown of these, and to which, if you pursue them in a right spirit, they will lead, I know not whether you will be able to attain. But I will do my utmost to inform you, and do you follow if you can. For he who would proceed aright in this matter should begin in youth to visit beautiful forms;

and first, if he be guided by his instructor aright to love one such form only — out of that he should create fair thoughts; and soon he will of himself perceive that the beauty of one form is akin to the beauty of another; and then if beauty of form in general is his pursuit, how foolish would he be not to recognize that the beauty in every form is one and the same! And when he perceives this he will abate his violent love of the one, which he will despise and deem a small thing, and will become a lover of all beautiful forms; in the next stage he will consider that the beauty of the mind is more honorable than the beauty of the outward form. So that if a virtuous soul have but a little comeliness, he will be content to love and tend him, and will search out and bring to the birth thoughts which may improve the young, until he is compelled to contemplate and see the beauty of institutions and laws, and to understand that the beauty of them all is of one family, and that personal beauty is a trifle; and after laws and institutions he will go on to the sciences, that he may see their beauty, being not like a servant in love with the beauty of one youth or man or institution, himself a slave, mean and narrow-minded, but drawing toward and contemplating the vast sea of beauty, he will create many fair and noble thoughts and notions in boundless love of wisdom; until on that shore he grows and waxes strong, and at last the vision is revealed to him of a single science, which is the science of beauty everywhere. To this I will proceed; please to give me your very best attention. He who has been instructed thus far in the things of love, and who has learned to see the beautiful in due order and succession, when he comes toward the end will suddenly perceive a nature of wondrous beauty — (and this, Socrates, is the final cause of all our former toils,) a nature which in the first place is everlasting, not growing and decaying, or waxing and waning; in the next place not fair in one point of view and foul in another, or at one time or in one relation or at one place fair, at another time or in another relation or at another place foul, as if fair to some and foul to others, or in the likeness of a face or hands or any other part of the bodily frame, or in any form of speech or knowledge, or existing in any other being; as for example, in an animal, or in heaven or in earth, or in any other place, but beauty only, absolute, separate, simple, and everlasting, which without diminution and without increase, or any change, is imparted to the ever-grow-

ing and perishing beauties of all other things. He who under the influence of true love rising upward from these begins to see that beauty, is not far from the end. And the true order of going or being led by another to the things of love, is to use the beauties of earth as steps along which he mounts upwards for the sake of that other beauty, going from one to two, and from two to all fair forms, and from fair forms to fair practices, and from fair practices to fair notions, until from fair notions he arrives at the notion of absolute beauty, and at last knows what the essence of beauty is. This, my dear Socrates," said the stranger of Mantineia, " is that life above all others which man should live, in the contemplation of beauty absolute ; a beauty which if you once beheld, you would see not to be after the measure of gold, and garments, and fair boys and youths, whose presence now entrances you ; and you and many a one would be content to live seeing only and conversing with them without meat or drink, if that were possible — you only want to be with them and to look at them. But what if man had eyes to see the true beauty — the divine beauty, I mean, pure and clear and unalloyed, not clogged with the pollutions of mortality, and all the colors and vanities of human life — thither looking, and holding converse with the true beauty divine and simple ? Do you not see that in that communion only, beholding beauty with the eye of the mind, he will be enabled to bring forth, not images of beauty, but realities ; (for he has hold not of an image but of a reality,) and bringing forth and nourishing true virtue to become the friend of God and be immortal, if mortal man may. Would that be an ignoble life ? "
— *The Symposium*, i. 502.

Beauty, madness of.

—— Thus far I have been speaking of the fourth and last kind of madness, which is imputed to him who, when he sees the beauty of earth, is transported with the recollection of the true beauty ; he would like to fly away, but he cannot ; he is like a bird fluttering and looking upward and careless of the world below ; and he is therefore esteemed mad. And I have shown this is of all inspirations to be the noblest and highest, and the offspring of the highest, and that he who loves the beautiful is called a lover because he partakes of it. For, as has been already said, every soul of man has in the way of nature beheld true being ; this was the condition of her passing into the form of man. But all souls do not easily recall the things of the other world; they may have seen them for a short time only, or they may have been unfortunate in their earthly lot, and may have lost the memory of the holy things which they saw there, through some evil and corrupting association. Few only retain an adequate remembrance of them; and they, when they behold any image of that other world, are rapt in amazement; but they are ignorant of what this rapture means, because they do not clearly perceive. For there is no light in the earthly copies of justice or temperance or any of the higher qualities which are precious to souls: they are seen but through a glass dimly; and there are few who, going to the images, behold in them the realities, and they only with difficulty. They might have seen beauty shining in brightness, when, with the happy band following in the train of Zeus, as we philosophers, or of other gods as others did, they saw a vision and were initiated into mysteries, which may be truly called most blessed, and which we celebrated in our state of innocence; having no experience of evils as yet to come; admitted to the sight of apparitions innocent and simple and calm and happy; shining in pure light, pure ourselves and not yet enshrined in that living tomb which we carry about, now that we are imprisoned in the body, like an oyster in his shell. Let me linger thus long over the memory of scenes which have passed away. — *Phaedrus*, i. 554.

Beauty, celestial.

—— But of beauty, I repeat again that we saw her there shining in company with the celestial forms; and coming to earth we find her here too, shining in clearness through the clearest aperture of sense. For sight is the keenest of our bodily senses;/though not by that is wisdom seen ;/ her loveliness would have been transporting if there had been a visible image of her, and the same is true of the loveliness of the other ideas as well. But this is the privilege of beauty that she is the loveliest and also the most palpable to sight. Now he who is not newly initiated, or who has become corrupted, does not easily rise out of this world to the sight of true beauty in the other; he looks only at her earthly namesake, instead of being awed at the sight of her, like a brutish beast he rushes on to enjoy and beget; he consorts with wantonness and is not afraid or ashamed of pursuing pleasure in violation of nature. But he whose initiation is recent, and who has been the spectator of many glories in the other world, is amazed when he sees any one having a godlike face or form, which is the expression of divine beauty; and at first a shudder runs through him, and again the old awe steals over him. — *Phaedrus*, i. 556.

Beauty, proportionate.

—— If we were painting a statue, and some one were to come and blame us for not putting the most beautiful colors on the most beautiful parts of the body — for the eyes, he would say, ought to be purple, but they are black — in that case we might fairly answer, "Sir, do not imagine that we ought to beautify the eyes to such a degree that they are no longer eyes; but see whether, by giving this and the other features their due, we make the whole beautiful." — *The Republic*, ii. 244.

Beauty of figure and melody.

—— *Ath.* What is beauty of figure, or beautiful melody? When a manly soul is in trouble, and when a cowardly soul is in a similar case, are they likely to use the same figures and gestures, or to give utterance to the same sounds?

Cle. How can they, when the very colors of their faces differ?

Ath. Good, my friend; I may observe, however, in passing, that in music there certainly are figures and there are melodies; and music is concerned with harmony and rhythm, so that you may speak of a melody or figure having rhythm or harmony; the term is correct enough, but you cannot speak correctly, as the masters of choruses have a way of talking metaphorically of the "color" of a melody or figure. Although you can speak of the melodies or figures of the brave and the coward, praising the one and censuring the other. And not to be tedious, the figures and melodies which are expressive of virtue of soul or body, or of images of virtue, are without exception good, and those which are expressive of vice are the reverse of good.

Cle. You are right in calling upon us to make that division.

Ath. But are all of us equally delighted with every sort of dance?

Cle. Far otherwise.

Ath. —— What is the cause of error or division among us? Are beautiful things not the same to us all, or are they the same in themselves, but not in our opinion of them? For no one will admit that forms of vice in the dance are more beautiful than forms of virtue, or that he himself delights in the forms of vice, and others in a muse of another character. And yet most persons say, that the excellence of music is to give pleasure to our souls. But this is intolerable and blasphemous; there is, however, a more plausible account of the delusion. — *Laws*, iv. 185.

↳ **Being, real.**

—— Which classes of things have a greater share in pure existence, in your judgment — those of which food and drink and condiments and all kinds of sustenance are examples, or the class which contains true opinion and mind and, in general, all virtue? Put the question in this way: — Which has a more pure being, — that which is concerned with the invariable, the immortal, and the true, and is found in the invariable, immortal, true; or that which is concerned with the variable and mortal, and is found in the variable and mortal?

Far purer, he replied, is that which is concerned with the invariable. — *The Republic*, ii. 416.

Belief and learning.

—— *Soc.* Let me raise this question: you would say that there is such a thing as " having learned? "

Gor. Yes.

Soc. And there is also " having believed? "

Gor. Yes.

Soc. And is the " having learned " the same as " having believed," and are learning and belief the same things?

Gor. In my judgment, Socrates, they are not the same.

Soc. And your judgment is right, as you may ascertain in this way: If a person were to say to you, " Is there, Gorgias, a false belief as well as a true? " you would reply, if I am not mistaken, that there is.

Gor. Yes.

Soc. Well, but is there a false knowledge as well as a true?

Gor. No.

Soc. No, indeed; and this again proves that knowledge and belief differ.

Gor. That is true.

Soc. And yet those who have learned as well as those who have believed are persuaded?

Gor. That is so.

Soc. Shall we then assume two sorts of persuasion, — one which is the source of belief without knowledge, as the other is of knowledge?

Gor. By all means. — *Gorgias*, iii. 39.

Beliefs and opinions, true.

—— Now when the Creator had framed the soul according to his will, he formed within her the corporeal universe, and brought them together, and united them centre to centre. The soul, interfused everywhere from the centre to the circumference of heaven, of which she is the external envelopment, herself turning in herself, began a divine beginning of never-ceasing and rational life enduring throughout all time. The body of heaven is visible, but the soul is invisible, and partakes of reason and harmony, and being made by the best of intellectual and everlasting natures is the best of things created. And because she is composed of the same and of the other and of the essence, these three, and divided and bound together in proportion, and is revolving backwards and forwards in herself, the soul, when touching anything which has essence, whether dispersed in parts or undivided, is stirred through all her powers to declare the sameness or difference of that and some other thing, and in relation to what and in what way and how and when individuals are connected or affected, both in the world of generation and in the world of immutable being. And when reason, which works with equal truth both in the circle of the diverse and of the same,—in the sphere of the self-moved in voiceless silence moving,— when reason, I say, is hovering around the sensible world and the circle of the diverse also moving truly imparts the intimations of sense to the whole soul, then arise fixed and true opinions and beliefs. But when reason is dwelling in the rational, and the circle of the same moving smoothly indicates this, then intelligence and knowledge are of necessity perfected. And if any one affirms that in which these are found to be other than the soul, he will say the very opposite of the truth. — *Timaeus*, ii. 529.

Bodily pleasures desired by men.

—— Consider, my friend, whether you and I are agreed about another question, which will probably throw light on our present inquiry : Do you think that the philosopher ought to care about the pleasures — if they are to be called pleasures — of eating and drinking?

Certainly not, answered Simmias.

And what do you say of the pleasures of love — should he care about them?

By no means.

And will he think much of the other ways of indulging the

body, for example, the acquisition of costly raiment, or sandals, or other adornments of the body? Instead of caring about them, does he not rather despise anything more than nature needs? What do you say?

I should say that the true philosopher would despise them.

Would you not say that he is entirely concerned with the soul and not with the body? He would like, as far as he can, to be quit of the body and turn to the soul.

That is true.

In matters of this sort philosophers, above all other men, may be observed in every sort of way to dissever the soul from the communion of the body.

That is true.

Whereas, Simmias, the rest of the world are of opinion that a life which has no share in bodily pleasures is not worth having; and that he who is indifferent about them is as good as dead.

That is quite true.

What again shall we say of the actual acquirement of knowledge? — is the body, if invited to share in the inquiry, a hinderer or a helper? I mean to say, have sight and hearing any truth in them? Are they not, as the poets are always telling us, inaccurate witnesses? and yet, if even they are inaccurate and indistinct, what is to be said of the other senses? — for you will allow that they are the best of them?

Certainly, he replied.

Then when does the soul attain truth? — for in attempting to consider anything in company with the body she is obviously deceived.

Yes, that is true.

Then must not existence be revealed to her in thought, if at all?

Yes.

And thought is best when the mind is gathered into herself and none of these things trouble her — neither sounds nor sights nor pain nor any pleasure, — when she has as little as possible to do with the body, and has no bodily sense or feeling, but is aspiring after true being?

Certainly.

And in this the philosopher dishonors the body; his soul runs away from the body and desires to be alone and by herself?

That is true. — *Phaedo*, i. 391.

Body, soul the life of. See *Soul*, etc.

Body and soul, their relative value. See *Soul*, etc.

——— If you were going to commit your body to some one, who might do good or harm to it, would you not carefully consider and ask the opinion of your friends and kindred, and deliberate many days as to whether you should give him the care of your body? But when the soul is in question, which you hold to be of far more value than the body, and upon the good or evil of which depends the well-being of your all;— about this you never consulted either with your father or with your brother or with any one of us who are your companions. But no sooner does this foreigner appear, than you instantly commit your soul to his keeping. In the evening, as you say, you hear of him, and in the morning you go to him, never deliberating, or taking the opinion of any one as to whether you ought to intrust yourself to him or not; you have quite made up your mind that you will be a pupil of Protagoras, and are prepared to expend all the property of yourself and of your friends in carrying out at any price this determination, although, as you admit, you do not know him, and have never spoken with him; and you call him a Sophist, but are manifestly ignorant of what a Sophist is; and yet you are going to commit yourself to his keeping. — *Protagoras*, i. 113.

Body, affecting soul.

——— The lovers of knowledge are conscious that their souls, when philosophy takes them in hand, are simply fastened and glued to their bodies: the soul is able to view real existence through the bars of a prison, and not of herself unhindered; she is wallowing in the mire of all ignorance; and philosophy beholding the terrible nature of her confinement, inasmuch as the captive through lust becomes a chief accomplice in her own captivity — for the lovers of knowledge are aware that this was the original state of the soul, but that when she was in this state philosophy adopted and comforted her, and wanted to release her, pointing out to her that the eye and the ear and the other senses are full of deceit, and persuading her to retire from them in all but the necessary use of them, and to be gathered up and collected into herself, and to trust only to herself and her own pure apprehensions of pure existence, and to mistrust whatever comes to her through other channels and is subject to vicissitude — philosophy, I say, shows her that all this is visible and tangible, but that what she sees in her own nature is intellectual and invisible. And the soul of the true philosopher thinks that she ought not to resist this deliverance, and therefore abstains from pleasure and desires and pains and fears, as far as she is able; reflecting that when a man has great joys or sorrows or fears or desires, he suffers from them, not merely the sort of evil which might be anticipated — as for example, the loss of his health or property which he had sacrificed to his lusts — but an evil greater far, which is the greatest and worst of all evils, and one of which he never thinks.

And what is that, Socrates? said Cebes.

Why, that when the feeling of pleasure or pain in the soul is most intense, all of us naturally suppose that the object of this intense feeling is then plainest and truest: but such is not the case.

Very true.

And this is the state in which the soul is most enthralled by the body.

How is that?

Why, because each pleasure and pain is a sort of nail which nails and rivets the soul to the body, until she becomes like the body and believes that to be true which the body affirms to be true; and from agreeing with the body and having the same delights, she is obliged to have the same habits and haunts, and is not likely ever to be pure at her departure to the world below, but is always infected by the body; and so she sinks into another body and there germinates and grows, and has therefore no part in the communion of the divine and pure and simple.

That is most true, Socrates, answered Cebes.

And this, Cebes, is the reason why the true lovers of knowledge are temperate and brave; and not for the reason which the world gives.

Certainly not.

Certainly not! For the soul of a philosopher will reason in another way; she will not ask philosophy to release her in order that when released she may deliver herself up again to the thralldom of pleasures and pains, doing a work only to be undone again, weaving instead of unweaving her Penelope's web. But she will calm passion and follow Reason, and dwell in her, beholding the true and divine (which is not matter of opinion), and thence derive nourishment. Thus she seeks to live while she lives, and after death she hopes to go to her own kindred and to a congenial world and to be freed from human ills. Never fear, Simmias and Cebes, that a soul which has been thus nurtured and has had these pursuits, will at her departure from the body be scattered and blown away by the winds and be nowhere and nothing.— *Phaedo*, i. 411.

Body, affections of the.

—— The most important of the affections which concern the whole body, remains to be considered. This is the cause of pleasure and pain in the things which we have mentioned, and in all other things which are perceived by sense through the parts of the body, and have pleasures and pains consequent upon them. Let us imagine the causes of every affection, whether of sense or not, to be of the following nature, remembering that we have already distinguished between the nature which moves and that which is immovable; for this is the direction in which we must hunt the prey which we mean to take. A body which is easily moved on receiving any slight impression communicates this to the parts affected, and these to other parts in an ever widening circle, until at last reaching the principle of mind they announce the power of the producing cause. But a body of the opposite kind, being at rest, and having no circular motion, is alone affected, and does not move any of the neighboring parts; and thus the parts not distributing their first impression to other parts, having no effect of motion on the whole animal, produce no effect on the patient. This is true of the bones and hair and other more earthly parts of the human body; whereas what was said above relates mainly to sight and hearing, because they have in them the greatest force of fire and air. Now, we must conceive of pleasure and pain in this way. An impression produced in us contrary to nature and violent, if sudden, is painful; and, again, the sudden return to nature is pleasant, and that which is gentle and gradual is imperceptible, and *vice versa*. But the impression which is most easily produced is most readily felt, and is not accompanied by pleasure or pain; such, for example, are the affections of the sight itself, which has been already said to be a kindred body communicating with us in the daytime; for cuttings and burnings and other affections which happen to the sight do not give pain, nor is their pleasure when the sight returns to its natural state; but the impressions are clearest and strongest according to the manner of the affection and the number of the objects perceived; for there is no violence either in the contraction or dilation of the eye. But bodies which are formed of larger particles yield to the agent only with a struggle; and then they impart their motions to the whole and cause pleasure and pain — pain when alienated from their natural conditions, and pleasure when restored to them. Things which experience gradual withdrawings and emptyings of their nature, and great and sudden replenishments, fail to perceive the emptying, and do perceive the replenishment; these occasion no pain, but the greatest pleasure to the mortal part of the human soul, as is manifest in the case of perfumes. But things which are changed all of a sudden, and only gradually and with difficulty return to their own nature, have all the opposite effects, as is evident in the case of burnings and cuttings of the body. — *Timaeus*, ii. 556.

Body; construction of the.

—— When all things were in disorder, God created in each thing, both internally in relation to itself and externally in relation to other things, certain harmonies in which were included all possible harmonies and proportions. For in those days nothing had any order except by accident; nor did any of the things which now have names deserve to be named at all — as, for example, fire, water, and the rest of the elements. All these the Creator first arranged, and out of them he constructed the universe, which was a single animal comprehending all other animals, mortal and immortal, in itself. Now of the divine, he himself was the Creator, but the creation of the mortal he committed to his offspring. And they, imitating him, received from him the immortal principle of the soul; and around this they fashioned a mortal body, and made the whole body to be a vehicle of the soul, and constructed within a soul of another nature which was mortal, subject to terrible and irresistible affections, — first of all, pleasure, the greatest incitement of evil; then pain, which deters from good; also rashness and fear, two foolish counselors, anger hard to be appeased and hope easily deceived by sense without reason and by all-daring love; these they mingled together according to necessary laws, and framed man. Wherefore, fearing to pollute the divine any more than is necessary, they separated the mortal nature, and to that gave a habitation in another part of the body, placing the neck between them to be the isthmus and boundary, which they constructed between the head and breast, in order that they might be kept distinct.

And in the breast, and in what is termed the thorax they encased the mortal soul, and as one part of this was superior and the other inferior they divided the cavity of the thorax into two parts, as the women's and men's apartments are divided in houses; and placed the midriff to be a wall of partition between them.

That part of the inferior soul which is endowed with courage and passion and loves contention they settled nearer the head, in the interval between the midriff and the neck, in order that it might be under the rule of reason, and might join with it in controlling and restraining the desires when they are no longer willing of their own accord to obey the word of command issuing from the citadel.

The heart, which is the knot of the veins and the fountain of the blood flowing rapidly through all the limbs, was set in the place of guard that when passion was roused by reason making proclamation of any wrong assailing them from without or being perpetrated by the desires within, quickly the whole power of feeling in the body, perceiving these commands and threats, might obey and follow through every turn and alley, and thus allow the principle of the best to have the command in all of them. But as the gods foreknew that the palpitation of the heart in the expectation of danger and the swelling and excitement of passion was caused by fire, they formed and implanted as a supporter to the heart the lung, which was, in the first place, soft and bloodless, and also had within hollows like the pores of a sponge, in order that, receiving the breath and the drink and cooling them, it might give the power of respiration and alleviate the heat. For which reason they cut the arteries or air vessels as passages to the lung, and placed the lung about the heart as a soft spring, that, when passion was rife within, the heart, beating against the yielding body, might be refreshed and suffer less, and might thus become more ready to enlist passion in the service of reason.

The part of the soul which desires meats and drinks and such things as the bodily frame needs, they placed between the midriff and the navel, contriving in all this region a sort of manger for the food of the body; and there they bound the desires down as a wild animal which was chained up with man, and must be nourished if man was to exist. They appointed this lower creation his place here in order that he might be always feeding at the manger, and have his dwelling as far as possible from the council chamber, making as little noise and disturbance as possible, and permitting the best part to advise quietly for the good of the whole. And knowing and considering that this lower principle in man would not listen to reason, and even if attaining to some degree of perception would never naturally care for any arguments, and was liable to be led away by phantoms and visions of the night and also by day, God framed the liver, to dwell in the same house with the lower nature, contriving that it should be solid and smooth, and bright and sweet, and also bitter, in order that the power of thought, which originates in the mind, might be reflected as in a mirror which receives and gives back images of them to the sight. And this power making use of the bitter part of the liver, to which it is akin, inspires terror, and comes threatening and invading, and suddenly mingling with the entire liver produces colors like bile, and contracts every part, and makes it wrinkled and rough; or, on the other hand, twisting out of their right place and contracting the lobe and receptacles and gates, or again, closing and shutting them up — in these and other ways creates pain and disgust. And the converse happens when some gentle inspiration of the understanding pictures images of an opposite character, and allays the bile and bitterness by not stirring them, and refuses to touch the nature opposed to itself, but by making use of the natural sweetness of the liver, corrects all things and makes them to be right and smooth and free, and makes the portion of the soul which resides about the liver happy and joyful, having in the night a time of peace and moderation, and the power of divination in dreams, inasmuch as it does not share in mind and reason. For the authors of our being, remembering the command of their father when he bade them make the human race as good as they could, thus ordered our inferior parts in order that they too might obtain a measure of truth, and in the liver placed their oracle, and herein is a proof that God has given the art of divination not to the wisdom, but to the foolishness of man. For no man, when in his wits, attains prophetic truth and inspiration; but when he receives the inspired word either his intelligence is enthralled by sleep, or he is demented by some distemper or possession. And he who would understand what he remembers to have been said, whether in a dream or when he was awake, by the prophetic and enthusiastic nature, or what he has seen, must first recover his wits; and then he will be able to explain rationally what all such words and apparitions mean, and what indications they afford to this man or that, of past, present, or future good and evil. But, while he continues demented, he cannot judge of the visions which he sees or the words which he utters; the ancient saying is very true, that "only a man who has his wits can act or judge about himself and his own affairs." And for this reason it is customary to appoint diviners or interpreters to be judges of the true inspiration. Some persons call them prophets; they do not know that they are only repeaters of dark sayings and visions, and are not to be called prophets at all, but only interpreters of prophecy.[1] — *Timaeus*, ii. 561.

Body and soul, health of.

—— *Soc.* What use is there, Callicles, in giving to the body of a sick man who is in a bad state of health a quantity of the most delightful food or drink or any other pleasant thing, which may be really as bad for him as if you gave him nothing, or even worse, if rightly estimated. Is not that true?

Cal. I will not say no to that.

Soc. For in my opinion there is no profit in a man's life if his body is in an evil plight — in that case his life also is evil: am I not right?

Cal. Yes.

Soc. When a man is in health the physicians will generally allow him to eat when he is hungry, and drink when he is thirsty, and to satisfy his desires as he likes, but when he is sick they hardly suffer him to satisfy his desires at all: even you will admit that?

Cal. Yes.

Soc. And does not the same argument hold of the soul, my good sir? While she is in a bad state and is senseless and intemperate and unjust and unholy, her desires ought to be controlled, and she ought to be prevented from doing anything which does not tend to her own improvement.

Cal. Yes.

Soc. And that will be for her true interests?

Cal. To be sure.

Soc. And controlling her desires is chastising her?

---

[1] Plato's ideas on the physical structure of man are given at large in succeeding pages too lengthily to be inserted here. Those who are curious to know in full his views on human physiology should read the whole of the "Timaeus."

Cal. Yes.

Soc. Then control or chastisement is better for the soul than intemperance or the absence of control. — *Gorgias*, iii. 96.

Body and soul, two processes of training.

—— Oh, my friend! I want you to see that the noble and the good may possibly be something different from saving and being saved, and that he who is truly a man ought not to care about living a certain time; he knows, as women say, that we must all die, and therefore he is not fond of life; he leaves all that with God, and considers in what way he can best spend his appointed term; whether by assimilating himself to that constitution under which he lives, as you at this moment have to consider, how you may become as like as possible to the Athenian people, if you intend to be dear to them, and to have power in the State; whereas I want you to think and see whether this is for the interest of either of us; I would not have us risk that which is dearest on the acquisition of this power, like the Thessalian enchantresses, who, as they say, bring down the moon from heaven at the risk of their own perdition. But if you suppose that any man will show you the art of becoming great in the city, and yet not conforming yourself to the ways of the city, whether for better or worse, then I can only say that you are mistaken, Callicles; for he who would deserve to be the true natural friend of the Athenian Demus, aye, or of Pyrilampes' darling, who is called after them, must be by nature like them, and not an imitator only. He, then, who will make you most like them, will make you as you desire, a statesman and orator: for every man is pleased, when he is spoken to in his own language and spirit, and dislikes any other. But perhaps you, sweet Callicles, may be of another mind. What do you say?

Cal. Somehow or other your words, Socrates, always appear to me to be good words; and yet, like the rest of the world, I am not quite convinced by you.

Soc. The reason is, Callicles, that the love of Demus which abides in your soul is an adversary to me; but I dare say that if we recur to these same matters, and consider them more thoroughly, you may be convinced for all that. Please, then, to remember that there are two processes of training all things, including body and soul; in the one, as we said, we treat them with a view to pleasure, and in the other with a view to the highest good, and then we do not indulge

but resist them: was not that the distinction which we drew?
Cal. Very true. — *Gorgias,* iii. 104.

Body after death.

—— Death, if I am right, is in the first place the separation from one another of two things, soul and body; nothing else. And after they are separated they retain their several characteristics, which are much the same as in life; the body has the same nature and ways and affections, all clearly discernible; for example, he who by nature or training or both was a tall man while he was alive, will remain as he was, after he is dead; and the fat man will remain fat; and so on; and the dead man, who in life had a fancy to have flowing hair, will have flowing hair. And if he was marked with the whip and had the prints of the scourge, or of wounds in him when he was alive, you might see the same in the dead body; and if his limbs were broken or misshapen when he was alive the same appearance would be visible in the dead. And in a word, whatever was the habit of the body during life would be distinguishable after death, either perfectly, or in a great measure and for a considerable time. And I should imagine that this is equally true of the soul, Callicles; when a man is stripped of the body. all the natural or acquired affections of the soul are laid open to view. — And when they come to the judge, as those from Asia come to Rhadamanthus, he places them near him and inspects them quite impartially, not knowing whose the soul is: perhaps he may lay hands on the soul of the great king, or of some other king or potentate, who has no soundness in him, but his soul is marked with the whip, and is full of the prints and scars of perjuries, and crimes with which each action has stained him, and he is all crooked with falsehood and imposture, and has no straightness, because he has lived without truth. Him Rhadamanthus beholds, full of all deformity and disproportion, which is caused by license and luxury and insolence and incontinence, and dispatches him ignominiously to his prison, and there he undergoes the punishment which he deserves.[1] — *Gorgias,* iii. 115.

Body and soul, mixtures of.

—— *Soc.* There are some mixtures which are of the body, and only in the body, and others which are of the soul, and

[1] The mythology of the Greeks as to the future state is largely given by Plato in his "Gorgias."

only in the soul; while there are other mixtures of pleasures with pains, common both to soul and body, which in their composite state are called sometimes pleasures and sometimes pains.

Pro. How is that?

Soc. Whenever, in the restoration or in the derangement of nature, a man experiences two opposite feelings; for example, when he is cold and is growing warm, or again, when he is hot and is being cooled, and he wants to have the one and be free from the other; the sweet has a bitter, as they say, and both together fasten upon him, and create irritation and in time drive him to distraction.

Pro. That description is very true to nature. — *Philebus*, iii. 185.

Body, honor of the.

—— Speaking generally, our glory is to follow the better and improve the inferior, which is susceptible of improvement, in the best manner possible. And of all the possessions which a man has, the soul is by nature most inclined to avoid the evil, and search out and find the chief good; and having found, to dwell with the good, during the remainder of life. Wherefore the soul also is second in honor; and third, as every one will perceive, comes the honor of the body in natural order. Having determined this, we have next to consider that there is a genuine honor of the body, and that of honors some are and some are not genuine. The legislator, as I suspect, ranks them in the following order: — Honor is not to be given to the fair, or the strong, or the swift, or the tall, or the healthy body (although many may think otherwise), any more than to their opposites; but the mean states of all these habits are by far the safest and most moderate; for the one extreme makes the soul braggart and insolent, and the other, illiberal and mean; and money, and property, and distinction, all go to the same tune. The excess of any of these things is apt to be a source of hatreds and divisions among states and individuals; and the defect of them is commonly a cause of slavery. — *Laws*, iv. 253.

Boldness of the Philosopher as to death.

—— Simmias, as the true philosophers are ever studying death, to them, of all men, death is the least terrible. Look at the matter in this way: if they have been always enemies of the body, and wanting to have the soul alone, when this is granted to them, how inconsistent would they be to be trembling and repining; instead of rejoicing at their departing to that place where, when they arrive, they hope to gain that which in life they loved (and this was wisdom), and at the same time to be rid of the company of their enemy. Many a man has been willing to go to the world below animated by the hope of seeing there an earthly love, or wife, or son, and conversing with them. And will he who is a true lover of wisdom, and is strongly persuaded in like manner that only in the world below he can worthily enjoy her, still repine at death? Will he not depart with joy? Surely he will, my friend, if he be a true philosopher. For he will have a firm conviction that there only, and nowhere else, he can find wisdom in her purity. And if this be true, he would be very absurd, as I was saying, if he were to fear death.

He would indeed, replied Simmias.

And when you see a man who is repining at the approach of death, is not his reluctance a sufficient proof that he is not a lover of wisdom, but a lover of the body, and probably at the same time a lover of either money or power, or both?

That is very true, he replied.

There is a virtue, Simmias, which is named courage. Is not that characteristic of the philosopher?

Certainly. — *Phaedo*, i. 394.

Boldness in thought.

—— *Theaet.* I cannot say, Socrates, that knowledge is all opinion, because there may be a false opinion; but I will venture to say, that knowledge is true opinion; let this then be my answer; and if this is hereafter disproved, I must try to find another.

Soc. That is the way in which you ought to answer, Theaetetus, and not in your former hesitating strain, for if we are bold we shall gain one of two advantages; either we shall find that which we seek, or we shall be less likely to think that we know what we do not know — and this surely is no mean reward. — *Theaetetus*, iii. 391.

Boundaries, removal of. See *Landmarks*.

Brave, honor to the. See *Battle, death in.*

—— There is another manner in which, according to Homer, brave youths should be honored; for he tells how Ajax, after he had distinguished himself in battle, was rewarded with long chines, which seems to be a complement appropriate to a hero in the flower of his age, being not only a tribute of honor but also a very strengthening thing.

Very true, he said.

Then in this, I said, Homer will be our teacher; and we too, at sacrifices and on the like occasions, will honor the brave, whether men or women, with hymns —

"and seats of precedence, and meats and flowing goblets;"

and in honoring them, we shall also be training them.

That, he replied, is excellent.

Yes, I said; and when a man dies gloriously in war shall we not say, in the first place, that he is of the golden race?

To be sure.

Nay, have we not the authority of Hesiod for affirming that when they are dead —

"They are holy angels upon the earth, authors of good, averters of ill, the guardians of speech-gifted men?"

Yes, and we believe him.

We must inquire of the God how we are to order the sepulture of divine and heroic personages, and do as he bids?

By all means.

And in ages to come we will do service to them and worship at their shrines as heroes. And not only they but any who are preëminently good, whether they die from age, or in any other way, shall be admitted to the same honors.

That is very right, he said.

Next, how shall our soldiers treat their enemies? What do you say about this?

In what respect do you mean?

I mean, shall they be made slaves? Do you think that Hellenes ought to enslave Hellenes, or allow others to enslave them, if they can help? Should not their custom be to spare them, considering the danger which there is that the whole race may one day fall under the yoke of the barbarians?

To spare them is infinitely better.— *The Republic*, ii. 296.

Brave sons of brave parents. See *State*, *Heroes*, etc.

Burial and remembrance of the dead.

—— At their death, the most moderate funeral is best, neither exceeding the customary expense, nor yet falling short of the honor which has been usually shown by the former generation to their parents; and let a man not forget to pay the yearly tribute of respect to the dead, honoring them chiefly by omitting nothing that conduces to a perpetual remembrance of them, and giving a reasonable portion of his fortune to the dead.

Doing this, and living after this manner, we shall receive our reward from the Gods and those who are above us; and we shall spend our days for the most part in good hope. — *Laws*, iv. 245.

Business, men of — their money-sting.

—— On the other hand, the men of business, stooping as they walk, and pretending not even to see those whom they have already ruined, insert the sting — that is, their money — into some one else who is not on his guard against them, and recover the parent sum many times over multiplied into a family of children: and so they make drone and pauper to abound in the State.

Yes, he said, there are plenty of them, that is certain.

The evil is like a fire which is blazing up, and which they will not extinguish. — *The Republic*, ii. 383.

Calmness in view of death. See *Courage*.

—— *Soc.* Why have you come at this hour, Crito? it must be quite early?

Crito. Yes, certainly.

Soc. What is the exact time?

Cr. The dawn is breaking.

Soc. I wonder the keeper of the prison would let you in.

Cr. He knows me because I often come, Socrates; moreover, I have done him a kindness.

Soc. And are you only just arrived?

Cr. No, I came some time ago.

Soc. Then why did you sit and say nothing, instead of at once awakening me?

Cr. By the Gods, Socrates, I would rather not myself have all this sleeplessness and sorrow. I have been wondering at your peaceful slumbers, which was the reason why I did not awaken you, because I wanted you to be out of pain. I have always thought you of a happy disposition; but never did I see anything like the easy, tranquil manner in which you bear this calamity.

Soc. Why, Crito, when a man has reached my age he ought not to be repining at the prospect of death.

Cr. And yet other old men find themselves in similar misfortunes, and age does not prevent them from repining. — *Crito*, i. 347.

Causes and conditions confounded.

—— I found my philosopher altogether forsaking mind or any other principle of order, but having recourse to air, and ether, and water, and other eccentricities. I might compare him to a person who began by maintaining generally that mind is the cause of the actions of Socrates, but who, when he endeavored to explain the causes of my several actions in detail, went on to show that I sit here because my body is made up of bones and muscles ; and the bones, as he would say, are hard and have joints which divide them, and the muscles are elastic, and they cover the bones, which have also a covering or environment of flesh and skin which contains them ; and as the bones are lifted at their joints by the contraction or relaxation of the muscles, I am able to bend my limbs, and this is why I· am sitting here in a curved posture ;—that is what he would say, and he would have a similar explanation of my talking to you, which he would attribute to sound, and air, and hearing, and he would assign ten thousand other causes of the same sort, forgetting to mention the true cause, which is, that the Athenians have thought fit to condemn me, and accordingly I have thought it better and more right to remain here and undergo my sentence ; for I am inclined to think that these muscles and bones of mine would have gone off long ago to Megara or Boeotia, — by the dog of Egypt they would, if they had been moved only by their own idea of what was best, and if I had not chosen as the better and nobler part, instead of playing truant and running away, to undergo any punishment which the State inflicts. There is surely a strange confusion of causes and conditions in all this. It may be said, indeed, that without bones and muscles and the other parts of the body I cannot execute my purposes. But to say that I do as I do because of them, and that this is the way in which mind acts, and not from the choice of the best, is a very careless and idle mode of speaking. I wonder that they cannot distinguish the cause from the condition, which the many, feeling about in the dark, are always mistaking and misnaming. — *Phaedo*, i. 427.

Cause, limit and, in the Universe. See *Limit*, etc.

Cause for every creation.

—— What is that which always is and has no becoming ; and what is that which is always becoming and never is ? That which is apprehended by intelligence and reason always is, and is the same ; but that which is conceived by opinion with the help of sensation and without reason, is always in a process of becoming and perishing, but never really is. Now everything that becomes or is created must of necessity be created by some cause, for nothing can be created without a cause. The work of the artificer who looks always to the abiding and the unchangeable, and who designs and fashions his work after an unchangeable pattern, must of necessity be made fair and perfect; but that of an artificer who looks to the created only, and fashions his work after a created pattern, is not fair or perfect. Was the heaven then or the world, whether called by this or any other more acceptable name — assuming the name, I am asking a question which has to be asked at the beginning of every inquiry — was the world, I say, always in existence and without beginning? or created and having a beginning? Created, I reply, being visible and tangible and having a body, and therefore sensible; and all sensible things which are apprehended by opinion and sense are in a process of creation and created. Now that which is created must of necessity be created by a cause. — *Timaeus*, ii. 523.

Cause, mind a. See *Mind*, etc.

Causes; two kinds of, intelligent and unintelligent.

—— These are the works of the second and coöperative causes which God, carrying into execution the idea of the best as far as possible, uses as his ministers. They are thought by most men not to be the second, but the prime causes of all things, because they freeze and heat, and contract and dilate, and the like. But they are not so, for they are incapable of reason or intellect; the only being which can properly have mind is the invisible soul, whereas fire and water, and earth and air, are all of them visible bodies. The lover of intellect and knowledge ought to explore causes of intelligent nature first of all, and, secondly, of those which are moved by others and of necessity move others. And this we too must now do. Both kinds of causes should be considered by us, but a distinction should be made between those which are endowed with mind and are the workers of things fair and good, and those which are deprived of intelligence and accomplish their several works by chance and without order. Of the second or concurrent causes of sight, which give to the eyes the power which they now possess, enough has been said. I will therefore now proceed to speak of the higher use and purpose for which God has given them to us. The sight in my opinion is the source of the greatest benefit to us, for had the eyes never seen the stars, and the sun, and the heaven, none of the words which we have spoken about the universe would ever have been uttered. But now the sight of day and night, and the revolution of the months and years, have given us the invention of number, and a conception of time, and the power of inquiring about the nature of the whole; and from this source we have derived philosophy, than which no greater good ever was or will be given by the gods to mortal man. This is the greatest boon of sight: and of the lesser benefits why should I speak, even the ordinary man if he were blind would in vain bewail the loss of them.

Thus much let me say however: God invented and gave us sight to the end, that we might behold the courses of intelligence in the heaven, and apply them to the courses of our own intelligence which are akin to them, the unperturbed to the perturbed; and that we, learning them and being partakers of the true computations of nature, might imitate the absolutely unerring courses of God and regulate our own vagaries. The same may be affirmed of speech and hearing; they have been given by the gods to the same end and for a like reason. For this is the principal end of speech, and there is a similar use of musical sound, which is given to the hearing for the sake of harmony. And harmony, which has motions akin to the revolutions of our souls, is not regarded by him who intelligently uses the Muses as given by them with a view to irrational pleasure, which is the prevailing opinion in our day, but with a view to the inharmonical course of the soul, and to be our ally in reducing this into harmony and agreement with itself; and rhythm was given by them for the same reason, on account of the irregular and graceless ways which prevail among mankind generally, and to help us against them.

Thus far in what we have been saying, with small exceptions the works of intelligence have been set forth; and now we must place by the side of them the things done from necessity — for the creation is mixed, being made up of necessity and mind. Mind, the ruling power, persuaded necessity to bring the greater part of created things to perfection, and thus in the beginning, when the influence of reason got the better of necessity, the universe was created. But if a person will truly tell of the way in which the work was accomplished, he must include the other influence of the variable cause as well. Wherefore, we must return again and find another suitable beginning, as about the former matters, so also about these. To which end we must consider the nature of fire, and water, and air, and earth, which were prior to the creation of the heavens, and what happened before there were elements; for no one has as yet explained them, but we speak of fire and the rest of them, whatever they mean, as though men knew their natures, and we maintain them to be the letters or elements of the whole, when they cannot reasonably be compared by a man of any sense even to the syllables or first compounds. And let me say thus much : I will not speak of the first principle·or principles of all things, or by whatever name they are to be called, for this reason, — because it is difficult to set forth my opinion according to the mode of discussion which we are at present employing. Do not imagine, any more than I can bring myself to imagine, that I should be right in undertaking so difficult a task. I will observe the rule of probability with which I began, not less but more than others and especially when I speak of the beginning of each and all. Once more, then, I call upon God, at the beginning of my discourse, and beg him to be our saviour out of a strange and unwonted inquiry, and to bring us to probability.— *Timaeus*, ii. 539.

Censorship of Fiction. See *Fiction*.

Censure, right and good.

—— *Ath.* At our time of life, Cleinias, there should be no feeling of irritation.

Cle. Certainly not.

Ath. I will not at present determine whether he who censures the Cretan or Lacedaemonian polities is right or wrong. But I believe that I can tell better than either of you what the many say about them. For assuming that you have reasonably good laws, one of the best of them will be a law forbidding any young men to inquire which of them are right or wrong; but with one mouth and one voice, they must all agree that the laws are all good and of divine origin ; and any one who says the contrary is not to be listened to. But an old man who remarks any defect, may communicate his observation to a ruler or to an equal when no young man is present.

Cle. Exactly so, Stranger ; and like a diviner, although not there at the time, you seem to me quite to have hit the meaning of the legislator, and to say what is most true.

Ath. As there are no young men present, and the legislator has given old men free license, there will be no impropriety in our discussing these matters now that we are alone.

Cle. True. And, therefore, you may be as free as you like in your censure of our laws, for there is no discredit in knowing what is wrong; he who receives what is said in a generous and friendly spirit will be the better for it.

Ath. Very good; however, I am not going to censure your laws until to the best of my ability I have examined them, but I am going to raise doubts about them. For you are the only people known to us, whether Greek or barbarian, whom the legislator commanded to eschew all great pleasures and amusements; whereas in the matter of pains or fears which we have just been discussing, he thought that they who from infancy had always avoided the pains, and fears and sorrows which must be, when they were compelled to face them would run away from those who were hardened in them, and become their subjects.

Now the legislator ought to have considered that this was equally true of pleasure; he should have said to himself, that if our citizens are from their youth upward unacquainted with the greatest pleasure, and unused to endure amid the temptations of pleasure, and are not disciplined to refrain from all things evil, the sweet feeling of pleasure will overcome them just as fear would overcome the former class; and in another, and even a worse manner, they will be the servants of those who are able to endure amid pleasures, and have had the opportunity of enjoying them, they being often the worst of mankind. One half of their souls will be a slave, the other half free; and they will not be worthy to be called in the true sense men and freemen. Tell me whether you assent to my words?

Cle. On first hearing, what you say appears to be the truth; but to be hasty in coming to a conclusion about such important matters, would be very childish and simple. — *Laws,* iv. 165.

Chance and Nature. See *Nature.*
Chance in legislation. See *Legislation,* etc.
Changeableness of Youth.

—— When a young man who has been brought up as we were just now describing, in a vulgar and miserly way, has tasted drones' honey and has come to associate with fierce and dangerous natures who are able to provide for him all sorts of refinements and varieties of pleasure, — then, as you may imagine, the change will begin of the oligarchical principle within him into the democratical.

Inevitably.

And as in the city like was helping like, and the change was effected by an alliance from without assisting one division of the citizens, so the young man also changes by a class of desires from without assisting the unsatisfied desires within him, that which is akin and alike again helping that which is akin and alike.

Certainly.

And if there be any ally which aids the oligarchical principle within him, whether the influence of friends or kindred, advising or rebuking him, then there arises a faction and an opposite faction, and the result is a civil war.

It must be so.

And there are times when the democratical principle gives way to the oligarchical, and some of his desires die, and others are banished; a spirit of reverence enters into the young man's soul and order is restored.

Yes, he said, that sometimes happens.

And then, again, after the old desires have been driven out fresh ones spring up, which are akin to them ;· and because he their father does not know how to educate them, wax fierce and numerous.

Yes, he said, that is apt to be the way.

They draw him to his old associates, and holding secret intercourse with them, breed and multiply in him?

Very true.

At length they seize upon the citadel of the young man's soul, which they perceive to be void of all fair accomplishments and pursuits of every true word, which are the best guardians and sentinels in the minds of men who are dear to the gods.

None better.

False and boastful words and conceits mount upwards instead of them, and occupy the vacant post.

They are sure to do so.

And so the young man returns into the country of the lotus-eaters, and takes up his abode there in the face of all men, and if any help be sent by his friends to the oligarchical part of him, the same vain conceits shut the gate of the king's fastness; they will not allow the new allies to pass. And if private individuals, venerable for their age, come and parley, they do not receive them; there is a battle and they win: then modesty, which they call silliness, is ignominiously thrust into exile by them. They affirm temperance to be unmanliness, and her also they contemptuously eject; and they pretend that moderation and orderly expenditure are vulgarity and meanness; and, by the help of a rabble of evil appetites they drive them beyond the border.

Yes, with a will.

And when they have emptied and swept clean the soul of him who is now in their power, and is being initiated by them in great mysteries, the next thing is to bring back to their house insolence and anarchy and waste and impudence in bright array, having garlands on their heads, with a great company, while they hymn their praises and call them by sweet names; insolence they term breeding, and anarchy liberty, and waste magnificence, and impudence courage. And so the young man passes out of his original nature, which was trained in the school of necessity, into the freedom and libertinism of useless and unnecessary pleasures.

Yes, he said, the change in him is visible enough.

After this he lives on, spending his money and labor and time on unnecessary pleasures quite as much as on necessary ones; but if he be fortunate, and is not too much intoxicated with passion, when he gets older, after the great tumult has passed away — supposing that he then readmits into the city some part of the exiled virtues, and does not wholly give himself up to their successors — in that case he balances his pleasures and lives in a sort of equilibrium, putting the government of himself into the hands of the one which comes first and wins the turn; and when he has had enough of that, then into the hands of another, and is very impartial in his encouragement of them all.

Very true, he said.

Neither does he receive or let pass into the fortress any true word of advice; if any one says to him that some pleasures are the satisfactions of good and noble desires, and others of evil desires, and that he ought to use and honor some and curtail and reduce others — whenever this is repeated to him he shakes his head and says that they are all alike, and that one is as honorable as another.

Yes, he said; that is the way with him.

Yes, I said, he lives through the day indulging the appetite of the hour; and sometimes he is lapped in drink and strains of the flute; then he is for total abstinence, and tries to get thin; then, again, he is at gymnastics; sometimes idling and neglecting everything, then once more living the life of a philosopher; often he is at politics, and starts to his feet and says and does whatever comes into his head; and, if he is emulous of any one who is a warrior, off he is in that direction, or of men of business, once more in that. His life has neither order nor law; and so he goes on continually and he terms this joy and freedom and happiness.

Yes, his life is all liberty, and equality.

Yes, I said; and multiform and full of the most various characters; — he answers to the State which we described as fair and spangled. And many a man and many a woman will emulate him and many a constitution and many an example of life is contained in him. — *The Republic*, ii. 388.

Children, spoiled by friends.

—— *Soc.* The question is, Which of us is skillful or successful in the treatment of the soul, and which of us has had good teachers?

La. Well but, Socrates; did you never observe that some persons, who have had no teachers, are more skillful than those who have, in some things?

Soc. Yes, Laches, I have observed that; but you would not be very willing to trust them if they only professed to be masters of their art, unless they could show some proof of their skill or excellence in one or more works.

La. That is true.

Soc. And therefore, Laches and Nicias, as Lysimachus and Melesias, in their anxiety to improve the minds of their sons, have asked our advice about them, we too should tell them who our teachers were, if we say that we have had any, and prove them to be men of merit and experienced trainers of the minds of youth and really our teachers. Or if any of us says that he has no teacher, but that he has works to show of his own; then he should point out to them, what Athenians or strangers, bond or free, he is generally acknowledged to have improved. But if he can show neither teachers nor works, then he should tell them to look out for others; and not to run the risk of spoiling the children of friends, which is the most formidable accusation that can be brought against any one by those nearest to him. — *Laches*, i. 78.

Children, training of, not easy.

—— Just as I thought that I had finished, and was only too glad that I had laid this question to sleep, and was reflecting how fortunate I was in your acceptance of what I then said, you begin again, ignorant of what a hornet's nest of words, you are arousing. Now I foresaw this coming trouble, and avoided it.

For what do you think that we are here? said Thrasymachus; to find the philosopher's stone, or to hear discourse?

Yes, but discourse should have a limit.

Yes, Socrates, said Glaucon, and the whole of life is the only limit which wise men assign to the hearing of such discourses. But never mind about us; only get on and in your own way answer the question: What sort of community of women and children is this which is to prevail among the guardians? and how shall we manage the period between birth and education which seems to require the greatest care? Tell us how these things will be.

Yes, my simple friend, but the answer is the reverse of easy; many more doubts arise about this than about our previous speculations. For the practicability of what is said may be doubted; and looked at in another point of view, whether the scheme, if ever so practicable, will be for the best, is also doubtful. Hence there arises a fear, as we draw near, lest our aspiration should be a dream only. — *The Republic,* ii. 274.

Children, taught their letters.

—— *Str.* I will proceed, finding as I do, such a ready listener in you: when children are beginning to know their letters —

Y. Soc. What are you going to say?

Str. That they easily recognize the several letters in very short and easy syllables, and are able to tell you them correctly.

Y. Soc. Certainly.

Str. Whereas in other syllables they do not recognize them, and think and speak falsely of them.

Y. Soc. Very true.

Str. Will not the best and easiest way of guiding them to the letters which they do not as yet know, be to refer them to the same letters in the words which they know, and to compare these with the letters which as yet they do not know, and show them that they are the same, and have the same character in their different combinations, until the letters, which they do not know, have been all placed side by side with the letters which they do know? in this way they have examples, and are made to learn that every letter in every combination is pronounced always either as the same or not the same.— *Statesman*, iii. 562.

Children, what they owe to their parents. See *Parents*.

—— Next comes the honor of living parents, to whom, as is meet, we have to pay the first and greatest and oldest of all debts, considering that all which a man has belongs to those who gave him birth and brought him up, and that he must do all that he can to minister to them: first, in his property; secondly, in his person; and thirdly, in his soul; paying the debts due to them for the care and travail which they bestowed upon him of old, in the days of his infancy, and which he is now to pay back to them when they are old and in the extremity of their need. And all his life long he ought never to utter, or to have uttered, an unbecoming word to them; for of all light and winged words he will have to give an account; Nemesis, the messenger of Justice, is appointed to watch over them. When they are angry, and want to satisfy their feelings in word or deed, he should not resist them, for a father who thinks that he has been wronged by his son, may be reasonably expected to be very angry. — *Laws*, iv. 245.

Children, falsely trained.

—— *Ath.* I imagine that Cyrus, though a great and patriotic general, had never given his mind to education, and never attended to the order of his household.

Cle. What makes you say so?

Ath. I think that from his youth upwards he was a soldier, and intrusted the bringing up of his children to the women; and they brought them up from their childhood as the favorites of fortune, who were blessed already, and needed no more blessings. They thought that they were happy enough, and that no one should be allowed to oppose them in any way, and they compelled every one to praise all that they said or did. This was the manner in which they brought them up.

Cle. A splendid education truly!

Ath. Such an education as women were likely to give them, and especially princesses who had recently grown rich, and in the absence of the men, too, who were occupied in wars and dangers, and too busy to look after them.

Cle. What would you expect?

Ath. Their father had possessions of cattle and sheep, and many herds of men and other animals; but he did not consider that those to whom he was about to make them over, were not trained in his own calling, which was Persian; for the Persians are shepherds — sons of a rugged land, which was a stern mother, and well fitted to produce a sturdy race able to live in the open air and watch, and to fight also, if fighting was required. He did not observe that his sons were trained differently; through the so-called blessing of being royal, they were educated in the corrupt Median fashion by women and eunuchs, which led to their becoming such as people do become when they are brought up unreproved. And so, after the death of Cyrus, his sons, in the fullness of luxury and license, took the kingdom, and first one slew the other because he could not endure a rival; and, afterwards, the slayer himself, mad with wine and brutality, lost his kingdom through the Medes and the eunuch, as they called him, who despised the folly of Cambyses.

Cle. That is what is said, and is probably the truth.

Ath. Yes; and the tradition says, that the empire came back to the Persians, through Darius and the seven chiefs.

Cle. True.

Ath. Let us note the rest of the story. Observe, that Darius was not the son of a king, and had not received a luxurious education. When he came to the throne, being one of the seven, he divided the country into seven portions, and of this arrangement there are some shadowy traces still remaining; he made laws upon the principle of introducing universal equality in the order of the State, and he embodied in a law the settlement of the tribute which Cyrus promised, — thus creating a feeling of friendship and community among all the Persians, and attaching the people to him with money and gifts. Hence his armies cheerfully acquired for him countries as large as those which Cyrus had left behind him. Darius was succeeded by his son Xerxes, and he again was brought up in the royal and luxurious fashion. Might we not justly say, "O Darius, why did you not learn wisdom from the misfortunes of Cyrus, instead of bringing up Xerxes in the same way in which he brought up Cambyses?" For Xerxes being the creation of the same education, met with much the same fortune as Cambyses; and from that time to this there has never been a really great king among the Persians, although they are all called great. And their degeneracy is not to be attributed to chance, as I maintain; the reason is rather the evil life which is generally led by the sons of very rich and royal persons; for never will boy or man, young or old, excel in virtue, who has been thus educated. And this, I say, is what the legislator has to consider, and what at this moment has to be considered by us. Justly may you, O Lacedaemonians, be praised for this — that you do not give special honor or maintenance to wealth rather than to poverty in particular, or to a royal rather than to a private station, where the divine and inspired lawgiver has not originally commanded them to be given. For no man ought to have preëminent honor in a state because he surpasses others in wealth, any more than because he is swift or fair or strong, unless he have some virtue in him; nor even if he have virtue, unless he have this particular virtue of temperance. — *Laws*, iv. 223.

Children, riches an evil left to.

—— I would not have any one fond of heaping up riches for the sake of his children, in order that he may leave them as rich as possible. For the possession of great wealth is of no use, either to them or to the State. The condition of youth which is free from flattery, and at the same time not in need of the necessaries of life, is the best and most harmonious of all, being in accord and agreement with our nature, and making life to be most entirely free from sorrow. Let parents, then, bequeath to their children not riches, but the spirit of reverence. We, indeed, fancy that they will inherit reverence from us, if we rebuke them when they show a want of reverence. But this quality is not really imparted to them by the present style of admonition, which only tells them that the young ought always to be reverential. A sensible legislator will rather exhort the elders to reverence the younger, and above all to take heed that no young man sees or hears him doing or saying anything base; for where old men have no shame, there young men will most certainly be devoid of reverence. The best way of training the young, is to train yourself at the same time; not to admonish them, but to be always carrying out your own principles in practice. — *Laws*, iv. 254.

Children; education of. See *Youth*, etc.

—— And now, assuming that children of both sexes have been born, their nurture and education will properly follow next in order; this cannot be left altogether unnoticed, and yet may be thought to be rather a subject for precept and admonition than for law. In private life there are many little things, not always apparent, arising out of the pleasures and desires and pains of individuals, which are contrary to the intention of the legislator ; these minutiæ alter and discompose the characters of the citizens, and cause great evil in states; for they are so small and of such frequent occurrence, that there would be an unseemliness and want of propriety in making them penal by law ; and if made penal, they are the destruction of the written law, because mankind get the habit of frequently transgressing in small matters. The result is that you cannot legislate about them, and still less can you say nothing. I speak somewhat darkly, but I shall endeavor also to bring my wares into the light of day, for I acknowledge that at present there is a want of clearness in what I am saying.

Cle. Very true.

Ath. Am I not right in maintaining that a good education is that which tends most to the improvement of mind and body ?

Cle. Undoubtedly.

Ath. And nothing can be plainer than that the fairest bodies ought to grow up from infancy in the best and straightest manner ?

Cle. Very true.

Ath. And do we not further observe that the first shoot of every living thing is by far the greatest and fullest ? Many will even contend that a man at twenty-five does not grow to twice the height which he attained at five.

Cle. True.[1] — *Laws*, iv. 306.

Choral song; harmony in.

—— *Ath.* I was speaking at the commencement of our discourse, as you will remember, of the fiery nature of young creatures ; I said that they were unable to keep quiet either in limb or voice, and that they called out and jumped about in a disorderly manner ; and that no other animal attained to any perception of order, but man only. Now the order of motion is called rhythm, and the order of the voice, in which high and low are duly mingled, is called harmony ; and both together are termed choric song. And I said that the gods had

---

[1] In Book vii. of his " Laws," Plato discusses quite extensively the education of children.

pity on us, and gave us Apollo and the Muses to be our playfellows and leaders in the dance; and Dionysus, as I dare say that you will remember, was the third.

Cle. I quite remember.

Ath. Thus far I have spoken of the chorus of Apollo and the Muses, and I have still to speak of the remaining chorus, which is that of Dionysus.

Cle. How is that arranged? There is something strange, at any rate, on first hearing, in a Dionysiac chorus of old men, if you really mean that those who are above thirty, and may be fifty, or from fifty to sixty years of age, are to form a dance in his honor.

Ath. That is very true; and I think with you that some reason should be given for the proposal.

Cle. Certainly.

Ath. Are we agreed thus far?

Cle. About what?

Ath. That every man and boy, slave and free, both sexes, and the whole city, should never cease charming themselves with the strains of which we have spoken; and that there should be every sort of change and variation of them in order to take away the effect of sameness, so that the singers may always receive pleasure from their hymns, and may never weary of them. — *Laws,* iv. 194.

Choristers; how they should sing.

—— Music is more celebrated than any other kind of imitation, and therefore requires the greatest care of them all. For if a man makes a mistake here, he may do himself the greatest injury by welcoming evil dispositions, and the mistake may be very difficult to discern, because the poets are artists very inferior in character to the Muses themselves, who would never fall into the monstrous error of assigning to the words of men the gestures and songs of women; nor combine the melodies and gestures of freemen with the rhythms of slaves and men of the baser sort; or, beginning with the rhythms and gestures of freemen, assign to them a melody or words which are of an opposite character; nor would they mix up the voices and sounds of animals and of men and instruments, and every other sort of noise, as if they were all one. But human poets are fond of introducing this sort of inconsistent mixture, and thus make themselves ridiculous in the eyes of those who, as Orpheus says, "are ripe for pleasure." The experienced see all this confusion, and yet the poets go on and make still further havoc by separating the rhythm and the figure of the dance from the melody, setting words to metre without music, and also separating the melody and rhythm from the words, using the lyre or the flute alone. For when there are no words, it is very difficult to recognize the meaning of the harmony and rhythm, or to see that any worthy object is imitated by them. And we must acknowledge that all this sort of thing, which aims only at swiftness and smoothness and a brutish noise, and uses the flute and the lyre not as the mere accompaniments of the dance and song, is exceedingly rude and coarse. The use of either, when unaccompanied by the others, leads to every sort of irregularity and trickery. This is all true enough. But we are considering not how our choristers, who are from thirty to fifty years of age, and may be over fifty, are not to use the Muses, but how are they to use them. And the considerations which we have urged seem to show in what way these fifty years' old choristers who are to sing, may be expected to be better trained. For they need to have a quick perception and knowledge of harmonies and rhythms; otherwise, how will they ever know which melodies would be rightly sung to the Dorian mode, or to the rhythm which the poet has assigned to them? — *Laws*, iv. 199.

Christ, unconsciously described. See *Just man*.

Cities, maritime, evil of,

—— *Ath. Str.* And now, what will this city be? I do not mean to ask what is or will be the name of the place; that may be determined by the accident of locality or of the original settlement, — a river or fountain, or some local deity may give the sanction of a name to the newly founded city; but I do want to know what the situation is; whether maritime or inland?

Cleinias. I should imagine, Stranger, that the city of which we are speaking is about eighty stadia distant from the sea.

Ath. And are there harbors on the seaboard?

Cle. Excellent harbors, Stranger; there could not be better.

Ath. You don't say so! And is the surrounding country productive, or in need of importations?

Cle. Hardly in need of anything.

Ath. And is there any neighboring State?

Cle. None whatever, and that is the reason for selecting the place; in days of old, there was a migration of the inhabitants, and the region has been deserted from time immemorial.

Ath. And has the place a fair proportion of hill, and plain, and wood?

Cle. Like the rest of Crete in that.

Ath. You mean to say that there is more rock than plain?

Cle. Exactly.

Ath. Then there is some hope that your citizens may be virtuous; had you been on the sea, and well provided with harbors, and an importing rather than a producing country, some mighty saviour would have been needed, and lawgivers more than mortal, if you were ever to have a chance of preserving your state from degeneracy and discordance of manners. But there is comfort in the eighty stadia: although the sea is too near, especially if, as you say, the harbors are so good. Still we must be satisfied. The sea is pleasant enough as a daily companion, but has also a bitter and brackish quality; filling the streets with merchants and shopkeepers, and begetting in the souls of men uncertain and unfaithful ways — making the State unfriendly and unfaithful both to her own citizens, and also to other nations. There is a consolation, therefore, in the country producing all things at home; and yet, owing to the ruggedness of the soil, not providing anything in great abundance. Had there been abundance there might have been a great export trade, and a great return of gold and silver; which, as we may safely affirm, has the most fatal result on a state whose aim is the attainment of just and noble sentiments; this was said by us, if you remember, in the previous discussion. — *Laws*, iv. 233.

Cities need faithful watchers.

—— Thus, O my friends, and for the reasons given, should a state act which would endure and be saved. But as a ship sailing on the sea has to be watched night and day, in like manner a city also is sailing on a sea of politics, and is liable to all sorts of insidious assaults; and therefore from morning to night, and from night to morning, rulers must join hands with rulers, and watchers succeed watchers, receiving and giving up their trust in a perpetual order. A multitude can never fulfil a duty of this sort with anything like energy; moreover, the greater number of the senators will have to be left during the greater part of the year to order their concerns at their own homes. They must be arranged in twelve portions, answering to twelve months, and serve as guardians each portion for a single month. Their business is to be at hand and receive any foreigner or citizen who comes to them, whether to give information, or to put questions of which other states are to receive the answers; or when the city desires to ask a question and receive an answer, or again, when there is a likelihood of internal commotions, which are always liable to happen in some form or other, they will, if they can, prevent their occurring; or if they have already occurred, will lose no time in making them known to the city, and healing the evil. Wherefore, also, this which is the presiding body of the State, ought always to have the control of their assemblies, and the dissolutions of them, regular as well as occasional. All this is to be ordered by the twelfth part of the council, which is always to keep watch together with the officers of the State during one portion of the year and to rest during the remaining eleven portions.

Thus will the city be fairly ordered. — *Laws*, iv. 280.

Citizen, right of the State to the. See *Authority*.

Citizen, obligation of the.

—— *Soc.* Then the laws will say: " Consider, Socrates, if we are speaking truly, that in your present attempt you are going to do us an injury. For, after having brought you into the world, and nurtured and educated you, and given you and every other citizen a share in every good which we had to give, we further proclaim to every Athenian, that if he does not like us when he has come of age and has seen the ways of the city, and made our acquaintance, he may go where he pleases and take his goods with him; and none of us laws will forbid him or interfere with him. Any of you who does not like us and the city, and who wants to emigrate to a colony or to any other city, may go where he likes, and take his goods with him. But he who has experience of the manner in which we order justice and administer the State, and still remains, has entered into an implied contract that he will do as we command him. And he who disobeys us is, as we maintain, thrice wrong: first, because in disobeying us he is disobeying his parents; secondly, because we are the authors of his education; thirdly because he has made an agreement with us that he will duly obey our commands; and he neither obeys them nor convinces us that our commands are unjust; and we do not rudely impose them, but give him the alternative of obeying or convincing us; that is what we offer, and he does neither.

These are the sort of accusations to which, as we were saying, you, Socrates, will be exposed if you accomplish your intentions; you, above all other Athenians." Suppose I ask, why is this? they will justly retort upon me that I above all other men have acknowledged the agreement. "There is clear proof," they will say, " Socrates, that we and the city were not displeasing to you. Of all Athenians you have been the most constant resident in the city, which, as you never leave, you may be supposed to love. For you never went out of the city either to see the games, except once when you went to the Isthmus, or to any other place unless when you were on military service; nor did you travel as other men do. Nor had you any curiosity to know other states or their laws : your affections did not go beyond us and our State; we were your special favorites, and you acquiesced in our government of you; and here in this city you begat your children, which is a proof of your satisfaction. Moreover, you might, if you had liked, have fixed the penalty at banishment in the course of the trial — the State which refuses to let you go now would have let you go then. But you pretended that you preferred death to exile, and that you were not grieved at death. And now you have forgotten these fine sentiments, and pay no respect to us the laws, of whom you are the destroyer; and are doing what only a miserable slave would do, running away and turning your back upon the compacts and agreements which you made as a citizen. And first of all answer this very question : Are we right in saying that you agreed to be governed according to us in deed, and not in word only? Is that true or not?" How shall we answer that, Crito? Must we not assent?

Cr. There is no help, Socrates.— *Crito,* i. 356.

Citizen, improvement of the.

—— *Soc.* And now, my friend, as you are already beginning to be a public character, and are admonishing and reproaching me for not being one, suppose that we ask a few questions of one another. Tell me, then, Callicles, how about making any of the citizens better? Was there ever a man who was once vicious, or unjust, or intemperate, or foolish, and became by the help of Callicles good and noble? Was there ever such a man, whether citizen or stranger, slave or freeman? Tell me, Callicles, if a person were to ask these questions of you, what would you answer? Whom would you say that you had improved by your conversation? There may have been good deeds of this sort which were done by you as a private person, before you came forward in public. Why will you not answer? *Cal.* You are contentious, Socrates.

Soc. Nay, I ask you, not from a love of contention, but because I really want to know in what way you think that affairs should be administered among us — whether, when you come to the administration of them, you have any other aim but the improvement of the citizens? Have we not already admitted many times over that such is the duty of a public man? Nay, we have surely said so; for if you will not answer for yourself I must answer for you. But if this is what the good man ought to effect for the benefit of his own State, allow me to recall to you the names of those whom you were just now mentioning, Pericles, and Cimon, and Miltiades, and Themistocles, and ask whether you still think that they were good citizens.

Cal. I do. — *Gorgias*, iii. 106.

City, heavenly. See *Heavenly idea of the earth.*
City — the mother of her citizens. See *State, a parent,* etc.
Clever unjust, the.

—— Look at things as they really are and you will see that the clever unjust are in the case of runners, who run well from the starting-place to the goal, but not back again from the goal: they go off at a great pace, but in the end only look foolish, slinking away with their ears down on their shoulders, and without a crown; but the true runner comes to the finish and receives the prize and is crowned. And this is the way with the just; he who endures to the end of every action and occasion of his entire life has a good report and carries off the prize which men bestow.

True.

And now you must allow me to repeat the blessings which you attributed to the fortunate unjust. I shall say of the just as you were saying of them, that as they grow older, if that is their desire, they become rulers in their own city, if they care to be; they marry whom they like and give in marriage to whomsoever they like; all that you said of the others I now say of these. And, on the other hand, I say of the unjust that the greater number, even though they escape in their youth, are found out at last and look foolish at the end of their course, and when they come to be old and miserable are flouted alike by stranger and citizen; they are beaten and then come those things unfit for ears polite, as you truly term them; they will be racked and burned, as you were saying — but I shall ask you to imagine that I have repeated your tale of horrors. — *The Republic*, ii. 445.

Cognitions, ideas that are.

—— But may not the ideas, asked Socrates, be thoughts only, and have no proper existence except in our minds, Parmenides? For in that case each idea may still be one, and not experience this infinite subdivision.

And can there be individual thoughts which are thoughts of nothing?

That is impossible, he said.

The thought must be of something?

Yes.

Of something that is or is not?

Of something that is.

Must it not be of a single something, which the thought recognizes as attaching to all, being a single form or nature?

Yes.

And will not this something, so apprehended which is always the same in all, be an idea?

From that, again, there is no escape.

Then, said Parmenides, if you say that everything else participates in the ideas, must you not say either that everything is made up of thoughts and that all things think; or that they are thoughts having no thought?

But that, Parmenides, is no more rational than the other. The more probable view is, that the ideas are, as it were, patterns fixed in nature, and that other things are like them, and resemblances of them; and that what is meant by the participation of other things in the ideas, is really assimilation to them. — *Parmenides*, iii. 249.

Colonization, a means of purification. See *Purification*.

Colonization, the best kind of.

—— Cities find colonization in some respects easier when the colonists are of one race, which like a swarm of bees is sent out from a single country, friends from friends, owing to some pressure of population, or other similar necessity, or because a portion of a state is driven by factions to emigrate. And there have been whole cities which have taken flight, when utterly conquered by a superior power in war. This, however, which is in one way an advantage to the colonist or legislator, in another point of view creates a difficulty. There is an element of friendship in the community of race, and language, and laws, and in common sacrifices, and the like; but colonies which are of this homogeneous sort are apt to kick against any laws different from their own; and although the badness of their own laws has undone them, yet because of the force of habit they would fain preserve the very customs which were their ruin; and the leader of the colony, who is their legislator, finds them troublesome and rebellious. On the other hand, the conflux of several populations might be more disposed to listen to new laws; but then, to make them combine and pull together, as they say of horses, is a most difficult task, and the work of years. And yet there is nothing which perfects the virtue of men like legislation and colonization.— *Laws*, iv. 235.

Color what is it?

— *Soc.* And now, as Pindar says, "Read my meaning:" color is an effluence of form, commensurate with sight, and sensible.

Theaet. I believe, Socrates, that you have truly explained his meaning.

Soc. Then apply his doctrine to perception, my good friend, and first of all to vision; that which you call white color is not in your eyes, and is not a distinct thing which exists out of them, nor can you assign any place to it; for if it had position it would be and be at rest, and there would be no process of becoming.

Theaet. Then what is color?

Soc. Let us carry out the principle which has just been affirmed, that nothing is self-existent, and then we shall see that every color, white, black, and every other color, arises out of the eye meeting the appropriate motion, and that what we term the substance of each color is neither the active nor the passive element, but something which passes between them, and is peculiar to each percipient; are you certain that the several colors appear to every animal — say to a dog — as they appear to you?

Theaet. Indeed I am not.

Soc. Or that anything appears the same to you as to another man? Would you not rather question whether you yourself see the same thing at different times, because you are never exactly the same?

Theaet. I should.

Soc. And if that with which I compare myself in size, or which I apprehend, were great or white or hot, it could not without actually changing become different by mere contact with another; nor again, if the apprehending or comparing subject were great or white or hot, could this, when unchanged from within, become changed by any approximation or affection of any other thing. For in our ordinary way of speaking we allow ourselves to be driven into most ridiculous and wonderful contradictions, as Protagoras and all who take his line of thought would remark. — *Theaetetus,* iii. 354.

Colors.

—— There is a fourth class of sensible things, having many varieties, which have now to be distinguished. They are called by the general name of colors, and are a flame which emanates from all bodies and has particles corresponding to the sense of sight. I have spoken already, in what has preceded, of the generation of sight, and this will be a natural and suitable place in which to give some account of colors.

Of the particles coming from other bodies which fall upon the sight, some are less and some are larger, and some are equal to the parts of the sight itself. Those which are equal are imperceptible, or transparent, as they are called by us; whereas the larger produce contraction, the smaller dilation, in the sight, by the exercise of a power akin to that of hot and cold bodies on the flesh, or of astringent bodies on the tongue, or of those heating bodies which are termed pungent by us. White and black, although they are found in another class of objects, and for this reason are imagined to be different, are affections of the same kind. Wherefore, we ought to term white that which dilates the visual ray, and the opposite of this black. There is also a swifter motion and impact of another sort of fire which dilates the ray of sight and reaches the eyes, forcing a way through their passages and melting them, and eliciting from them a union of fire and water which we call tears, being itself an opposite fire which comes to them from without — the inner fire flashes forth like lightning, and the outer finds a way in and is extinguished in the tear-drop, and all sorts of colors are generated by the mixture. This affection is termed dazzling, and the object which produces it is called bright and flashing. There is another sort of fire which is intermediate, and which reaches and mingles with the moisture of the eye without flashing; and in this the fire mingling with the ray of the tear-drop produces a color like blood, to which we give the name of red. A bright hue mingled with red and white gives the color called auburn (ξανθόν). The law of proportion, however, according to which the several colors are formed, even if a man knew he would be foolish if he attempted to tell, as he could not give any necessary reason, nor even any tolerable or probable account of them. Again, red, when mingled with black and white, gives a purple hue, which becomes umber (ὄρφνινον) when the colors are burnt as well as mingled and the black is more thoroughly mixed with them. Flame color (πυρρὸν) is produced by a union of auburn and dun (φαιὸν) and dun by an admixture of black and white; yellow (ὠχρὸν) by an admixture of white and auburn. White and bright meeting, and falling upon a full black, become dark blue (κυανοῦν), and when dark blue mingles with white, light blue (γλαυκὸν) color is formed, as leek green (πράσιον) is formed also out of the union of flame color and black. There will be no difficulty in seeing how the colors derived from these are mingled and assimilated in accordance with probability. He, however, who should attempt to verify all this by experiment, would forget the difference of the human and divine nature. For God only has the knowledge and also the power which are able to combine many things into one and again dissolve the one into many. But no man either is or ever will be able to accomplish either the one or the other operation. — *Timaeus*, ii. 559.

Community of wives.

➤— Here, then, is one difficulty in our law about women which we have escaped; the wave has not swallowed us up alive for enacting that the guardians of either sex should have all their pursuits in common; to the utility and possibility of this the argument is its own witness.

Yes, that was a mighty wave which you have escaped.

Yes, I said, but a much greater is coming; you will not think much of this when you see the next.

Go on, let me see.

The law, I said, which is the sequel of this and of all that has preceded, is to the following effect, — "that the wives of these guardians are to be common, and their children also common, and no parent is to know his own child, nor any child his parent."

Yes, he said, that is a much greater wave than the other; and the utility as well as the possibility of such a law is far more doubtful.

I do not think, I said, that there can be any dispute about the very great utility of having wives and children in common; the possibility is quite another matter, and will be very much disputed. — *The Republic*, ii. 282.

Community, the first form of government.

—— The first and highest form of the State and of the government and of the law is that in which there prevails most widely the ancient saying, that " Friends have all things in common." Whether there is now, or ever will be, this communion of women and children and of property, in which the private and individual is altogether banished from life, and things which are by nature private, such as eyes and ears and hands, have become common, and in some way see and hear and act in common, and all men express praise and blame, and feel joy and sorrow, on the same occasions, and the laws unite the city to the utmost, — whether all this is possible or not, I say that no man, acting upon any other principle, will ever constitute a state more exalted in virtue, or truer or better than this. Such a state, whether inhabited by Gods or sons of Gods, will make them blessed who dwell therein; and therefore to this we are to look for the pattern of the State, and to cling to this, and, as far as possible, to seek for one which is like this. The State which we have now in hand, when created, will be nearest immortality and unity in the next degree; and, after that, by the grace of God, we will complete the third one. And, we will begin by speaking of the nature and origin of the second.

Let them at once distribute their land and houses, and not till the land in common, since a community of goods goes beyond their proposed origin, and nurture, and education. But in making the distribution, let the several possessors feel that their particular lots also belong to the whole city; and seeing that the earth is their parent, let them tend her more carefully than children do their mother. For she is a goddess and their queen, and they are her mortal subjects. — *Laws*, iv. 264.

Comparatives.

—— *Soc.* Ever, as we say, into the hotter and the colder there enters a more and a less.

Pro. True.

Soc. Then, says the argument, they have never any end, and being endless must also be infinite.

Pro. Yes, Socrates, that is exceedingly true.

Soc. Yes, my dear Protarchus, and the word which you have just uttered suggests to me that such expressions as " exceedingly " and also the term " mildly " mean the same as more or less; for whenever they occur they do not allow of the existence of quantity — they are always introducing degrees into actions, instituting a comparison of the more or less violent or more or less mild, and at each creation of more or less, quantity disappears. For, as I was just now saying, if quantity and measure did not disappear, but were allowed to intrude in the sphere of more and less and the other comparatives, these last would themselves be driven out of their own domain. When definite quantity is once admitted, there can be no longer a " hotter " or a " colder " (for these are always progressing, and are never in one stay); but definite quantity is at rest, and progresses not. Which proves that comparatives, such as the hotter and the colder, are to be ranked in the class of the infinite. — *Philebus*, iii. 159.

Compulsory and voluntary care of men. See *Education, compulsion in*.

—— *Str.* Our first duty, as we were saying, was to remodel the name, so as to have the notion of care rather than of feeding, and then to divide, for there may be still considerable divisions.

Y. Soc. How can they be made?

Str. First by separating the divine shepherd from the human guardian or manager.

Y. Soc. True.

Str. And the art of management which is assigned to man would again have to be subdivided.

Y. Soc. On what principle?

Str. On the principle of voluntary and compulsory.

Y. Soc. Why?

Str. Because, if I am not mistaken, there has been an error here; for our simplicity led us to rank them together, whereas they are utterly different, and their modes of government are different.

Y. Soc. True.

Str. Then, now, as I said, let us make the correction and divide human care into two parts, on the principle of voluntary and compulsory.

Y. Soc. Certainly.

Str. And if we call the management of violent rulers tyranny, and the voluntary management of voluntary bipeds politics, may we not further assert that he who has this latter art of management is the true king and statesman?

Y. Soc. I think, Stranger, that we have now completed the account of the Statesman. — *Statesman*, iii. 560.

Concealment of evil.

—— Probably the youth will say to himself in the words of Pindar: —

" Can I by justice or by crooked ways of deceit ascend a loftier tower, which may be a fortress to me all my life ? "

For what men say is that, if I am really just without being thought just, this is no profit, but evident pain and loss. But if, though unjust, I acquire the character of justice, a heavenly life is to be mine. Since then, as philosophers say, appearance tyrannizes over truth and is the lord of happiness, to appearance I must wholly devote myself. I will have in front of me the painted form and figure of virtue; behind I will trail the subtle and crafty fox, as Archilochus, first of sages, counsels. But I hear some one exclaiming that wickedness is not easily concealed; to which I answer, — Nothing great is easy. Nevertheless, this must be the way to happiness, and the way by which we must go, if we follow in the steps of the argument. As to concealment, that may be secured by the formation of societies and political clubs. And there are professors of rhetoric who teach the philosophy of persuading courts and assemblies; and so, partly by persuasion and partly by force, I shall make unlawful gains and not be punished. Still I hear a voice saying that the gods cannot be deceived, neither can they be compelled. But what if there are no gods? or, suppose that the gods have no care about human things — why in either case should we care about concealment? And even if there are gods, and they have a care of us, yet we know about them only from tradition and the genealogies of the poets; and the poets are the persons who say that they may be influenced and turned by " sacrifices and soothing entreaties." Let us be consistent then, and either believe both or neither. And if we believe them, why then we had better be unjust, and offer of the fruits of injustice; for if we are just we shall indeed escape the vengeance of heaven, but we shall lose the gains of injustice; whereas, if we are unjust, we shall keep the gains, and by our sinning and praying, and praying and sinning, the gods will be propitiated, and we shall be forgiven. "But there is a world below in which either we or our children will suffer for our deeds." Yes, my friend, will be the reply, but there are mysteries and atoning deities, and these have great power. That is what mighty cities declare; and the children of the gods, who were their poets and prophets, affirm the same. — *The Republic*, ii. 187.

Conception and generation, divine nature of.

———— "There is a certain age at which human nature is desirous of procreation — procreation which must be in beauty and not in deformity; and this procreation is the union of man and woman, and is a divine thing; for conception and generation are an immortal principle in the mortal creature, and in the inharmonious they can never be. But the deformed is always inharmonious with the divine, and the beautiful harmonious. Beauty, then, is the destiny or goddess of parturition who presides at birth, and therefore when approaching beauty the conceiving power is propitious, and diffuse, and benign, and begets and bears fruit: at the sight of ugliness it frowns and contracts in pain, and is averted and morose, and shrinks up, and not without a pang refrains from conception. And this is the reason why, when the hour of conception arrives, and the teeming nature is full, there is such a flutter and ecstasy about beauty whose approach is the alleviation of the pain of travail. For love, Socrates, is not, as you imagine, the love of the beautiful only." "What then?" "The love of generation and of birth in beauty." "Yes," I said. "Yes, indeed," she replied. "But why of generation?" I said. "Because to the mortal, generation is a sort of eternity and immortality," she replied; "and if as has been already admitted, love is of the everlasting possession of the good, all men will necessarily desire immortality together with good, wherefore love is of immortality."

All this she taught me at various times when she spoke of love. And I remember that she once said to me, "What is the cause, Socrates, of love, and the attendant desire? See you not how all animals, birds as well as beasts, in their desire of procreation, are in agony when they take the infection of love; this begins with the desire of union; whereto is added the care of offspring, on behalf of whom the weakest are ready to battle against the strongest even to the uttermost, and to die for them, and will let themselves be tormented with hunger or suffer anything in order to maintain their offspring." — *The Symposium*, i. 498.

Concupiscent nature ruled.

—— Ought not the rational principle, which is wise, and has the care of the whole soul, to rule, and the passionate or spirited principle to be the subject and ally?

Certainly.

And, as we were saying, the united influence of music and gymnastic will bring them into accord, nerving and sustaining the reason with noble words and lessons, and moderating and soothing and civilizing the wildness of passion by harmony and rhythm?

Quite true, he said.

And these two, thus nurtured and educated, and having learned truly to know their own functions, will rule over the concupiscent part of every man, which is the largest and of all things most insatiable; over this they will keep guard, lest, waxing great with the fullness of bodily pleasures, as they are termed, and no longer confined to her own sphere, the concupiscent soul should attempt to enslave and rule those who are not her natural-born subjects, and overturn the whole life of man?

Very true, he said.

The two will be the defenders of the whole soul and the whole body against attacks from without; the one counseling, and the other fighting under his leader, and courageously executing his commands and counsels. — *The Republic*, ii. 268.

Confidence and courage. See *Ability*, etc.

Conjecture in art.

—— *Soc.* I mean to say, that if arithmetic, mensuration, and weighing be taken away from any art, that which remains will not be much.

Pro. Not much, certainly.

Soc. The rest will be only conjecture, and the better use of the senses, which is given by experience and exercise in addition to a certain power of guessing, which is commonly called art, and is perfected by attention and practice.

Pro. Nothing more assuredly.

Soc. Music, for instance, is full of this empiricism; as is seen in the harmonizing of sounds, not by rule, but by conjecture; the music of the flute is always trying to guess the pitch of each vibrating note, and is therefore mixed up with much that is doubtful and has very little certainty. — *Philebus*, iii. 196.

Consonances and harmonies.

—— I conceive that as the eyes are designed to look up at the stars, so are the ears to hear harmonious motions, and these are sister sciences — as the Pythagoreans say, and we, Glaucon, agree with them?

Yes, he replied.

But this, I said, is a laborious study, and therefore we had better go and learn of them; and they will tell us whether there are any other applications of these sciences. At the same time, we must not lose sight of our own higher object.

What is that?

There is a perfection which all knowledge ought to reach, and which our pupils ought also to attain, and not to fall short of, as I was saying that they did in astronomy. For in the science of harmony, as you probably know, they are equally empirical. The sounds and consonances which they compare are those which are heard only, and their labor, like that of the astronomers, is in vain.

Yes, by heaven! he said; and 'tis as good as a play to hear them talking about their condensed notes, as they call them; they put their ears alongside of their neighbors as if to get a sound out of them — one set of them declaring that they catch an intermediate note and have found the least interval which should be the unit of measurement; the others maintaining the opposite theory that the two sounds have passed into the same — either party setting their ears before their understanding.

You mean, I said, those gentlemen who tease and torture the strings and rack them on the pegs of the instrument: I might carry on the metaphor and speak after their manner of the blows which the plectrum gives, and make accusations against the strings, both of backwardness and forwardness to sound; but this would be tedious, and therefore I will only say that these are not the men, but that I am speaking of the Pythagoreans, of whom I was just now proposing to inquire about harmony. For they too are in error, like the astronomers; they investigate the numbers of the harmonies which are heard, but they never attain to problems — that is to say, they never reach the natural harmonies of number, or reflect why some numbers are harmonious and others not. — *The Republic*, ii. 358.

Conspirators and traitors.

—— Whoever by promoting a man to power enslaves the laws, and subjects the city to factions, using violence and stirring up sedition contrary to law, him we will deem the greatest enemy of the whole State. But he who takes no part in such proceedings, and yet being the chief magistrate of the State, knowing of them or not knowing of them, by reason of cowardice does not interfere on behalf of his country, such an one we must consider nearly as bad. Every man who is worth anything will inform the magistrates, and bring the conspirator to trial for making a violent and illegal attempt to change the government. The judges of the traitor shall be the same as of the robbers of temples; and let the whole proceeding be carried on in the same way, and the vote of the majority condemn to death. But let there be a general rule, that the disgrace and punishment of the father is not to be visited on the children, except in the case of some one whose father, grandfather, and great-grandfather have successively undergone the penalty of death. Such persons the city shall send away with all their possessions, reserving only and wholly their appointed lot to their original city and country. And out of the citizens who have more than one son of not less than ten years of age, they shall select ten whom their father or grandfather by the mother's or father's side shall appoint, and let them send to Delphi the names of those who are selected, and him whom the God appoints they shall establish as heir of the house which has failed; and may he have better fortune than his predecessors! — *Laws*, iv. 369.

Constituency, legislators not always to obey their.

——*Str.* They say, that if any one knows how the ancient laws may be improved, he must first persuade his own State of the improvement, and then he may legislate, but not otherwise.

Y. Soc. And are they not right?

Str. I dare say. But supposing that he does use some gentle violence for their good, what is this violence to be called? Or rather, before you answer, let me ask the same question in reference to our previous instance.

Y. Soc. What do you mean?

Str. Suppose that a skillful physician has a patient, of whatever sex or age, whom he compels against his will to do something for his good which is contrary to the written rules, what is this compulsion to be called? Would you ever dream of calling it a violation of the art, or breach of the laws of health? Nothing could be more unjust than for the patient to whom such a gentle violence is applied, to charge the physician who practices the violence with wanting skill or aggravating his disease.

Y. Soc. Most true.

Str. In the political art the error is not called disease, but evil, or disgrace, or injustice.

Y. Soc. Quite true.

Str. And when the citizen, contrary to law and custom, is compelled to do what is juster and better and nobler than he did before, and this sort of violence is blamed, the last and most absurd thing which he could say, is that he has incurred disgrace or evil or injustice at the hands of the legislator who uses the violence.

Y. Soc. That is very true.

Str. And shall we say that the violence, if exercised by a rich man, is just, and if by a poor man, unjust? May not any man, rich or poor, with or without written laws, with the will of the citizens or against the will of the citizens, do what is for their interest? Is not this the true principle of government, in accordance with which the wise and good man will order the affairs of his subjects? As the pilot watches over the interests of the ship, or of the crew, and preserves the lives of his fellow-sailors, not by laying down rules, but by making his art a law — even so, and in the self-same way, may there not be a true form of polity created by those who are able to govern in a similar spirit, and who show a strength of art which is superior to the law? Nor can wise rulers ever err while they regard the one great rule of distributing justice to the citizens with intelligence and art, and are able to preserve, and, so far as that is possible, to improve them. — *Statesman*, iii. 582.

Contradiction, the art of.

―― Verily, Glaucon, I said, glorious is the power of the art of contradiction!

Why do you say so?

Because I think that many a man falls into the practice against his will. When he thinks that he is reasoning he is really disputing, just because he cannot define and divide, and so know that of which he is speaking; and he will pursue a merely verbal opposition in the spirit of contention and not of fair discussion.

Yes, he replied, such is very often the case ; but what has that to do with us and our argument ?

A great deal ; for there is certainly a danger of our getting unintentionally into a verbal opposition.

In what way ?

Why we valiantly and pugnaciously insist upon the verbal truth, that different natures ought to have different pursuits, but we never considered at all what was the meaning of sameness or difference of nature or why we distinguished them when we assigned different pursuits to different natures. — *The Republic*, ii. 278.

Controversy.

—— *Str.* Let us consider once more whether there may not be another aspect of sophistry ?

Theaet. What is that ?

Str. In the acquisitive there was a subdivision of the combative or fighting art.

Theaet. There was.

Str. Perhaps we had better divide it.

Theaet. What shall be the divisions ?

Str. There shall be one division of the competitive, and the other of the pugnacious.

Theaet. Very good.

Str. That part of the pugnacious which is a contest of bodily strength may be properly called by some such name as violent.

Theaet. True.

Str. And when the war is one of words, that may be termed controversy ?

Theaet. Yes.

Str. And controversy may be of two kinds.

Theaet. What are they ?

Str. When long speeches are answered by long speeches, and there is public discussion about the just and unjust, that is forensic controversy.

Theaet. Yes.

Str. And there is a private sort of controversy, which is cut up into questions and answers, and this is commonly called disputation ?

Theaet. Yes, that is the name.

Str. And of disputation, that sort which is only a discussion about contracts, and is carried on at random, and without rules of art, is recognized by dialectic to be a distinct class, but has hitherto had no distinctive name, and does not deserve to receive one at our hands.

Theaet. No; for the different species are too minute and heterogeneous.

Str. But that which proceeds by rules of art to dispute about justice and injustice in their own nature and about things in general, have we not been accustomed to call argumentation (Eristic)?

Theaet. Very true. — *Sophist,* iii. 459.

Conventional notions of right.

—— *Soc.* I declare, O Callicles, that Callicles will never be at one with himself, but that his whole life will be a discord. And yet, my friend, I would rather that my lyre should be inharmonious, and that there should be no music in the chorus which I provided; aye, or that the whole world should be at odds with me, and oppose me, rather than that I myself should be at odds with myself, and contradict myself.

Cal. O, Socrates, you are a regular declaimer, and are manifestly running riot in the argument. And now you are declaiming in this way because Polus has met with the same evil fate himself which he accused you of bringing upon Gorgias: he said, if I remember rightly, that when Gorgias was asked by you, whether, if some one came to him who wanted to learn rhetoric, and did not know justice, he would teach him justice? And Gorgias in his modesty replied that he would, because he thought that mankind in general would expect this of him, and would be displeased if he said "No;" in consequence of this admission, Gorgias was compelled to contradict himself, and you were delighted; Polus laughed at you at the time, deservedly, as I think; and now he has himself experienced the same misfortune. I cannot say very much for his wit when he conceded to you, that to do is more dishonorable than to suffer injustice, for this was what led to his being entangled by you; and because he was too modest to say what he thought, he had his mouth stopped. For the truth is, Socrates, that you, who pretend to be engaged in the pursuit of truth, are appealing now to the popular and vulgar notions of right, which are not natural, but only conventional. Convention and nature are generally at variance with one another: and hence, if a person is too modest to say what he thinks, he is compelled to contradict himself; and you, in your ingenuity, perceiving the advantage to be hereby gained, slyly ask of him who is arguing con-

ventionally a question which is to be determined by the rule of
nature; and if he is talking of the rule of nature, you slip away
to custom: as you did in this very discussion about doing and
suffering injustice. When Polus was speaking of the conventionally dishonorable, you assailed him from the point of view
of nature; for by the rule of nature, to suffer injustice is the
greater disgrace, because the greater evil; but conventionally,
to do evil is the more disgraceful. For the suffering of injustice is not the part of a man, but of a slave, who indeed had
better die than live; since when he is wronged and trampled
upon, he is unable to help himself, or any other about whom
he cares.

The reason, as I conceive, is that the makers of laws are the
majority who are weak; and they make laws and distribute
praises and censures with a view to themselves and to their own
interests; and they terrify the stronger sort of men, and those
who are able to get the better of them, in order that they may
not get the better of them; and they say, that dishonesty is
shameful and unjust; meaning, by the word injustice, the desire of a man to have more than his neighbors; for knowing
their own inferiority I suspect they are too glad of equality.
And therefore the endeavor to have more than the many, is
conventionally said to be shameful and unjust, and is called injustice, whereas nature herself intimates that it is just for the
better to have more than the worse, the more powerful than
the weaker; and in many ways she shows, among men as well
as among animals, and indeed among whole cities and races,
that justice consists in the superior ruling over and having more
than the inferior. For on what principle of justice did Xerxes
invade Hellas, or his father the Scythians (not to speak of
numberless other examples)? These are men who act according to nature; yes, by Heaven, and according to the law of
nature: not, perhaps, according to that artificial law, which we
forge and impose upon our fellows of whom we take the best
and strongest from their youth upwards, and tame them like
young lions, charming them with the sound of the voice, and
saying to them, that with equality they must be content, and
that the equal is the honorable and the just. But if there
were a man who had sufficient force, he would shake off and
break through, and escape from all this; he would trample
under foot all our formulas and spells and charms, and all our
laws, sinning against nature: the slave would rise in rebellion

and be lord over us, and the light of natural justice would shine forth. And this I take to be the sentiment of Pindar, in the poem in which he says that —

"Law is the king of all, mortals as well as immortals."
— *Gorgias*, iii. 71.

Conversion, the process of.

—— Whether I am right or not God only knows. But, whether true or false, my opinion is that in the world of knowledge the idea of good appears last of all, and is seen only with an effort; and, when seen, is also inferred to be the universal author of all things beautiful and right, parent of light and of the lord of light in this world, and the source of truth and reason in the other;. and is the power upon which he who would act rationally either in public or private life must have his eye fixed.

I agree, he said, as far as I am able to understand you.

Moreover, you must not wonder that those who attain to this beatific vision are unwilling to descend to human affairs; for their souls are ever hastening into the upper world where they desire to dwell; and this desire of theirs is very natural, if our allegory may be trusted.

Yes, very natural.

And is there anything surprising in one who passes from divine contemplations to the evil state of man, misbehaving himself in a ridiculous manner; if, while his eyes are blinking and before he has become accustomed to the surrounding darkness, he is compelled to fight in courts of law, or in other places, about the images or shadows of images of justice, and is endeavoring to meet the conceptions of those who have never yet seen the absolute justice?

Anything but surprising, he replied.

Any one who has common sense will remember that the bewilderments of the eyes are of two kinds, and arise from two causes, either from coming out of the light or from going into the light, which is true of the mind's eye, quite as much as of the bodily eye; and he who remembers this when he sees any one whose vision is perplexed and weak, will not be too ready to laugh; he will first ask whether that soul of man has come out of the brighter life, and is unable to see because unaccustomed to the dark, or having turned from darkness to the day is dazzled by excess of light. And he will count the one happy in his condition and state of being, and he will pity the other; or, if he have a mind to laugh at the soul which comes from below into the light, there will be more reason in this than in the laugh which greets the other coming from above into the den.

That, he said, is a very just remark.

But if I am right, then certain professors of education must be mistaken in saying that they can put a knowledge into the soul which was not there before, like sight into blind eyes.

Nevertheless, they do say so, he replied.

Whereas, I said, our argument shows that the power is already in the soul; and that as the eye may be imagined unable to turn from darkness to light without the whole body, so too, when the eye of the soul is turned round, the whole soul must be turned round from the world of becoming into that of being, and learn by degrees to endure the sight of being, and of the brightest and best of being — or in other words, of the good.

Very true.

And there must be some art which will affect conversion in the easiest, quickest manner; not implanting eyes, for they exist already, but giving them a right direction, which they have not. — *The Republic*, ii. 344.

Cookery, not an art.

—— *Soc.* Let me now remind you of what I was saying to Gorgias and Polus; I was saying, as you will not have forgotten, that there were some processes which aim at pleasure, and at pleasure only, and know nothing of good and evil, and there are other processes which know good and evil. And I considered that cookery, which I do not call art, but only an experience, was of the former class, which is concerned with pleasure, and the art of medicine was of the class which is concerned with the good. And now, by the god of friendship, I must beg you, Callicles, not to jest, or to imagine that I am jesting with you; do not answer at random what is not your real opinion; for you will observe that we are arguing about the way of human life; and to a man who has any sense at all what question can be more serious than this? whether he should follow after that way of life to which you exhort me, and act what you call the manly part of speaking in the assembly, and cultivating rhetoric, and engaging in public affairs, after your manner; or whether he should pursue the life of philosophy; and in what the latter way of life differs from the former. But perhaps we had better distinguish them first, as I attempted to do before, and when we come to an agreement that they are distinct, we may proceed to consider in what they differ from one another, and which of them we should choose. Perhaps, however, you do not even now understand what I mean?

Cal. No, I do not.

Soc. Then I will explain myself more clearly: seeing that you and I have agreed that there is such a thing as good, and that there is such a thing as pleasure, and that pleasure is not the same as good, and that the pursuit and process of acquisition of the one, that is pleasure, is different from the pursuit and process of acquisition of the other, which is good — I wish that you would tell me whether you agree thus far or not?

Cal. Yes, I agree.

Soc. Then I will proceed, and ask whether you also agree with me, and whether you think that I spoke the truth when I further said to Gorgias and Polus — that cookery in my opinion is only an experience, not an art at all; and that whereas medicine is an art, and attends to the nature and constitution of the patient, and has principles of action and reason in each case, cookery, in attending upon pleasure, never regards either the nature or the reason of that pleasure to which she devotes herself, nor ever considers or calculates anything, but works by experience and routine, and just preserves the recollection of what she had usually done when producing pleasure. And first I would have you consider whether I have proved what I was saying, and then whether there are not other similar processes which have to do with the soul — some of them processes of art, making a provision for the soul's highest interest — others despising the interest, and, as in the previous case, considering only the pleasure of the soul, and how this may be acquired, but not considering what pleasures are good or bad, and having no other aim but to afford gratification, whether good or bad. In my opinion, Callicles, there are such processes, and this is the sort of thing which I term flattery, whether concerned with the body or the soul, or whenever employed with a view to pleasure, and without any consideration of good and evil. — *Gorgias*, iii. 91.

Cookery, medicine, etc.

—— Now, seeing that there are these four arts which are ever ministering to the body and the soul for their highest good; flattery knowing or rather guessing their natures, has distributed herself into four shams or simulations of them;

she puts on the likeness of one or other of them, and pretends to be that which she simulates, and has no regard for men's highest interests, but is ever making pleasure the bait of the unwary, and deceiving them into the belief that she is of the highest value to them. Cookery simulates the disguise of medicine, and pretends to know what food is the best for the body; and if the physician and the cook had to enter into a competition in which children were the judges, or men who had no more sense than children, as to which of them best understands the goodness or badness of food, the physician would be starved to death. A flattery I deem this and an ignoble sort of thing, Polus, for to you I am now addressing myself, because it aims at pleasure instead of good. An art I do not call it but only an experience because it is unable to explain or to give a reason of the nature of its own applications. And I do not call any irrational thing an art; if you dispute my words, I am prepared to argue in defense of them.

Cookery, then, as I maintain, is a flattery which takes the form of medicine, and dressing up, in like manner, is a flattery which takes the form of gymnastic, and is knavish, false, ignoble, illiberal, working deceitfully by the help of lines, and colors, and enamels, and garments, and making men affect a spurious beauty to the neglect of the true beauty which is given by gymnastic.

I would rather not be tedious, and therefore I will only say, after the manner of the geometricians (for I think that by this time you will be able to follow),

As dressing up : gymnastic : : cookery : medicine; or rather —

As dressing up : gymnastic : : sophistry : legislation; and —

As cookery : medicine : : rhetoric : justice.

And this, I say, is the natural difference between the rhetorician and the sophist, but by reason of their near connection, they are apt to be jumbled up together neither do they know what to make of themselves, nor do other men know what to make of them. For if the body presided over itself, and were not under the guidance of the soul, and the soul did not discern and discriminate between cookery and medicine, but the body was made the judge of them, and the rule of judgment was the bodily delight which was given by them, then the word of Anaxagoras, that word with which you, friend

Polus, are so well acquainted, would come true; Chaos would return, and cookery, health, and medicine would mingle in an indiscriminate mass. And now I have told you my notion of rhetoric, which is in relation to the soul what cookery is to the body. — *Gorgias*, iii. 51.

Corporeal, and spiritual essence.

―― Now God did not make the soul after the body, although we have spoken of them in this order; for when he put them together he would never have allowed that the elder should serve the younger, but this is a random manner of speaking which we have, because we ourselves too are very largely affected by chance. Whereas he made the soul in origin and excellence prior to and older than the body, to be the ruler and mistress, of whom the body was to be the subject. And he made her out of the following elements and on this manner: of the unchangeable and indivisible, and also of the divisible and corporeal he made a third sort of intermediate essence, partaking of the same and of the other or diverse, and this compound in like manner he placed in a mean between the indivisible and the divisible or corporeal. He took the three elements of the same, the other, and the essence, and mingled them all together, compressing the reluctant and unsociable nature of the other into the same. And when he had mixed them and out of all the three made one, he again divided this whole into as many portions as was fitting, each of them containing an admixture of all three. — *Timaeus*, iii. 528.

Counterparts and antagonisms in nature making harmony. See *Antagonisms*.

Country, motherhood of. See *Motherhood*.

Courage, a man of.

―― *Soc.* Laches, suppose that we first set about determining the nature of courage, and in the second place proceed to inquire how the young men may attain this quality by the help of studies and pursuits. Try, and see whether you can tell me what is courage.

La. Indeed, Socrates, that is soon answered: he is a man of courage who remains at his post, and does not run away, but fights against the enemy; of that you may be very certain.

Soc. That is good, Laches; and yet I fear that I did not express myself clearly; and therefore you have answered not the question which I intended to ask, but another.

La. What do you mean, Socrates?

Soc. I will endeavor to explain; you would call a man courageous, who remains at his post, and fights with the enemy?

La. Certainly I should.

Soc. And so should I; but what would you say of another man who fights flying, instead of remaining?

La. How flying?

Soc. Why, as the Scythians are said to fight, flying as well as pursuing; and as Homer says in praise of the horses of Aeneas, that they knew "how to pursue, and fly quickly hither and thither;" and he passes an encomium on Aeneas himself, as having a knowledge of fear or flight, and calls him "an author of fear or flight."

La. Yes, Socrates, and there Homer is right; for he was speaking of chariots, as you were speaking of the Scythian cavalry, who have that way of fighting; but the heavy-armed Greek fights, as I say, remaining in his rank.

Soc. And yet, Laches, you must except the Lacedaemonians at Plataea, who, when they came upon the light shields of the Persians, are said not to have been willing to stand and fight, and to have fled; but when the ranks of the Persians were broken, they turned upon them like cavalry, and won the battle.

La. That is true.

Soc. That was my meaning when I said that I was to blame in having put my question badly, and that this was the reason of your answering badly. For I meant to ask you not only about the courage of heavy-armed soldiers, but about the courage of cavalry and every other style of soldier; and not only who are courageous in war, but who are courageous in perils by sea, and who in disease, or in poverty, or again in politics, are courageous; and not only who are courageous against pain or fear, but mighty to contend against desires and pleasures, either fixed in their rank or turning upon their enemy. There is this sort of courage, is there not, Laches?

La. Certainly, Socrates.

Soc. And all these are courageous, but some have courage in pleasures, and some in pains; some in desires, and some in fears; and some are cowards under the same conditions, as I should imagine.

La. Very true. — *Laches,* i. 83.

Courage, generic.

Soc. Now I was asking about courage and cowardice in general. And I will begin with courage, and once more ask, What is that common quality, which is the same in all these cases, and which is called courage? Do you understand now what I mean?

La. Not over well.

Soc. I mean this: As I might ask what is that quality which is called quickness, and which is found in running, playing the lyre, in speaking, in learning, and in many other similar actions, or rather which we possess in nearly every action that is worth mentioning of arms, legs, mouth, voice, mind; would you not apply the term quickness to all of them?

La. Quite true.

Soc. And suppose I were to be asked by some one: What is that common quality, Socrates, which, in all these uses of the word, you call quickness? I should say that which accomplishes much in a little time — that I call quickness in running, speaking, and every other sort of action.

La. You would be quite correct.

Soc. And now, Laches, do you try and tell me, What is that common quality which is called courage, and which includes all the various uses of the term when applied both to pleasure and pain, and in all the cases which I was just now mentioning?

La. I should say that courage is a sort of endurance of the soul, if I am to speak of the universal nature which pervades them all.

Soc. But that is what we must do if we are to answer the question. And yet I cannot say that every kind of endurance is, in my opinion, to be deemed courage. Hear my reason: I am sure, Laches, that you would consider courage to be a very noble quality.

La. Most noble, certainly.

Soc. And you would say that a wise endurance is also good and noble?

La. Very noble.

Soc. But what would you say of a foolish endurance? Is not that, on the other hand, to be regarded as evil and hurtful?

La. True.

Soc. And is anything noble which is evil and hurtful?

La. I ought not to say that, Socrates.

Soc. Then you would not admit that sort of endurance to be courage — for that is not noble, but courage is noble?

La. You are right.

Soc. Then, according to you, only the wise endurance is courage?

La. True.

Soc. But as to the epithet "wise,"— wise in what? In all things small as well as great? For example, if a man endures in spending his money wisely, knowing that by spending he will acquire more in the end, do you call him courageous?

La. Assuredly not.

Soc. Or, for example, if a man is a physician, and his son, or some patient of his, has inflammation of the lungs, and begs that he may be allowed to eat or drink something, and the other refuses; is that courage?

La. No; that is not courage at all, any more than the last.

Soc. Again, take the case of one who endures in war, and is willing to fight, and wisely calculates and knows that others will help him, and that there will be fewer and inferior men against him than there are with him; and suppose that he has also advantages of position; would you say of such an one who endures with all this wisdom and preparation, that he, or some man in the opposing army who is in the opposite circumstances to these and yet endures and remains at his post, is the braver?

La. I should say that the latter, Socrates, was the braver.

Soc. But, surely, this is a foolish endurance in comparison with the other?

La. That is true.

Soc. And you would say that he who in an engagement of cavalry endures, having the knowledge of horsemanship, is not so courageous as he who endures, having no knowledge of horsemanship?

La. That is my view.

Soc. And he who endures, having a knowledge of the use of the sling, or the bow, or any other art, is not so courageous as he who endures, not having such a knowledge?

La. True.

Soc. And he who descends into a well, and dives, and holds out in this or any similar action, having no knowledge of diving, or the like, is, as you would say, more courageous than those who have this knowledge?

La. Why, Socrates, what else can a man say?

Soc. Nothing, if that is what he thinks.

La. But that is what I do think.

Soc. And yet men who thus run risks and endure are foolish, Laches, in comparison of those who do the same things, having the skill to do them.

La. That is true.

Soc. But foolish boldness and endurance appeared before to be base and hurtful to us.

La. Quite true.

Soc. Whereas courage was acknowledged to be a noble quality.

La. True.

Soc. And now on the contrary we are saying that the foolish endurance, which was before held in dishonor, is courage.

La. Very true.

Soc. And are we right in saying that?

La. Indeed, Socrates, I am sure we that are not right.

Soc. Then according to your statement, you and I, Laches, are not attuned to the Dorian mode, which is a harmony of words and deeds; for our deeds are not in accordance with our words. Any one would say that we had courage who saw us in action, but not, I imagine, he who heard us talking about courage just now.

La. That is most true.

Soc. And is this condition of ours satisfactory?

La. Quite the reverse.

Soc. Suppose, however, that we admit the principle to a certain extent.

La. What principle? And to what extent?

Soc. The principle of endurance. We too must endure and persevere in the inquiry, and then courage will not laugh at our faint-heartedness in searching for courage; which after all may, very likely, be endurance.

La. I am ready to go on, Socrates; and yet I am unused to investigations of this sort. But the spirit of controversy has been aroused in me by what has been said; and I am really grieved at being thus unable to express my meaning. For I fancy that I do know the nature of courage; but, somehow or other, she has slipped away from me, and I cannot get hold of her and tell her nature. — *Laches*, i. 84.

Courage, a special trait of the philosopher. See *Calmness*.

—— The true philosophers, and they only, are ever seeking to release the soul. Is not the separation and release of the soul from the body their especial study?

That is true.

And, as I was saying at first, there would be a ridiculous contradiction in men studying to live as nearly as they can in a state of death, and yet repining when death comes.

Certainly.

Then, Simmias, as the true philosophers are ever studying death; to them, of all men, death is the least terrible. Look at the matter in this way; if they have always been enemies of the body, and wanting to have the soul alone, when this is granted to them, how inconsistent would they be, to be trembling and repining; instead of rejoicing at their departing to that place where, when they arrive, they hope to gain that which in life they loved (and this was wisdom), and at the same time to be rid of the company of their enemy. Many a man has been willing to go to the world below in the hope of seeing there an earthly love, or wife, or son, and conversing with them. And will he who is a true lover of wisdom, and is strongly persuaded in like manner that only in the world below he can worthily enjoy her, still repine at death? Will he not depart with joy? Surely, he will, my friend, if he be a true philosopher. For he will have a firm conviction that there only, and nowhere else, he can find wisdom in her purity. And if this be true, he would be very absurd, as I was saying, if he were to fear death.

He would indeed, replied Simmias.

And when you see a man who is repining at the approach of death, is not his reluctance a sufficient proof that he is not a lover of wisdom, but a lover of the body, and probably at the same time a lover of either money or power, or both?

That is very true, he replied.

There is a virtue, Simmias, which is named courage. Is not that a characteristic of the philosopher?

Certainly. — *Phaedo*, i. 394.

Courage improved by love.

—— I say that a lover who is detected in doing any dishonorable act, or submitting through cowardice when any dishonor is done him by another, will be more pained at being detected by his beloved than at being seen by his father, or by his companions, or by any one else. The beloved, too, when he is seen in any disgraceful situation, has the same feeling about his lover. And if there were only some way of contriving that a state or an army should be made up of lovers and their loves, they would be the very best governors of their own city, abstaining from all dishonor, and emulating one another in honor ; and when fighting at one another's side, although a mere handful, they would overcome the world. For what lover would not choose rather to be seen by all mankind than by his beloved, either when abandoning his post or throwing away his arms? He would be ready to die a thousand deaths rather than endure this. Or who would desert his beloved or fail him in the hour of danger? The veriest coward would become an inspired hero, equal to the bravest, at such a time ; Love would inspire him. That courage which, as Homer says, the God breathes into the soul of heroes, Love of his own nature infuses into the lover.

Love will make men dare to die for their beloved — love alone; and women as well as men. Of this Alcestis the daughter of Pelias is a monument to all Hellas ; for she was willing to lay down her life on behalf of her husband, when no one else would, although he had a father and mother; but the tenderness of her love so far exceeded theirs, that she made them seem to be as strangers in blood to their own son, and in name only related to him ; and so noble did this action of hers appear to the gods, as well as to men, that among the many who have done virtuously she was one of the very few to whom the gods have granted the privilege of returning to earth, in admiration of her virtue ; such exceeding honor is paid by them to the devotion and virtue of love. But Orpheus, the son of Oeagrus, the harper, they sent empty away, and showed him an apparition only of her whom he sought, but herself they would not give up ; because he appeared to them to be enervated by his art and not daring like Alcestis to die for love, to have been contriving how he might enter Hades alive ; moreover, they afterward caused him to suffer death at the hands of women, as the punishment of his cowardliness. — *The Symposium*, i. 473.

Courage in the State.

——— Again, I said, there is no difficulty in seeing the nature of courage, and in what part that quality resides which gives the name of courageous to the State.

How do you mean?

Why, I said, every one who calls any State courageous or cowardly, will be thinking of the part which fights and goes out to battle on the State's behalf.

No one, he replied, would ever think of any other.

The rest of the citizens may be courageous or may be cowardly, but their courage or cowardice will not, as I conceive, have the effect of making the city either one or the other.

Certainly not.

The city will be courageous in virtue of a portion of the citizens in whom resides a never-failing quality preservative of that opinion about things to be feared and not to be feared, in which the legislator educated them; and this is what you term courage.

I should like to hear what you are saying once more, for I do not think that I perfectly understand you.

I mean that courage is a kind of salvation.

Salvation of what?

The salvation, I said, of the opinion about proper objects of fear which the law implants through education; and I mean by the word "never-failing," to intimate that in pleasure or in pain, or under the influence of desire or fear, a man preserves, and does not lose this opinion. — *The Republic*, ii. 254.

Courage and confidence. See *Ability*, etc.

Courage and cowardice.

—— *Al.* I rather think, Socrates, that some honorable things are evil.

Soc. And are some dishonorable things good?

Al. Yes.

Soc. You mean in such a case as the following: In time of war, men have been wounded or have died in rescuing a companion or kinsman, when others who have neglected the duty of rescuing them have escaped in safety?

Al. True.

Soc. And to rescue another under such circumstances is honorable, because of the attempt to save those whom we ought to save; and this is courage?

Al. True.

Soc. But evil because of death and wounds?

Al. Yes.

Soc. And the courage which is shown in the rescue is one thing, and the death another.

Al. Certainly.

Soc. Then the rescue of one's friends is honorable in one point of view, but evil in another?

Al. True.

Soc. And if honorable, then also good: Will you consider now whether I may not be right, for you were acknowledging that the courage which is shown in the rescue is honorable? Now is this courage good or evil? Look at the matter thus: which would you rather choose, good or evil?

Al. Good.

Soc. And the greatest goods you would be most ready to choose, and would least like to be deprived of them?

Al. Certainly.

Soc. What would you say of courage? At what price would you be willing to be deprived of courage?

Al. I would rather die than be a coward.

Soc. Then you think that cowardice is the worst of evils?

Al. I do.

Soc. As bad as death, I suppose?

Al. Yes.

Soc. And life and courage are the extreme opposites of death and cowardice?

Al. Yes.

Soc. And they are what you would most desire to have, and the opposites you would least desire?

Al. Yes.

Soc. Is this because you think life and courage the best, and death and cowardice the worst?

Al. Yes.

Soc. And you would regard the rescue of a friend in battle as good, because of the courage which is there shown?

Al. I should.

Soc. But evil because of the death which ensues?

Al. Yes.

Soc. Might we not describe their different effects as follows: You may call either of them evil in respect of the evil which is the effect, and good in respect of the good which is the effect of either of them?

Al. Yes.

Soc. And they are honorable in so far as they are good, and dishonorable in so far as they are evil?

Al. True.

Soc. Then when you say that the rescue of a friend in battle is honorable and yet evil, that is equivalent to saying that the rescue is good and yet evil?

Al. I believe that you are right, Socrates.

Soc. Nothing honorable, regarded as honorable, is evil; nor anything base, regarded as base, good.

Al. Clearly not. — *Alcibiades I.* iv. 530.

Courage untempered.

—— *Str.* Courage, when untempered by the gentler nature during many generations, may at first bloom and strengthen, but at last bursts forth into every sort of madness.

Y. Soc. Like enough.

Str. And then, again, the soul which is over-full of modesty and has no element of courage in many successive generations, is apt to grow very indolent, and at last to become utterly paralyzed and useless.

Y. Soc. That, again, is quite likely.

Str. It was of these bonds I said that there would be no difficulty in creating them, if only both classes originally held the same opinion about the honorable and good; indeed, in this single word, the whole process of royal weaving is comprised — never to allow temperate natures to be separated from the brave, but to weave them together, like the warp and the woof, by common sentiments and honors and opinions, and by the giving of pledges to one another; and out of them forming one smooth and even web, to intrust to them the offices of State.

Y. Soc. How do you mean?

Str. Where one officer only is needed, you must choose a ruler who has both these qualities; when many, you must mingle some of each, for the temperate ruler is very careful and just and safe, but is wanting in thoroughness and go.

Y. Soc. Certainly, that is very true.

Str. The character of the courageous, on the other hand, falls short of the former in justice and caution, but has the power of action in a remarkable degree, and where either of these two qualities is wanting, there cities cannot altogether prosper either in their public or private life. — *Statesman,* iii. 598.

Courts of Law and lawyers.

—— In courts of law men literally care nothing about truth, but only about conviction : and this is based on probability, to which he who would be a skillful orator should therefore give his whole attention. And they say also that there are cases in which the actual facts ought to be withheld, and only the probabilities should be told either in accusation or defense, and that always in speaking the orator should keep probability in view, and say good-bye to the truth. And the observance of this principle throughout a speech furnishes the whole art.

Phaedr. That is what the professors of rhetoric do actually say, Socrates. I remember that we have touched lightly upon this matter already, but with them the point is all-important.

Soc. I dare say that you are familiar with Tisias. Does he not define probability to be that which the many think?

Phaedr. Certainly he does.

Soc. I believe that he has a clever and ingenious case of this sort : He supposes a feeble and valiant man to have assaulted a strong and cowardly one, and to have robbed him of his coat or of something or other ; he is brought into court, and then Tisias says that both parties should tell lies : the coward should say that he was assaulted by more men than one ; the other should prove that they were alone, and should use this argument : " How could a man like me have assaulted a man like him ? " The complainant will not like to confess his own cowardice, and will therefore invent some other lie which his adversary will thus gain an opportunity of refuting. And there are other devices of the same kind which have a place in the system. Am I not right, Phaedrus?

Phaedr. Certainly. — *Phaedrus,* i. 578.

Courts of justice, establishment of.

—— A city which has no regular courts of law ceases to be a city ; and again, if a judge is silent and says no more than the litigants in preliminary trials and in private arbitrations, he will never be able to decide justly ; wherefore a multitude of judges will not easily judge well, nor a few if they are not good judges. The point in dispute should be made clear by both parties, and time, and deliberation, and repeated examination, greatly tend to clear up doubts. For this reason, he who goes to law with another, should go first of all to his neighbors and friends who know best the questions at issue. And if he be unable to obtain from them a satisfactory decision, let him have recourse to another court; and if the two courts cannot settle the matter, let the third put an end to the suit.

Now the establishment of courts of justice may be regarded as a choice of magistrates, for every magistrate must also be a judge of some things ; and the judge, though he be not a magistrate, yet in certain respects is a very important magistrate on the day on which he is determining a suit. Regarding then the judges also as magistrates, let us say who are fit to be judges, and of what they are to be judges, and how many of them are to judge in each suit. Let that be the supreme tribunal which the ligitants agree to appoint in common for themselves. And let there be two other tribunals : one for private individuals, who desire to have causes of action decided against one another ; the other for public causes, in which some citizen is of opinion that the public has been wronged by an individual, and is willing to vindicate the common interests. — *Laws*, iv. 288.

Cowards, children made. See *Courage*.

—— I said, my dear friend, let none of the poets tell us that

" The gods, taking the disguise of strangers, haunt cities in all sorts of forms; "

and let no one slander Proteus and Thetis, neither let any one, either in tragedy or any other kind of poetry, introduce Here disguised in the likeness of a priestess, —

" Asking an alms for the life-giving daughters of the river Inachus; "

let us have no more lies of that sort. Neither must we have mothers under the influence of the poets scaring their children with abominable tales of certain gods who, as they say,

" Go about by night in the likeness of strangers from every land; "

let them beware lest they blaspheme against the gods and at the same time make cowards of their children. — *The Republic*, ii. 204.

Creation, beginning and reason of the.

—— If the world be indeed fair and the artificer good, then, as is plain, he must have looked to that which is eternal. But if what cannot be said without blasphemy is true, then he looked to the created pattern. Every one will see that he must have looked to the eternal, for the world is the fairest of creations and He is the best of causes. And having been created in this way the world has been framed with a view to that which is apprehended by reason and mind and is unchangeable, and must, if this be admitted, of necessity be the copy of something. Now that the beginning of everything should be according to nature is a great matter. And in speaking of the copy and original we may assume that words are akin to the matter which they describe, when they relate to the lasting and permanent and intelligible, they ought to be lasting and unfailing, and as far as is in their nature irrefutable and immovable — nothing less. But when they express only the copy or image and not the eternal things themselves, they need only be probable and analogous to the real words. As being is to becoming, so is truth to belief. If then, Socrates, amid the many opinions about the gods and the generation of the universe, we are not able to give notions which are in every way exact and consistent with one another, do not be surprised. Enough, if we adduce probabilities as likely as any others, for we must remember that I who am the speaker, and you who are the judges, are only mortal men, and we ought to accept the tale which is probable and not inquire further. — *Timaeus*, ii. 524.

Creations of God indissoluble.

—— Oceanus and Tethys were the children of Earth and Heaven, and from these sprang Phorcys and Cronos and Rhea, and many more with them; and from Cronos and Rhea sprang Zeus and Herè, and all those whom we know as their brethren, and others who were their children.

Now, when all of them, both those who visibly appear in their revolutions as well as those other gods who are of a more retiring nature, had come into being, the Creator of the universe spoke to them as follows : Gods and sons of gods who are my works, and of whom I am the artificer and father, my creations are indissoluble, if so I will. All that is bound may be dissolved, but only an evil being would wish to dissolve that which is harmonious and happy. And although being created, ye are not altogether immortal and indissoluble, ye shall certainly not be dissolved, nor be liable to the fate of death ; having in my will a greater and mightier bond than those which bound you at the time of creation. — *Timaeus*, ii. 533.

Creator, artist.

—— There is another artist, — I should like to know what you would say of him.

Who is he?

One who is the maker of all the works of all other workmen.

What an extraordinary man!

Wait a little, and there will be more reason for your saying so. For this is he who makes not only vessels of every kind, but plants and animals, himself and all other things — the earth and heaven, and the things which are in heaven, or under the earth; he makes the gods also.

He must be a rare master of his art.

Oh! you are unbelieving, are you? Do you mean that there is no such maker or creator, or that in one sense there might be a maker of all these things but not in another? Do you not see that there is a way in which you could make them yourself?

What way?

An easy way enough; or rather, there are many ways in which the feat might be accomplished, none quicker than that of turning a mirror round and round, you would soon make the sun and the heavens, and the earth and yourself, and other animals and plants, and all the other creations of art as well as nature, in the mirror.

Yes, he said, but that is an appearance only.

Very good,.I said, you are coming to the point now; and the painter, as I concèive, is just a creator of this sort, is he not?

Of course. — *The Republic,* ii. 426.

Crimes and criminals — treatment of.

—— There is a sense of disgrace in legislating, as we are about to do, for all the details of crime in a state which, as we say, is to be well regulated and will be perfectly adapted to the practice of virtue. To assume that in such a state there will arise some accomplice in crimes as great as any which are ever perpetrated in other states, and that we must legislate for him by anticipation, and threaten and make laws against him if he should arise; in order to deter him, and punish his acts, under the idea that he will arise — this, as I was saying, is in a manner disgraceful. But seeing that we are not like the ancient legislators, who gave laws to demi-gods and sons of Gods, being themselves, according to the popular belief, the offspring of the gods, and legislating for others, who were also the children of divine parents, whereas we are only men who are legislating for the sons of men, there is no uncharitableness in apprehending that some one of our citizens may be like a seed which has touched the ox's horn, and have a heart which cannot be softened any more than those seeds can be softened by fire.

Among our citizens there may be those who cannot be subdued by all the strength of the laws; and for their sake, though an ungracious task, I will proclaim my first law about the robbing of temples, in case such a crime should ever be committed. I do not expect or imagine that any well-brought-up citizen will ever take the infection, but their servants, and strangers, and strangers' servants, may be guilty of many impieties. And with a view to them especially, and yet not without a provident eye to the weakness of human nature generally, I will proclaim the law about robbers of temples and similar incurable, or almost incurable criminals. Having already agreed that such enactments ought always to have a short prelude, we may speak to the criminal whom some tormenting desire by night and by day tempts to go and rob a temple, in words of admonition and exhortation: O sir, we will say to him, the impulse which moves you to rob temples is not an ordinary human malady, nor yet a visitation of Heaven, but a madness which is begotten in men from ancient and unexpiated crimes of his race, destroying him when his time is come; against this you must guard as well as you can, and how you are to guard I will explain to you. When any such thought comes into your mind, go and perform expiations, go as a supliant to the temples of the Gods who avert evils, go to the society of those who are called good men among you; hear them tell and yourself try to repeat after them, that every man should honor the noble and the just. Fly from the company of the wicked — fly, and turn not back; and if thy disorder is lightened sensibly by these remedies, well and good, but if not, then acknowledge death to be nobler than life, and depart hence.

Such are the preludes which we sing to all who have thoughts of unholy and treasonable actions, and to him who hearkens to them the law has nothing more to say. But to him who is disobedient when the prelude is over, cry with a loud voice, — He who is taken in the act of robbing temples, if he be a slave or stranger, shall have his evil deed engraven on his face and hands, and shall be beaten with as many stripes as may seem good to the judges, and be cast naked beyond the borders of the land. And if he suffers this punishment he will probably be corrected and improved; for no penalty which the law inflicts is designed for evil, but always makes him who suffers either better or not so bad. But if any citizen be found guilty of any great or unmentionable wrong, either in relation to the Gods or his parents, or the State, let the judge deem him to be incurable, remembering what an education and training he has had from youth, upward, and yet has not abstained from the greatest of crimes. The penalty of death is to him the least of evils; and others will be benefited by his example, if he be put away out of the land with infamy.— *Laws*, iv. 366.

Crimnality and punishment of bad public men.

—— Of these fearful examples, most, as I believe, are taken from the class of tyrants and kings and potentates and public men, for they are the authors of the greatest and most impious crimes, because they have the power. And Homer witnesses to the truth of this; for they are always kings and potentates whom he has described as suffering everlasting punishment in the world below;—such were Tantalus, and Sisyphus, and Tityus. But no one ever described Thersites, or any private person who was a villain, as suffering everlasting punishment or as incurable. For to commit the worst crimes, as I am inclined to think, was not in his power, and he was happier than those who had the power. Yes, Callicles, the very bad men come from the class of those who have power. And yet in that very class there may arise good men, and worthy of all admiration they are, for where there is a great power to do wrong, to live and to die justly is a hard thing, and greatly to be praised, and few there are who attain this. Such good and true men, however, there have been, and will be again, in Athens and in other states, who have fulfilled their trust righteously; and there is one who is quite famous all over Hellas, Aristides, the son of Lysimachus. But, in general, great men are also bad, my friend.

And, as I was saying, Rhadamanthus, when he gets a soul of the bad kind, knows nothing about him, neither who he is, nor who his parents are; he knows only that he has got hold of a villain; and seeing this, he stamps him as curable or incurable, and sends him away to Tartarus, whither he goes and receives his recompense. — *Gorgias*, iii. 117.

Criminals co-existing with paupers.

—— God has made the flying drones, Adeimantus, all without stings, whereas of the walking drones he has made some without stings and others with dreadful stings; of the stingless class are those who in their old age end as paupers; of the stingers come all the criminal class, as they are termed.

Most true, he said.

Clearly then, whenever you see paupers in a state, somewhere in that neighborhood there are hidden away thieves and cut-purses, and robbers of temples, and other malefactors.

Clearly.

Well, I said, and in oligarchical states do you not find paupers?

Yes, he said; nearly everybody is a pauper who is not a ruler.

And may we be so bold as to suppose that there are also many criminals to be found in them, rogues who have stings, and whom the authorities are careful to restrain by force?

Certainly, we may be so bold.

The existence of such persons is to be attributed to want of education, ill-training, and an evil constitution of the State?

True. — *The Republic*, ii. 380.

Cures, why unknown to physicians.

—— This Thracian told me that in these notions of theirs, which I was mentioning, the Greek physicians are quite right as far as they go; but Zamolxis, he added, our king, who is also a god, says further, " that as you ought not to attempt to cure the eyes without the head, or the head without the eyes, so neither ought you to attempt to cure the body without the soul; and this," he said, "is the reason why the cure of many diseases is unknown to the physicians of Hellas, because they are ignorant of the whole, which ought to be studied also; for the part can never be well unless the whole is well." For all good and evil, whether in the body or in human nature, originates, as he declared, in the soul, and overflows from thence, as from the head into the eyes. And therefore if the head and the body are to be well, you must begin by curing the soul; that is the first thing. And the cure, my dear youth, has to be effected by the use of certain charms, and these charms are fair words; and by them temperance is implanted in the soul, and where temperance is, there health is speedily imparted, not only to the head, but to the whole body. And he who taught me the cure and the charm at the same time added a special direction : "Let no one," he said, " persuade you to cure the head, until he has first given you his soul to be cured by the charm. For this," he said, "is the great error of our day in the treatment of the human body, that physicians separate the soul from the body." — *Charmides*, i. 10.

Curiosity does not make a philosopher.

—— May we not say of the philosopher that he is a lover, not of a part of wisdom only, but of the whole?

True.

Then he who dislikes knowledge, especially in youth, when he has no power of judging what is good and what is not, such an one we maintain not to be a philosopher or a lover of knowledge, just as he who refuses his food is not hungry, and may be said to have a bad appetite, and not a good one?

There we are right, he said.

Whereas he who has a taste for every sort of knowledge and who is curious to learn and is never satisfied, may be justly termed a philosopher? Am I not right?

Glaucon said: If curiosity makes a philosopher, you will find many a strange being claiming the name. For all the lovers of sights have a delight in learning, and will therefore have to be included. Musical amateurs, too, are a folk wonderfully out of place among philosophers, for they are the last persons in the world who would come to anything like a philosophical discussion, if they could help, while they run about at the Dionysiac festivals as if they had let out their ears to hear every chorus; whether the performance is in town or country — that makes no difference — they are there. Now are we to maintain that all these and any who have similar tastes, as well as the professors of minor arts, are philosophers?

Certainly not, I replied, they are only an imitation. — *The Republic*, ii. 303.

Custom and **Law.** See *Colonization*, etc.

Dancing, natural.

—— The Gods, pitying the toils which our race is born to undergo, have appointed holy festivals, in which men alternate rest with labor; and have given them the Muses, and Apollo the leader of the Muses, and Dionysus, to be partners in their revels, that they may improve what education they have, at the festivals of the gods, and by their aid. I should like to know whether a common saying is true to nature or not. For what men say is that the young of all creatures cannot be quiet in their bodies or in their voices; they are always wanting to move, and cry out; at one time leaping and skipping, and overflowing with sportiveness and delight at something, and then again uttering all sorts of cries. But, whereas other animals have no perception of order or disorder in their movements, that is, of rhythm or harmony, as they are called, to us the Gods, who, as we say, have been appointed to be our partners in the dance, have given the pleasurable sense of harmony and rhythm; and so they stir us into life, and we follow them and join hands with one another in dances and songs; and these they call choruses, which is a term naturally expressive of cheerfulness. Shall we begin, then, with the acknowledgment that education is first given through Apollo and the Muses? What do you say?

Cle. I assent. — *Laws*, iv. 183.

Dead, burial and remembrance of the. See *Burial*, etc.

Dead, they are our shades and images.

—— Now we must believe the legislator when he tells us that the soul is in all respects superior to the body, and that even in life what makes each one of us to be what we are is only the soul; and that the body follows us about in the likeness of each of us, and therefore, when we are dead, the bodies of the dead are rightly said to be our shades or images; for that the true and immortal being of each one of us which is called the soul goes on her way to other gods — that before them she may give an account — an inspiring hope to the good, but very terrible to the bad, as the laws of our fathers tell us, which also say that not much can be done in the way of helping a man after he is dead. But the living — he should be helped by all his kindred, that while in life he may be the holiest and justest of men, and after death may have no great sins to be punished in the world below. If this be true, a man ought not to waste his substance under the idea that all this lifeless mass of flesh which is in process of burial is connected with him; he should consider that the son, or brother, or the beloved one, whoever he may be, whom he thinks he is laying in the earth, has gone away to complete and fulfill his own destiny, and that his duty is rightly to order the present, and to spend moderately on the lifeless altar of the Gods below. — *Laws*, iv. 468.

Dead; heroic. See *Battle, death in.*

Death, escape from, not always right.

—— Not much time will be gained, O Athenians, in return for the evil name which you will get from the detractors of the city, who will say that you killed Socrates, a wise man; for they will call me wise even although I am not wise, when they want to reproach you. If you had waited a little while, your desire would have been fulfilled in the course of nature. For I am far advanced in years, as you may perceive, and not far from death. I am speaking now only to those of you who have condemned me to death. And I have another thing to say to them: You think that I was convicted because I had no words of the sort which would have procured my acquittal — I mean, if I had thought fit to leave nothing undone or unsaid. Not so; the deficiency which led to my conviction was not of words — certainly not. But I had not the boldness or impudence or inclination to address you as you would have liked me to address you, weeping and wailing and lamenting, and saying and doing many things which you have been accustomed to hear from others, and which, as I maintain, are unworthy of me. I thought at the time that I ought not to do anything common or mean when in danger: nor do I now repent of the manner of my defense, and I would rather die having spoken after my manner, than speak in your manner and live. For neither in war nor yet at law ought any man to use every way of escaping death. Often in battle there can be no doubt that if a man will throw away his arms, and fall on his knees before his pursuers, he may escape death; and in other dangers there are other ways of escaping death, if a man is willing to say and do anything. The difficulty, my friends, is not in avoiding death, but in avoiding unrighteousness; for that runs faster than death. I am old and move slowly, and the slower runner has overtaken me, and my accusers are keen and quick, and the faster runner, who is unrighteousness, has overtaken them. And now I depart hence condemned by you to suffer the penalty of death, and they too go their ways condemned by the truth to suffer the penalty of villainy and wrong; and I must abide by my award — let them abide by theirs. I suppose that these things may be regarded as fated, — and I think that they are well. — *Apology*, i. 336.

Death and life, chances of, not to be calculated.

—— Some one will say: And are you not ashamed, Socrates, of a course of life which is likely to bring you to an untimely end? To him I may fairly answer: There you are mistaken: a man who is good for anything ought not to calculate the chance of living or dying; he ought only to consider whether in doing anything he is doing right or wrong — acting the part of a good man or of a bad. Whereas, according to your view, the heroes who fell at Troy were not good for much, and the son of Thetis above all, who altogether despised danger in comparison with disgrace; and when his goddess mother said to him, in his eagerness to slay Hector, that if he avenged his companion Patroclus, and slew Hector, he would die himself, — "Fate," as she said, "waits upon you next after Hector;" he, hearing this, utterly despised danger and death, and instead of fearing them, feared rather to live in dishonor, and not to avenge his friend. "Let me die next," he replies, "and be avenged of my enemy, rather than abide here by the beaked ships, a scorn and a burden of the earth." Had Achilles any any thought of death and danger? For wherever a man's place is, whether the place which he has chosen or that in which he has been placed by a commander, there he ought to remain in the hour of danger: he should not think of death or of anything, but of disgrace. And this, O men of Athens, is a true saying. — *Apology,* i. 326.

Death, fear of, no wisdom.

—— Strange, indeed, would be my conduct, O men of Athens, if I who, when I was ordered by the generals whom you chose to command me at Potidaea and Amphipolis and Delium, remained where they placed me, like any other man, facing death, — if, I say, now, when, as I conceive and imagine, God orders me to fulfill the philosopher's mission of searching into myself and other men, I were to desert my post through fear of death, or any other fear; that would indeed be strange, and I might justly be arraigned in court for denying the existence of the Gods, if I disobeyed the oracle because I was afraid of death: then I should be fancying that I was wise when I was not wise. For the fear of death is indeed the pretense of wisdom, and not real wisdom, being a pretended knowledge of the unknown; and no one knows whether death, which men in their fear apprehend to be the greatest evil, may not be the greatest good. Is there not here conceit of knowledge, which is a disgraceful sort of ignorance? And this is the point in which, as I think, I differ from others and in which I might perhaps fancy myself wiser than men in general, — that whereas I know but little of the world below, I do not suppose that I know: but I do know that injustice and disobedience to a better, whether God or man, is evil and dishonorable, and I will never fear or avoid a possible good rather than a certain evil. And therefore if you let me go now, and reject the counsels of Anytus, who said that if I were not put to death I ought not to have been prosecuted, and that if I escape now, your sons will all be utterly ruined by listening to my words, — if you say to me, Socrates, this time we will not mind Anytus, and will let you off, but upon one condition, that you are not to inquire and speculate in this way any more, and that if you are caught doing this again you shall die ; — if this was the condition on which you let me go, I should reply : Men of Athens, I honor and love you ; but I shall obey God rather than you, and while I have life and strength I shall never cease from the practice and teaching of philosophy, exhorting any one whom I meet after my manner, and convincing him. — *Apology*, i. 327.

Death, calmness in view of. See *Calmness*, etc.

Death and life not to be considered in questions of duty.

—— I proceed to argue the question whether I ought or ought not to try and escape without the consent of the Athenians : and if I am clearly right in escaping, then I will make the attempt; but if not, I will abstain. The other considerations which you mention, of money and loss of character and the duty of educating one's children, are, as I fear, only the doctrines of the multitude, who would be as ready to call people to life, if they were able, as they are to put them to death — and with as little reason. But now, since the argument has thus far prevailed, the only question which remains to be considered is, whether we shall do rightly either in escaping or in suffering others to aid in our escape and paying them in money and thanks, or whether we shall not do rightly ; and if the latter, then death or any other calamity which may ensue on my remaining here must not be allowed to enter into the calculation. — *Crito*, i. 353.

Death, presentiment of in Socrates. See *Presentiment*.

Death, life from.

—— Here is a new way in which we arrive at the inference that the living come from the dead, just as the dead come from the living ; and this, if true, affords the satisfactory proof that the souls of the dead must exist in some place out of which they come again.

Yes, Socrates, he said ; the conclusion seems to flow necessarily out of our previous admissions.

And that these admissions were not unfair, Cebes, he said, may be shown, I think, as follows: If generation were in a straight line only, and there were no compensation or circle in nature, no turn or return of elements into one another, then you know that all things would at last have the same form and pass into the same state, and there would be no more generation of them.

What do you mean? he said.

A simple thing enough, which I will illustrate by the case of sleep, he replied. You know that if there were no alternation of sleeping and waking, the story of the sleeping Endymion would in the end have no meaning, because all other things would be asleep too, and he would not be distinguishable from the rest. Or if there were composition only, and no division of substances, then the chaos of Anaxagoras would come again. And in like manner, my dear Cebes, if all things which partook of life were to die, and after they were dead remained in the form of death, and did not come to life again, all would at last die, and nothing would be alive — how could this be otherwise? For if the living spring from any others who are not the dead, and they die, must not all things at last be swallowed up in death?

There is no escape from that, Socrates, said Cebes; and I think that what you say is entirely true.

Yes, he said, Cebes, I entirely think so too; nor is this a delusion in which we are agreeing: but I am confident in the belief that there truly is such a thing as living again, and that the living spring from the dead, and that the souls of the dead are in existence, and that the good souls have a better portion than the evil. — *Phaedo*, i. 399.

Death in age; nearness of. See *Age, as viewing eternity.*

Death, willingness for, how consistent.

—— There may be reason in saying that a man should wait, and not take his own life until God summons him, as he is now summoning me.

Yes, Socrates, said Cebes, there is surely reason in that. And yet how can you reconcile the seemingly true belief that God is our guardian and we his possessions, with this willingness to die which we were attributing to the philosopher? That the wisest of men should be willing to leave a service in which they are ruled by the Gods who are the best of rulers, is not reasonable, for surely no wise man thinks that when set at liberty he can take better care of himself than the Gods take of him. A fool may perhaps think so — he may argue that he had better run away from his master, not considering that his duty is to remain to the end, and not to run away from the good, and that there would be no sense in his running away. But the wise man will want to be ever with him who is better than himself. Now this, Socrates, is the reverse of what was just now said; for upon this view the wise man should sorrow and the fool rejoice at passing out of life. — *Phaedo*, i. 388.

Death, fear of, contrary to courage. See *Courage*.

—— Herodicus, being a trainer, and himself of a sickly constitution, by a happy combination of training and doctoring, found out a way of torturing first and chiefly himself, and secondly the rest of the world.

How was that? he said.

By the invention of lingering death; for he had a mortal disease which he perpetually tended, and as recovery was out of the question, he passed his entire life as a valetudinarian; he could do nothing but attend upon himself, and he was in constant torment whenever he departed in anything from his usual regimen, and so dying hard, by the help of science he struggled on to old age.

A rare reward of his skill!

Yes, I said; such a reward as a man might fairly expect who could not be made to see that if Asclepius did not instruct his descendants in valetudinarian arts, the omission arose not from ignorance or inexperience of such a department of medicine, but because he knew that in all well-ordered states every individual had an occupation to which he must attend, and therefore has no leisure to spend in continually being ill. This we remark in the case of the artisan, but, ludicrously enough, do not apply the same rule to people of the richer sort. — *The Republic*, ii. 230.

Death, welcome to the philosopher. See *Philosopher*, and *Boldness*.

Death may be life.

—— *Soc.* But surely according to you, life is an awful thing; and indeed I think that Euripides may have been right in saying, —

"Who knows if life be not death and death life;"

and that we are very likely dead; I have heard a philosopher say that at this very moment we *are* dead, and that the body (σῶμα) is a tomb (σῆμα), and that the part of the soul which is the seat of the desires is liable to be blown and tossed about; and some ingenious man, probably a Sicilian or Italian, playing with the word, invented a tale; in which he called the soul a vessel (πίθος), meaning a believing vessel (πιστικὸς), and the ignorant he called the uninitiated or leaky, and the place in the souls of the uninitiated in which the desires are seated, being the intemperate and incontinent part, he compared to a vessel full of holes, because they can never be satisfied. He is not of your way of thinking, Callicles, for he declares, that of all the souls in Hades, meaning the invisible world (ἀειδὲς), these uninitiated or leaky persons are the most miserable, and that they carry water to a vessel which is full of holes in a similarly holey colander. The colander, as he declares, is the soul, and the soul which he compares to a colander is the soul of the ignorant, which is full of holes, and therefore incontinent, owing to a bad memory and want of faith. These are strange words, but still they show what, if I can, I desire to prove to you; that you should change your mind, and, instead, of the intemperate and insatiate life, you should choose that which is orderly and sufficient, and has a due provision for daily needs. — *Gorgias*, iii. 81.

Death in battle. See *Battle*.
Deceit and falsehood.
—— *Str.* Not-being has been acknowledged by us to be one among many classes of being, diffused over all being.
Theaet. True.
Str. And thence arises the question, whether not-being mingles with opinion and language.
Theaet. How so?
Str. If not-being has no part in the proposition, then all things must be true; but if not-being has a part, then false opinion and false speech are possible, for to think or to say what is not, is falsehood, which thus arises in the region of thought and in speech.
Theaet. That is quite true.
Str. And if there is falsehood there is deceit.
Theaet. Yes.
Str. And if there is deceit, then all things must be full of idols and images and fancies.
Theaet. To be sure.
Str. Into that region the Sophist, as we said, made his es-

cape, and when he had got there, denied the very possibility of falsehood; no one, he argued, either conceived or uttered falsehood, inasmuch as not-being did not in any way partake of being. — *Sophist*, iii. 500.

Deceiver as to truth.

—— To know and to declare the truth in matters of high interest which a man loves, among wise men who love him, is a safe thing and gives confidence; but to carry on an argument when you are yourself only a doubting inquirer, which is my case, is a dangerous and slippery thing; and the danger is not that I shall be laughed at (of which the fear would be childish), but that I shall miss the truth where I most need to be sure of my footing, and drag my friends after me in my fall. And I pray Nemesis not to visit upon me the words which I am going to utter. For I do indeed believe that to be an involuntary homicide is a less crime than to be a deceiver about the beauty or goodness or justice of institutions. And that is a risk which I would rather run among enemies than among friends, and therefore you do well to console me.

Glaucon laughed and said: Well then, Socrates, in case you and your argument do us any serious injury you shall be acquitted beforehand of the homicide, and shall not be held to be a deceiver; take courage then and speak.

Well, I said, the law says that when a man is acquitted he is free from guilt, and what holds in the one case may hold in the other. — *The Republic*, ii. 275.

Deception. See *Concealment of evil.*

Deception, how practiced and avoided.

—— *Soc.* The art of disputation, then, is not confined to the courts and the assembly, but is one and the same in every use of language; this is that art, if such an art there be, which finds a likeness of everything to which a likeness can be found, and draws into the light of day the likenesses and disguises which are used by others?

Phaedr. How do you mean?

Soc. Let me put the matter thus: When will there be more chance of deception — when the difference is large or small?

Phaedr. When the difference is small.

Soc. And you will be less likely to be discovered in passing by degrees into the other extreme than when you go all at once?

Phaedr. Of course.

Soc. He, then, who would deceive others, and not bo deceived, must exactly know the real likenesses and differences of things?

Phaedr. Yes, he must.

Soc. And if he is ignorant of the true nature of anything, how can he ever distinguish the greater or less degree of likeness to other things of that which he does not know?

Phaedr. He cannot.

Soc. And when men are deceived, and their notions are at variance with realities, it is clear that the error slips in through some resemblances?

Phaedr. Yes, that is the way.

Soc. Then he who would be a master of the art must know the real nature of everything; or he will never know either how to make the gradual departure from truth into the opposite of truth which is effected by the help of resemblances, or how to avoid it?

Phaedr. He will not.

Soc. He then, who being ignorant of the truth aims at appearances, will only attain an art of rhetoric which is ridiculous and is not an art at all?

Phaedr. That may be expected. — *Phaedrus,* i. 566.

Deception in the soul, detestable, and in God impossible.

—— But although the gods are themselves unchangeable, still by witchcraft and deception they may make us think that they appear in various forms?

Suppose that, he replied.

Well, but can you imagine that God will be willing to lie, or make a false representation of himself whether in word or deed?

I cannot say, he replied.

Do you not know, I said, that the true lie, if I may use such an expression, is hated of gods and men?

What do you mean? he said.

I mean this, I said, — that no one will admit falsehood into that which is the truest and highest part of himself, or about the truest and highest matters; there he is most afraid of a lie having possession of him.

Still, he said, I do not comprehend you.

The reason is, I replied, that you attribute some grand meaning to me; I am but saying only that deception, or being deceived or uninformed about realities in the highest faculty, which is the soul, and in that part of them to have and to hold the lie, is what mankind least like, — that, I say, is what they utterly detest.

There is nothing more hateful to them.

And, as I was just now remarking, this ignorance in the soul of him who is deceived may be called the true lie ; for the lie in words is only a kind of imitation and shadowy image of a previous affection of the soul, not pure unadulterated falsehood. Am I not right?

Perfectly right.

The true lie is hated not only by the gods, but also by men?

Yes.

Whereas the lie in words is in certain cases useful and not hateful ; in dealing with enemies — that would be an instance ; or again, as a cure or preventive of the madness of those who are called your friends ; also in the tales of mythology, of which we were just now speaking — because we do not know the truth about ancient traditions, we make falsehood as much like truth as may be, and so of use.

Very true, he said.

But can any of these reasons apply to God? Can we suppose that he is ignorant of antiquity, and therefore has recourse to invention?

That would be ridiculous, he said.

The lying poet then has no place in our idea of God?

I should say not.

But peradventure again he may tell a lie because he is afraid of enemies?

That is inconceivable.

But he may have friends who are senseless or mad?

But no mad or senseless person can be a friend of God.

Then no motive can be imagined why God should lie?

None.

Then the superhuman and divine is absolutely incapable of falsehood?

Yes.

Then is God perfectly simple and true both in deed and word ; he changes not ; he deceives not, either by dream or waking vision, by sign or word. — *The Republic*, ii. 205.

Deeds and **Words**, tribute of.

—— There is a tribute of deeds and of words. The departed

have already had the first, when going forth on their destined journey they were attended on their way by the State and by their friends ; the tribute of words remains to be given to them, as is meet and by law ordained. For noble words are a memorial and a crown of noble actions, which are given to the doers of them by the hearers. A word is needed which will duly praise the dead and gently admonish the living, exhorting the brethren and descendants of the departed to imitate their virtue and consoling their fathers and mothers and the survivors, if any, who may chance to be alive of the previous generation. What sort of a word will this be, and how shall we rightly begin the praises of these brave men ? In their life they rejoiced their own friends with their virtue, and their death they gave in exchange for the salvation of the living. And I think that we should praise them in the order in which nature made them good, for they were good because they were sprung from good fathers. Wherefore let us first of all praise the goodness of their birth; secondly, their nurture and education; and then let us set forth how noble their actions were, and how worthy of the education which they had received. — *Menexenus*, iv. 567.

Definition needed for knowledge.

—— *Soc.* Methought that I too had a dream, and I heard in my dream that the primeval letters or elements out of which you and I and all other things are compounded, have no reason or explanation, but are names only, of which not even existence or non-existence can be predicated ; you cannot say of them that they are or are not, for either of the two implies existence, which must not be added on, if one means to speak of this or that thing taken by itself alone. You may not say itself, or that, or each, or alone, or this, or the like ; for these go about everywhere and are applied to all things, and are distinct from them ; whereas, if the first elements could be described, and had a definition suitable to them, they would be spoken of apart from all else. But none of these primeval elements can be defined ; they can only be named, for they have nothing but a name, and the things which are compounded of them, as they are complex, are expressed by a combination of names, for the combination of names is the essence of a proposition. Thus, then, the elements or letters are only objects of perception, and cannot be defined or known ; but the combinations or syllables of them are known and expressed and apprehended by true opinion. When, therefore, any one forms the true opinion of anything without definition, you may say that his mind is truly exercised, but has no knowledge; for he who cannot give and receive a definition of a thing, has no knowledge of that thing; but when he adds the definition; then he is perfected in knowledge, and may be all that I have been denying of him. Was that the form in which the dream appeared to you?

Theaet. Precisely.

Soc. And you allow and maintain that true opinion, combined with definition, is knowledge?

Theaet. Exactly.

Soc. Then may we assume, Theaetetus, that to-day, and in this casual manner, we have found a truth which in former times many wise men have grown old and have not found?

Theaet. At any rate, Socrates, I am satisfied with the present statement.

Soc. Which is probably correct, — for how can there be knowledge apart from definition and true opinion? — *Theaetetus,* iii. 408.

Definition, how attained

—— *Soc.* Understand why; — just now the reason is, as I was saying, that if you get at the difference and distinguishing characteristic of each thing, then, as many persons affirm, you will get at the definition or explanation of it; but while you lay hold only of the common and not of the characteristic notion, you will only have the definition of those things to which this common quality belongs.

Theaet. I understand you, and your account of definition is, in my judgment, correct.

Soc. But he who, having a right opinion about anything, can find out the difference which distinguishes it from other things, will know that of which before he had only an opinion.

Theaet. Yes, that is what we are maintaining.

Soc. Nevertheless, Theaetetus, on a nearer view, I find myself quite disappointed in the picture, which at a distance was not so bad.

Theaet. What do you mean?

Soc. I will endeavor to explain: I will suppose myself to have true opinion of you, and if to this I add your definition, then I have knowledge, but if not, opinion only.

Theaet. Yes.

Soc. The definition was assumed to be the interpretation of your difference. — *Theaetetus,* iii. 417.

Deluge, tradition and effects of the.

—— *Ath.* Do you believe that there is any truth in ancient traditions?

Cle. What traditions?

Ath. The traditions about the many destructions of mankind which have been occasioned by deluges and diseases, and in many other ways, and of the preservation of a remnant.

Cle. Every one is disposed to believe them.

Ath. Let us imagine one of them: I will take the famous one which was caused by a deluge.

Cle. What is to be remarked in them?

Ath. I mean to say that those who then escaped would only be hill-shepherds, — small sparks of the human race preserved on the tops of mountains.

Cle. Clearly.

Ath. Such survivors would necessarily be unacquainted with the arts of those who live in cities, and with the various devices which are suggested to them by interest or ambition, and all the wrongs which they contrive against one another?

Cle. Very true.

Ath. Let us suppose, then, that the cities in the plain and on the sea-coast were utterly destroyed at that time.

Cle. Very good.

Ath. Would not all implements perish and every other excellent invention of political or any other sort of wisdom utterly fail at that time?

Cle. Why, yes, my friend; and if things had always continued as they are at present ordered, how could any discovery have ever been made even in the least particular? For it is evident that the arts were unknown during thousands and thousands of years. And no more than a thousand or two thousand years have elapsed since the discoveries of Daedalus, Orpheus, and Palamades, — since Marsyas and Olympus invented music, and Amphion the lyre, — not to speak of numberless other inventions which are but of yesterday. — *Laws,* iv. 205.

Demons, Hesiod's use of the term.

—— *Soc.* I wish that you would consider what is the real meaning of this word "demons." I wonder whether you would think my view right?

Her. Let me hear.

Soc. You know how Hesiod uses the word?

Her. Indeed I do not.

Soc. Do you not remember that he speaks of a golden race of men who came first?

Her. Yes, I know that.

Soc. He says of them, —

> "But now that fate has closed over this race,
> They are holy demons upon the earth,
> Beneficent, averters of ills, guardians of mortal men."

Her. What of that?

Soc. What of that! Why, I suppose that he means by the golden men, not men literally made of gold, but good and noble; and I am convinced of this, because he further says that we are the iron race.

Her. That is true.

Soc. And do you not suppose that good men of our own day would by him be said to be of that golden race?

Her. Very likely.

Soc. And are not the good wise?

Her. Yes, they are wise.

Soc. And therefore I have the most entire conviction that he called them demons, because they were δαήμονες (knowing or wise), and in the ancient Attic dialect this is the very form of the word. Now he and other poets say truly, that when a good man dies he has honor and a mighty portion among the dead, and becomes a demon; which is a name given to him signifying wisdom. And I say too that every wise man who happens to be a good man is more than human (δαιμόνιον) both in life and death, and is rightly called a demon. — *Cratylus*, i. 636.

Democracy.

Next comes democracy and the democratical man: the origin and nature of them we have still to learn, that we may compare the individual and the State, and so pronounce upon them.

That, he said, is our method.

Well, I said, and how does the change from oligarchy into democracy arise? — Is it not on this wise? The end which such state desires is to become as rich as possible; and the rulers, who are aware that their own power rests upon property, refuse to curtail by law the extravagance of the spendthrift youth because they will gain by their ruin; they lend them money, and buy their land, and grow more wealthy and honorable than ever?

Exactly.

There can be no doubt that you cannot have in the citizens of the same state the love of wealth and the spirit of moderation; one or the other will have to be disregarded.

That is tolerably clear. . . . .

Now in this state of things the rulers and their subjects come in one another's way, whether on a journey or some other occasion of meeting, or on a pilgrimage or a march as fellow-soldiers or fellow-sailors; they observe each other in the moment of danger (and where danger is there is no fear that the poor will be despised by the rich), and very likely the wiry, sunburnt poor man, may be placed in battle at the side of a wealthy one who has never spoilt his complexion, and has plenty of superfluous flesh — when he sees such an one puffing and at his wits'-end, can he avoid drawing the conclusion that men like him are only rich because no one has the courage to despoil them? And when they meet in private will not people be saying to one another that our "warriors are not good for much?"

Yes, he said, I am quite aware that this is their way of talking.

And, as where a body is weak the addition of a touch from without may bring on illness, and sometimes even when there is no external provocation a commotion may arise within, in the same way where there is weakness in the State there is also likely to be illness, of which the occasion may be very slight, one party introducing their democratical, the other their oligarchical allies, and the State falls sick, and is at war with herself; and may be at times distracted, even when there is no external cause?

Yes, surely.

And then democracy comes into being after the poor have conquered their opponents, slaughtering some and banishing some, while to the remainder they give an equal share of freedom and power; and this is the form of government in which the magistrates are commonly elected by lot.

Yes, he said, that is the nature of democracy, whether the revolution has been affected by arms or whether fear has caused the opposite party to withdraw.

And now what is their manner of life, and what sort of a government have they? For as the government is, such will be the man.

Clearly, he said.

In the first place, are they not free? and the city is full of freedom and frankness — a man may do as he likes.

They say so, he replied.

And where freedom is, the individual is clearly able to order his own life as he pleases?

Clearly.

Then in this kind of State there will be the greatest variety of human natures?

There will.

This, then, is likely to be the fairest of States; and will appear the fairest, being spangled with the manners and characters of mankind like an embroidered robe which is spangled with every sort of flowers. And just as women and children think variety charming, so there are many men who will deem this to be the fairest of States.

Yes.

Yes, my good sir, and there will be no better in which to look for a government.

Why?

Because of the liberty which reigns there: they have a complete assortment of constitutions: and he who has a mind to establish a State, as we have been doing, must go to a democracy as he would to a bazaar at which they sell them, and pick out one that suits him; then when he has made his choice, he may found his State.

He will be sure to have patterns enough.

And there being no necessity, I said, for you to govern in this State, even if you have the capacity, or to be governed unless you like, or to go to war when the others go to war, or to be at peace when others are at peace, unless you are disposed — there being no necessity also because some law forbids you to hold office or be a dicast, that you should not hold office or be a dicast, if you take a fancy — is not that a way of life which for the moment is supremely delightful?

For the moment, yes.

And is not their humanity to the condemned often charming? Under such a government there are men who, when they have been sentenced to death or exile, stay where they are and walk about the world; the gentleman parades like a hero, as though nobody saw or cared.

Yes, he replied, many and many a one.

See too, I said, the forgiving spirit of democracy, and the

"don't care" about trifles, and the disregard which she shows of all the fine principles which we were solemnly affirming at the foundation of the city — as when we said that, except in the case of some rare natures, never will there be a good man who in his early youth has not made things of beauty a delight and a study — how grandly does she trample our words under her feet, never giving a thought to the pursuits which make a statesman, and promoting to honor any one who professes to be the people's friend.

Yes, she is of a noble spirit.

These and other kindred characteristics are proper to democracy, which is a charming form of government, full of variety and disorder, and dispensing equality to equals and unequals alike. — *The Republic*, ii. 382.

Despot. See *King.*

Dialectic, what is it?

—— *Pro.* What is dialectic?

Soc. Clearly the science which knows all that knowledge of which we are now speaking; for I am sure that all men who have a grain of intelligence will admit that the knowledge which has to do with being and reality, and sameness and unchangeableness, is by far the truest of all. And would you, Protarchus, say or decide otherwise?

Pro. I have often heard Gorgias maintain, Socrates, that the art of persuasion far surpassed every other; this, as he says, is by far the best of them all, for to it all things submit, not by compulsion, but of their own free will. — *Philebus*, iii. 198.

Dialectic, power of. See *Science,* etc.

Dialectical skill of Socrates.

—— *Nic.* You do not seem to be aware that any one who has an intellectual affinity to Socrates, and enters into conversation with him, is liable to be drawn into an argument; and whatever subject he may start will be continually carried round and round by him, until at last he finds that he has to give an account both of his present and past life; and when he is once entangled, Socrates will not let him go until he has completely and thoroughly sifted him. Now I am used to his ways; and I know that he will certainly do as I say and also that I myself will be the sufferer; for I am fond of his conversation, Lysimachus. Neither do I think that there is any harm in being reminded of the evil which we are, or have been doing:

he who does not fly from reproof will be sure to take more heed of his after life; as Solon says, he will wish and desire to be learning so long as he lives, and will not think that old age of itself brings wisdom. To me, to be cross-examined by Socrates is neither unusual nor unpleasant; indeed, I knew all along that where Socrates was, the argument would soon pass from our sons to ourselves; and therefore, as I say, that for my part, I am quite willing to discourse with Socrates in his own manner; but you had better ask our friend Laches what his feeling may be.

La. I have but one feeling, Nicias, or (shall I say?) two feelings about discussions. Some would think that I am a lover, and to others I may seem to be a hater of discourse; for when I hear a man discoursing of virtue, or of any sort of wisdom, who is a true man and worthy of his theme, I am delighted beyond measure: and I compare the man and his words, and note the harmony and correspondence of them.— *Laches,* i. 80.

Dialecticians and Rhetoric. See *Rhetoric.*
Dialectic progress.

—— But do you imagine that men who are unable to give and take a reason will have the knowledge which we require of them?

Neither can this be said any more than the other.

And so, Glaucon, we have at last arrived at dialectic. This is that strain which is of the intellect only, but which the faculty of sight will nevertheless be found to imitate; for sight, as you may remember, was finally imagined by us to behold real animals and the stars, and last of all the sun himself; and so with dialectic; when a person starts on the discovery of the absolute by the light of reason only, and without any assistance of sense, if he perseveres by pure intelligence, he attains at last to the idea of good, and finds himself at the end of the intellectual world, as in the other case at the end of the visible.

Exactly, he said.

Then this is the progress which you call dialectic?

True. — *The Republic,* ii. 359.

Differences as to right opinion.

—— *Soc.* Then right opinion implies the perception of differences?

Theaet. Clearly.

Soc. What, then, shall we say of adding reason or explanation to right opinion? If the meaning is that we should form an opinion of the way in which something differs from another thing, the proposal is ridiculous.

Theaet. How so?

Soc. We are required to have a right opinion of the differences which distinguish one thing from another when we have already a right opinion of them, and so we go round and round; the revolution of the scytal, or pestle, or any other rotatory engine, in the same circles, is as nothing compared to our mode of proceeding; and we may be truly described as the blind directing the blind; for to add those things which we already have, in order that we may learn what we already think, implies a depth of darkness.

Theaet. Tell me, then; what were you going to say just now, when you asked the question?

Soc. If, my boy, the argument, when speaking of adding the definition, had used the word to "know," and not merely "have an opinion" of the difference, this which is the most promising of all the definitions of knowledge would have come to a pretty end, for to know is surely to get knowledge. — *Theaetetus,* iii. 418.

Discord and war.

—— There is a difference in the names "discord" and "war," and I imagine there is also a difference in their natures; the one is expressive of what is internal and domestic, the other of what is external and foreign; and the first of the two is properly termed discord, and only the second, war.

That is a very just distinction, he replied.

Shall I further add that the Hellenic race is all united together by ties of blood and friendship, and alien and strange to the barbarians?

Very good, he said.

And therefore when Hellenes fight with barbarians and barbarians with Hellenes, they will be described by us as being at war when they fight, and by nature enemies, and this kind of antagonism should be called war; but when Hellenes fight with one another we shall say that Hellas is then in a state of disorder and discord, and such enmity is to be called discord, they being by nature friends.

I agree.

Consider then, I said, when that which is now acknowledged

by us to be discord occurs, and a city is divided, if both parties destroy the lands and burn the houses of one another, how wicked does the strife appear, — how can either of them be a lover of his country? for no true lover of his country would tear in pieces his nurse and mother; there might be reason in the conqueror depriving the conquered of their harvest, but still they would have the idea of peace in their hearts, and not go on fighting forever.

Yes, he said, a better temper than the other.

And when you found a State, will it not be an Hellenic State?

It ought to be, he replied.

Then will not the citizens be good and civilized?

To be sure.

And will they not be lovers of Hellas, and think of Hellas as their own land, and share in the common temples?

Most certainly.

And any difference that arises among Hellenes will be regarded by them as discord only, — a quarrel among friends, which is not to be called a war?

Certainly not. — *The Republic*, ii. 297.

Discord and disease.

—— *Str.* In the soul there are two kinds of evil.

Theaet. What are they?

Str. The one may be compared to disease in the body, the other to deformity.

Theaet. I do not understand.

Str. Perhaps you have never reflected that disease and discord are the same.

Theaet. To this, again, I know not what I should reply.

Str. Do you not conceive discord to be a dissolution of kindred elements originating in some disagreement?

Theaet. Just that.

Str. And is deformity anything but the want of measure, which is always unsightly?

Theaet. Exactly.

Str. And do we not see that opinion is opposed to desire, pleasure to anger, reason to pain, and that all similar elements are opposed to one another in the souls of bad men?

Theaet. Certainly.

Str. And yet they must all be akin?

Theaet. Of course.

Str. Then we shall be right in calling vice a discord and disease of the soul? Most true. — *Sophist*, iii. 462.

Discourse, Rhetoric the art of. See *Rhetoric*.

Discourses, long or short.

—— *Str.* I would like to observe that you and I, remembering what has been said, would praise or blame the shortness of discussions, not by comparing them with one another, but according to a standard of measure, having in view what is fitting, which as we were saying, must be borne in mind.

Y. Soc. Very true.

Str. And yet, not everything is to be judged even with a view to what is fitting in all respects; for we do not want such a length as is suited to give pleasure — which is quite a secondary matter; and reason tells us that we should be contented to make the ease or rapidity with which an inquiry is attained, not the first but the second object; the first and highest of all being to assert the great method of division according to species, — whether the discourse be shorter or longer is not to the point. No offense should be taken at length, but the longer and shorter are to be employed indifferently, according as either of them is better calculated to sharpen the wits of the auditors. Reason would also say to him who censures the length of discourses and cannot away with their circumlocution, that he should not at once lay them aside or censure them as tedious, but he should prove that if they had been shorter they would have made those who took part in them better dialecticians, and more capable of expressing the truth of things, — about any other praise and blame, he need not trouble himself; he need not be supposed to hear them. — *Statesman*, iii. 571.

Diseases, cures of, why unknown.

Diseases. See *Cures*, etc.

Diseases, how originating.

—— Now every one can see whence diseases arise. There are four natures out of which the body is compacted — earth and fire and water and air, and the unnatural excess and defect of these, or the change of any one of them from their own natural place into another (for there are more kinds than one), and the assumption of that which does not belong to them, or any similar irregularity, produces diseases and disorders; for each being produced or changed in a manner contrary to nature, the elements which were previously cool grow warm, and those which were dry become moist, and the light becomes heavy, and the heavy light; all sorts of changes occur. For we affirm that only the same, in the same and like manner and proportion added or subtracted to or from the same, will allow the body to remain in the same state, whole and sound, and that whatever comes or goes away in violation of these rules causes all manner of changes and infinite diseases and disorders. — *Timaeus*, ii. 572.

Disorders and excesses.

— *Cle.* The probability is that ignorance will be a more prevalent disorder among kings, because they lead a proud and luxurious life.

Ath. Is it not palpable that the kings of that time were guilty of trying to be above the established laws, and that they did not consistently observe what they had agreed to observe by word and oath? This inconsistency of theirs may have had the appearance of wisdom, but was really, as we assert, the greatest ignorance, and utterly overthrew the whole empire through fatal error and perversity.

Cle. Very likely.

Ath. Good; and what ought the then legislator to have done in order to avert this calamity? Truly there is no great wisdom in knowing, and no great difficulty in telling, after the evil has happened; but to have foreseen the remedy at the time would have taken a much wiser head than ours.

Meg. What do you mean?

Ath. Any one who looks at what has occurred with you, Megillus, may easily know and may easily say what ought to have been done at that time.

Meg. Speak a little more clearly.

Ath. Nothing can be clearer than the observation which I am about to make.

Meg. What is it?

Ath. That if any one gives too great a power to anything, too large a sail to a vessel, too much food to the body, too much authority to the mind, and is regardless of the mean, everything is overthrown, and, in the wantonness of excess, runs in the one case to disorder, and in the other to injustice, which is the child of excess. I mean to say, my dear friends, that there is no soul of man, young and irresponsible, who will be able to sustain the temptation of arbitrary power — no one who will not, under such circumstances, become filled with folly, that worst of diseases, and be hated by his nearest and dearest friends: when this happens his kingdom is undermined, and all his power vanishes from him. And great legislators who know the mean should take heed of the danger. — *Laws*, iv. 220.

Disorders of the soul. See *Mind*.

Disputers, self-wise.

—— I was led on by you to say more than I had intended; but the point of comparison was, that when a simple man who has no skill in dialectics believes an argument to be true which he afterward imagines to be false, whether really false or not, and then another and another, he has no longer any faith left, and great disputers, as you know, come to think at last that they have grown to be the wisest of mankind; for they alone perceive the utter unsoundness and instability of all arguments, or indeed, of all things, which, like the currents in the Euripus, are going up and down in never-ceasing ebb and flow.

That is quite true, I said.

Yes, Phaedo, he replied, and very melancholy too, if there be such a thing as truth or certainty or possibility of knowledge, that a man should have lighted upon some argument or other which at first seemed true and then turned out to be false, and instead of blaming himself and his own want of wit, because he is annoyed, should at last be too glad to transfer the blame from himself to arguments in general; and forever afterwards should hate and revile them, and lose truth and the knowledge of realities. — *Phaedo*, i. 419.

Dissembler, the.

—— *Str.* Let us, then, examine our imitator of appearance, and see whether he is all of a piece, or whether there is any cleft in him.

Theaet. Let us examine him.

Str. Indeed, there is a very considerable cleft in him; for if you unfold him you find that one of the two classes of imitators is a simple being, who thinks that he knows that which he only fancies; the other sort has knocked about among arguments, until he suspects and fears that he is ignorant of that which to the many he pretends to know.

Theaet. There are certainly the two kinds which you describe.

Str. Shall we regard one as the simple imitator — the other as the dissembling or ironical imitator?

Theaet. That is good.

Str. And shall we further speak of this latter class as having one or two members?

Theaet. Answer yourself.

Str. Upon consideration, then, there appear to me to be two; there is the dissembler, who harangues a multitude in public in a long speech, and the dissembler, who in private and in short speeches compels the person who is conversing with him to contradict himself.

Theaet. What you say is most true.

Str. And who is the maker of the long speeches? Is he the statesman or the public orator?

Theaet. The latter.

Str. And what shall we call the other? Is he the philosopher or the Sophist?

Theaet. The philosopher he cannot be, for upon our view he is ignorant; but since he is an imitator of the wise he will have a name which is formed by an adaptation of the word σοφός. What shall we name him? I am pretty sure that I cannot be mistaken in terming him the true and very Sophist.

Str. Shall we bind up his name as we did before, making a chain from one end to the other?

Theaet. By all means.

Str. He, then, who traces the pedigree of his art as follows: He who, belonging to the conscious or dissembling section of the art of making contradictions, is an imitator of appearance and has divided off from the art of image-making which is a branch of phantastic, that further division of creative art, the juggling of words, a creation human, and not divine — any one who affirms the real Sophist to be of this blood and lineage will say the very truth.

Theaet. Undoubtedly. — *Sophist,* iii. 509.

Diversities of opinion.

—— O Euthydemus, I said, I have but a dull conception of these subtleties and excellent devices of wisdom; I am afraid that I hardly understand them, and you must forgive me therefore if I ask a very stupid question : if there be no falsehood or false opinion or ignorance, there can be no such thing as erroneous action, for a man cannot fail of acting as he is acting — that is what you mean ?

Yes, he replied.

And now, I said, I will ask my stupid question : If there is no such thing as error in deed, word, or thought, then what, in the name of goodness, do you come hither to teach ? And were you not just now saying that you could teach virtue, best of all men, to any one who could learn ?

And are you such an old fool, Socrates, rejoined Dionysodorus, that you bring up now what I said at first — and if I had said anything last year, I suppose that you would bring that up — but are nonplussed at the words I have just uttered?

Why, I said, they are not easy to answer; for they are the words of wise men: and indeed I know not what to make of this word " nonplussed " which you used last. What do you mean by that, Dionysodorus? You must mean that I cannot refute your argument. Tell me if the words have any other sense.

Certainly, he said; that is my meaning; and I wish that you would answer.

What, before you, Dionysodorus? I said.

Answer, said he.

And is that fair?

Yes, quite fair, he said.

Upon what principle? I said. I can only suppose that you are a very wise man, who comes to us in the character of a great logician, and who knows when to answer and when not to answer — and now you will not open your mouth at all, because you know that you ought not.

You prate, he said, instead of answering. But if, my good sir, you admit that I am wise, answer as I tell you.

I suppose that I must obey, for you are master. Put the question.

Are the things which have sense alive or lifeless?

They are alive.

And do you know of any word which is alive?

I cannot say that I do.

They why did you ask me what sense my words had?

Why, because I was stupid and made a mistake. And yet, perhaps, I was right after all in saying that words have a sense; what do you say, wise man? If I was not in error, you will not refute me, and all your wisdom will be nonplussed; but if I did fall into error, then again you are wrong in saying that there is no error, — and this remark was made by you not quite a year ago. I am inclined to think, however, Dionysodorus and Euthydemus, that this argument is not very likely to advance; even your skill in the subtleties of logic, which is really amazing, has not found out the way of throwing another and not falling yourself. — *Euthydemus,* i. 190.

Diversities of pleasure.

—— *Soc.* The awe which I feel, Protarchus, about the names of the Gods is more than human, and now I would not sin against Aphrodite by naming her amiss; of her, then, I say nothing. But I will begin with Pleasure which I know to be diverse, and will consider and ask what her nature is. She has one name and therefore you will imagine that she is one, and yet surely she takes the most various and even unlike forms. For do we not say that the intemperate has pleasure, and that the temperate has pleasure in his very temperance, and that the fool is pleased when he is full of foolish fancies and hopes, and that the wise man has pleasure in his wisdom; and how foolish would any one be who affirmed that all these opposite pleasures are severally alike.

Pro. Why, Socrates, they are opposed in so far as they spring from opposite causes, but they are not in themselves opposite, for must not pleasure be of all things most absolutely like pleasure, — that is, like itself?

Soc. Yes, my good friend, just as color is like color; in so far as they are colors, there is no difference between them; and yet we all know that black is not only unlike, but even absolutely opposed to white; or again, as figure is like figure, for they are all comprehended under one class; and yet some figures are absolutely opposed to one another, and there is an infinite diversity of them. And we might find similar examples in many other things; therefore do not rely upon this argument, which would go to prove the unity of the most extreme opposites. And I suspect that we shall find a similar opposition among pleasures.

Pro. Very likely; but how will this invalidate the argument?

Soc. Why, I shall reply, that dissimilar as they are, you apply to them a new predicate, for you say that all pleasant things are good; now although no one can argue that pleasure is not pleasure, he may argue, as we are doing, that pleasures are oftener bad than good; but you call them all good (he would say), and at the same time are compelled, if you are pressed, to acknowledge that they are unlike. And he will want to know what is that identical quality existing alike in good and bad pleasures, which makes you designate all of them as good.

Pro. What do you mean, Socrates? Do you think that any

one who asserts pleasure to be the good, will even tolerate the notion that some pleasures are good and some bad?

Soc. And yet you will acknowledge that they are different from one another, and even opposite to one another?

Pro. Not in so far as they are pleasures.

Soc. That is a return to the old position, Protarchus, and so we are to say (are we) that there is no difference in pleasures, but that they are all alike; and the examples which have just been cited do not pierce our dull minds, but we go on arguing all the same, like the weakest and most inexperienced reasoners?

Pro. What do you mean?

Soc. Why, I mean to say, that in self-defense I may, if I like, follow your example, and assert boldly that the two things most unlike are most absolutely alike, and the result will be that you and I will prove ourselves to be very tyros in the art of disputing; and the argument will be blown away and lost. — *Philebus,* iii. 146.

Divination, the work of.

———— Furthermore all sacrifices and the whole province of divination, which is the art of communion between Gods and men, — these, I say, are concerned only with the preservation of the good and the cure of the evil love. For all impiety is likely to ensue if, instead of accepting and honoring and reverencing the harmonious love in all his actions, a man honors the other love, whether in his feelings towards Gods or parents, towards the living or the dead. Wherefore the business of divination is to see to these loves and to heal them, and divination is the peacemaker of Gods and men working by a knowledge of the religious or irreligious tendencies which exist in human loves. — *The Symposium,* i. 482.

Divine power of the poet.

———— I am conscious in my own self and the general opinion is that I do not speak better and have more to say about Homer than any other man. But I do not speak equally well about others — tell me the reason of this?

Soc. I perceive, Ion; and I will proceed to explain to you what I imagine to be the reason of this. The gift which you possess of speaking excellently about Homer is not an art, but, as I was just saying, an inspiration; there is a divinity moving you, like that in the stone which Euripides calls a magnet, but which is commonly known as the stone of Heraclea.

For that stone not only attracts iron rings, but also imparts to them a similar power of attracting other rings; and sometimes you may see a number of pieces of iron and rings suspended from one another so as to form quite a long chain; and all of them derive their power of suspension from the original stone. Now this is like the Muse, who first of all inspires men herself; and from these inspired persons a chain of other persons is suspended, who take the inspiration from them. For all good poets, epic as well as lyric, compose their beautiful poems not as works of art, but because they are inspired and possessed. And as the Corybantian revelers when they dance are not in their right mind, so the lyric poets are not in their right mind when they are composing their beautiful strains; but when falling under the power of music and metre they are inspired and possessed; like Bacchic maidens who draw milk and honey from the rivers, when they are under the influence of Dionysus, but not when they are in their right mind. And the soul of the lyric poet does the same, as they themselves tell us; for they tell us that they bring songs from honeyed fountains, culling them out of the gardens and dells of the Muses; whither, like the bees, they wing their way. And this is true. For the poet is a light and winged and holy thing, and there is no invention in him until he has been inspired and is out of his senses, and the mind is no longer in him; when he has not attained to this state, he is powerless and is unable to utter his oracles. Many are the noble words in which poets speak of the actions which they record, like your own words about Homer; but they do not speak of them by any rules of art; they are inspired to utter that to which the Muse impels them, and that only; and when inspired, one of them will make dithyrambs, another hymns of praise, another choral strains, another epic or iambic verses — and he who is good at one is not good at any other kind of verse; for not by art does the poet sing, but by power divine. Had he learned by rules of art, he would have known how to speak, not of one theme only, but of all; and therefore God takes away the minds of poets, and uses them as his ministers, as he also uses diviners and holy prophets, in order that we who hear them may know that they speak not of themselves who utter these priceless words in a state of unconsciousness, but that God is the speaker, and that through them he is conversing with us. And Tynnichus the Chalcidian affords a striking instance of what I am saying; he wrote nothing that any one would care to remember but the famous pæan which is in every one's mouth, and is one of the finest poems ever written, and truly an invention of the Muses, as he himself says. For in this way the God would seem to indicate to us and not allow us to doubt that these beautiful poems are not human or the work of man, but divine and the work of God; and that the poets are only the interpreters of the Gods by whom they are severally possessed. Was not this the lesson which the God intended to teach when by the mouth of the worst of poets he sang the best of songs? Am I not right, Ion?

Ion. Yes, indeed, Socrates, I feel that you are; for your words touch my soul, and I am persuaded somehow that good poets are the inspired interpreters of the Gods. — *Ion,* i. 223.

Divine mind, good in the. See *Mind.*
Divine, the soul resembling the.

—— When the soul and the body are united, then nature orders the soul to rule and govern, and the body to obey and serve. Now which of these two functions is akin to the divine? and which to the mortal? Does not the divine appear to you to be that which naturally orders and rules, and the mortal to be that which is subject and servant?

True.

And which does the soul resemble?

The soul resembles the divine, and the body the mortal, — there can be no doubt of that, Socrates.

Then reflect, Cebes: of all that has been said is not this the conclusion, — that the soul is in the very likeness of the divine and immortal, and intellectual, and uniform, and indissoluble, and unchangeable; and that the body is in the very likeness of the human, and mortal, and unintellectual and multiform, and dissoluble, and changeable. — *Phaedo,* i. 408.

Divine nature of generation and conception. See *Conception.*
Divine madness. See *Madness,* etc.
Divine, Statesman called. See *Statesman.*
Divine things only unchangeable.

—— Only the most divine things of all are unchangeable, and body is not included in this class. Heaven and the universe, as we have termed them, although they have been endowed by the Creator with many glories, partake of a bodily nature, and therefore cannot be entirely free from perturbations. But the heavenly motion is, as far as possible, single and in the same place, and in relation to the same; and is therefore only subject to a reversal, which is the least alteration possible. For the lord of all moving things is alone able to move of himself; and to think that he can go at one time in one direction and at another time in another, is unlawful. Hence we must not say that the world is either self-moved always, or all made to go round by God in two opposite courses; or that two Gods, having opposite purposes, make it move round. But as I have already said (and this is the only remaining alternative) the world is governed by an accompanying divine power, and receives life and immortality by the appointment of the Creator, and then, when let go again, moves spontaneously, being let go at such a time as to have, during infinite cycles of years, a reverse movement: this is due to exquisite perfection of balance, and the size of the universe, which is the greatest of bodies, and turns on the smallest pivot. — *Statesman*, iii. 554.

Divine bonds in the State.

—— *Str.* Can we say that such a connection as this will lastingly unite the evil with one another or with the good, or that there is any science which would seriously think of using a bond of this kind to join such materials?

Y. Soc. Impossible.

Str. But in those which were originally noble natures, and have been trained accordingly, in those only may we not say that the bond of union is implanted by law, and that this is the medicine which art prescribes for them, and the divine bond, which, as I was saying, heals and unites dissimilar and contrary parts of virtue?

Y. Soc. Very true.

Str. Where this divine bond exists there is no difficulty in imagining, or when you have imagined, in creating the other human bonds.

Y. Soc. How is that, and of what bonds do you speak?

Str. Those of intermarriage, and those which are formed between States by giving and taking children in marriage, as well as by private betrothals and espousals. For many persons form unions of an improper kind, with a view to the procreation of children.

Y. Soc. In what way?

Str. They seek after wealth and power, which in matrimony are objects not worthy even of a serious censure.

Y. Soc. There is no need to consider them at all. . . . .

Str. It was of these bonds I said that there would be no difficulty in creating them, if only both classes originally held the same opinion about the honorable and the good; indeed, in this single word, the whole process of royal weaving is comprised — never to allow temperate natures to be separated from the brave, but to weave them together, like the warp and the woof, by common sentiments and honors and opinions, and by the giving of pledges to one another; and out of them forming one smooth and even web, to intrust them to the offices of state.— *Statesman,* iii. 597.

Divining of truth *instinctive.* See *Instinctive.*

Doctors and **patients.**

—— *Ath.* Of doctors, as you doubtless know, there are two kinds, a gentler and a ruder, and two modes of cure; and as children ask the doctor to be gentle with them, so we will ask the legislator to cure our disorders with the gentlest remedies. What I mean to say is, that besides doctors, there are their assistants, who are also styled doctors.

Cle. Very true.

Ath. And whether they are slaves or freemen makes no difference; they acquire their knowledge of medicine by obeying and observing their masters, empirically and not rationally, as the manner of freemen is, who have learned scientifically themselves the art which they impart to their pupils. You are aware that there are these two classes of doctors?

Cle. To be sure.

Ath. And did you ever observe that there are two classes of patients in States, slaves and freemen; and the slave doctors run about and cure the slaves, and wait for them in the dispensaries — practitioners of this sort never talk to their patients individually, or let them talk about their own individual complaints? The doctor prescribes what he thinks good, out of the abundance of his experience, as if he had no manner of doubt; and when he has given his orders, like a tyrant, he rushes off with equal assurance to some other servant who is ill; and so he relieves the master of the house of the care of his invalid slaves. But the other doctor, who is a freeman, attends and practices upon freemen; and he carries his inquiries far back, and goes into the nature of the disorder; he enters into discourse with the patient and with his friends, and is at once getting information from the sick man, and also instructing him as far as he is able, and he will not prescribe for him until he has first convinced him; at last, when he has brought the patient more and more under his persuasive influences and set him on the road to health, he attempts to effect a cure. Now, which is the better way of proceeding in a physician and in a trainer? Is he the better who accomplishes his ends in a double way, or he who works in one way, and that the ruder and inferior?

Cle. I should say, Stranger, that the double way is far better. — *Laws*, iv. 247.

Dog, — a true philosopher.

—— The trait of which I am speaking, I replied, may be also seen in the dog, and is remarkable in an animal.

What trait?

Why a dog, whenever he sees a stranger, is angry; when an acquaintance, he welcomes him, although the one has never done him any harm, nor the other any good. Did this never strike you as curious?

I never before thought of it, though I quite recognize the truth of your remark.

And surely this instinct of the dog is very charming, — your dog is a true philosopher.

Why?

Why, because he distinguishes the face of a friend and of an enemy only by the criterion of knowing and not knowing. And must not the creature be fond of learning who determines what is friendly and what is unfriendly by the test of knowledge and ignorance? — *The Republic*, ii. 198.

Dorian kings, the cause of their ruin.

—— I remember, and you will remember what I said at first, that a statesman and legislator ought to ordain laws with a view to wisdom; whereas you were arguing that the good lawgiver ought to order all with a view to war. And to this I replied that there were four virtues, whereas your regards were fixed on one of the four only; but that you ought to regard all virtue, and especially that which comes first, and is the guide of all the rest — I mean wisdom and mind and opinion, united with the affection and desire which waits upon them. And now the argument returns to the same point, and I say once more, in jest if you like, or in earnest if you like, that the prayer of a fool is full of danger, being likely to end in the opposite of what he desires. And if you would rather receive my words in earnest, I am willing that you should; and you will find, as I have said already, that not cowardice was the cause of the ruin of the Dorian kings and of their whole design, nor ignorance of military matters, either on the part of the rulers or of their subjects; but the cause was the corrupting influence of the other vices, and especially their ignorance of the most important human affairs. — *Laws*, iv. 217.

Dreams, sleep free from fanciful.

—— Certain of the unnecessary pleasures and appetites are deemed to be unlawful; every one appears to have them, but in some persons they are controlled by the laws and by reason, and the better desires prevail over them, — either they are wholly banished or they are few and weak; while in the case of others they are stronger, and there are more of them.

Which appetites do you mean?

I mean those which are awake when the reasoning and human and ruling power is asleep; when the wild beast in our nature, gorged with meat or drink, starts up and leaps about, and seeks to go and satisfy his desires, there is no conceivable folly or crime, however shameless or unnatural — not excepting incest or parricide, or the eating of forbidden food — of which at such a time, you know, a man may not believe himself to be capable.

Most true, he said.

But when a man's pulse is healthy and temperate, and when before going to sleep he has awakened his rational powers and fed them on noble thoughts and inquiries, collecting himself in meditation after having first indulged his appetites neither too much nor too little, but just enough to lay them to sleep, and prevent them and their enjoyments and pains from interfering with the higher principle — which he leaves in the solitude of pure abstraction, free to contemplate and aspire to the knowledge of the unknown, whether in past, present, or future: when again he has allayed the passionate element, if he has a quarrel against any one — I say, when, after pacifying the two irrational principles, he rouses up the third, which is reason, before he takes his rest, then, as you know, he attains truth most nearly, and is least likely to be the sport of fanciful and lawless visions. — *The Republic*, ii. 400.

Drinking wine condemned. See *Wine forbidden.*

Drunkenness condemned in Sparta.

—— *Meg.* The laws of Sparta, in as far as they relate to pleasure, appear to me to be the best in the world; for that which leads mankind in general into the wildest pleasure and license, and every other folly, the law has clean driven out; and neither in the country nor in towns which are under the control of Sparta, will you find revelries and the many incitements of every kind of pleasure which accompany them, and any one who meets a drunken and disorderly person will immediately have him most severely punished, and will not let him off on any pretense, not even at the time of a Dionysiac festival; although I have remarked that this may happen at your performances "on the cart," as they are called; and among our Tarentine colonists I have seen the whole city drunk at a Dionysiac festival; but nothing of that sort happens among us.

Ath. O Lacedæmonian Stranger, these festivities are praiseworthy where there is a spirit of endurance, but are very senseless when they are under no regulations. In order to retaliate, an Athenian has only to point out the license which exists among your women. To all such accusations, whether they are brought against the Tarentines, or us, or you, there is one answer which exonerates the practice in question from impropriety. When a stranger expresses wonder at the singularity of what he sees, any inhabitant will naturally answer him: Wonder not, O stranger; this is our custom, and you may very likely have some other custom about the same things. Now we are speaking, my friends, not about men in general, but about the merits and defects of the lawgivers themselves. Let us then discourse a little more at length about them, and about the nature of intoxication at large, which is a very important matter, and will seriously task the discrimination of the legislator. I am not talking of the mere practice of drinking or not drinking wine in general, but about downright intoxication: are we to follow the custom of the Scythians, and Persians, and Carthaginians, and Celts, and Iberians, who are all warlike nations, or that of your countrymen who, as you say, wholly abstain? Whereas the Scythians and Thracians, both men and women, drink unmixed wine, which they also pour on their garments, and this they think a happy and glorious institution. The Persians, again, are much given to other practices of luxury which you reject, but they have more moderation in them than the Thracians and Scythians. — *Laws,* iv. 167.

Dualism.

—— You have to imagine, then, that there are two ruling powers, and that one of them is set over the intellectual world, the other over the visible. I do not say heaven, lest you should fancy that I am playing upon the name (οὐρανός, ὁρατός). May I suppose that you have this distinction of the visible and intelligible fixed in your mind?

I have.

Now take a line which has been cut into two unequal parts, and divide each of them again in the same proportion, and suppose the two main divisions to answer, one to the visible and the other to the intelligible, and then compare the subdivisions as to their relative clearness and want of clearness, and you will find that the first section in the sphere of the visible consists of images. And by images I mean, in the first place, shadows, and in the second place, reflections in water and in solid, smooth, and polished bodies, and the like: do you understand?

Yes, I understand.

Imagine, now, the other section, of which this is only the resemblance, to include ourselves and the animals, and everything in nature and everything in art.

Very good.

Would you not admit that this latter section has a different degree of truth, and that the copy is to the object which is copied as the sphere of opinion is to the sphere of knowledge?

Most undoubtedly.

Next proceed to consider the manner in which the sphere of the intellectual is to be divided.

In what manner?

As thus: there are two subdivisions, in the lower of which the soul uses the figures given by the former divisions as images; the inquiry can only be hypothetical, and instead of going upwards to a principle, descends to the other end; in the higher of the two, the soul passes out of hypotheses, and goes up to a principle which is above hypotheses, making no use of images, as in the former case, but proceeding only in and by the ideas themselves. — *The Republic*, ii. 337.

Duty, questions of.

—— *Soc.* Are we to say that we are never intentionally to do wrong, or that in one way we ought and in another way we ought not to do wrong, or is doing wrong always evil and dishonorable, as I was just now saying, and as has been already acknowledged by us? Are all our former admissions which were made within a few days to be thrown away? And have we, at our age, been earnestly discoursing with one another all our life long only to discover that we are no better than children? Or, in spite of the opinion of the many, and in spite of consequences, whether better or worse, shall we insist on the truth of what was then said, that injustice is always an evil and dishonor to him who acts unjustly? Shall we say so or not?

Cr. Yes.

Soc. Then we must do no wrong?

Cr. Certainly not.

Soc. Nor when injured injure in return, as the many imagine; for we must injure no one at all?

Cr. Clearly not.

Soc. Again, Crito, may we do evil?

Cr. Surely not, Socrates.

Soc. And what of doing evil in return for evil, which is the morality of the many — is that just or not?

Cr. Not just.

Soc. For doing evil to another is the same as injuring him?

Cr. Very true.

Soc. Then we ought not to retaliate or render evil for evil to any one, whatever evil we may have suffered from him. But I would have you consider, Crito, whether you really mean what you are saying. For this opinion has never been held, and never will be held, by any considerable number of persons; and those who are agreed and those who are not agreed upon this point have no common ground, and can only despise one another when they see how widely they differ. Tell me, then, whether you agree with and assent to my first principle, that neither injury nor retaliation nor warding off evil by evil is ever right. And shall that be the premise of our argument? Or do you decline and dissent from this? For thus have I ever thought and still think; but, if you are of another opinion, let me hear what you have you to say. — *Crito,* i. 353.

Earth, the rotundity of the.

—— I may describe to. you, however, the form and regions of the earth according to my conception of them.

That, said Simmias, will be enough.

Well then, he said, my conviction is, that the earth is a round body in the centre of the heavens, and therefore has no need of air or any similar force as a support, but is kept there and hindered from falling or inclining any way by the equability of the surrounding heaven and by her own equipoise. For that which, being in equipoise, is in the centre of that which is equably diffused, will not incline any way in any degree, but will always remain in the same state and not deviate.[1] — *Phaedo*, i. 439.

Earth, likeness of the. See *Animals*, etc.
Earth, heavenly idea of.

—— For I should say that in all parts of the earth there are hollows of various forms and sizes, into which the water and the mist and the lower air collect; and that the true earth is pure and in the pure heaven, in which also are the stars — that is the heaven which is commonly spoken of as the ether, of which this is but the sediment gathering in the hollows of the earth. But we who live in these hollows are deceived into the notion that we are dwelling above on the surface of the earth; which is just as if a creature who was at the bottom of the sea were to fancy that he was on the surface of the water, and that the sea was the heaven through which he saw the sun and the other stars, — he having never come to the surface by reason of his feebleness and sluggishness, and having never lifted up his head and seen, nor ever heard from one who had seen, how much purer and fairer the world above is than his own. And such is exactly our case; for we are dwelling in a hollow of the earth, and fancy that we are on the surface; and the air we call the heaven, wherein we imagine that the stars move. But this again is owing to our feebleness and sluggishness, which prevent our reaching the surface of the air; for if any man could arrive at the exterior limit, or take the wings of a a bird and fly upward, then like a fish who puts his head out and sees this world, he would see a world beyond; and, if the nature of man could sustain the sight, he would acknowledge that this other world was the place of the true heaven and the true light and the true earth. For our earth, and the stones, and the entire region which surrounds us, are spoilt and corroded, as in the sea all things are corroded by the brine; for in the sea too there is hardly any noble or perfect growth, but clefts only, and sand, and an endless slough of mud: and even the shore is not to be compared to the fairer sights of this world. — *Phaedo*, i. 439.

[1] Plato's cosmogonic ideas are largely given in the Dialogues of "Phaedo" and "Timaeus."

Earthly and sensual soul.

—— But the soul which has been polluted, and is impure at the time of her departure, and is the companion and servant of the body always, and is in love with and fascinated by the body and by the desires and pleasures of the body, until she is led to believe that the truth only exists in a bodily form, which a man may touch and see and taste and use for the purposes of his lusts, — the soul, I mean, accustomed to hate and fear and avoid the intellectual principle, which to the bodily eye is dark and invisible, and can be attained only by philosophy ; — do you suppose that such a soul will depart pure and unalloyed ?

That is impossible, he replied.

She is held fast by the corporeal, which the continual association and constant care of the body have wrought into her nature.

Very true.

And this corporeal element, my friend, is heavy and weighty and earthy, and is that element of sight by which such a soul is depressed and dragged down again into the visible world, because she is afraid of the invisible and of the world below — prowling about tombs and sepulchres, in the neighborhood of which, as they tell us, are seen certain ghostly apparitions of souls which have not departed pure, but are cloyed with sight and therefore visible.

That is very likely, Socrates.

Yes, that is very likely, Cebes ; and these must be the souls, not of the good, but of the evil, who are compelled to wander about such places in payment of the penalty of their former evil way of life ; and they continue to wander until through the craving after the corporeal which never leaves them, they are imprisoned finally in another body. And they may be supposed to find their prisons in the same natures which they have had in their former lives.

What do you mean, Socrates ?

I mean to say that men who have followed after gluttony, and wantonness, and drunkenness, and have had no thought of avoiding them, would pass into asses and animals of that sort. — *Phaedo*, i. 409.

Education, compulsion in.

—— Solon was under a delusion when he said that a man as he is growing older may learn many things, — for he can no more learn than he can run ; youth is the time of toil.

Very true.

And, therefore, calculation and geometry, and all the other elements of instruction, which are a preparation for dialectic, should be presented to the mind in childhood; not, however, under any notion of forcing them.

Why not?

Because a freeman ought to be a freeman in the acquisition of knowledge. Bodily exercise, when compulsory, does no harm; but knowledge which is acquired under compulsion has no hold on the mind.

Very true.

Then my good friend, I said, do not use compulsion, but let early education be a sort of amusement; you will then be better able to find out the natural bent.

You are right there. — *The Republic*, ii. 364.

Education, sign of a liberal.

—— *Soc.* Theaetetus, I take another view of the subject: you answered that knowledge is perception?

Theaet. I did.

Soc. And if any one were to ask you: With what does a man see black and white colors? and with what does he hear sharp and flat sounds? — you would say, if I am not mistaken, " With the eyes and with the ears."

Theaet. I should.

Soc. The free use of words and phrases, rather than minute precision, is generally characteristic of a liberal education, and the opposite is pedantic; but sometimes precision is necessary, and I believe that the answer which you have just given is open to the charge of incorrectness; for which is more correct, to say that we see or hear with the eyes and with the ears, or through the eyes and through the ears?

Theaet. I should say, Socrates, "through," rather than " with."

Soc. Yes, my boy; for no one can suppose that we are Trojan horses, in whom are perched several unconnected senses, not meeting in some one nature, of which they are the instruments, whether you term this soul or not, with which through these we perceive objects of sense. — *Theaetetus*, iii. 387.

Education, early.

—— *Ath.* According to my view, he who would be good at any thing must practice that thing from his youth upwards, both in sport and earnest, in the particular manner which the work requires; for example, he who is to be a good builder, should play at building children's houses; and he who is to be a good husbandman, at tilling the ground; those who have the care of their education should provide them when young with mimic tools. And they should learn beforehand the knowledge which they will afterwards require for their art. For example, the future carpenter should learn to measure or apply the line in play; and the future warrior should learn riding, or some other exercise for amusement, and the teacher should endeavor to direct the children's inclinations and pleasures by the help of amusements, to their final aim in life. The most important part of education is right training in the nursery.) The soul of the child in his play should be trained to that sort of excellence in which, when he grows up to manhood, he will have to be perfected. Do you agree with me thus far?

Cle. Certainly.

Ath. Then let us not leave the meaning of education ambiguous or ill-defined. At present, when we speak in terms of praise or blame about the bringing-up of each person, we call one man educated and another uneducated, although the uneducated man may be sometimes very well educated for the calling of a retail trader, or of a captain of a ship, and the like. For we are not speaking of education in this narrower sense, but of that other education in virtue from youth upwards, which makes a man eagerly pursue the ideal perfection of citizenship, and teaches him how rightly to rule and how to obey. This is the only education which, upon our view, deserves the name; that other sort of training, which aims at the acquisition of wealth or bodily strength, or mere cleverness apart from intelligence and justice, is mean and illiberal, and is not worthy to be called education at all. But let us not quarrel with one another about a word, provided that the proposition which has just been granted hold good; to wit, that those who are rightly educated generally become good men. Neither must we cast a slight upon education, which is the first and fairest thing that the best of men can ever have, and which, though liable to take a wrong direction, is capable of reformation. And this work of reformation is the great business of every man while he lives.
— *Laws,* iv. 173.

Education of youth and children. See *Youth,* etc.

Education, the benefit of, to the State.

—— If you mean to ask what great good accrues to the State

from the right training of a single youth, or of a single chorus, — when the question is put in that form, we cannot deny that the good is not very great in any particular instance. But if you ask what is the good of education in general, the answer is easy — that education makes good men, and that good men act nobly, and conquer their enemies in battle, because they are good. Education certainly gives victory, although victory sometimes produces forgetfulness of education ; for many have grown insolent from victory in war, and this insolence has engendered in them innumerable evils ; and many a victory has been and will be suicidal to the victors; but education is never suicidal. — *Laws*, iv. 172.

Elevation of self.

—— Do you see any way in which the philosopher can be preserved in his calling to the end? and remember what we were saying of him, that he was to have knowledge and memory and courage and magnanimity — these were admitted by us to be the true philosopher's gifts.

Yes.

Now, will not such an one be, from the first, in all things first among all, especially if his bodily endowments are like his mental ones ?

Certainly, he said.

And his friends and fellow-citizens will want to use him as he gets older for their own purposes?

No question.

Falling at his feet, they will make requests to him and do him honor and flatter him, because they want to get into their hands now, the power which he will one day possess.

That often happens, he said.

And what will he do under such circumstances, especially if he be a citizen of a great city, rich and noble, and a tall, proper youth ? Will he not be full of boundless aspirations, and fancy himself able to manage the affairs of Hellenes and of barbarians, and therefore will he not dilate and elevate himself in the fullness of vain pomp and senseless pride ?

To be sure he will.

Now, when he is in this state of mind, if some one gently comes to him and tells him that he is without sense, which he must have, but can only get it by slaving for it, do you think that, under such adverse circumstances, he will be easily induced to listen?

He would be very unlikely to listen.

But suppose further that there is one person who has feeling, and who, either from some excellence of disposition or natural affinity, is inclined or drawn towards philosophy, and his friends think that they are likely to lose the advantages which they were going to reap from his friendship, what will be the effect upon them ? Will they not do and say anything to prevent his learning and to make the teacher powerless, using to this end private intrigues as well as public prosecutions?

There can be no doubt of it.

And how can one who is thus circumstanced ever become a philosopher?

Impossible.

Then, were we not right in saying that even the very qualities which make a man a philosopher may, if he be ill-educated, serve to divert him from philosophy, no less than riches and their accompaniments and the other so-called goods of life?

We were quite right.

Thus, my excellent friend, is brought about the ruin and failure of the natures best adapted to the best of all pursuits, who, as we assert, are rare at any time; and this is the class out of whom come those who are the authors of the greatest evil to States and individuals; and also of the greatest good when the tide carries them in the direction of good; but a small man never was the doer of any great thing either to individuals or States.

That is most true, he said.

They fall away, and philosophy is left desolate, with her marriage rite incomplete: for her own have forsaken her, and while they are leading a false and unbecoming life, other unworthy persons, seeing that she has no protector, enter in and dishonor her; and fasten upon her the reproaches which her reprovers utter; who say of her votaries that some of them are good for nothing, and the greater number deserving of everything that is bad.

That is certainly said.

Yes; and what else would you expect, I said, when you think of the puny creatures who, seeing this land open to them — a land well stocked with fair names and showy titles — like prisoners who run away out of prison into a sanctuary, take a leap out of the arts into philosophy; those who do so being probably the cleverest hands at their own miserable crafts?

For, although philosophy be in this evil case, still there remains a dignity about her which is not found in the other arts. And many are thus attracted by her whose natures are imperfect and whose souls are marred and disfigured by their meanness, as their bodies are by their arts and crafts. Is not that true? Yes. — *The Republic*, ii. 321.

Eloquence, its force of truth.

—— How you, O Athenians, have been affected by my accusers, I cannot tell; but I know that they almost made me forget myself — so persuasively did they speak; and yet they have hardly uttered a word of truth. But many as their falsehoods were, there was one of them which quite amazed me: — I mean when they told you to be upon your guard, and not allow yourselves be deceived by the force of my eloquence. To use such language, when they were sure to be detected as soon as I opened my lips and displayed my deficiency, did certainly appear to me most shameless, — unless by the force of eloquence they mean the force of truth; for if this is their meaning, I admit that I am eloquent. But in how different a way from theirs! Well, as I was saying, they have hardly uttered a word, or not more than a word, of truth; but you shall hear from me the whole truth: not, however, delivered after their manner, in a set oration duly ornamented with words and phrases. No, by heaven! but I shall use the words and arguments which occur to me at the moment; for I am certain that I am right in this; and that at my time of life I ought not to be appearing before you, O men of Athens, in the character of a juvenile orator: let no one expect it of me. — *Apology*, i. 315.

Eloquence, power of. See *Battle.*

Endurance. See *Courage.*

Enemies and friends, treatment of.

—— Well, there is another question: Are friends to be interpreted as real or seeming, enemies as real or seeming?

Surely, he said, a man may be expected to love those whom he thinks good, and to hate those whom he thinks evil.

Yes, but do not persons often err in their judgment of good and evil; many who are not good appear to them to be good, and conversely?

That is true.

Then to them the good will be enemies, and the evil will be their friends?

True.

And in that case they will be right in doing good to the evil and evil to the good?

Apparently.

But the good are just and would not do an injustice?

True.

Then according to your argument it is just to injure those who do no wrong?

Nay, Socrates; the doctrine is immoral.

Then I suppose that they ought to do good to the just and harm to the unjust?

I like that better.

But see the consequence: Many a man who is ignorant of the world has friends who are friends, and then he ought to do harm to them; and he has good enemies whom he ought to benefit; but if so, we shall be saying the very opposite of that which we affirm to be the meaning of Simonides.

That is true, he said; and I think that we had better correct an error into which we have fallen in the use of the words "friend" and "enemy."

What was the error, Polemarchus? I replied.

The error lay in the assumption that he is a friend who seems or is thought good.

And how is the error to be corrected?

We should rather say that he is a friend who is, as well as seems, good; and that he who seems only, and is not good, only seems to be and is not a friend; and of an enemy the same may be said.

You would argue that the good are our friends and the bad our enemies?

Yes.

And instead of saying simply, as we did at first, that it is just to do good to your friends and harm to your enemies, you would now say, it is just to do good to your friends when they are good, and harm to your enemies when they are evil?

Yes, that appears to me to be the truth.

But then ought the just to injure any one at all?

Undoubtedly he ought to injure the wicked who are his enemies.

And when horses are injured, are they improved or deteriorated?

The latter.

Deteriorated, that is to say, in the good qualities of horses, not of dogs?

Yes, of horses.

And dogs are deteriorated in the good qualities of dogs, and not of horses?

Of course.

And will not men who are injured be deteriorated in that which is the proper virtue of man?

Certainly.

And that human virtue is justice?

To be sure.

Then men who are injured are of necessity made unjust?

That is the result.

But can the musician by his art make men unmusical?

Certainly not.

Or the horseman by his art make bad horsemen?

Impossible.

And can the just by justice make men unjust, or, speaking generally, can the good by virtue make them bad?

Assuredly not.

Nor can heat produce cold?

No.

Nor drought moisture?

Never.

Nor can the good harm any one?

Clearly not.

And the just is the good?

Certainly.

Then to injure a friend or any one else is not the act of a just man, but of the opposite, who is the unjust?

I think that what you say is quite true, Socrates.

Then if a man says that justice consists in repaying a debt, meaning that a just man ought to do good to his friends and injure his enemies, he is not really wise; for he says what is not true, if, as has been clearly shown, the injuring of another can be in no case just.

I agree with you, said Polemarchus.

Then you and I are prepared to take up arms against any one who attributes such a saying to Simonides or Bias or Pittacus, or any other wise man or seer?

I am quite ready to join with you, he said.

Shall I whisper in your ear whose I believe the saying to be?

Whose?

I believe that Periander, or Perdiccas, or Xerxes, or Ismenias, the Theban, or some other rich and mighty man, who had a great opinion of his own power, first said that justice is doing good to your friends and harm to your enemies.

Most true, he said.

Yes, I said; but if this definition of justice also breaks down, what other can be offered?

Several times in the middle of our discourse Thrasymachus had made an attempt to get the argument into his own hands by interrupting us, and had been put down by the rest of the company, who wanted to hear the end. But when I had done speaking and there was a pause, he could no longer hold his peace; and, gathering himself up, he came at us like a wild beast seeking to devour us. Polemarchus and I cowered in fear. — *The Republic*, ii. 155.

Enemies, all men are.

—— *Ath.* Are we to conceive each man as warring against himself: or how is that to be?

Cle. O Athenian Stranger, inhabitant of Attica I will not call you, who seem to me worthy to be named after the goddess Athene, because you go back to first principles; you, from the light which you have thrown upon the argument, will more readily recognize the truth of my assertion, when I said just now that all men are the enemies of all other men, both in public and private, and every individual of himself.

Ath. My good sir, what do you mean?

Cle. I mean what I say; and, further, that there is a victory and defeat, — the first and best of victories, the lowest and worst of defeats, — which each man gains or sustains at the hands, not of another, but of himself; this shows that there is a war against ourselves going on in every one of us. — *Laws*, iv. 157.

Enslaving power of money.

—— Come, now, and let us reason with the unjust, who is not intentionally in error. "Sweet Sir," we will say to him, "what think you of things esteemed noble and ignoble? Is not the noble that which subjects the beast to the man, or rather to the god in man; and the ignoble that which subjects the man to the beast?" He can hardly avoid saying Yes, — can he now?

Not if he has any regard for my opinion.

But, if he admit this, we may ask him another question:

How would a man profit if he received gold and silver on the condition that he was to enslave the noblest part of him to the worst? Who can imagine that a man who sold his son or daughter into slavery for money, especially if he sold them into the hands of fierce and evil men, would be the gainer, however large might be the sum which he received? And will any one say that he is not a miserable caitiff who sells his own divine being to that which is most atheistical and detestable, and has no pity? Eriphyle took the necklace as the price of her husband's life, but he is taking a bribe in order to compass a worse ruin. — *The Republic*, ii. 421.

Envy causing the death of good men.

—— I have said enough in answer to the charge of Meletus: any elaborate defense is unnecessary; but as I was saying before, I certainly have many enemies, and this is what will be my destruction if I am destroyed; of that I am certain; not Meletus, nor yet Anytus, but the envy and detraction of the world, which has been the death of many good men, and will probably be the death of many more; there is no danger of my being the last of them. — *Apology*, i. 326.

Envy, a pain of the soul.

—— *Soc.* Do we not speak of anger, fear, desire, sorrow, love, emulation, envy, and the like, as pains which belong to the soul only?

Pro. Yes.

Soc. And shall we not find them also full of the most wonderful pleasures? need I remind you of the anger

" Which stirs even a wise man to violence,
And sweeter is than honey and the honeycomb?"

And you remember how pleasures mingle with pains in lamentation and bereavement?

Pro. Yes, there is a natural connection between them.

Soc. And you remember also how at the sight of tragedies the spectators smile through their tears?

Pro. Certainly, I do.

Soc. And are you aware that even at a comedy the soul experiences a mixed feeling of pain and pleasure?

Pro. I do not understand you.

Soc. I admit, Protarchus, that there is some difficulty in recognizing this mixture of feelings at a comedy.

Pro. There is, I think.

Soc. And the greater the difficulty the more desirable is the examination of the case, because the difficulty of examining other cases of mixed pleasures and pains will be less.

Pro. Proceed.

Soc. I have just mentioned envy; would you not call that a pain of the soul?

Pro. Yes.

Soc. And yet the envious man finds something in the misfortunes of his neighbors at which he is pleased?

Pro. Certainly. — *Philebus,* iii. 187.

Envy and injustice.

—— Worthy of honor, too, is he who does no injustice, and of more than twofold honor if he not only does no injustice himself, but hinders others from doing any; the first may count as one man, the second is worth many men, because he informs the rulers of the injustice of others. And yet more highly to be esteemed is he who coöperates with the rulers in correcting the citizens as far as he can — he shall be proclaimed the great and perfect citizen, and bear away the palm of virtue. The same praise may be given about temperance and wisdom, and all other goods which may be imparted to others, as well as acquired by a man for himself; he who imparts them shall be honored as the man of men, and he who is willing yet is not able, may be allowed the second place; but he who is jealous and will not, if he can help, allow others to partake in a friendly way of any good, is deserving of blame: the good, however, which he has, is not to be undervalued because possessed by him, but to be acquired by us to the utmost of our power. Let every man, then, freely strive for the prize of virtue, and let there no envy. For the unenvious nature increases the greatness of States — he himself contends in the race and defames no man; but the envious, who thinks that he ought to get the better by defaming others, is less energetic himself in the pursuit of true virtue, and reduces his rivals to despair by his unjust slanders of them. And thus he deprives the whole city of the proper training for the contest of virtue, and diminishes her glory as far as in him lies. — *Laws,* iv. 256.

Equality not the same as impartiality.

—— When Alcibiades had done speaking, some one — Critias, I believe — went on to say: O Prodicus and Hippias, Callias appears to me to be a partisan of Protagoras. And this led

Alcibiades, who loves opposition, to take the other side. But we should not be partisans either of Socrates or Protagoras; let us rather unite in entreating both of them not to break up the discussion.

Prodicus added: That, Critias, seems to me to be well said, for those who are present at such discussions ought to be impartial hearers of both the speakers; remembering, however, that impartiality is not the same as equality, for both sides should be impartially heard, and yet an equal meed should not be assigned to both of them; but to the wiser a higher meed should be given, and a lower to the less wise. And I as well as Critias would beg you, Protagoras and Socrates, to grant our request, which is, that you will argue with one another and not wrangle; for friends argue with friends out of goodwill, but only adversaries and enemies wrangle. — *Protagoras*, i. 137.

Equality and unequality.

—— Shall we proceed a step further, and affirm that there is such a thing as equality, not of one piece of wood or stone with another, but that, over and above this, there is equality in the abstract? Shall we say so?

Say so, yes, replied Simmias, and swear to it, with all the confidence in life.

And do we know the nature of this abstract essence?

To be sure, he said.

And whence did we obtain our knowledge? Did we not see equalities of material things, such as pieces of wood and stones, and gather from them the idea of an equality which is different from them? for you will acknowledge that there is a difference. Or look at the matter in another way: — Do not the same pieces of wood or stone appear at one time equal, and at another time unequal?

That is certain.

But are real equals ever unequal? or is the idea of equality the same as that of inequality?

Impossible, Socrates.

Then these (so-called) equals are not the same with the idea of equality?

I should say, clearly not, Socrates.

And yet from these equals, although differing from the idea of equality, you conceived and attained that idea?

Very true, he said.

Which might be like, or might be unlike them?

Yes.

But that makes no difference: whenever from seeing one thing you conceived another, whether like or unlike, there must surely have been an act of recollection?

Very true.

But what would you say of equal portions of wood and stone, or other material equals? and what is the impression produced by them? Are they equals in the same sense in which absolute equality is equal? or do they fall short of this equality in a measure?

Yes, he said, in a very great measure too. — *Phaedo*, i. 401.

Equality of anarchy.

—— When a democracy which is thirsting for freedom has evil cup-bearers presiding over the feast, and has drunk too deeply of the strong wine of freedom, then, unless her rulers are very amenable and give a plentiful draught, she calls them to account and punishes them, and says that they are cursed oligarchs.

Yes, he replied, a very common thing.

Yes, I said; and loyal citizens are insulted by her as lovers of slavery and men of naught; she would have subjects who are like rulers, and rulers who are like subjects: these are men after her own heart, whom she praises and honors both in private and public. Now, in such a State, can liberty have any limit?

Certainly not.

By degrees, the anarchy finds a way into private houses, and ends by getting among the animals and infecting them.

How do you mean?

I mean that the father gets accustomed to descend to the level of his sons and to fear them, and the son to be on a level with his father, he having no shame or fear of either of his parents; and this is his freedom, and the metic is equal with the citizen and the citizen with the metic, and the stranger on a level with either.

Yes, he said, that is true.

That is true; and, there are other light evils such as the following: the master fears and flatters his scholars, and the scholars despise their masters and tutors; and, in general, young and old are alike, and the young man is on a level with the old, and is ready to compete with him in word or deed;

and old men condescend to the young, and are full of pleasantry and gayety; they do not like to be thought morose and authoritative, and therefore they adopt the manners of the young. — *The Republic*, ii. 391.

Essence, individual.

—— Now God did not make the soul after the body, although we have spoken of them in this order; for when he put them together he would never have allowed that the elder should serve the younger, but this is a random manner of speaking, because we ourselves too are very largely affected by chance. Whereas he made the soul in origin and excellence prior to and older than the body, to be the ruler and mistress, of whom the body was to be the subject. And he made her out of the following elements and on this manner: of the unchangeable and indivisible, and also of the divisible and corporeal, he made a third sort of intermediate essence, partaking of the same and of the other or diverse, and this compounded in like manner he placed in a mean between the indivisible and the divisible or corporeal. He took these three elements of the same, the other and the essence, and mingled them all together, compressing the reluctant and unsociable nature of the other into the same. And when he had mixed them, and out of all the three made one, he again divided this whole into as many portions as was fitting, each of them containing an admixture of all three. — *Timaeus*, ii. 528.

Essence, war about.

—— *Str.* There appears to be a sort of war of Giants and Gods going on amongst them; they are fighting about the nature of essence.

Theaet. How is that?

Str. Some of them are dragging down all things from heaven and from the unseen to earth, and seem determined to grasp in their hands rocks and oaks; of these they lay hold, and are obstinate in maintaining, that the things only which can be touched or handled have being or essence, because they define being and body as one, and if any one else says that what is not a body exists they altogether despise him, and will hear of nothing but body.

Theaet. I have often met with such men, and terrible fellows they are.

Str. And that is the reason why their opponents cautiously defend themselves from above, out of an unseen world, mightily contending that true essence consists of certain intelligible and incorporeal ideas ; the bodies of the materialists, which by them are maintained to be the very truth, they break up into little bits by their arguments, and affirm them to be generation and not essence. O Theaetetus, there is an endless war upon this theme which is always being waged between the two armies. — *Sophist*, iii. 483.

Essence, nature of.

—— *Str.* If they will admit that any, even the smallest particle of being is incorporeal, that is enough ; they must then say what that nature is which is common to both the corporeal and incorporeal, which they have in their mind's eye when they say of both of them that they " are." Perhaps they may be in a difficulty ; and if this is the case, there is a possibility that they may accept a notion of ours respecting the nature of essence, having nothing of their own to offer.

Theaet. What is the notion ? Tell us, and we shall see.

Str. My notion would be, that anything which possesses any sort of power to affect another, or to be affected by another even for a moment, however trifling the cause and however slight and momentary the effect, has real existence ; and I hold that the definition of being is simply power.

Theaet. They accept your suggestion, having nothing better of their own to offer.

Str. Very good ; perhaps we, as well as they, may one day change our mind ; but, for the present, this may be regarded as the understanding which is established with them.

Theaet. Agreed. — *Sophist*, iii. 485.

Esteem and praise distinguished.

—— Then our meeting will be delightful ; for in this way you, who are the speakers, will be most likely to win esteem, and not praise only, among us who are your audience ; for esteem is a sincere conviction of the hearers' souls, but praise is often an insincere expression of men uttering falsehoods contrary to their conviction. And thus we who are the hearers will be gratified and not pleased ; for gratification is of the mind when receiving wisdom and knowledge, but pleasure is of the body when eating or experiencing some other bodily delight. Thus spoke Prodicus, and many of the company applauded his words. — *Protagoras*, i. 137.

Eternal, space is.

—— There is a third nature, which is space, and is eternal, and admits not of destruction, and provides a home for all created things, and is perceived without the help of sense, by a kind of spurious reason, and is hardly matter of belief, which we, beholding as in a dream, say, of all existence, that it must of necessity be in some place and occupy a space, but that what is neither in heaven nor in earth has no existence. — *Timaeus*, ii. 544.

Evil and good, the presence of.

—— Now I want to know whether in all cases a substance is assimilated by the presence of another substance; or must the presence be after a peculiar sort?

The latter, he said.

Then that which is neither good nor evil may be in the presence of evil, but not as yet evil, and that has happened before now?

True.

And when anything is in the presence of evil, not being as yet evil, the presence of good arouses the desire of good in that thing; but the presence of evil, which makes a thing evil, takes away the desire and friendship of the good; for that which was once both good and evil has now become evil only, and the good had no friendship with the evil?

None.

And therefore we say that those who are already wise, whether Gods or men, are no longer lovers of wisdom; nor can they be lovers of wisdom, who are ignorant to the extent of being evil, for no evil or ignorant person is a lover of wisdom. There remain those who have the misfortune to be ignorant, but are not yet hardened in their ignorance, or void of understanding, and do not as yet fancy that they know what they do not know; and therefore those who are the lovers of wisdom are as yet neither good nor bad. But the bad do not love wisdom any more than the good; for, as we have already seen, neither unlike is the friend of unlike, nor like of like. You remember that?

Yes, they both said. — *Lysis*, i. 58.

Evil, concealment of. See *Concealment*, etc.
Evil, God not the author of. See *God*.

—— Let us equally refuse to believe, or allow to be repeated, the tale of Theseus son of Poseidon, or of Peirithous son of Zeus, going forth to perpetrate such a horrid rape; or of any other hero or son of a God daring to do such impious and horrible things as they falsely ascribe to them in our day: and let us compel the poets to declare either that these acts were not done by them, or that they were not the sons of Gods:—both in the same breath they shall not be permitted to affirm. We will not have them teaching our youth that the gods are the authors of evil, and that heroes are no better than men; undoubtedly, these sentiments, as we were saying, are neither pious nor true, for they are at variance with our demonstration that evil cannot come from God. Undoubtedly.

And further they are likely to have a bad effect on those who hear them; for everybody will begin to excuse his own vices when he is convinced that similar wickednesses are always being perpetrated by the kindred of the Gods,—

"The relatives of Zeus, whose paternal altar is in the heavens and on the mount of Ida,"

and who have —

"The blood of deity yet flowing in their veins."

And therefore let us put an end to such tales, lest they engender laxity of morals among the young. — *The Republic*, ii. 214.

Evil, suffering less than doing. See *Injustice*.
Evil-doers, justice among. See *Honor among theives*.
Evil-doers, effect of punishment on. See *Punishment*, etc.
Evil; the greatest in the State. See *Injustice, penalty of*.

—— Shall we begin by asking of ourselves what we conceive to be the greatest good, and what ought to be the chief aim of the legislator in the organization of a State, and what is the greatest evil, and then consider whether our previous description has the stamp of the good or of the evil.

By all means.

Can there be any greater evil than discord and distraction and plurality where unity ought to reign? or any greater good than the bond of unity?

There cannot.

And there is unity where there is community of pleasures and pains — where all the citizens are glad or sorry on the same occasions?

No doubt.

Yes; and where there is no common but only private feeling, a State is disorganized — when you have one half of the world triumphing and the other sorrowing at the same events happening to the city and the citizens?

Certainly.

Such differences commonly originate in a disagreement about the use of the terms "meum" and "tuum," mine and thine.

Exactly.

And is not that the best-ordered State in which the greatest number of persons apply the terms "mine" and "not mine" in the same way to the same thing?

True, very true.

Or that again which most nearly approaches to the condition of the individual — as in the body, when but a finger is hurt, the whole frame, drawn towards the soul and forming one realm under the ruling power therein, feels the hurt and sympathizes all together with the part affected, and we say that the man has a pain in his finger; and the same expression is used about any other part, which has a sensation of pain at suffering or of pleasure at the alleviation of suffering.

Very true, he replied; and I agree with you that in the best-ordered State there is the nearest approach to this common feeling which you describe.

Then when any one of the citizens experiences any good or evil, the whole State will make his case their own, and either rejoice or sorrow with him?

Yes, he said, that is what will happen in a well-ordered State. — *The Republic*, ii. 287.

Evil and good, power for. See *Good*, etc.

Evil and good, when they are such.

—— *Soc.* And punishment is an evil?

Pol. Certainly.

Soc. And you would admit once more, my good sir, that great power is a benefit to a man if his actions turn out to his advantage, and that this is the meaning of great power; and if not, then his power is an evil and is no power. But let us look at the matter in another way: — do we not acknowledge that the things of which we were speaking, the infliction of death, and exile, and the deprivation of property, are sometimes a good and sometimes not a good?

Pol. Certainly.

Soc. About that you and I may be supposed to agree?

Pol. Yes.

Soc. Tell me, then, when do you say that they are good and when that they are evil: what principle do you lay down?

Pol. I would rather, Socrates, that you should answer as well as ask that question.

Soc. Well, Polus, since you would rather have the answer from me, I say that they are good when they are just, and evil when they are unjust. — *Gorgias,* iii. 56.

Evils imperishable.

—— *Soc.* Evils, Theodorus, can never pass away; for there must always remain something which is antagonistic to good. Having no place among the Gods in heaven, of necessity they hover around the earthly nature and this mortal sphere. Wherefore we ought to fly away from earth to heaven as quickly as we can; and to fly away is to become like God, as far as this is possible; and to become like him, is to become holy and just and wise. But, O my friend, you cannot easily convince mankind that they should pursue virtue or avoid vice, not in order that a man may seem to be good, which is the reason given by the world, and in my judgment is only a repetition of an old wives' fable, whereas, the truth is that God is never unrighteous at all — he is perfect righteousness; and he of us who is the most righteous is most like him. Herein is seen the true cleverness of a man, and also his nothingness and want of manhood. — *Theaetetus,* iii. 378.

Excess in pleasures.

—— *Soc.* Then if we want to see the true nature of pleasures as a class, we should not look at the most diluted pleasures, but at the most extreme and most vehement?

Pro. In that every one will be ready to agree.

Soc. And the obvious instances of the greatest pleasure, as we have often said, are pleasures of the body?

Pro. Certainly.

Soc. And are they felt by us to be or become greater, when we are sick or when we are in health? And here we must be careful in our answer, and not make a mistake.

Pro. How are we likely to mistake?

Soc. Why, because we might be tempted to answer rashly, "when we are in health."

Pro. Yes, that is the natural answer.

Soc. Well, but are not those pleasures the greatest of which mankind have the greatest desires?

Pro. True.

Soc. And do not people who are in a fever, or any similar illness, feel cold or thirst or other bodily affection more intensely? Am I not right in saying that they have a deeper want and great pleasure in the satisfaction of their want?

Pro. That is clear when you say so.

Soc. Well, then, shall we not be right in saying, that if a person would wish to see the greatest pleasures he ought to go and look, not at health, but at disease? And here you must distinguish: do not imagine that I am asking whether those who are very ill have more pleasure than those who are well, but understand that I am speaking of the intensity of pleasure; I want to know where pleasures are found to be most in excess. For, as I say, we have to discover what is pleasure, and what nature they attribute to her who deny her very existence.

Pro. I believe that I follow you.

Soc. We shall soon see whether you do or not, Protarchus, for you shall answer me; tell me, then, whether you see, I will not say more, but more intense and excessive pleasures in wantonness than in temperance? and please to think before you speak.

Pro. I understand you, and see that there is a great difference between them; the temperate are restrained by the wise man's aphorisms of "never too much," which is their rule, but excess of pleasure possessing the minds of fools and wantons quite maddens and infuriates them. — *Philebus,* iii. 183.

Exchange, art of.

—— *Str.* Take another branch of his (the Sophist's) genealogy; for he is a professor of a great and many-sided art; and if we look back at what has preceded, we see that he presents another aspect, besides that of which we are speaking.

Theaet. In what respect?

Str. There were two sorts of acquisitive art; the one concerned with hunting, the other with exchange.

Theaet. There were.

Str. And of the art of exchange there are two divisions, the one of giving, and the other of selling.

Theaet. Let us assume that.

Str. Further, we will suppose that the art of selling is divided into two parts.

Theaet. How?

Str. There is one part which is distinguished as the sale of a man's own productions; another, which is the exchange of the works of others.

Theaet. Certainly.

Str. And is not that part of exchange which takes place in the city, being about half of the whole, termed retailing?

Theaet. Yes.

Str. And that which exchanges the goods of one city for those of another by selling and buying is the exchange of the merchant?

Theaet. To be sure.

Str. And this exchange of the merchant is partly an exchange of food for the use of the body, and partly of the food of the soul which is bartered and received in exchange for money.

Theaet. What do you mean?

Str. You want to know what is the meaning of food for the soul; the other kind you understand.

Theaet. Yes.

Str. Take music in general and painting and marionette playing and many other things, which are purchased in one city, and carried away and sold in another — wares of the soul which are hawked about either for the sake of instruction or amusement; — may not he who takes them about and sells them be quite as truly called a merchant as he who sells meats and drinks?

Theaet. To be sure he may.

Str. And would you not call by the same name him who goes about from city to city, buying knowledge from all quarters and exchanging his wares for money?

Theaet. Certainly I should.

Str. Of this merchandise of the soul, may not one part be fairly termed the art of display? And there is another which is certainly not less ridiculous, but being a trade in learning must be called by some name germane to the matter?

Theaet. Certainly.

Str. There should be two names for them, one descriptive of the sale of the knowledge of virtue, and the other of the sale of other kinds of knowledge.

Theaet. Of course.

Str. The name of art seller corresponds well enough to the one; and I hope that you will tell me the name of the other.

Theaet. He must be the Sophist, whom we are seeking; no other name can possibly be right.

Str. No other; and so this trader in virtue again turns out to be our friend the Sophist, whose art may now be traced a second time, through the art of acquisition — exchange — buying and selling, — by the merchant, not forgetting that there is a merchandise of the soul which is concerned with speech and knowledge.

Theaet. Certainly.

Str. And there may be a third reappearance of him; for he may have settled down in a city, and partly fabricate as well as buy these same wares, intending to live by selling them, and he would still be called a Sophist?

Theaet. Certainly.

Str. Then that part of the acquisitive art which exchanges, and of exchange which either sells a man's own productions or retails those of others, as the case may be, and in either way sells knowledge, you would again term Sophistry?

Theaet. I must if I am to keep up with the argument. — *Sophist,* iii. 457.

Existence, recollection a proof of previous.

—— Yes, he said, Cebes, I entirely think so too; nor is this a delusion in which we are agreeing; but I am confident in the belief that there truly is such a thing as living again, and that the living spring from the dead, and that the souls of the dead are in existence, and that the good souls have a better portion than the evil.

Cebes added: Your favorite doctrine, Socrates, that knowledge is simply recollection, if true, also necessarily implies a previous time in which we learned that which we now recollect. But this would be impossible unless our soul was in some place before existing in the human form; here then is another argument of the soul's immortality.

But tell me, Cebes, said Simmias interposing, what proofs are given of this doctrine of recollection? I am not very sure at this moment that I remember them.

One excellent proof, said Cebes, is afforded by questions. If you put a question to a person in a right way, he will give a true answer of himself, but how could he do this unless there were knowledge and right reason already in him? And this is most clearly shown when he is taken to a diagram or to anything of that sort.

But if, said Socrates, you are still incredulous, Simmias, I would ask you whether you may not agree with me when you look at the matter in another way; I mean, if you are still incredulous as to whether knowledge is recollection?

Incredulous, I am not, said Simmias; but I want to have this doctrine of recollection brought to my own recollection, and, from what Cebes has said, I am beginning to recollect and be convinced; but I should still like to hear what you were going to say.

This is what I should say, he replied: — We should agree, if I am not mistaken, that what a man recollects he must have known at some previous time.

Very true.

And what is the nature of this knowledge or recollection? I mean to ask, whether when a person has already seen or heard, or in any way perceived anything, and he knows not only that, but something else of which he has not the same but another knowledge, we may not fairly say that he recollects that which comes into his mind. Are we agreed about that? — *Phaedo*, i. 399.

Existence, pure and real.

—— Which classes of things have a greater share of pure existence in your judgment, — those of which food and drink and condiments and all kinds of sustenance are examples, or the class which contains true opinion and mind, and, in general, all virtue? Put the question in this way: Which has a more pure being, — that which is concerned with the invariable, the immortal, and the true, and is found in the invariable, immortal, true; or that which is concerned with the variable and mortal, and is found in the variable and mortal?

Far purer, he replied, is the being of that which is concerned with the invariable.

And does the essence of the invariable partake of knowledge in the same degree as of essence?

Yes, of knowledge in the same degree.

And of truth in the same degree?

Yes.

And, conversely, that which has less of truth will also have less of essence?

Necessarily.

Then, in general, those kinds of things which are in the service of the body have less of truth and essence than those which are in the service of the soul?

Far less.

And has not the body itself less of truth and essence than the soul?

Yes.

What is filled with more real existence, and actually has a more real existence, is more really filled than that which is filled with less real existence and is less real?

Of course.

And if there be a pleasure in being filled with that which is according to nature, that which is more really filled with more real being will have more real and true joy and pleasure; whereas that which participates in less real· being will be less truly and surely satisfied, and will participate in a less true and real pleasure?

Unquestionably. — *The Republic*, ii. 416.

Str. Let us push the question; for if they will admit that any, even the smallest particle of being, is incorporeal, that is enough; they must then say what that nature is which is common to both the corporeal and incorporeal, and which they have in their mind's eye when they say of both of them that they "are." Perhaps they may be in a difficulty; and if this is the case, there is a possibility that they may accept a notion of ours respecting the nature of essence, having nothing of their own to offer.

Theaet. What is the notion? Tell us, and we shall see.

Str. My notion would be, that anything which possesses any sort of power to affect another, or to be affected by another even for a moment, however trifling the cause and however slight and momentary the effect, has real existence; and I hold that the definition of being is simply power. — *Sophist*, iii. 485.

Existences, separation of.

—— *Str.* But to show that somehow and in some sense the same is other, or the other same, or the great small, or the like unlike; and to delight in always thus bringing forward oppositions in argument, is no true refutation, but only proves that he who uses such arguments is a neophyte who has got but a little way in the investigation of truth.

Theaet. To be sure.

Str. For certainly, my friend, the attempt to separate all existences from one another is not only tasteless but also illiterate and unphilosophical.

Theaet. Why so?

Str. The attempt at universal separation is the final annihilation of all reason ; for only by the union of conceptions with one another do we attain to discourse of reason.

Theaet. True.

Str. And observe that we were only just in time in making a resistance to such separatists, and compelling them to make the admission that other did mingle with other. — *Sophist,* iii. 499.

Faculties ; what are they?

—— Do we admit the existence of opinion?

Undoubtedly.

As being the same with knowledge, or another faculty?

Another faculty.

Then opinion and knowledge have to do with different kinds of matter corresponding to this difference of faculties?

Yes.

And knowledge is relative to being, and knows being; but before I proceed, I will first make a division.

What division?

I will begin by placing faculties in a class by themselves; they are powers in us and in all other things by which we do as we do. Sight and hearing, for example, I should call faculties. Have I clearly explained the class which I mean?

Yes, I quite understand.

Then let me tell you my view about them. I do not see them, and therefore the distinctions of figure, color, and the like, which enable me to discern the differences of some things, do not apply to them. In speaking of a faculty I think only of the end and the operation ; and that which has the same end and the same operation I call the same faculty, but that which has another end and another operation I call different. Would that be your way of speaking?

Yes.

To return. Would you place knowledge among faculties, or in some other class?

Certainly knowledge is a faculty, and the most powerful of all faculties.

And is opinion also a faculty?

Certainly, he said ; for opinion is that with which we are able to form an opinion.

And yet you were surely admitting a little while ago that knowledge is not the same as opinion?

Why, yes, said he : for how can any reasonable being ever identify that which is infallible with that which errs?

That is very good, I said, and clearly shows that we are conscious of a distinction between them?

Yes.

Then knowledge and opinion, having distinct powers, have also distinct ends or subject-matters?

That is certain. — *The Republic*, ii. 305.

False oaths. See *Oaths*.

False opinion and true. See *Heterodoxy*.

—— What do you mean, Dionysodorus? I have often heard, and have been amazed, to hear this thesis of yours, which is maintained and employed by the disciples of Protagoras, and others before them, and which to me appears to be quite wonderful and suicidal, as well as destructive, and I think that I am most likely to hear the truth of this from you. The dictum is that there is no such thing as falsehood; a man must either say what is true or say nothing. Is not that your position?

He assented.

But if he cannot speak falsely, may he not think falsely?

No, he cannot, he said.

Then there is no such thing as false opinion?

No, he said. — *Euthedymus*, i. 189.

Soc. Let us then put into more precise terms the question which has arisen about pleasure and opinion. Is there such a thing as opinion?

Pro. Yes.

Soc. And such a thing as pleasure?

Pro. Yes.

Soc. And there must be something about which a man has an opinion?

Pro. True.

Soc. And something which gives pleasure?

Pro. Quite correct.

Soc. And whether his opinion is right or wrong, makes no difference; he will still always have an opinion?

Pro. Certainly.

Soc. And he who is pleased, whether he is rightly pleased or not, will always have a real feeling of pleasure?

Pro. Yes : that is also quite true.

Soc. Then, how can opinion be true and false, and pleasure only true; and yet the state of being pleased, or holding an opinion may be both real?

Pro. Yes; that is the question.

Soc. You mean that opinion has the attributes of true and false, and hence becomes not merely opinion, but opinion of a certain quality; and this is what you think should be examined?

Pro. Yes. — *Philebus,* iii. 174.

Falsehood, when committed. See *Fiction,* etc.
Falsehood, God incapable of. See *Deception.*
Falsehood for the State. See *Lies,* etc.
Fame, immortality of fame. See *Immortality,* etc.
Family ties in the State.

—— Did you ever know an example in other States of a ruler who would speak of one of his colleagues as a friend and of another as not a friend to him?

Yes, very often.

And the friend he describes and regards as one in whom he has an interest, and the other as one in whom he has no interest?

Exactly.

But would any of your guardians speak of one of their fellows as a friend and of another as not a friend to him?

Certainly not; for every one whom they meet will be regarded by them either as a brother or sister, or father or mother, or son or daughter, or as the child or parent of those who are thus connected with him.

Capital, I said; but let me ask you once more: Shall they be a family in name only, or shall they always act as if they were a family? For example, in the use of the word "father," would the care of a father be implied and the filial reverence and duty and obedience to him which the law commands; and is the violator of these duties to be regarded as an impious and unrighteous person who is not likely to receive much good either from the hands of God or man? Are these to be the strains which the children will hear repeated in their ears by all the citizens about their parents and kindred when they are pointed out to them?

These, he said, and none other; for what can be more ridiculous than for them to utter the names of family ties with the lips only, and not to act upon them?

Then in our city the language of harmony and concord will be more often heard than in any other. As I was describing before, when any one is well or ill, the universal word will be, "mine is well" or "mine is ill."

Most true.

And agreeably to this mode of thinking or speaking, were we not saying also that they will have their pleasures and pains in common?

Yes, and so they will.

And they will have a common interest in the same which they will call "my own," and having this common interest they will have a common feeling of pleasure and pain?

Yes, they will have a far greater community of feeling.— *The Republic*, ii. 289.

Fancies of people.

—— But first I must tell you that I am one who from my childhood upward have set my heart upon a certain thing. All people have their fancies; some desire horses, and others dogs; and some are fond of gold and others of honor. Now, I have no violent desire for any of these things; but I have a passion for friends; and I would rather have a good friend than the best cock or quail in the world: I would even go further, and say than a horse or dog. Yea, by the dog of Egypt, I should greatly prefer a real friend to all the gold of Darius, or even to Darius himself; I am such a lover of friends as that. And when I see you and Lysis, at your early age, so easily possessed of this treasure, and so soon, he of you, and you of him, I am amazed and delighted, seeing that I myself, although I am now advanced in years, am so far from having made a similar acquisition, that I do not even know in what way a friend is acquired. But I want to ask you a question about this, for you have experience: tell me then, when one loves another, is the lover or the beloved the friend; or may either be the friend?

I think that either may be the friend.

Do you mean, I said, that if only one of them loves the other, they are mutual friends?

Yes, he said; that is my meaning.

But what if the lover is not loved in return? That is a possible case.

Yes.

Or is, perhaps, even hated? for that is a fancy which lovers sometimes have, Nothing can exceed their love; and yet they imagine either that they are not loved in return, or that they are hated. Is not that true?

Yes, he said, quite true. —*Lysis*, i. 50.

Fancies of hope.

—— *Soc.* All men, as we were saying just now, are always filled with hopes?
Pro. Certainly.
Soc. And these hopes, as they are termed, are propositions which exist in the minds of each of us?
Pro. Yes.
Soc. And the fancies of hope are also pictured in us; a man may often have a vision of a heap of gold, and pleasures ensuing, and in the picture there may be a likeness of himself mightily rejoicing over his good fortune.
Pro. True.
Soc. And may we not say that the good, being friends of the Gods, have generally true pictures presented to them, and the bad false pictures?
Pro. Certainly.
Soc. And yet the bad have pleasures painted in their fancy as well as the good; but I presume that they are false pleasures?
Pro. They are. — *Philebus*, iii. 178.

Fathers, brave sons of brave. See *State, heroes*, etc.
Fathers, sons of good, why they turn out ill.

—— But why do the sons of good fathers often turn out ill? Let me explain that, — which is far from being wonderful, if, as I have been saying, the very existence of the State implies that virtue is not any man's private possession. If this be true — and nothing can be truer — then I will ask you to imagine, as an illustration, some other pursuit or branch of knowledge which may be assumed equally to be the condition of the existence of a State. Suppose that there could be no State unless we were all flute-players, as far as each had the capacity, and everybody was freely teaching everybody the art, both in private and public, and reproving the bad player as freely and openly as every man now teaches justice and the laws, not concealing them as he would conceal the other arts, but imparting them — for all of us have a mutual interest in the justice and virtue of one another, and this is the reason why every one is ready to teach justice and the laws; suppose, I say, that there were the same readiness and liberality among us in teaching one another flute-playing, do you imagine, Socrates, that the sons of good flute-players would be more likely to be good than the sons of bad ones? I think not. Would not their sons grow up to be distinguished or undistinguished according to their own natural capacities as flute-players, and the son of a good player would often turn out to be a bad one, and the son of a bad player to be a good one, and all flute-players would be good enough in comparison of those who were ignorant and unacquainted with the art of flute-playing? In like manner I would have you consider that he who appears to you to be the worst of those who have been brought up in laws and humanities, would appear to be a just man and a master of justice if he were to be compared with men who had no education, or courts of justice, or laws, or any restraints upon them which compelled them to practice virtue — with the savages, for example, whom the poet Pherecrates exhibited on the stage at the last year's Lenaean festival. If you were living among men such as the man-haters in his Chorus, you would be only too glad to meet with Eurybates and Phrynondas, and you would sorrowfully long to revisit the rascality of this part of the world. And you, Socrates, are discontented, and why? Because all men are teachers of virtue, each one according to his ability, and you say that there is no teacher. You might as well ask, Who teaches Greek? For of that too there will not be any teachers found. Or you might ask, Who is to teach the sons of our artisans this same art which they have learned of their fathers? He and his fellow-workmen have taught them to the best of their ability, — but who will carry them further in their arts? And you would certainly have a difficulty, Socrates, in finding a teacher of them; but there would be no difficulty in finding a teacher of those who are wholly ignorant. And this is true of virtue or of anything; and if a man is better able than we are to promote virtue ever so little, that is as much as we can expect. A teacher of this sort I believe myself to be, and above all other men to have the knowledge which makes a man noble and good; and I give my pupils their money's-worth, and even more, as they themselves confess. And therefore I have introduced the following mode of payment: When a man has been my pupil, if he likes he pays my price, but there is no compulsion; and if he does not like, he has only to go into a temple and take an oath of the value of the instructions, and he pays no more than he declares to be their value.

Such is my Apologue, Socrates, and such is the argument by which I endeavor to show that virtue may be taught, and that this is the opinion of the Athenians. And I have also attempted to show that you are not to wonder at good sons having bad fathers, or at good fathers having bad sons, of which the sons of Polycleitus afford an example, who are the companions of our friends here, Paralus and Xanthippus, but are nothing in comparison with their father; and this is true of the sons of many other artists.— *Protagoras*, i. 126.

Faultless man not to be found.

—— All this relates to Pittacus, as is further proved by the sequel. For he adds: " Therefore I will not throw away my life in searching after the impossible, hoping in vain to find a perfectly faultless man among those who partake of the fruit of the broad-bosomed earth; and when I have found him to tell you of him" (this is the vehement way in which he pursues his attack upon Pittacus throughout the whole poem): " but him who does no evil, voluntarily I praise and love; not even the Gods war against necessity." All this has a similar drift, for Simonides was not so ignorant as to say that he praised those who did no evil voluntarily, as though there were some who did evil voluntarily. For no wise man, as I believe, will allow that any human being errs voluntarily, or voluntarily does evil and dishonorable actions; but they are very well aware that all who do evil and dishonorable things do them against their will. And Simonides never says that he praises him who does no evil voluntarily; the word "voluntarily" applies to himself. For he was under the impression that a good man might often compel himself to love and praise another, and to be the friend and approver of another; and that there might be an involuntary love, such as a man might feel to an unnatural father or mother, or his country, or the like. Now bad men, when their parents or country have any defects, rejoice at the sight of them and find fault with them and expose and denounce them to others under the idea that the rest of mankind will be less likely to take themselves to task and accuse them of neglect; and they blame their defects far more than they deserve in order that the odium which is necessarily incurred by them may be increased: but the good man dissembles his feelings, and constrains himself to praise them; and if they have wronged him and he is angry, he pacifies his anger and is reconciled, and compels himself to love and praise his own flesh and blood. And Simonides, as is probable, considered that he himself had often had to praise and magnify a tyrant or the like, much against his will, and he also wishes to imply to Pittacus that he is not censorious and does not censure him. "For I am satisfied," he says, "when a man is neither bad nor very stupid, and when he knows justice (which is the health of States), and is of sound mind, I will find no fault with him, for I am not given to finding fault, and there are innumerable fools" (implying that if he delighted in censure he might have abundant opportunity of finding fault). "All things are good with which evil is unmingled." In these latter words he does not mean to say that all things are good which have no evil in them, as you might say "All things are white which have no black in them," for that would be ridiculous; but he means to say that he accepts and finds no fault with the moderate or intermediate state. "I do not hope," he says, "to find a perfectly blameless man among those who partake of the fruits of the broad-bosomed earth, and when I have found him to tell you of him; in this sense I praise no man. But he who is moderately good, and does no evil, is good enough for me, who love and approve every one" (and here observe that he uses a Lesbian word ἐπαίνημι, because he is addressing Pittacus, — "who love and approve every one voluntarily, who does no evil:" and that the stop should be put after "voluntarily"); "but there are some whom I involuntarily praise and love. And you, Pittacus, I would never have blamed, if you had spoken what was moderately good and true; but I do blame you because, wearing the appearance of truth, you are speaking falsely about the greatest matters." And this, I said, Prodicus and Protagoras, I take to be the true meaning of Simonides in this poem. — *Protagoras*, i. 145.

Fear, its object. See *Courage, Bravery*.

—— *Soc.* Now, let us proceed a step, and see whether we are equally agreed about the fearful and the hopeful. Let me tell you my own opinion, and if I am wrong you shall set me right; in my opinion the terrible and the hopeful are the things which do or do not create fear, and fear is not of the present, nor of the past, but is of future and expected evil. Do you not agree to that, Laches?

La. Yes, Socrates, entirely.

Soc. That is my view, Nicias; the terrible things, as I should say, are the evils which are future; and the hopeful are the good or not evil things which are future. Do you or do you not agree with me? — *Laches*, i. 92.

Fear, its source and influence.

—— *Ath.* Fear springs out of an evil habit of the soul. And when some one applies external agitation to affections of this sort, the motion coming from without gets the better of the terrible and violent internal one, and produces a peace and calm in the soul, and quiets the restless palpitation of the heart, which is a thing much to be desired, sending some to sleep, and making others who are awake to dance to the pipe, with the help of the Gods, to whom they offer acceptable sacrifices, and producing in them a sound mind, which takes the place of their former agitations. And in this, as I would shortly say, there is a considerable amount of sense.

Cle. Certainly.

Ath. But if fear has such a power we ought to consider further, that every soul which from youth upward has been familiar with fears, will be made more liable to fear, and every one will admit that this is the way to form a habit of cowardice and not of courage.

Cle. Certainly.

Ath. And, on the other hand, the habit of overcoming, from our youth upwards, the fears and terrors which beset us, may be said to be an exercise of courage?

Cle. True. — *Laws*, iv. 309.

Few, the government of the, only true.

—— *Str.* The several forms of government cannot be defined by the words few or many, voluntary or compulsory, poverty or riches; but some notion of science must enter in, if we are to be consistent with what has preceded.

Y. Soc. And we must be consistent.

Str. Well, then, in which of these various forms of States may the science of government, which is among the greatest and most difficult of all sciences, be supposed to reside? That we must discover, and then we shall see who are the false politicians who win popularity and pretend to be politicians and are not, and separate them from the wise king.

Y. Soc. That, as the argument has already intimated, is our duty.

Str. Do you think that the multitude in a State can attain political science?

Y. Soc. Impossible.

Str. But, perhaps, in a city of a thousand men, there would be a hundred, or say fifty, who could?

Y. Soc. In that case political science would certainly be the easiest of all sciences; there could not be found in a city of that number as many really first-rate draught-players, if judged by the standard of the rest of Hellas, and there would certainly not be as many kings. For kings we may truly call those who possess royal science, whether they rule or not, as was shown in the previous argument.

Str. Thank you for reminding me; and the consequence is that any true form of government can only be supposed to be the government of one, two, or, at any rate, of a few.

Y. Soc. Certainly. — *Statesman*, iii. 578.

Fickleness of youth. See *Changeableness*.

Fiction, censorship of.

—— You know also that the beginning is the chiefest part of any work, especially in a young and tender thing; for that is the time at which the character is formed and most readily receives the desired impression.

Quite true.

And shall we just carelessly allow children to hear any casual tales which may be framed by casual persons, and to receive into their minds notions which are the very opposite of those which are to be held by them when they are grown up?

We cannot.

Then the first thing will be to have a censorship of the writers of fiction, and let the censors receive any tale of fiction which is good, and reject the bad; and we will desire mothers and nurses to tell their children the authorized ones only. Let them fashion the mind with these tales, even more fondly than they form the body with their hands. And most of those which are now in use must be discarded.

Of what tales are you speaking? he said.

You may find a model of the lesser in the greater, I said; for they are necessarily cast in the same mould, and there is the same spirit in both of them.

That may be very true, he replied; but I do not as yet know what you would term the greater.

Those, I said, which are narrated by Homer and Hesiod, and the rest of the poets, who have ever been the great story-tellers of mankind.

But which stories do you mean, he said; and what fault do you find with them?

A fault which is most serious, I said; the fault of telling a lie, and what is more, a bad lie.

But when is this fault committed?

Whenever an erroneous representation is made of the nature of gods and heroes, — like the drawing of a limner which has not the shadow of a likeness to the truth.

Yes, he said, that sort of thing is certainly very blameable. — *The Republic*, ii. 200.

Figure and melody.

—— I may observe, however, in passing, that in music there certainly are figures and there are melodies; and music is concerned with harmony and rhythm, so that you may speak of a melody or figure having rhythm or harmony; the term is correct enough, but you cannot speak correctly, as the masters of choruses have a way of talking metaphorically of the "color" of a melody or figure, although you can speak of the melodies or figures of the brave and the coward, praising the one and censuring the other. And not to be tedious, the figures and melodies which are expressive of virtue of soul or body, or of images of virtue, are without exception good, and those which are expressive of vice are the reverse of good. — *Laws*, iv. 184.

Filial monsters.

—— But we are digressing. Let us therefore return and inquire how the tyrant will maintain that fair and numerous and various and ever-changing army of his.

If, he said, there are sacred treasures in the city, he will confiscate them and spend the proceeds; that is obvious. And in so far as they suffice, he will be able to diminish the taxes which he would otherwise have to impose.

And when these fail?

Why, clearly, he said, then he and his boon companions, whether male or female, will be maintained out of his father's estate.

I see your meaning, I said. You mean that the people from whom he has derived his being, will maintain him and his companions?

Yes, he said; he must be maintained by them.

But what if the people go into a passion, and aver that a grown-up son ought not to be supported by his father, but that the father should be supported by the son? He did not bring his son into the world in order that when he was grown up he himself should be the servant of his own servants, and should support him and his rabble of slaves and companions; but that, having such a protector, he might be emancipated from the government of the rich and aristocratic, as they are termed. And so, bids him and his companions depart, just as any other father might drive out of his house a riotous son and his party of revelers.

By heaven, he said, then the parent will discover what a monster he has been fostering in his bosom; and when he wants to drive him out, he will find that he is weak and his son strong.

Why, you do not mean to say that the tyrant will use violence? What! beat his father if he opposes him?

Yes, he will; and he will begin by taking away his arms.

Then he is a parricide, and a cruel, unnatural son to an aged parent whom he ought to cherish; and this is real tyranny, about which there is no mistake; as the saying is, the people who would escape the smoke which is the slavery of freemen, have fallen into the fire which is the tyranny of slaves. Thus liberty, getting out of all order and reason, passes into the harshest and bitterest form of slavery. — *The Republic*, ii. 398.

But, O heavens! Adeimantus, on account of some new-fangled love of a harlot, who is anything but a necessary connection, can you believe that he would strike the mother who is his ancient friend and necessary to his very existence, and would place her under the authority of the other, when she is brought under the same roof with her; or that, under like circumstances, he would do the same to his withered old father, first and most indispensable of friends, for the sake of some newly-found, blooming youth who is the reverse of indispensable? — *The Republic*, ii. 403.

Filial regards and duties. See *Children, what they owe to their parents*. See *Parents*, etc.

Finite and infinite.

—— *Soc.* Were we not saying that God revealed a finite element of existence, and also an infinite?

Pro. Certainly.

Soc. Let us assume these two principles, and also a third, which is compounded out of them; but I fear that I am very clumsy at these processes of division and enumeration.

Pro. What are you saying, my good friend?

Soc. I say that still a fourth class is wanted.

Pro. And what will that be?

Soc. Find the cause of the third or compound, and add this as a fourth class to the three others.

Pro. And would you like to have a fifth class or cause of resolution, as well as a cause of composition?

Soc. Not, I think, at present;. but if I want a fifth at some future time you shall allow me to have one.

Pro. Certainly.

Soc. Let us begin with the three first; and as we find two out of the three greatly divided and dispersed, let us endeavor to reunite them, and see how in each of them there is a one and many.

Pro. If you would explain to me a little more about them, perhaps I might be able to follow you.

Soc. Well, the two classes are the same, which I mentioned before; one the finite, and the other the infinite, and I will first show that the infinite is in a certain sense many, and the finite may be hereafter discussed.

Pro. I agree.

Soc. And now consider well; for the question to which I invite your attention is difficult and controverted. When you speak of hotter and colder, can you conceive any limit in those qualities? Does not the more and less, which dwells in their very nature, prevent their having any end? for if they had an end, the more and less would themselves have an end.

Pro. That is most true.

Soc. Ever, as we say, into the hotter and the colder there enters a more and a less.

Pro. True.

Soc. Then, says the argument, they have never any end, and being endless must also be infinite. — *Philebus*, iii. 158.

Fire in the Universe.

—— *Soc.* We see the elements which enter into the nature of the bodies of all animals, fire, water, air, and, as the storm-tossed sailor cries, " Land ahead," in the constitution of the world.

Pro. The proverb may be applied to us; for truly the storm gathers us and we are at our wit's end.

Soc. Consider now that each of the elements, as they exist in us, is but a small fraction of any one of them, and of a mean sort, and not in any way pure, or having any power worthy of its nature. One instance will prove this of all of them; there is a fire within us, and in the universe.

Pro. True.

Soc. And is not our fire small and weak and mean, but the fire in the universe is wonderful in quantity and beauty, and in every power that fire has?

Pro. Most true.

Soc. And is that universal element nourished and generated and ruled by our fire, or is the fire in you and me, and in other animals, dependent on the universal fire?

Pro. That is a question which does not deserve an answer.

Soc. Right; and you would say the same, if I am not mistaken, of the earth which is in animals and the earth which is in the universe, and you would give a similar reply about all the other elements?

Pro. Why, how could any man who gave any other be deemed in his senses?

Soc. I do not think that he could, — but now go a step further; when we see those elements of which we have been speaking gathered up in one, do we not call them a body?

Pro. Very true.

Soc. And the same may be said of the cosmos, which for the same reason may be considered as a body, because made up of the same elements.

Pro. Very true. — *Philebus,* iii. 164.

Fire and friction.

—— *Soc.* There are plenty of other proofs which will show that motion is the source of that which is said to be and become, and rest of not-being and destruction; for fire and warmth, which are supposed to be the parent and nurse of all other things, are born of friction, which is a kind of motion; is not this the origin of fire?

Theaet. Yes. — *Theaetetus,* iii. 353.

Flattery and shams. See *Cookery.*

Flattery in rhetoric.

—— *Soc.* In my opinion, Gorgias, the whole of which rhetoric is a part is not an art at all, but the habit of a bold and ready wit, which knows how to 'manage mankind: this habit I sum up under the word "flattery;" and it appears to me to have many other parts, one of which is cookery, which may seem to be an art, but, as I maintain, is only an experience or routine, and not an art: another part is rhetoric, and the art of dressing up and sophistry are two others: thus there are four branches, and four different things answering to them. And Polus may ask, if he likes, for he has not as yet been informed, what part of flattery is rhetoric: he did not see that I had not yet answered him when he proceeded to ask a further question:— Whether I do not think rhetoric a fine thing? But I shall not tell him whether rhetoric is a fine thing or not, until I have first answered, "What is rhetoric?" For that would not be right, Polus; but I shall be happy to answer, if you will ask me, What part of flattery is rhetoric?

Pol. I will ask, and do you answer; what part of flattery is rhetoric?

Soc. Will you understand my answer? Rhetoric, according to my view, is the shadow of a part of politics.—*Gorgias,* iii. 48.

Flesh rejected as food.

—— *Ath.* The practice of men sacrificing one another still exists among many nations: and, on the other hand, we hear of other human beings who do not even venture to taste the flesh of a cow and had no animal sacrifices, but only cakes and fruits swimming in honey, and similar pure offerings, but no flesh or animals; from these they abstained under the idea that they ought not to eat them, and might not stain the altars of the Gods with blood. In former days men are said to have lived a sort of Orphic life, having the use of all lifeless things, but abstaining from all living things.—*Laws,* iv. 303.

Flux and change.

—— *Soc.* We may leave the rest of their theory unexamined, but we must not forget to ask them the only question with which we are concerned: Are all things in motion and flux?

Theod. Yes, they will reply.

Soc. And they are moved in both those ways which we distinguished; that is to say, they move and are also changed?

Theod. Of course, if the motion is to be perfect.

Soc. If they only moved, and were not changed, we should be able to say what are the kinds of things which are in motion and flux?

Theod. Exactly.

Soc. But now, since not even white continues to flow white, and the very whiteness is a flux or change which is passing into another color, and will not remain white, can the name of any color be rightly used at all?

Theod. How is that possible, Socrates, either in the case of this or of any other quality, if while we are using the word the object is escaping in the flux? — *Theaetetus*, iii. 385.

Food, flesh rejected as. See *Flesh*.

Force and persuasion in legislation. See *Legislation*, etc.

Forgetfulness and memory.

—— *Soc.* The other class of pleasures, which, as we were saying is purely mental, is entirely derived from memory.

Pro. What do you mean?

Soc. I must first of all analyze memory or rather perception which is prior to memory if the nature of these mental states is ever to be properly cleared up.

Pro. How will you proceed.

Soc. Let us imagine affections of the body that are extinguished before they reach the soul, which remains unaffected by them; and again, other affections which vibrate through both soul and body, and impart a shock to both of them.

Pro. Granted.

Soc. And the soul may be said to be oblivious of the first but not of the second?

Pro. Quite true.

Soc. When I say oblivious do not suppose that I mean forgetfulness in a literal sense; for forgetfulness is the exit of memory, which in this case has not yet entered; and to speak of the loss of that which is not yet in existence, and never has been, is a contradiction; do you see?

Pro. Yes.

Soc. Then just be so good as change the terms.

Pro. To what shall I change them?

Soc. Instead of the oblivion of the soul, when you are describing the state in which she is unaffected by the shocks of the body, say unconsciousness. — *Philebus*, iii. 169.

Form, harmony of soul and.

—— I maintain that neither we nor our guardians, whom we have to educate, can ever become musical until we and they know the essential forms of temperance, courage, liberality, magnificence, and then kindred as well as the contrary forms, in all their combinations, and can recognize them and their images wherever they are found, not slighting them either in small things or great, but believing them all to be within the sphere of one art and study.

Most assuredly.

And when a beautiful soul harmonizes with a beautiful form,

and the two are cast in one mould, that will be the fairest of sights to him who has an eye to contemplate the vision?
The fairest indeed.
And the fairest is also the loveliest?
That may be assumed.
And the man who has the spirit of harmony will be most in love with the loveliest; but he will not love him who is of an inharmonious soul?
That is true, he replied, if the deficiency be in his soul, but any merely personal defect he will not mind, and will love all the same. — *The Republic*, ii. 226.

Forms of government unessential.

—— We seem to have reached a height from which a man may look down and see that virtue is one but that the forms of vice are innumerable; there being four special ones which are deserving of note.

What do you mean? he said.

I mean, I replied, that there appear to be as many forms of the soul as there are forms of the State.

How many?

There are five of the State, and five of the soul, I said.

What are they?

The first, I said, is that which we have been describing, and which may be said to have two names, monarchy and aristocracy, accordingly as rule is exercised by one or many.

True, he replied.

But I regard the two names as describing one form only; for whether the government is in the hands of one or many, if the governors have been trained in the manner which we have described, the fundamental laws of the State will be maintained.

That is true, he replied. — *The Republic*, ii. 272.

Forms of government, four.

—— I shall particularly wish to hear what were the four constitutions of which you were speaking.

That, I said, is easily answered: the four governments of which I spoke, so far as they have distinct names, are, first, the Cretan and Spartan, which are generally applauded : next, there is oligarchy; this is not equally approved, and is a form of government which has many evils: thirdly, democracy, which naturally follows oligarchy, although different; and lastly comes tyranny, great and famous, which is different from them all, and is the fourth and worst disorder of a State. I do not know of any other constitution which can be said to have a distinct form. There are lordships and principalities which are bought and sold, and some other intermediate forms of government. But these nondescripts are oftener found among barbarians than among Hellenes. — *The Republic*, ii. 371.

Fortunate unjust, the. See *Clever*.

Free use of words and phrases. See *Education, the sign of a liberal*.

Freedom, artificers of.

—— If then we would retain the notion with which we began, that our guardians are to be released from every other art, and to be the special artificers of freedom, and to minister to this and have no other end, they ought not to practice or imitate anything else; and, if they imitate at all, they should imitate from youth upward the characters which are suitable to their profession — the temperate, holy, free, courageous, and the like;- but they should not depict or be skillful at imitating any kind of illiberality or other baseness, lest from imitation they should come to be what they imitate. Did you never observe how imitations, beginning in early youth, at last sink into the constitution and become a second nature of body, voice, and mind? — *The Republic*, ii. 218.

Freedom, anarchy, resulting from. See *Anarchy*.

Freedom unknown to the tyrant.

—— The people are such fools, and this noxious class and their followers grow numerous and become aware of their numbers, and then they choose him who has most of the tyrant in his soul, and make him their leader.

Yes, he said, they will choose him because he will be the most fit to be a tyrant.

If the people yield, well and good; but if they resist him, as he began by beating his own father and mother, so now, if he has the power, he beats them, and will maintain his dear old fatherland and motherland, as the Cretans say, in subjection to his young retainer whom he has introduced to be their rulers and masters. Such is the end of his passions and desires.

Exactly.

Even in early days and before they get power, this is their character; they associate only with their own flatterers or ready tools; or, if they want anything from anybody, they in their turn are equally ready to fall down before them; there is no attitude of kindness which they will not assume, but when they have gained their point they know them no more.

Yes, truly.

They are always either the masters or servants and never the friends of anybody; the tyrant never tastes of true freedom or true friendship.

Certainly not. — *The Republic*, ii. 404.

Freedom of Philosophy

——— *Soc.* Those who have been trained in philosophy and liberal pursuits compared with those who from their youth upwards have been knocking about in the courts and such like places, are in their way of life as freemen are to slaves.

Theod. In what is the difference seen?

Soc. In the leisure spoken of by you, which a freeman can always command; he has his talk out in peace, and, like ourselves, wanders at will from one subject to another, and from a second to a third if his fancy prefers a new one, caring not whether his words are many or few; his only aim is to attain the truth. But the lawyer is always in a hurry; there is the water of the clepsydra driving him on, and not allowing him to expatiate at will; and there is his adversary standing over him, enforcing his rights; the affidavit, which in their phraseology is termed the brief, is recited; and from this he must not deviate. He is a servant, and is disputing about a fellow-servant before his master, who is seated, and has the cause in his hands; the trial is never about some indifferent matter, but always concerns himself; and often the race is for his life. The consequence has been, that he has become keen and shrewd; he has learned how to flatter his master in word and indulge him in deed; but his soul is small and unrighteous. His slavish condition has deprived him of growth and uprightness and independence; dangers and fears, which were too much for his truth and honesty, came upon him in early years, when the tenderness of youth was unequal to them, and he has been driven into crooked ways; from the first he has practiced deception and retaliation, and has become stunted and warped. And so he has passed out of youth into manhood, having no soundness in him; and is now, as he thinks, a master in wisdom. Such is the lawyer, Theodorus. Will you have the companion picture of the philosopher, who is of our brotherhood; or shall we return to the argument? Do not let us abuse the freedom of digression which we claim.

Theod. Nay, Socrates, let us finish what we are about; for you truly said that we belong to a brotherhood which is free, and are not the servants of the argument; but the argument is our servant, and must wait our leisure. Who is our judge? Or where is the spectator having any right to censure or control us, as he might the poets? — *Theaetetus,* iii. 375.

Freedom in the Persian State.

—— *Ath.* The State which has become exclusively and excessively attached to monarchy or to freedom has neither of them in moderation; but your States, the Laconian and Cretan, have a certain moderation; and the Athenians and Persians having had more at first, have now less. Shall I tell you why?

Cle. By all means, if it will tend to the elucidation of our subject.

Ath. Hear, then: — There was a time when the Persians had more of the state which is a mean between slavery and freedom. In the reign of Cyrus they were freemen and also lords of many others; the rulers gave a share of freedom to the subjects, and being treated as equals, the soldiers were on better terms with their generals, and showed themselves more ready in the hour of danger. And if there was any wise councilor among them, he imparted his wisdom to the public; for the king was not jealous, but allowed him full liberty of speech and gave honor to those who were able to be his counselors in anything, and allowed all men equally to participate in wisdom. And the nation waxed in all respects, because there was freedom and friendship and communion of soul among them. — *Laws,* iv. 223.

Freedom growing to license.

—— *Ath.* As time went on, the poets themselves introduced the reign of ignorance and misrule. They were men of genius, but they had no knowledge of what is just and lawful in music; raging like Bacchanals and possessed with inordinate delights — mingling lamentations with hymns, and pæans with dithyrambs; imitating the sounds of the flute on the lyre, and making one general confusion; ignorantly affirming that music has no truth, and whether good or bad, can only be judged of rightly by the pleasure of the hearer. And by composing such licentious poems, and adding to them words as licentious, they have inspired the multitude with lawlessness and boldness, and made them fancy that they can judge for themselves about melody and song. And in this way, the theatres from being mute have become vocal, as though they had understanding of good and bad in music and poetry ; and instead of an aristocracy, an evil sort of theatrocracy has grown up. For if the democracy which judged had only consisted of freemen, there would have been no fatal harm done ; but in music there first arose the universal conceit of omniscience and general lawlessness ; freedom came following afterwards, and men fancying that they knew what they did not know, had no longer any fear, and the absence of fear begets shamelessness. For what is shamelessness but the insolent refusal to regard the opinion of the better by reason of an overdaring sort of liberty?

Meg. That is most true.

Ath. Consequent upon this freedom comes the other freedom of disobedience to rulers ; and then the attempt to escape the control and exhortation of father, mother, elders, and when near the end, the control of the laws also ; and at the very end there is the contempt of oaths and pledges, and no regard at all for the Gods, — herein they exhibit and imitate the old Titanic nature ; and thus they return again to the old, and lead a life of evils which have no end. Why do I say so ? Because I think that the argument ought to be pulled up from time to time, and not be allowed to run away, but held with bit and bridle, and then we shall not, as the proverb says, fall off our ass. — *Laws*, iv. 230.

Friends and enemies, — treatment of. See *Enemies*.

Friendship dearer than money. See *Fancies*, etc.

—— Oh ! my beloved Socrates, let me entreat you once more to take my advice and escape. For if you die I shall not only lose a friend who can never be replaced, but there is another evil ; people who do not know you and me will believe that I might have saved you if I had been willing to give money, but that I did not care. Now, can there be a worse disgrace than this — that I should be thought to value money more than the life of a friend? For the many will not be persuaded that I wanted you to escape, and that you refused. — *Crito*, i. 348.

Friendship, the principle of.

—— *Ath.* He who would rightly consider these matters must see the nature of friendship and·desire, and of these so-called loves, for they are of two kinds, and out of the two arises a third kind, having the same name; and this similarity of name causes all the difficulty and obscurity.

Cle. How is that?

Ath. Dear is the like in virtue to the like, and the equal to the equal; dear also, though after another fashion, is he who has abundance to him who is in want. And when either of these friendships becomes excessive, we term the excess love.

Cle. Very true.

Ath. The friendship which arises from contraries is horrible and coarse, and has often no tie of communion ; but that which arises from likeness is gentle, and has a tie of communion, which lasts through life. As to the mixed sort, which is made up of them both, there is, first of all, a difficulty in determining what he who is possessed by this third love desires ; moreover, he is drawn different ways, and is in doubt between the two principles; the one exhorting him to enjoy the beauty of youth, and the other forbidding him. For the one is a lover of the body, and hungers after beauty, like ripe fruit, and would feign satisfy himself without any regard to the character of the beloved; the other holds the desire of the body to be a secondary matter, and looking rather than loving with his soul, and desiring the soul of the other in a becoming manner, regards the satisfaction of the bodily love as wantonness; he reverences and respects temperance, and courage, and magnanimity, and wisdom, and wishes to live chastely with the chaste object of his affection. Now the sort of love which is made up of the other two is that which we have described as the third. Seeing then that there are these three sorts of love, ought the law to prohibit and forbid them all to exist among us? Is it not rather clear that we should wish to have in the State the love which is of virtue and which desires the beloved youth to be the best possible; and the other two, if possible, we should hinder? What do you say, friend Megillus?

Meg. I think, Stranger, you are altogether right in what you have been now saying. — *Laws,* iv. 352.

Funerals, three kinds of.

—— Of three kinds of funerals, there is one which is too extravagant, another is too niggardly, the third in a mean; and you choose and approve and order the last without qualification. But if I had an extremely rich wife, and she bade me bury her, and I were to describe her burial in poetry, I should praise the extravagant sort; and a poor miserly man, who had not much to spend, would approve of the niggardly; and the man of moderate means, who was himself moderate, would praise a moderate funeral. Now you in the capacity of legis-

lator must not barely say "a moderate funeral," but you must define what moderation is, and how much; unless you are definite, you must not suppose that you are speaking a language that can become law. — *Laws*, iv. 247.
Funeral orations. See *Battle, death in.*
Future state and world.

—— Such is the nature of the other world; and when the dead arrive at the place to which the genius of each severally conveys them, first of all, they have sentence passed upon them, as they have lived well and piously or not. And those who appear to have lived neither well nor ill, go to the river Acheron, and using such means of conveyance as they have, are carried in them to the lake, and there they dwell and are purified of their evil deeds, and suffer the penalty of the wrongs which they have done to others, and are absolved, and receive the rewards of their good deeds according to their deserts. But those who appear to be incurable by reason of the greatness of their crimes — who have committed many and terrible deeds of sacrilege, murders foul and violent, or the like — such are hurled into Tartarus which is their suitable destiny, and they never come out. Those again who have committed crimes, which, although great, are not irremediable — who in a moment of anger, for example, have done violence to a father or a mother, and have repented for the remainder of their lives, or who have taken the life of another under the like extenuating circumstances — these are plunged into Tartarus, the pains of which they are compelled to undergo for a year, but at the end of the year the wave casts them forth — mere homicides by way of Cocytus, parricides and matricides by Pyriphlegethon — and they are borne to the Acherusian lake, and there they lift up their voices and call upon the victims whom they have slain or wronged, to have pity on them, and to be kind to them, and to let them come out into the lake. And if they prevail, then they come forth and cease from their troubles; but if not, they are carried back again into Tartarus and from thence into the rivers unceasingly, until they obtain mercy from those whom they have wronged; for that is the sentence inflicted upon them by their judges. Those too who have been preëminent for holiness of life, are released from this earthly prison, and go to their pure home which is above, and dwell in the purer earth; and those who have duly purified themselves with philosophy, live henceforth altogether without the body, in mansions fairer far than these, which may not be described, and of which the time would fail me to tell.

Wherefore, Simmias, seeing all these things, what ought not we to do in order to obtain virtue and wisdom in this life? Fair is the prize, and the hope great.

A man of sense ought not to say, nor will I be too confident, that the description which I have given of the soul and her mansions is exactly true. But I do say that, inasmuch as the soul is shown to be immortal, he may venture to think, not improperly or unworthily, that something of the kind is true. The venture is a glorious one, and he ought to comfort himself with words like these, which is the reason why I lengthen out the tale. Wherefore, I say, let a man be of good cheer about his soul, who has cast away the pleasures and ornaments of the body as alien to him, and hurtful rather in their effects, and has followed after the pleasures of knowledge in this life; who has arrayed the soul in her own proper jewels, which are temperance, and justice, and courage, and nobility, and truth — thus adorned, she is ready to go on her journey to the world below, when her hour comes. — *Phaedo*, i. 443.

Gain, the lover of.

—— Has the lover of gain greater experience of the pleasure of knowledge which is imparted by the truth than the philosopher has of the pleasure of gain?

The philosopher, he replied, has greatly the advantage; for he has always known the taste of the other pleasures from his youth upwards: but the lover of gain in all his experience has not of necessity tasted — or, I should rather say, even if he desired could hardly have tasted by any process of learning truth — the sweetness of intellectual pleasures.

Then the lover of wisdom has a great advantage over the lover of gain, for he has a double experience?

Very great indeed. — *The Republic*, ii. 412.

Generation and conception, divine nature of. See *Conception*.

Generation of opposites.

—— Are not all things which have opposites generated out of their opposites? I mean such things as good and evil, just and unjust — and there are innumerable other opposites which are generated out of opposites. And I want to show that in all opposites there is a similar alternative; I mean to say, for example, that anything which becomes greater must become greater after being less.

True.

And that which becomes less must have been once greater and then have become less.

Yes.

And the weaker is generated from the stronger, and the swifter from the slower.

Very true.

And the worse is from the better, and the more just is from the more unjust?

Of course.

And is this true of all opposites? and are we convinced that all of them are generated out of opposites?

Yes.

And in this universal opposition of all things, are there not also two intermediate processes which are ever going on, from one to the other, and back again; where there is a greater and a less there is also an intermediate process of increase and diminution, and that which grows is said to wax, and that which decays to wane?

Yes, he said.

And there are many other processes, such as division and composition, cooling and heating, which equally involve a passage into and out of one another. And this holds of all opposites, even though not always expressed in words — they are generated out of one another, and there is a passing or process from one to the other of them?

Very true, he replied.

Well, and is there not an opposite of life, as sleep is the opposite of waking?

True, he said.

And what is that?

Death, he answered.

And these then are generated, if they are opposites, the one from the other, and have there their two intermediate processes also?

Of course.

Now, said Socrates, I will analyze one of the two pairs of opposites which I have mentioned to you, and also its intermediate processes, and you shall analyze the other to me. The state of sleep is opposed to the state of waking, and out of sleeping waking is generated, and out of waking, sleeping; and the process of generation is in the one case falling asleep, and in the other waking up. Are you agreed about that?

Quite agreed.

Then, suppose that you analyze life and death to me in the same manner. Is not death opposed to life?

Yes.

And they are generated one from the other?

Yes.

What is generated from the living?

The dead.

And what from the dead?

I can only say in answer — the living.

Then the living, whether things or persons, Cebes, are generated from the dead?

That is clear, he replied.

Then the inference is that our souls exist in the world below?

That is true.

And one of the two processes or generations is visible — for surely the act of dying is visible?

Surely, he said. — *Phaedo*, i. 397.

Generation, spontaneous. See *Life, spontaneous.*

Generation of all things.

—— *Soc.* Here are two new principles.

Pro. What are they?

Soc. One is the generation of all things, and another is essence.

Pro. I readily accept both generation and essence at your hands.

Soc. Very right; and would you say that generation is for the sake of essence, or essence for the sake of generation?

Pro. You want to know whether that which is called essence is, properly speaking, for the sake of generation?

Soc. Yes.

Pro. By the Gods, I wish that you would repeat your question.

Soc. I mean, O my Protarchus, to ask whether you would tell me that ship-building is for the sake of ships, or are ships for the sake of ship-building? and in all similar cases I should ask the same question.

Pro. Why do you not answer yourself, Socrates?

Soc. I have no objection, but you must take your part.

Pro. Certainly.

Soc. My answer is, that all things instrumental, remedial, material, are always used with a view to generation, and that each generation is relative to, or for the sake of, some being or essence, and the whole of generation relative to the whole of essence.

Pro. Assuredly.

Soc. Then pleasure, being a generation, will surely be for the sake of some essence?

Pro. True.

Soc. And that for the sake of which something is done must be placed in the class of good, and that which is done for the sake of another thing, in some other class, my good friend.

Pro. Most certainly.

Soc. Then pleasure, being a generation, will be rightly placed in some other class than that of good?

Pro. Quite right.

Soc. Then, as I said at first, we ought to be very grateful to him who first pointed out that pleasure was a generation only, and had no true being; for he is clearly one who laughs at the notion of pleasure being a good.

Pro. Assuredly.

Soc. And he would surely laugh also at those who make generation their highest end.

Pro. Of whom are you speaking and what do you mean?

Soc. I am speaking of those who when they cure hunger or thirst or any other defect, by some process of generation, are as much delighted as if the generation were itself pleasure; and they say that they would not wish to live without these and the like feelings.

Pro. That is certainly what they appear to think.

Soc. And is not destruction universally admitted to be the opposite of generation?

Pro. Certainly.

Soc. Then he who chooses thus, would choose generation and destruction rather than that third sort of life, in which, as we were saying, was neither pleasure nor pain, but only the purest possible thought. — *Philebus*, iii. 194.

Genius, a youthful.

—— Socrates, I have become acquainted with one very remarkable Athenian youth whom I commend to you as well worthy of your attention. If he had been a beauty I should have been afraid to praise him, lest you should suppose that I was in love with him; but he is no beauty, and you must not be offended if I say that he is very like you; for he has a snub nose and projecting eyes, although these features are less marked in him than in you. Seeing, then, that he has no personal attractions, I may freely say, that in all my acquaintance, which is very large, I never knew any one who was his equal in natural gifts : for he has a quickness of apprehension which is almost unrivaled, and he is exceedingly gentle, and also the most courageous of men ; there is a union of qualities in him such as I have never seen in any other, and should scarcely have thought possible ; for those who, like him, have quick and ready and retentive wits, have generally also quick tempers ; they are ships without ballast, which go darting about, and grow mad rather than courageous ; and the steadier sort, when they have to face study, are stupid and cannot remember. Whereas he moves surely and smoothly and successfully in the path of knowledge and inquiry ; he is full of gentleness, and flows on silently like a river of oil ; at his age, it is wonderful. — *Theaetetus*, iii. 343.

Gentleness and greatness seemingly inconsistent.

—— We shall have to select natures which are suited to their task of guarding the city ?

We shall.

And the selection will be no easy task I said ; but still we must endeavor to do our best as far as we can ?

We must.

The dog is a watcher, I said, and the guardian is also a watcher ; and in this point of view, is not the noble youth very like a well-bred dog ?

How do you mean ?

I mean that both of them ought to be quick to see, and swift to overtake the enemy ; and strong too, if, when they have caught him, they have to fight with him.

All these qualities, he replied, will certainly be required.

Well, and your guardian must be brave if he is to fight well?

Certainly.

And is he likely to be brave who has no spirit, whether horse or dog or any other animal ? Have you never observed how the presence of spirit makes the soul of any creature absolutely fearless and invincible ?

I have.

Then now we have a clear idea of the bodily qualities which are required in the guardian.

True.

And also of the mental ones; his soul is to be full of spirit?

Yes.

But then, Glaucon, those spirited natures are apt to be furious with one another, and with everybody else.

There is a difficulty, he replied.

Whereas, I said, they ought to be gentle to their friends, and dangerous to their enemies; or, instead of their enemies destroying them, they will destroy themselves.

True, he said.

What is to be done then, I said; how shall we find a gentle nature which has also a great spirit, for they seem to be inconsistent with one another?

True.

And yet he will not be a good guardian who is wanting in either of these two qualities; and, as the combination of them appears to be impossible, this is equivalent to saying that to be a good guardian is also impossible. — *The Republic*, ii. 197.

Gentleness of warriors and rulers.

—— *Soc.* We spoke of those who were intended to be our warriors, and said that they were to be guardians of the city against the attacks of enemies internal as well as external, and to have no other employment; they were to be merciful in judging their subjects, of whom they were by nature friends, but when they came in the way of their enemies in battle they were to be fierce with them.

Tim. Exactly.

Soc. We said, if I am not mistaken, that the guardians should be doubly gifted with a passionate and also with a philosophical temper, and that then they would be as they ought to be, gentle to their friends and fierce to their enemies. — *Timaeus*, ii. 514.

Geometry, its study and uses.

—— Shall we inquire whether the kindred science also concerns us?

You mean geometry?

Yes.

Certainly, he said; that part of geometry which relates to war is clearly our concern; for in pitching a camp, or taking up a position, or closing or extending the lines of an army, or any other military manœuvre, whether in actual battle or on a march, there will be a great difference in a general, according as he is or is not a geometrician.

Yes, I said, but for that purpose a very little of either geometry or calculation will be enough; the question is rather of the higher and greater part of geometry, whether that tends towards the great end — I mean towards the vision of the idea of good; and thither, as I was saying, all things tend which compel the soul to turn her gaze towards that place, where is the full perfection of being, of which she ought, by all means, to attain the vision.

True, he said.

Then if geometry compels us to view being, it concerns us; if becoming only, it does not concern us?

Yes, that is what we assert.

Nevertheless, such a conception of the science is in flat contradiction to the ordinary language of geometricians, as will hardly be denied by those who have any acquaintance with their study: for they speak of squaring and applying and adding, having in view use only, and absurdly confuse the necessities of geometry with those of daily life; whereas knowledge is the real object of the whole science.

Certainly, he said.

Then must not a further admission be made?

What admission?

The admission that this knowledge at which geometry aims is of the eternal, and not of the perishing and transient.

That, he replied, may be readily allowed, and is true.

Then, my noble friend, geometry will draw the soul towards truth, and create the spirit of philosophy, and raise up that which is now unhappily allowed to fall down.

Nothing will be more effectual.

Then nothing should be more effectually enacted, than that the inhabitants of your fair city should learn geometry. — *The Republic*, ii. 354.

Giants and Gods. See *Essence, war about*.

Gifted minds, ill-educated, become the worst.

—— There is reason in supposing that the finest natures, when under alien conditions, receive more injury than the inferior, because the contrast is greater.

Very true.

And may we not say, Adeimantus, that the most gifted minds, when they are ill-educated, become the worst? Do not great crimes and the spirit of pure evil spring out of a fullness of nature ruined by education rather than from any inferiority, whereas weak natures are scarcely capable of any very great good or very great evil?

There I think that you are right.

And our philosopher follows the same analogy — he is like a plant which, having proper nurture, grows and matures into all virtue, but, if sown and planted in an alien soil, becomes the most noxious of all weeds, unless saved by some divine help. — *The Republic*, ii. 318.

Gifts of the pure and impure. See *Impure*.
Gifts, natural. See *Talents*, etc.
Globe, the world, a. See *Earth, rotundity of the*.
Gluttony and sensuality.

—— Those then who know not wisdom and virtue, and are always busy with gluttony and sensuality, go down and up again as far as the mean; and in this region they move at random throughout life, but they never pass into the true upper world; thither they neither look, nor do they ever find their way, neither are they truly filled with true being, nor do they taste of true and abiding pleasure. Like cattle with their eyes looking down and their heads stooping, not indeed to the earth, but to the dining-table, they fatten and feed and breed, and, in their excessive love of these delights, they kick and butt at one another with horns and hoofs which are made of iron; and they kill one another by reason of their insatiable lust. For they fill themselves with that which is not substantial, and the part of themselves which they fill is also unsubstantial and incontinent.

Verily, Socrates, said Glaucon, you describe the life of the many like an oracle.

Their pleasures are mixed with pains. How can they be otherwise? For they are mere images and pictures of the true, and are colored only by contrast, which exaggerates both light and shade, and so they implant in the minds of fools insane desires of themselves; and they are fought about as Stesichorus says that the Greeks fought about the shadow of Helen at Troy in ignorance of the truth. — *The Republic*, ii. 417.

God, not the author of evil. See *Evil, concealment of*.

—— Then God, if he be good, is not the author of all things, as the many assert, but he is the cause of a few things only, and not of most things that occur to men. For few are the goods of human life, and many are the evils, and the good only is to be attributed to God alone; of the evils the cause is to be sought elsewhere and not in him.

That appears to me to be most true, he said.

Then we must not listen to Homer or any other poet who is guilty of the folly of saying that two casks

"Lie at the threshold of Zeus, full of lots, one of good, the other of evil lots;"

and that he to whom Zeus gives a mixture of the two,

"Sometimes meets with evil fortune at other times with good,"

but that he to whom is given the cup of unmingled ill,

"Him wild hunger drives over the divine earth."

And again

"Zeus, who is the dispenser of good and evil to us."

And if any one asserts that the violation of oaths and treaties of which Pandarus was the real author, was brought about by Athene and Zeus, or that the strife and conflict of the Gods was instigated by Themis and Zeus, he shall not have our approval; neither will we allow our young men to hear the words of Aeschylus, that

"God plants guilt among men when he desires utterly to destroy a house."

And if a poet writes of the sufferings of Niobe, which is the subject of the tragedy in which these iambic verses occur, or of the house of Pelops, or of the Trojan War, or any similar theme, either we must not permit him to say that these are the works of God, or, if they are of God, he must devise some such explanation of them as we are seeking: he must say that God did what was just and right, and they were the better for being punished; but that those who are punished are miserable, and God is the author of their misery,— the poet is not to be permitted to say, though he may say that the wicked are miserable because they require to be punished, and are benefited by receiving punishment from God; but that God being good is the author of evil to any one, that is to be strenuously denied, and not allowed to be sung or said in any well-ordered commonwealth by old or young. Such a fiction is suicidal, ruinous, impious. — *The Republic*, ii. 202.

God unchangeable.

—— What do you think of another principle? Shall I ask you whether God is a magician, and of a nature to appear insidiously now in one shape, and now in another — sometimes himself changing and becoming different in form, sometimes deceiving us with the semblance of such transformations: or is he one and the same, immutably fixed in his own proper image?

I cannot answer you without more thought.

Well, I said; but if we suppose a change in anything that change must be effected either by the thing itself, or by some other thing?

That is most certain.

And things which are at their best are also least liable to be altered or discomposed; for example, when healthiest and strongest, the human frame is least liable to be affected by meats and drinks and labors, and the plant which is in the fullest vigor also suffers least from heat or wind, or other similar accidents.

Of course.

And this is true of the soul as well as of the body; the bravest and wisest soul will be least confused or deranged by any external influence.

True.

And further, as I should suppose, the same principle applies to all works of art — vessels, houses, garments; and that when well made and in good condition, they are least altered by time and circumstances.

Very true.

Then everything which is good, whether made by art or nature, or both, is liable to receive the least change at the hands of others?

True.

But surely God and the things of God are absolutely perfect?

Of course they are.

He is therefore least likely to take many forms.

He is.

But suppose again that he changes and transforms himself?

Clearly, he said, that must be the case if he is changed at all.

And will he then change himself for the better, or for the worse?

If he change at all he must change for the worse, for we cannot suppose that he is deficient in virtue or beauty.

Very true, Adeimantus; but then, would any one, whether God or man, desire to change for the worse?

Impossible.

Then God too cannot be willing to change; being, as is supposed, the fairest and best that is conceivable, every God remains absolutely and forever in his own form.

That necessarily follows, he said, in my judgment. — *The Republic*, ii. 203.

God incapable of falsehood. See *Deception*.
God, absolute knowledge in. See *Absolute knowledge*, etc.
Gods, impassiveness of the.

—— *Soc.* Well, then, assuming that pain ensues on the dissolution, and pleasure on the restoration of the harmony, let us now ask what will be the condition of animated beings who are neither in process of restoration nor of dissolution. And mind what you are going to say : I ask whether any animal who is in that condition can possibly have any feeling of pleasure or pain, great or small?

Pro. Certainly not.

Soc. Then here we have a third state, over and above that of pleasure and of pain?

Pro. Very true.

Soc. And do not forget that there is such a state of which the recognition will very considerably affect our judgment of pleasure, and I should like to say a word or two about it.

Pro. What have you to say?

Soc. Why, you know that if a man chooses the life of wisdom, there is no reason why he should not live in this neutral state.

Pro. You mean that he may live neither rejoicing nor sorrowing?

Soc. Yes; and if I remember rightly, when the lives were compared, no degree of pleasure, whether great or small, was thought to be necessary to him who chose the life of thought and wisdom.

Pro. Yes certainly, that was said.

Soc. Then he may live without pleasure; and who knows whether this may not be the most divine of all lives?

Pro. At any rate, the Gods cannot be supposed to have either joy or sorrow.

Soc. Certainly not. There would be great impropriety in their having either. — *Philebus*, iii. 169.

Gods, war of Giants and. See *Essence, war about*.
Gods, existence of the.

—— *Ath.* They will make some provoking speech of this sort: O inhabitants of Athens, and Sparta, and Cnosus, they will reply, in that, you speak truly; for some of us deny the very existence of the Gods, while others, as you say, are of opinion that they do not care about us; and others that they are turned from their course by gifts. Now we have a right to claim, as you yourself allowed, in the matter of the laws, that before you are hard upon us and threaten us, you should argue with us and convince us — you should first attempt to teach and persuade us that there are Gods by reasonable evidences — and also that they are too good to be unrighteous, or to be propitiated, or turned from their course by gifts. For when we hear these and the like things said of them by those who are esteemed to be the best of poets, and orators, and prophets, and priests, and innumerable others, the thoughts of most of us are not set upon abstaining from unrighteous acts, but upon doing them and making atonement for them. When lawgivers profess that they are gentle and not stern, we think that they should first of all use persuasion to us, and show us the existence of Gods, if not in a better manner than other men, at any rate in a truer; and who knows but that we shall hearken to them? — *Laws,* iv. 397.

Good and evil, the presence of. See *Evil and good,* etc.

Good, all men desire the.

―――― " When a man loves the beautiful, what does he desire?" I answered her, "That the beautiful may be his." " Still," she said, " the answer suggests a further question : " What is given by the possession of beauty?" "To what you have asked," I replied, " I have no answer ready." " Then," she said, " let me put the word 'good' in the place of the beautiful, and repeat the question once more: He who loves the good loves, what does he love?" " The possession of the good," I said. " And what does he gain who possesses the good?" " Happiness," I replied; " there is no difficulty in answering that." " Yes," she said, " the happy are made happy by the acquisition of good things. Nor is there any need to ask why a man desires happiness; the answer is already final." " You are right" I said. " And is this wish and this desire common to all? and do all men always desire their own good, or only some men? — what say you?" " All men," I replied; " the desire is common to all." — *The Symposium,* i. 497.

Good, sufficiency of the. See *Sufficiency,* etc.

Good, the idea of, the highest knowledge.

―――― What, he said, is there a knowledge still higher than these — higher than justice and the other virtues?

Yes, I said, there is. And of these too we must behold not

the outline merely, as at present — nothing short of the most finished work should satisfy us. When little things are elaborated with an infinity of pains, in order that they may appear in full clearness and precision, how ridiculous that the highest truths should not be held worthy of the greatest exactness !

A right noble thought ; but do you suppose that we shall refrain from asking you which are the highest ?

Nay, I said, ask if you will ; but I am certain that you have often heard the answer, and now you either do not understand or you mean to be troublesome ; I incline to think the latter, for you have been often told that the *idea* of good is the highest knowledge, and that all other things become useful and advantageous only by their use of this. You must have already guessed that of this I am about to speak, concerning which, as you have often heard me say, we know so little; and, without which, any other knowledge or possession of any kind will profit us nothing. Do you think that the possession of the whole world is of any value without the good? or of all knowledge, without the beautiful and good?

Assuredly not.

You are doubtless aware that most people call pleasure good, and the finer sort of wits say knowledge ? And are you aware that the latter cannot explain the nature of knowledge, but are obliged after all to say that knowledge is of the good?

How ridiculous.

Yes, I said, that they should begin by reproaching us with our ignorance of the good, and then presume our knowledge of it — for good, they say, is the knowledge of the good, which implies that we understand them when they use the term "good," — is certainly ridiculous. — *The Republic*, ii. 332.

Good, beautiful and true, the. See *Beautiful*.

Good counsel.

—— The law would say that to be patient under suffering is best, and that we should not give way to impatience, as there is no knowing whether such things are good or evil ; and nothing is gained by impatience ; also, because no human thing is of serious importance ; and grief stands in the way of that which at the moment is most required.

What is most required ? he asked.

That we should take counsel about the past, and when the dice has been thrown, order our affairs accordingly by the advice of reason ; not like children who have had a fall, keeping hold of the part struck and wasting time in setting up a howl, but accustoming the soul forthwith to apply a remedy, raising up that which is sickly and fallen, banishing the cry of sorrow by a real cure.

Yes, he said, that is the best way of meeting the attacks of fortune. — *The Republic*, ii. 435.

Good, the greatest. See *Evil, the greatest*, etc.

—— *Soc.* I am still in the dark; for which are the greatest and best of human things? I dare say that you have heard men singing at feasts the old drinking song, in which the singers enumerate the goods of life, first health, beauty next, thirdly, as the writer of the song says, wealth honestly obtained.

Gor. Yes, I know the song; but what is your drift?

Soc. I mean to say, that the producers of those things which the author of the song praises, that is to say, the physician, the trainer, the money-maker, will at once come to you, and first the physician will say, "O Socrates, Gorgias is deceiving you, for my art is concerned with the greatest good of men, and not his." And when I ask, Who are you? he will reply, "I am a physician." What do you mean? I shall say. Do you mean that your art produces the greatest good? "Certainly," he will answer, "for is not health the greatest good? What greater good can men have, Socrates?" And after him the trainer will come and say, "I, too, Socrates, shall be greatly surprised if Gorgias can show more good of his art than I can show of mine." To him I shall say, Who are you, my friend, and what is your business? "I am a trainer," he will reply, "and my business is to make men beautiful and strong in body." When I have done with the trainer, there arrives the money-maker, and he, as I expect, will utterly despise them all. "Consider, Socrates," he will say, "whether Gorgias or any one else can produce any greater good than wealth." Well, you and I say to him, And are you a creator of wealth? "Yes," he replies. And who are you? "A money-maker." And do you consider wealth to be the greatest good of man? "Yes," he will reply, "of course." And we shall rejoin: Yes; but our friend Gorgias contends that his art produces a greater good than yours; and then he will be sure to go on and ask, "What good? Let Gorgias answer." Now I want you, Gorgias, to imagine that this question is asked of you by them and by me: What is that which, as you say, is the greatest good of man, and of which you are the creator? Answer us.

Gor. That good, Socrates, which is truly the greatest, being that which gives to men freedom in their own persons, and to rulers the power of ruling over others in their several States. — *Gorgias*, iii. 36.

Good and evil; when they are such. See *Evil, and good; when*, etc.

Good or evil, power for.

—— Of those fearful examples, most, as I believe, are taken from the class of tyrants, and kings, and potentates, and public men, for they are the authors of the greatest and most impious crimes, because they have the power. And Homer witnesses to the truth of this; for they are always kings and potentates, whom he has described as suffering everlasting punishment in the world below; such were Tantalus and Sisyphus and Tityus. But no one ever described Thersites, or any private person who was a villain, as suffering everlasting punishment or as incurable. For to commit the worst crimes, as I am inclined to think, was not in his power, and he was happier than those who had the power. Yes, Callicles, the very bad men come from the class of those who have power. And yet in that very class there may arise good men, and worthy of all admiration they are, for where there is great power to do wrong, to live and die justly is a hard thing, and greatly to be praised, and few there are who attain this. Such good and true men, however, there have been, and will be again, at Athens, and in other States, who have fulfilled their trust righteously. — *Gorgias*, iii. 117.

Good, highest in the State. See *Evil, the greatest*, etc.

Good, in the divine mind.

—— *Soc.* And now have I not sufficiently shown that Philebus' goddess is not to be regarded as identical with the good?

Phi. Neither is your "mind" the good, Socrates, for that will be open to the same objections.

Soc. Perhaps, Philebus, you may be right in saying of so my "mind," but of the true, which is also the divine mind — far otherwise. However, I will not at present claim the first place for mind as against the mixed life, but we must come to some understanding about the second place. For you might affirm pleasure and I mind to be the cause of the mixed life, and that case, although neither of them would be good, one of them might be imagined to be the cause of the good. And I might proceed further to argue in opposition to Philebus that the element which makes this mixed life eligible and good, is more akin and more similar to mind than to pleasure. And if this is true, pleasure cannot be truly said to share either in the first or second place, and does not, if I may trust my own mind, attain even to the third. — *Philebus*, iii. 157.

✗ **Good and pleasant, a unity in nature.**

—— Philebus says that pleasure is the true end of all living beings, at which all ought to aim, and moreover, that it is the chief good of all, and that the two names "good" and "pleasant," are correctly given to one thing and one nature; Socrates, on the other hand, begins by denying this, and further says, that in nature as in name, they are two, and that wisdom partakes more than pleasure of the good. — *Philebus*, iii. 200.

Good, truth the beginning of every.

—— Truth is the beginning of every good thing, both in heaven and on earth; and he who would be blessed and happy, should be from the first a partaker of the truth, that he may live a true man as long as possible, for then he can be trusted; but he is not to be trusted who loves voluntary falsehood, and he who loves involuntary falsehood is a fool. Neither condition is to be desired, for the untrustworthy and ignorant has no friend, and as time advances he becomes known, and lays up in store for himself isolation in crabbed age when life is on the wane; so that, whether his children or friends are alive or not, he is equally solitary. — *Laws*, iv. 255.

Good men, simplicity of.

—— I should like to put a question to you. Ought there not to be good physicians in a State, and are not the best those who have treated the greatest number of constitutions good and bad, just as good judges are those who are acquainted with all sorts of moral natures?

Yes, I said, I quite agree about the necessity of having good judges and good physicians. But do you know whom I think good?

Will you inform me?

Yes, if I can. Let me however note that in the same question you join two things which are not the same.

How so? he asked.

Why, I said, you join physicians and judges. Now skillful physicians are those who, from their youth upwards, have combined with the knowledge of their art, the greatest experience of disease; they had better not be robust in health, and should have had all manner of diseases in their own persons. For the body, as I conceive, is not the instrument with which they cure the body; in that case we would not allow them ever to be sickly; but they cure the body with the mind, and the mind which is or has become sick can cure nothing.

That is very true, he said.

But with the judge the case is different; he governs mind by mind, and he ought not therefore to have been reared among vicious minds, and to have associated with them from youth upwards, in order that, having gone through the whole calendar of crime, he may infer the crimes of others like their diseases from the knowledge of himself; but the honorable mind which is to form a healthy judgment ought rather to have had no experience or contamination of evil habits when young. And this is the reason why in youth good men often appear to be simple, and are easily practiced upon by the evil, because they have no examples of what evil is in their own souls. — *The Republic*, ii. 233.

Goods of life.

—— Now goods are of two kinds: there are human and there are divine goods, and the human hang upon the divine; and the State which attains the greater, at the same time acquires the less, or not having the greater loses both. Of the lesser goods the first is health, the second beauty, the third strength, including swiftness in running and bodily agility generally, and the fourth is wealth, not the blind god [Pluto], but one who is keen of sight, because he has wisdom for a companion. For wisdom is chief and leader of the divine class of goods, and next follows temperance; and from the union of these two with courage springs justice, and fourth in the scale of virtue is courage. The four naturally take precedence of the other goods, and this is the order in which the legislator must place them; and after these he will enjoin the rest of his ordinances on the citizens with a view to these, the human looking to the divine, and the divine looking to their leader mind. . . . . For the goods of which the many speak are not really good: first in the catalogue is placed health, beauty next, wealth third, and then innumerable others, as for example to have a keen eye, or a quick ear and in general to have all the senses perfect; or, again, to be a tyrant and do as you like; and the final consummation of happiness is to have acquired all these things, and as soon as you are possessed of them to be immortal. But you and I say, that while to the just and holy all these things are the best of possessions, to the unjust they are all, including even health, the greatest of evils. For in truth to have sight, and hearing, and the use of the senses, or to live at all, without justice and virtue, even though a man be rich in all the so-called goods of fortune, is the greatest of evils, if life be immortal; but not so great, if the bad man lives a very short time. These are the truths of which you must persuade or if they will not be persuaded, must compel your poets, to sing with suitable accompaniments of harmony and rhythm, and in these they must train up your youth. Am I not right? For I plainly declare that evils, as they are termed, are goods to the unjust, and only evils to the just, and that goods are truly good to the good, but evil to the evil. — *Laws,* iv. 162, 190.

Government, forms of, unessential. See *Forms.*

Government, four kinds of. See *Forms.*

Government, property in.

———— What manner of government do you term oligarchy?

A government resting on a valuation of property, in which the rich have power and the poor are deprived of power.

I understand, he replied.

Ought I not to describe, first of all, how the change from timocracy to oligarchy arises?

Yes.

Well, I said, no eyes are required in order to see how the one passes into the other.

How?

The accumulation of gold in the treasury of private individuals is the ruin of timocracy: they invent illegal modes of expenditure, but what do they or their wives care about the law?

Very true.

And then one seeing another prepares to rival him, and thus the whole body of the citizens acquires a similar character.

Likely enough.

After that they get on in trade, and the more they think of making a fortune the less they think of virtue; for when riches and virtue are placed together in the scales of the balance, the one always rises as the other falls.

True.

And in proportion as riches and rich men are honored in the State, virtue and the virtuous are dishonored. — *The Republic,* ii. 377.

Government, the beginning of. See *Legislation, beginning of.*
Government, science of.

—— *Str.* The several forms of government cannot be defined by the words few or many, voluntary or compulsory, poverty or riches ; but some notion of science must enter in, if we are to be consistent with what has preceded.

Y. Soc. And we must be consistent.

Str. Well, then, in which of these various forms of States may the science of government, which is among the greatest and most difficult of all sciences, be supposed to reside ? That we must discover, and then we shall see who are the false politicians who win popularity and pretend to be politicians and are not, and separate them from the wise king.

Y. Soc. That, as the argument has already intimated, is our duty.

Str. Do you think that the multitude in a State can attain political science?

Y. Soc. Impossible.

Str. But, perhaps, in a city of a thousand men, there would be a hundred, or say fifty, who could ?

Y. Soc. In that case political science would certainly be the easiest of all sciences ; there could not be found in a city of that number as many really good draught-players, if judged by the standard of the rest of Hellas, and there would certainly not be as many kings. For kings we may truly call those who possess royal science, whether they rule or not, as was shown in the previous argument. — *Statesman,* iii. 578.

Government of the few, only true. See *Few.*
Government, with or without laws.

—— *Str.* That can be the only true form of government in which the governors are found to possess true science, and are not mere pretenders, whether they rule according to law, or without law, over willing or unwilling subjects, and are rich or poor themselves, — none of these things can properly be included in the notion of the ruler.

Y. Soc. True.

Str. And whether with a view to the public good they purge the State by killing some, or exiling some; whether they lower or increase the body corporate, by sending out or receiving into the hive swarms of citizens, while they act according to the rules of wisdom and justice, whether with or without laws, if they use their power with a view to the general security and improvement, then the city over which they rule, and which has these characteristics, may be described as the only true State. All other governments are not genuine or real, but only imitations of this, and some of them are better and some of them are worse; the better are said to be well governed, but they are mere imitations like the others.

Y. Soc. I agree, Stranger, in the greater part of what you say; but as to their ruling without laws — the expression has a harsh sound.

Str. I was just going to ask, Socrates, whether you objected to any of my statements; and now I see that this notion of there being good government without laws will require some further consideration.

Y. Soc. Certainly.

Str. There can be no doubt that legislation is in a manner the business of a king, and yet the best thing of all is not that the law should rule, but that a man should rule, supposing him to have wisdom and royal power. Do you see why this is?

Y. Soc. Why?

Str. Because the law in aiming at what is noblest or most just cannot at once comprise what is best for all. The differences of men and actions, and the endless irregular movements of human things, do not admit of any universal and simple rule. No art can lay down a rule which will last for all time.

Y. Soc. Of course not.

Str. But this the law is always striving to make one; like an obstinate and ignorant tyrant, who will not allow anything to be done contrary to his appointment, or any question to be asked — not even in sudden changes of circumstances, when something happens to be better than what he commanded for some one.

Y. Soc. True; such is the manner in which the law treats us.

Str. A perfectly simple principle can never be applied to a state of things which is the reverse of simple.

Y. Soc. True.

Str. Then if the law is not the perfection of right, why are we compelled to make laws at all? — *Statesman*, iii. 579.

Government of Sparta, doubtful

—— *Meg.* Stranger, I perceive that I cannot say, without more thought, what I should call the government of Lacedaemon. for it seems to me to be like a tyranny; the power of our

Ephors is marvelously tyrannical; and sometimes it appears to me to be of all cities the most democratical; and who can reasonably deny that it is an aristocracy? We have also a monarchy which is held for life, and is said by all mankind, and not by ourselves only, to be the most ancient of all monarchies; and, therefore, when asked on a sudden, I cannot precisely say which form of government the Spartan is.

Cle. I am in the same difficulty, Megillus, for I do not feel confident that the polity of Cnosus is any of these.

Ath. The reason is, my excellent friends, that you really have polities, but the cities of which we were speaking are mere aggregations of citizens who are the subjects and servants of parts of their own State; they are named after their several ruling powers, and are not polities at all. But if States are to be named after their rulers, the true State ought to be called by the name of the God who rules over wise men. — *Laws*, iv. 240.

Government, necessity for.

—— Mankind must have laws, and conform to them, or their life would be as bad as that of the most savage beast. And the reason of this is, that no man's nature is able to know what is best for the social state of man; or knowing, always able to do what is best. In the first place, there is a difficulty in apprehending that the true art of politics is concerned, not with private but with public good; — for public good binds together States, but private only distracts them, — nor do men always see that the gain is greater both to the individual and the State, when the State and not the individual is first considered. In the second place, even if a person know as a matter of science that this is the truth, but is possessed of absolute and irresponsible power, he will never be able to abide in this principle or to persist in regarding the public good as primary in the State, and the private good as secondary. Human nature will be always drawing him into avarice and selfishness, avoiding pain and pursuing pleasure without any reason, and will bring these to the front, obscuring the juster and better; and so, working darkness in his soul, will at last fill with evils both him and the whole city. For if a man were born so divinely gifted that he could naturally apprehend the truth, he would have no need of laws to rule over him; for there is no law or order which is above knowledge, nor can mind, without impiety, be deemed the subject or slave of any man, but rather the lord of all. — *Laws*, iv. 388.

Governors. See *Kings, Rulers, Legislators.*
Greatness and gentleness seemingly inconsistent. See *Gentleness,* etc.
Greatness, the idea of.
—— You see a number of great objects, and when you look at them together, there seems to you to be one and the same idea (or nature) in them all; hence you conceive of a greatness as one.

Very true, said Socrates.

And if you go on and allow your mind in like manner to embrace in one view the idea of greatness and of great things which are not the idea, and to compare them, will not another greatness arise, which will appear to be the source of all these?

That is true.

Then another kind of greatness now comes into view over and above absolute greatness, and the individuals which partake of it; and then another over and above all these, by virtue of which they will all be great, and so each idea, instead of being one, will be infinitely subdivided. — *Parmenides,* iii. 249.

Grief, manifestations of.
—— Shall we proceed to get rid of the weepings and wailings of famous men?

They will go with the others.

But shall we be right in getting rid of them? Reflect: our principle is that the good man will not consider death terrible to a good man.

Yes; that is our principle.

And therefore he will not sorrow for his departed friend as though he had suffered anything terrible?

He will not.

Such an one, as we further maintain, is enough for himself and his own happiness, and therefore is least in need of other men.

True, he said.

And for this reason the loss of a son or brother, or the deprivation of fortune, is to him of all men least terrible.

Assuredly.

And therefore he will be least likely to lament, and will bear with the greatest equanimity any misfortune of this sort which may befall him.

Yes, he will feel such a misfortune less than another.

Then we shall be right in getting rid of the lamentations of famous men, and making them over to women (and not even to women who are good for anything), or to men of a baser sort, that those who are being educated by us to be the defenders of their country may scorn to do the like.

That will be very right.

Then we will once more entreat Homer and the other poets not to depict Achilles, who is the son of a goddess, first lying on his side, then on his back, and then on his face; then starting up and sailing in a frenzy along the shores of the barren sea; now taking the dusky ashes in both his hands and pouring them over his head, or bewailing and sorrowing in the various modes which Homer has delineated. Nor should he describe Priam, the kinsman of the Gods, as praying and beseeching —

"Rolling in the dirt, calling each man loudly by his name."

Still more earnestly will we beg of him not to introduce the Gods lamenting and saying, —

"Alas! my misery! Alas! that I bore the bravest to my sorrow."

But if he must introduce the Gods, at any rate let him not dare so completely to represent the greatest of the Gods as to make him say —

"O heavens! with my eyes I behold a dear friend of mine driven round and round the city, and my heart is sorrowful."

Or again : —

"Woe is me that I am fated to have Sarpedon, dearest of men to me, subdued at the hands of Patroclus the son of Menoetius."

For if, my sweet Adeimantus, our youth seriously believe in such unworthy representations of the Gods, instead of laughing at them as they ought, hardly will any of them deem that he himself, being but a man, can be dishonored by similar actions; neither will he rebuke any inclination that may arise in his mind to say and do the like. And instead of having any shame or self-control, he will be always whining and lamenting on slight occasions. — *The Republic,* ii. 209.

Gyges, story of.

—— Now that justice is only the inability to do injustice will best appear if we imagine something of this kind; suppose we give both the just and the unjust entire liberty to do what they will, and let us attend and see whither desire will lead them; then we shall detect the just man in the very act; the just and unjust will be found going the same way, — following their interest, which all natures follow as a good, and are only diverted into the path of justice by the force of law. The liberty

which we are supposing may be most conveniently given to them in the form of such a power as is said to have been possessed by Gyges, the ancestor of Croesus the Lydian. According to the tradition, Gyges was a shepherd in the service of the king of Lydia, and, while he was in the field, there was a storm and earthquake, which made an opening in the earth at the place where he was feeding his flock. Amazed at the sight, he descended into the opening, where, among other marvels, he beheld a hollow brazen horse, having doors, at which he stooping and looking in saw a dead body, of stature, as appeared to him, more than human, and having nothing on but a gold ring; this he took from the finger of the dead and reascended. Now the shepherds met together, according to custom, that they might send their monthly report concerning the flock to the king; and into their assembly he came having the ring on his finger, and as he was sitting among them he chanced to turn the collet of the ring towards the inner side of the hand, when instantly he became invisible, and the others began to speak of him as if he were no longer there. He was astonished at this, and again touching the ring he turned the collet outwards and reappeared; thereupon he made trials of the ring, and always with the same result; when he turned the collet inwards he became invisible, when outwards he reappeared. Perceiving this, he immediately contrived to be chosen one of the messengers sent to the court, where he no sooner arrived than he seduced the queen, and with her help conspired against the king and slew him and took the kingdom. Suppose now that there were two such magic rings, and the just put on one of them and the unjust the other; no man they say is of such an iron nature that he would stand fast in justice. — *The Republic*, ii. 181.
Gymnastics and music.

—— In speaking of education, the law means to speak of those who have the care of order and instruction in gymnasia and schools, and of the going to school and lodging of boys and girls; and in speaking of contests, the law refers to the judges of gymnastics and of music; these again are divided into two classes, the one having to do with music, the other with gymnastic. — *Laws*, iv. 286.

After music comes gymnastic, in which our youth are next to be trained.

Certainly.

And gymnastic as well as music should receive careful attention in childhood, and continue through life. Now my belief is, — and this is a matter upon which I should like to have your opinion, but my own belief is, — not that the good body improves the soul, but that the good soul improves the body. What do you say?

Yes, I agree.

Then if we have educated the mind, the minuter care of the body may properly be committed to the mind, and we need only describe the outlines of the subject for brevity's sake.

Very good.

That they must abstain from intoxication has been already remarked by us, for of all persons a guardian should be the last to get drunk and not know where in the world he is.

Yes, he said; that a guardian should require another to guard him is ridiculous indeed.

But next, what shall we say of their food; for the men are athletes in the great contest of all, are they not?

Yes, he said.

And will the usual gymnastic exercises be suited to them?

I cannot say.

I am afraid, I said, that such exercise is but a sleepy sort of thing, and rather perilous to health. Do you not observe that athletes sleep away their lives, and are liable to most dangerous illnesses if they depart, in ever so slight a degree, from their customary regimen?

Yes, I do.

Then, I said, a finer sort of training will be required for our warrior athletes, who are to be like wakeful dogs, and to see and hear with the utmost keenness; in the many changes of water and also of food, of summer heat and winter cold, which they will have to endure, they must not be liable to break down in health.

That is quite my view, he said.

The really excellent gymnastic is twin sister of that simple music which we were just now describing.

How so.

Why, I conceive that there is a gymnastic also which is simple and good; and that such ought to be the military gymnastic.

What do you mean?

My meaning may be learned from Homer; he, you know, feeds his heroes, when they are campaigning, on soldiers' fare; they have no fish, although they are on the shores of the Hellespont, and they are allowed nothing but roast meat — which only requires a fire, and is therefore the most convenient diet for soldiers — and not boiled, as this would involve a carrying about of pots and pans.

True.

And I can hardly be mistaken in saying that sweet sauces are not even mentioned in Homer. In proscribing them, however, he is not singular, as all professional athletes know that a man who is to be in good condition should take nothing of the kind. — *The Republic*, ii. 227.

Habit, mental and bodily. See *Mental*, etc.
Happiness gained by Wisdom.

—— Let us consider this further point, I said : Seeing that all men desire happiness, and happiness, as has been shown, is gained by a use, and a right use, of the things of life, and the right use of them, and good fortune in the use of them, is given by knowledge, the inference is that every man ought by all means to try and make himself as wise as he can?

Yes, he said.

And the desire to obtain this treasure, which is far more precious than money, from a father or a guardian or a friend or a suitor, whether citizen or stranger — the eager desire and prayer to them that they would impart wisdom to you, is not at all dishonorable, Cleinias ; nor is any one to be blamed for doing any honorable service or ministration to any man, whether a lover or not, if his aim is to get wisdom. Do you agree to that? I said.

Yes, he said, I quite agree, and think that you are right.

Yes, I said, Cleinias, if only wisdom can be taught, and does not come to man spontaneously; for that is a point which has still to be considered, and is not yet agreed upon by you and me.

But I think, Socrates, that wisdom can be taught, he said.

Best of men, I said, I am delighted to hear you say that; and I am also grateful to you for having saved me from a long and tiresome speculation as to whether wisdom can be taught or not. But now, as you think that wisdom can be taught, and that wisdom only can make a man happy and fortunate, will you not acknowledge that all of us ought to love wisdom, and you individually will try to love her?

Certainly, Socrates, he said ; and I will do my best. — *Euthydemus*, i. 184.

Harmony.

—— Might not a person say that harmony is a thing invisible, incorporeal, perfect, divine, existing in the lyre which is harmonized, but that the lyre and the strings are matter and material, composite, earthy, and akin to mortality? And when some one breaks the lyre, or cuts and rends the strings, then he who takes this view would argue as you do, and on the same analogy, that the harmony survives and has not perished; for you cannot imagine, as he would say, that the lyre without the strings, and the broken strings themselves which are mortal, remain, and yet that the harmony, which is of heavenly and immortal nature and kindred, has perished — and perished too before the mortal. That harmony, he would say, must still exist somewhere, and the wood and strings will decay before that decays. . . . . Now there is an absurdity in saying that harmony is discord, or is composed of elements which are still in a state of discord. But perhaps what he really meant to say was that harmony is composed of differing notes of higher or lower pitch which disagreed once, but are now reconciled by the art of music; for if the higher and lower notes still disagreed, there could be no harmony, as is indeed evident. For harmony is a symphony, and symphony is an agreement; but an agreement of disagreements while they disagree, there cannot be; you cannot harmonize that which disagrees. This may be illustrated by rhythm, which is composed of elements short and long, once differing and now in accord; which accordance, as in the former instance, medicine, so in this, music implants, making love and unison to grow up among them; and thus music, too, is concerned with the principles of love in their application to harmony and rhythm. Again, in the essential nature of harmony and rhythm there is no difficulty in discerning love which has not yet become double. But when you want to use them in actual life, either in the composition of music or in the correct performance of airs or metres composed already, which latter is called education, then the difficulty begins, and the good artist is needed. Then the old tale has to be repeated of fair and heavenly love — the love of Urania the fair and heavenly muse, and of the duty of accepting the temperate, and those who are as yet intemperate only that they may become temperate, and of preserving their love; and again, of the vulgar Polyhymnia, who must be used with circumspection that the pleasure may not generate licentiousness. — *Phaedo*, i. 414, 481.

Harmony of soul and form. See *Form*.
Harmony of temperance.

—— Do you observe that we were pretty right in our anticipation that temperance was a sort of harmony?

Why so?

Why, because temperance is unlike courage and wisdom, each of which resides in a part only, the one making the State wise and the other valiant; but that is not the way with temperance, which extends to the whole, and runs through the notes of the scale, and produces a harmony of the weaker and the stronger and the middle class, whether you suppose them to be stronger or weaker in wisdom or strength or numbers or wealth, or whatever else may be the measure of them. Most truly then do we describe temperance as the natural agreement of superior and inferior, both in States and individuals, about which of the two elements shall rule. — *The Republic*, ii. 257.

Harmony civilizing.

—— And ought not the rational principle, which is wise, and has the care of the whole soul, to rule, and the passionate or spirited principle to be the subject and ally?

Certainly.

And, as we were saying, the united influence of music and gymnastic will bring them into accord, nerving and sustaining the reason with noble words and lessons, and moderating, and soothing and civilizing the wildness of passion by harmony and rhythm?

Quite true, he said. — *The Republic*, ii. 268.

Harmony of the inner man.

—— As we were saying at the beginning of our work of construction, some divine power must have conducted us to a primary form of justice — that suspicion of ours has been now verified?

Yes, certainly. . . . .

And justice was the reality, and was concerned not with the outward man, but with the inward, which is the true self and concernment of man; for the just man does not permit the several elements within him to interfere with one another, or any of them to do the work of others, but he sets in order his own inner life, and is his own master, and at peace with himself; and when he has bound together the three principles within him, which may be compared to the higher, lower, and middle notes of the scale, and the intermediate intervals —

when he has bound together all these, and is no longer many, but has become one entirely temperate and perfectly adjusted nature, then he will begin to act, if he has to act, whether in a matter of property, or in the treatment of the body, or some affair of politics or private business; in all which cases he will think and call that which preserves and coöperates with this harmonious condition, just and good action; and the knowledge which presides over it, wisdom; and that which at any time destroys this condition, he will call unjust action, and the opinion which presides over it, ignorance. — *The Republic*, ii. 270.
Harmony of health and wealth.

—— On this higher end the man of understanding will concentrate the energies of his life. And in the first place, he will honor studies which impress these qualities on his soul, and will disregard others?

Clearly, he said.

In the next place, he will regulate his bodily habit, and so far will he be from yielding to brutal and irrational pleasures, that he will regard even health as quite a secondary matter; his first object will be not that he may be fair or strong or well, unless he is likely thereby to gain temperance, but he will be always desirous of preserving ·the harmony of the body for the sake of the concord of the soul?

Certainly he will, he replied, if he has true music in him.

And there is a principle of order and harmony in the acquisition of wealth; this also he will observe, and will not allow himself to be dazzled by the opinion of the world, and heap up riches to his own infinite harm?

I should think not, he said.

He will look at the city which is within him, and take care to avoid any change of his own institutions, such as might arise either from superfluity or from want; and with a view to this only gain or spend in so far as he is able?

Very true.

And, for the same reason, he will accept such honors as he deems likely to make him a better man; but those which are likely to disorder his constitution, whether private or public honors, he will avoid. — *The Republic*, ii. 423.
Harmony in the soul.

—— *Soc.* What would you say of the soul? Will the good soul be that in which disorder is prevalent, or that in which there is harmony and order?

Cal. The latter follows from our previous admissions.

Soc. What is the name which is given to the effect of harmony and order in the body?

Cal. I suppose that you mean health and strength?

Soc. Yes, I do; and what is the name which you would give to the effect of harmony and order in the soul? Try and discover a name for this as well as for the other.

Cal. Why do you not give the name yourself, Socrates?

Soc. Well, if you would rather, I will; and you shall say whether you agree with me, and if not you shall refute and answer me. Healthy, as I conceive, is the name which is given to the regular order of the body, and from this comes health and every other bodily excellence: is that true or not?

Cal. True.

Soc. And "lawful" and "law" are the names which are given to the regular order and action of the soul, and these make men lawful and orderly: and so we have temperance and justice? have we not?

Cal. Yes. — *Gorgias*, iii. 95.

Harmony, counterparts and antagonisms in the soul, making. See *Antagonisms.*

Harmony dissolved, a generation of pain.

—— *Soc.* I say that when the harmony in animals is dissolved, there is also a dissolution of nature and a generation of pain.

Pro. That is very probable.

Soc. And the restoration of harmony and return to nature is the source of pleasure, if I may be allowed to speak in the fewest and shortest words about matters of the greatest moment. — *Philebus*, iii. 167.

Harmony in choral song. See *Choral.*

Harmonies and consonances. See *Consonances.*

Harmonies of divers kinds.

—— We were saying, as you may remember, in speaking of the words, that we had no need of lamentation and strains of sorrow?

True.

And which are the harmonies expressive of sorrow? As you are a musician, I wish that you would tell me.

The harmonies which you mean are the mixed or tenor Lydian, and the full-toned or bass Lydian, and others which are like them.

These then, I said, must be banished; even to women of virtue and character they are of no use, and much less to men.

Certainly.

In the next place, drunkenness and softness and indolence are utterly at variance with the character of our guardians.
Of course.
Then I must ask you again, which are the soft or drinking harmonies?
The Ionian, he replied, and the Lydian; they are termed "solute."
Well, and are these of any military use?
Quite the reverse, he replied; but then the Dorian and the Phrygian appear to be the only ones which remain.
I answered: Of the harmonies I know nothing, but I want to have one warlike, which will sound the word or note which a brave man utters in the hour of danger and stern resolve, or when his cause is failing and he is going to wounds or death or is overtaken by some other evil, and at every such crisis meets fortune with calmness and endurance; and another to be used by him in times of peace and freedom of action, when there is no pressure of necessity; and he is seeking to persuade God by prayer or man by instruction and advice; or on the other hand, which expresses his willingness to listen to persuasion or entreaty and advice; and which represents him when he has accomplished his aim, not carried away by success, but acting moderately and wisely, and acquiescing in the event. These two harmonies I ask you to leave; the strain of necessity and the strain of freedom, the strain of the unfortunate and the strain of the fortunate, the strain of courage, and the strain of temperance; these, I say, leave.
And these, he replied, are the very ones of which I was speaking.
Then, I said, if only the Dorian and Phrygian harmonies are used in our songs and melodies, we shall not want multiplicity of notes or a panharmonic scale?
I suppose not. — *The Republic*, ii. 222.

"**Having**" and "**possessing**," distinction between.

—— *Soc.* You have heard the common explanation of the verb " to know ? "

Theaet. I do not know that I remember at the moment.

Soc. They explain the word " to know " as meaning " to have knowledge."

Theaet. True.

Soc. I should like to make a slight change, and say " to possess " knowledge.

Theaet. How do the two expressions differ?

Soc. Perhaps there may be no difference; but still I should like you to hear and help to test my view.

Theaet. I will, if I can.

Soc. I should distinguish "having" from "possessing:" for example, a man may buy and keep under his control a garment which he does not wear; and then we should say, not that he has, but that he possesses the garment.

Theaet. That would be the correct expression.

Soc. Well, may not a man "possess" and yet not "have" knowledge in the sense of which I am speaking? As you may suppose a man to have caught wild birds — doves or any other birds — and to be keeping them in an aviary which he has constructed at home; and then we might say, in one sense, that he always has them because he possesses them, might we not?

Theaet. Yes.

Soc. And yet, in another sense, he has none of them; but he has power over them, and has them under his hand in an inclosure of his own, and can take and have them whenever he likes; he can catch any which he likes, and again let them go, and he may do so as often as he pleases.

Theaet. True.

Soc. Once more, then, as in what preceded, we made a sort of waxen figment in the mind, so let us now suppose that in the mind of each man there is an aviary of all sorts of birds — some flocking together apart from the rest, others in small groups, others solitary, flying anywhere and everywhere.

Theaet. Let us imagine such an aviary; and what is to follow?

Soc. We may suppose this receptacle to be empty while we are young, and that the birds are kinds of knowledge; when a man has gotten and detained in the inclosure any of those different kinds of knowledge, then he may be said to have learned or discovered the thing of which that knowledge is: and this is to know. — *Theaetetus,* iii. 403.

Health, harmony of wealth and. See *Harmony,* etc.

Health of body and soul. See *Body,* etc.

Heavenly idea of the Earth. See *Earth,* etc.

Heavenly bodies, beheld as symbols of truths and means of education.

——— Socrates, as you rebuked the vulgar manner in which I

praised astronomy before, my praise shall be more worthy of your spirit. For every one, as I think, must feel that astronomy compels the soul to look upwards, and leads us from this world to another.

I am an exception then, for I should rather say that those who elevate astronomy into philosophy make us look downwards and not upwards.

What do you mean ? he asked.

You, I replied, have in your mind a sublime conception of how we know the things above. And I dare say that if a person were to throw his head back and study the fretted ceiling, you would still think that his mind was the percipient, and not his eyes. And you are very likely right, and I may be a simpleton : but, in my opinion, that knowledge only which is of being and of the unseen can make the soul look upwards, and whether a man gapes at the heavens or blinks on the ground, seeking to learn some particular of sense, I would deny that he can learn, for nothing of that sort is matter of science; his soul is looking, not upwards, but downwards, whether his way to knowledge is by water or by land, and in whichever element he may lie on his back and float.

I acknowledge, he said, the justice of your rebuke. Still, I should like to know how astronomy can be learned in any other way more conducive to that knowledge of which we speak ?

I answered ; the starry heaven which we behold is wrought upon a visible ground, and therefore, although the fairest and most perfect of visible things, must necessarily be deemed inferior far to the true motions of absolute swiftness and absolute slowness, which are relative to each other, and carry with them that which is contained in them, in the true number and in every true figure. Now, these are to be apprehended by reason and intelligence, but not by sight.

True, he replied.

The spangled heavens should be used as a pattern and with a view to that higher knowledge; their beauty is like the beauty of figures or pictures wrought by the hand of Daedalus, or some other great artist, which we may chance to behold ; any geometrician who saw them would appreciate the exquisiteness of their workmanship, but he would never dream of thinking that in them he could find the true equal or the true double, or the truth of any other proportion.

No, he said, to think so would be ridiculous.

And will not a true astronomer have the same feeling when he looks at the movements of the stars? Will he not think that heaven and the things in heaven are framed by the Creator in the most perfect manner? But when he reflects that the proportions of night and day, or of both to the month, or of the month to the year, or of the other stars to these and to one another, are of the visible and material, he will never fall into the error of supposing that they are eternal and liable to no deviation — that would be monstrous; he will rather seek in every possible way to discover the truth of them.

I quite agree now that you tell me so.

Then, I said, in astronomy, as in geometry, we should use problems and let the heavens alone — if we desire to have a real knowledge of the science and to train the reasoning faculty by the aid of it. — *The Republic*, ii. 356.

Heirships of wealth, an evil. See *Inheritances*.

Heracles and Iolaus.

—— I am no Heracles; and even Heracles could not fight against the Hydra, who was a she-Sophist, and had the wit to shoot up many new heads when one of them was cut off; especially when he saw a second monster of a sea-crab, who was also a Sophist, and appeared to have newly arrived from a sea voyage, bearing down upon him from the left, opening his mouth and biting. Then he called Iolaus, his nephew, to his help, and he ably succored him; but if my Iolaus, who is Patrocles the statuary, were to come, he would make a bad business worse.

And now that you have delivered yourself of this strain, said Dionysodorus, will you inform me whether Iolaus was the nephew of Heracles any more than he is yours?

I suppose that I had best answer you, Dionysodorus, I said, for you will insist on asking — that I pretty well know — out of envy, in order to prevent me from learning the wisdom of Euthydemus.

Then answer me, he said.

Well then, I said, I can only reply, that Iolaus was not my nephew at all, but the nephew of Heracles; and his father was not my brother Patrocles, but Iphicles, who has a name rather like his, and was the brother of Heracles. — *Euthydemus*, i. 201.

Heroic sons of heroic fathers. See *State, heroes*.

Heroic men to be kissed and honored by all. See *Brave, honor to the*.

—— But the hero who has distinguished himself, what shall be done to him? In the first place, he shall receive honor in the army from his youthful comrades; every one of them in succession shall crown him. What do you say to that?

I approve.

And what do you say to his receiving the right hand of fellowship?

To that too, I agree.

But you will hardly agree to my next proposal.

What is your proposal?

That he should kiss and be kissed by them.

Most certainly, and I should be disposed to go further and say: Let no one whom he has a mind to kiss refuse to be kissed by him while the expedition lasts. So that if there be a lover in the army, whether his love be youth or maiden, he may be more eager to win the prize of valor.

That is good, I said. That the brave man is to have more wives than others has been already determined; and he is to have first choices in such matters more than others, in order that he may have as many children as possible.

Agreed. — *The Republic*, ii. 295.

Heterodoxy and false opinion. See *False opinion*.

—— *Soc.* If thinking is speaking to one's self, no one speaking and thinking of two objects, and apprehending them both in his soul, will say and think that the one is the other of them, and I must add, that you will have to let the word "other" alone [*i. e.* not insist that "one" and "other" are both in Greek called "other," ἕτερον]. I mean to say, that no one thinks the noble to be base, or anything of the kind.

Theaet. I will give up the word "other," Socrates; and I agree in what you say.

Soc. If a man has both of them in his thoughts, he cannot think that the one of them is the other?

Theaet. True.

Soc. Neither, if he has one of them in his mind and not the other, can he think that one is the other?

Theaet. True; for we should have to suppose that he apprehends that which is not in his thoughts at all.

Soc. Then no one who knows either both or only one of the two objects in his mind can think that the one is the other. And therefore, he who maintains that false "doxy" is heterodoxy is talking nonsense; for neither in this, any more than in the previous way, can false opinion exist in us. . . . . . The only possibility of erroneous opinion is, when knowing you and Theodorus, and having the seal or impression of both of you in the wax block, but seeing you both imperfectly and at a distance, I try to assign the right impression of memory visual to the right impression, and fit this into the proper mould; if I ·succeed, recognition will take place ; but if I fail and transpose them, putting the foot into the wrong shoe,—that is to say, putting the vision of either of you on to the wrong seal, or seeing you as in a mirror when the sight flows from right to left — then "heterodoxy" and false opinion ensues. —*Theaetetus*, iii. 395–398.

Highest good in the State. See *Evil*, etc.
Hippias, self-assertion of. See *Self-assertion*, etc.
Holiness, resembling Justice.

—— Suppose that he went on to say : Well now, is there such a thing as holiness ? — we should answer, Yes, if I am not mistaken?

Yes, he said.

And that you acknowledge to be a thing — should we admit that?

He assented.

And is this a sort of thing which is of the nature of the holy, or of the nature of the unholy ? I should be angry at his putting such a question, and should say, Peace, man ; nothing can be holy if holiness is not holy. What do you say to that ? Would you not answer in the same way?

Certainly, he said.

And then after this suppose that he came and asked us, What were you saying just now ? Perhaps I may not have heard you rightly, but you seemed to me to be saying that the parts of virtue were not the same as one another. I should reply, You certainly heard that said, but not, as you imagine, said by me ; for Protagoras gave the answer, and I only asked the question. And suppose that he turned to you and said, Is this true, Protagoras? and do you maintain that one part of virtue is unlike another, and is this your position ? how would you answer him?

I could not help acknowledging the truth of what he said, Socrates.

Well then, Protagoras, we will assume this ; and now supposing that he proceeded to say further, Then holiness is not of the nature of justice, nor justice of the nature of holiness, but of the nature of unholiness; and holiness is of the nature of the not just, and therefore of the unjust, and the unjust is unholy; — how shall we answer him? I should certainly answer him on my own behalf that justice is holy, and that holiness is just; and I would say in like manner on your behalf also, if you would allow me, that justice is either the same with holiness, or very nearly the same; and above all I would assert that justice is like holiness and holiness is like justice; and I wish that you would tell me whether I may be permitted to give this answer on your behalf, and whether you would agree with me.

He replied, I cannot simply agree, Socrates, to the proposition that justice is holy and that holiness is just, for there appears to me to be a difference between them. But what matter? if you please I please; and let us assume, if you will, that justice is holy, and that holiness is just.

Pardon me, I said; I do not want this " if you wish " or " if you will " sort of argument to be proven, but I want you and me to be proven; I mean to say that the argument will be best proven if there be no " if."

Well, he said, I admit that justice bears a resemblance to holiness, for there is always some point of view in which everything is like every other thing; white is in a certain way like black, and hard is like soft, and the most extreme opposites have some qualities in common; even the parts of the face which, as we were saying before, are distinct and have different functions, are still in a certain point of view similar, and one of them is like another of them. And you may prove that they are like one another on the same principle that all things are like one another; and yet things which are alike in some particular ought not to be called alike, nor things which are unlike in some particular, however slight, unlike.

And do you think, I said in a tone of surprise, that justice and holiness have but a small degree of likeness?

Certainly not, he said; but I do not agree with what I understand to be your view. — *Protagoras*, i. 130.

Holiness; the essence of.

—— *Soc.* What do you say of piety, Euthyphro: is not piety, according to your definition, loved by all the Gods?

Euth. Yes.

Soc. Because it is pious or holy, or for some other reason?

Euth. No, that is the reason.

Soc. It is loved because it is holy, not holy because it is loved?

Euth. Yes.

Soc. And that which is in a state to be loved of the Gods, and is dear to them, is in a state to be loved of them because it is loved of them?

Euth. Certainly.

Soc. Then that which is loved of God, Euthyphro, is not holy, nor is that which is holy loved of God, as you affirm; but they are two different things.

Euth. How do you mean, Socrates?

Soc. I mean to say that the holy has been acknowledged by us to be loved of God because it is holy, not to be holy because it is loved.

Euth. Yes.

Soc. But that which is dear to the Gods is dear to them because it is loved by them, not loved by them because it is dear to them.

Euth. True.

Soc. But, friend Euthyphro, if that which is holy is the same as that which is dear to God, and that which is holy is loved as being holy, then that which is dear to God would have been loved as being dear to God; but if that which is dear to God is dear to him because loved by him, then that which is holy would have been holy because loved by him. But now you see that the reverse is the case, and that they are quite different from one another. For one (θεοφιλὲς) is of a kind to be loved because it is loved, and the other (ὅσιον) is loved because it is of a kind to be loved. Thus you appear to me, Euthyphro, when I ask you what is the essence of holiness, to offer an attribute only, and not the essence — the attribute of being loved by all the Gods. But you still refuse to explain to me the nature of holiness. And therefore, if you please, I will ask you not to hide your treasure, but to tell me once more what piety or holiness really is, whether dear to the Gods or not (for that is a matter about which we will not quarrel). And what is impiety?

Euth. I really do not know, Socrates, how to say what I mean. For somehow or other our arguments, on whatever ground we rest them, seem to turn round and walk away. — *Euthyphro*, i. 294.

Homer, the best of poets. See *Imitative poetry*.

—— *Soc.* I often envy the profession of a rhapsode, Ion; for you have always to wear fine clothes, and to look as beautiful as you can is a part of your art. Then, again, you are obliged to be continually in the company of many good poets; and especially of Homer, who is the best and most divine of them; and to understand him, and not merely learn his words by rote, is a thing greatly to be envied. And no man can be a rhapsode who does not understand the meaning of the poet. For the rhapsode ought to interpret the mind of the poet to his hearers, but how can he interpret him well unless he knows what he means? All this is greatly to be envied.

Ion. That is true, Socrates; interpretation has certainly been the most laborious of my art; and I believe myself able to speak about Homer better than any man. . . . .

Soc. But how did you come to have this skill about Homer, and not about Hesiod or the other poets? Does not Homer speak of the same themes which all other poets handle? Is not war his great argument? and does he not speak of human society and of intercourse of men, good and bad, skilled and unskilled, and of the Gods conversing with one another and with mankind, and about what happens in heaven and in the world below, and the generations of Gods and heroes? Are not these the themes of which Homer sings?

Ion. Very true, Socrates.

Soc. And do not the other poets sing of the same?

Ion. Yes, Socrates; but not in the same way as Homer.

Soc. What! in a worse way?

Ion. Yes, in a far worse.

Soc. And Homer is better?

Ion. He is incomparably better. — *Ion*, i. 219.

Homer, not a legislator. See *Legislator*.

Homicide, less criminal than deception. See *Deceiver as to truth*.

Honesty professed.

—— That you may not suppose yourself to be deceived in thinking that all men regard every man as having a share of justice and of every other political virtue, let me give you a further proof, which is this. In other cases, as you are aware, if a man says that he is a good flute-player, or skillful in any other art in which he has no skill, people either laugh at him or are angry with him, and his relations think that he is mad and go and admonish him; but when honesty is in question, or some other political virtue, even if they know that he is dishonest, yet, if the man comes publicly forward and tells the truth about his dishonesty, in this case they deem that to be madness which in the other case was held by them to be good sense. They say that men ought to profess honesty whether they are honest or not, and that a man is mad who does not make such a profession. Their notion is, that a man must have some degree of honesty; and that if he has none at all he ought not to be in the world. — *Protagoras*, i. 123.

Honor due to parents. See *Children*, etc., and *Parents*.
Honor and justice among thieves.

—— We have already shown that the just are clearly wiser and better and abler than the unjust, and that the unjust are incapable of common action; nay more, that to speak as we did of evil-doers, ever acting vigorously together, is not strictly true, for if they had been perfectly evil, they would have laid hands upon one another; but there must evidently have been some remnant of justice in them, or they would have injured one another as well as their victims, and then they would have been unable to act together; they were but semi-villainous, for had they been whole villains, wholly unjust, they would have been wholly incapable of action. That, as I believe, is the truth of the matter, and not what you said at first. But whether the just have a better and happier life than the unjust is a further question which we also proposed to consider. I think that they have, and for the reasons which I have given; but still I should like to examine further, for this is no light matter, concerning nothing less than the true rule of life. — *The Republic*, ii. 175.

Honor and dishonor in love. See *Love, Honor*, etc.
Honor to the brave. See *Death in battle*, and *Heroic*.
Hope, fancies of. See *Fancies*.
Human life, in what consists the salvation of.

—— Suppose, again, the salvation of human life to depend on the choice of odd and even, and on the knowledge of when men ought to choose the greater or less, either in reference to themselves or to each other, whether near or at a distance; what would be the saving principle of our lives? Would not knowledge? — a knowledge of measuring, when the question is one of excess and defect, and a knowledge of number, when the question is of odd and even? The world will acknowledge that, will they not?

Protagoras himself thought that they would.

Well, then, my friends, I say to them, seeing that the salvation of human life has been found to consist in the right choice of pleasures and pains, — in the choice of the more and the fewer and the greater and the less, and the nearer and remoter, must not this measuring be a consideration of excess and defect, and equality in relation to each other?

That is undeniably true. — *Protagoras,* i. 156.

Hypotheses, used by reason.

—— Of this kind I still spoke as intelligible, although in inquiring into it the soul is compelled to use hypotheses; not proceeding to a first principle because she is unable to ascend above hypotheses, but employing the objects of which the shadows below are resemblances in their turn as images, they having in relation to the shadows a greater distinctness and therefore a higher value.

I understand, he said, that you are speaking of geometry and the sister arts.

And when I speak of the other division of the intellectual, you will also understand me to speak of that knowledge, which reason herself attains by the power of dialectic, using the hypotheses not as first principles, but only as hypotheses — that is to say, as steps and points of departure into a region which is above hypotheses, in order that she may soar beyond them to the first principle of the whole; and clinging to this and then to that which depends on this, by successive steps she descends again without the aid of any sensible object, beginning and ending in ideas.

I understand you, he replied; not perfectly, for you seem to me to be describing a task far from easy; but, at any rate, I understand you to say that knowledge and being, which the science of dialectic contemplates, are clearer than the notions of the arts, as they are termed, which proceed from hypotheses only: these are also contemplated by the understanding, and not by the senses: yet, because they start from hypotheses and do not ascend to a principle, those who contemplate them appear to you not to exercise the higher reason upon them, although when a first principle is added to them they are cognizable by the higher reason. And the habit which is concerned with geometry and the cognate sciences I suppose that you would term understanding and not reason, as being intermediate between opinion and reason. — *The Republic,* ii. 389.

Human life, progression of. See *Progression of,* etc.

Ibycus, his love in old age.

—— I feel like Ibycus who, when in his old age, against his will, he fell in love, compared himself to an old race-horse, who was about to run in a chariot race, shaking with fear at the course he knew so well — this was his simile of himself.— *Parmenides*, iii. 254.

Ideal State, Philosophers to be kings in the. See *Rulers in the State, who should be.*

Ideas, abstract.

—— Socrates, he said, I admire the bent of your mind towards philosophy ; tell me now, was this your own distinction between ideas in themselves and the things which partake of them? and do you think that there is an idea of likeness apart from the likeness which we possess, or of the one and many, and of the other notions of which Zeno has been speaking?

I think that there are such ideas, said Socrates.

Parmenides proceeded. And would you also make ideas of the just and the beautiful and the good, and of all that class?

Yes, he said, I should.

And would you make an idea of man apart from us and from all other human creatures, or of fire and water?

I am often undecided, Parmenides, as to whether I ought to include them or not.

And would you feel equally undecided, Socrates, about things of which the mention may provoke a smile ? — I mean such things as hair, mud, dirt, or anything else that is foul and base ; would you suppose that each of these has an idea distinct from the actual objects with which we come into contact, or not ?

Certainly not, said Socrates ; visible things like these are such as they appear to us, and I am afraid that there would be an absurdity in assuming any idea of them, although I sometimes get disturbed, and begin to think that there is nothing without an idea ; but then again, when I have taken up this position, I run away, because I am afraid that I may fall into a bottomless pit of nonsense, and perish ; and so I return to the ideas of which I was just now speaking, and occupy myself with them.

Yes, Socrates, said Parmenides ; that is because you are still young ; the time will come when philosophy will have a firmer grasp of you, if I am not mistaken, and then you will not despise even the meanest things : at your age, you are too much disposed to regard the opinions of men. But I should like to know whether you mean that there are certain ideas of which all other things partake, and from which they are therefore named; that similars for example, become similar, because they partake of similarity; and great things become great, because they partake of greatness; and that just and beautiful things become just and beautiful, because they partake of justice and beauty?

Yes, certainly, said Socrates, that is my meaning. — *Parmenides*, iii. 246.

Ideas that are cognitions. See *Cognitions*.

Idle talking.

—— I certainly do not see my way at present.

Yes, said Parmenides; and I think that this arises, Socrates, out of your attempting to define the beautiful, the just, the good, and the ideas generally, without sufficient previous training. I noticed your deficiency, when I heard you talking here with your friend Aristoteles, the day before yesterday. The impulse that carries you towards philosophy is assuredly noble and divine; but still there is an art which often seems to be useless, and is called by the vulgar idle talking and is often imagined to be useless; in that you must train and exercise yourself, now that you are young, or truth will elude your grasp. — *Parmenides*, iii. 253.

Ignoble, the.

—— Come, now and let us reason with the unjust, who is not intentionally in error. "Sweet Sir," we will say to him, "what think you of things esteemed noble and ignoble? Is not the noble that which subjects the beast to the man, or rather to the God in man; and the ignoble that which subjects the man to the beast?" He can hardly avoid saying yes — can he now?

Not if he has any regard for my opinion.

But, if he admit this, we may ask him another question; How would a man profit if he received gold and silver on the condition that he was to enslave the noblest part of him to the worst? Who can imagine that a man who sold his son or daughter into slavery for money, especially if he sold them into the hands of fierce and evil men, would be the gainer, however large might be the sum which he received? And will any one say that he is not a miserable caitiff who sells his own divine being to that which is most atheistical and detestable, and has no pity? Eriphyle took the necklace as the price of her husband's life, but he is taking a bribe in order to compass a worse ruin.

Yes, said Glaucon, far worse, I will answer for him.

Has not the intemperate been censured of old, because in him that huge multiform monster is allowed to be too much at large?

Clearly.

And men are blamed for pride and sullenness, as when the growth and increase of the lion and serpent are out of proportion?

Yes.

And luxury and softness are blamed, because they relax and weaken this same creature, and make a coward of him?

Very true.

And is not a man reproached for flattery and meanness who subordinates the spirited animal to the unruly monster, and, for the sake of money, of which he can never have enough, habituates himself in the days of his youth to be trampled in the mud, and from being a lion to become a monkey?

True, he said.

And why are mean employments and handicraft arts a reproach? Only because they imply a natural weakness of the higher principle, and the individual is unable to control the creatures within him, but has to court them, and his only study is how to flatter them?

Such appears to be the reason. — *The Republic*, ii. 421.

Ignorance, legislative, destroying States. See *States, destroyed by ignorance*.

—— *Str.* When the foundation of politics is in the letter only and in custom, and knowledge is divorced from action, can we wonder, Socrates, at the miseries that there are, and always will be, in States? Any other art, built on such a foundation, would be utterly undermined, — there can be no doubt of that. Ought we not rather to wonder at the strength of the political bond? For States have endured all this, time out of mind, and yet some of them still remain and are not overthrown, though many of them, like ships foundering at sea, are perishing and have perished, and will hereafter perish, through the incapacity of their pilots and crews, who have the worst sort of ignorance of the highest truths — I mean to say, that they are wholly unacquainted with politics, of which, above all other sciences, they believe themselves to have acquired the most perfect knowledge. — *Statesman*, iii. 588.

Ignorance the cause of crimes.

—— A man may truly say that ignorance is a third cause of crimes. Ignorance, however, may be conveniently divided by the legislator into two sorts : There is simple ignorance, which is the source of lighter offenses, and double ignorance which is accompanied by conceit of wisdom ; and he who is under the influence of the latter, fancies that he knows all about matters of which he knows nothing. This second kind of ignorance, when possessed of power and strength, will be held by the legislator to be the source of great and monstrous crimes, but when attended with weakness will only result in the errors of children and old men ; and these he will treat as errors, and will make laws accordingly for those who commit them, which will be the mildest and most merciful of all laws. — *Laws*, iv. 376.

Images, sensible, some truths have not.

—— But people seem to forget that some things have sensible images, which may be easily shown, when any one desires to exhibit any of them or explain them to an inquirer, without any trouble or argument ; while the greatest and noblest truths have no outward image of themselves visible to man, which he who wishes to satisfy the longing soul of the inquirer can adapt to the eye of sense, and therefore we ought to practice reasoning ; for immaterial things, which are the highest and greatest, are shown only in thought and idea, and in no other way, and all that we are saying is said for the sake of them. Moreover, there is always less difficulty in fixing the mind on small matters than on great. — *Statesman*, iii. 571.

Imitation, a form of jest.

—— *Str.* Is there any more graceful or artistic form of jest than imitation ?

Theaet. Certainly not; and imitation is a very comprehensive term, which includes under one class the most diverse sorts of things.

Str. We know, of course, that he who professes by one art to make all things is really a painter, and by the painter's art makes resemblance of them which have the same name with them ; and he can deceive the less intelligent sort of young children, to whom he shows his pictures at a distance, into the belief that he has the absolute power of making whatever he likes.

Theaet. Certainly.

Str. And may there not be supposed to be an imitative art

of reasoning? Is there any impossibility in stealing the hearts of youths through their ears, when they are still at a distance from the truth, by showing them fictitious arguments, and making them think that they are true, and that the speaker is the wisest of men in all things?

Theaet. Yes; why should there not be another similar art?

Str. But as time goes on, and they advance in years, and come more into contact with realities, and have learnt by sad experience to see and feel the truth of things, are they not compelled to change many opinions which they had so that the great appears small to them, and the easy difficult, and all their seeming speculations are overturned by the facts of life?

Theaet. That is my view, as far as I can judge, although, at my age, I may be one of those who see things at a distance only.

Str. And the wish of all of us, who are your friends, is and always will be to bring you as near to the truth as we can without the sad reality. And now I should like you to tell me whether the Sophist is not visibly a magician and imitator of true being; or are we still disposed to think that he may have a true knowledge of the various matters about which he disputes?

Theaet. But how is that possible, Stranger? Is there any doubt, after what has been said, that he is to be located in one of the divisions of children's play?

Str. Then we must place him in the class of magicians and mimics.

Theaet. Certainly we must.

Str. And now our business is not to let the animal out, for we have got him in a sort of dialectical net, and there is one thing which he certainly will not escape.

Theaet. What is that?

Str. The inference that he is a juggler.

Theaet. Precisely my own opinion of him.

Str. Then, clearly, we ought as soon as possible to divide the image-making art, and go down into the net, and, if the Sophist does not run away from us, to seize him and deliver him over to reason, who is the lord of the hunt, and announce the capture of him; and if he creeps into the recesses of the imitative art, and secretes himself in one of them, to divide again and follow him up, until in some subsection of imitation he is caught. For our method of tackling each and all is one

which neither he nor any other creature will ever escape in triumph.
Theaet. That is good, and let us do as you say. — *Sophist,* iii. 469.

Imitation in painting.

—— All that is said by any of us can only be imitation and comparison. For if we consider how the works of the painter represent bodies divine and heavenly, and the different degrees of gratification with which the eye of the spectator receives them, we shall see that we are satisfied with the artist who is able in any degree to imitate the earth and its mountains, and the rivers, and the woods, and the universe, and the things that are and move therein, and further, that knowing nothing precise about such matters, we do not examine or analyze the painting ; all that is required is a sort of indistinct and deceptive mode of shadowing them forth. But when a person endeavors to paint the human form we are quick at finding out defects, and our familiar knowledge makes us severe judges of any one who does not render every point of similarity ; and we may observe the same thing to happen in discourse ; we are satisfied with a picture of divine and heavenly things which has very little likeness to them ; but we are more precise in our criticism of mortal and human things. — *Critias,* ii. 594.

Ath. And can he who does not know what the exact object is which is imitated, ever know whether the resemblance is truthfully executed? I mean, for example, whether a statue has the proportions of a body, and the true situation of the parts, what those proportions are, and how the parts fit into one another in due order ; also their colors and conformations, or whether this is all confused in the execution ? Do you think that any one can know about this, who does not know what the animal is which has been imitated?

Cle. Impossible.

Ath. But even if we know that the thing pictured or sculptured is a man, who has received at the hand of the artist all his proper parts and forms and colors, must we not also know whether the work is beautiful or in any respect deficient in beauty ?

Cle. If this were not required, Stranger, we should all of us be judges of beauty. — *Laws,* iv. 198.

Imitations becoming a second nature. See *Freedom,* etc.
Imitative art. See *Likeness-making.*

Imitative poetry.

—— Of the many excellences which I perceive in the order of our State, there is none which upon reflection pleases me better than the rule about poetry.

What rule?

The rule about rejecting imitative poetry, which certainly ought not to be received; as I see far more clearly now that the parts of the soul have been distinguished.

What do you mean?

Speaking in confidence, for I should not like to have my words repeated to the tragedians and the rest of the imitative tribe — but I do not mind saying to you that all poetical imitations are ruinous to the understanding of the hearers, and that the knowledge of what they are is the only antidote to them.

Explain the purport of your remark.

Well, I will tell you: although I have always from my earliest youth had an awe and love of Homer, which even now makes the words falter on my lips, for he is the great captain and teacher of the whole of that charming tragic company; but a man is not to be reverenced before the truth, and therefore I will speak out. — *The Republic*, ii. 425.

Imitators, Poets are.

—— It remains narrative both in the speeches which the poet recites and the passages between?

Quite true.

But when the poet speaks in the person of another, may we not say that he assimilates his style to that of the person who, as he informs you, is going to speak?

Certainly.

And this assimilation of himself to another either by the use of voice or gesture, is the imitation of the person whose character he assumes?

Of course.

Then in this case the narrative of the poet may be said to proceed by way of imitation?

Very true. — *The Republic*, ii. 216.

To me the wonder is rather that the poets, present as well as past, are no better — not that I mean to depreciate them, but every one can see that they are a tribe of imitators, and will imitate best and most easily the ways of life amid which they have been brought up; whereas that which is beyond the range of a man's education can hardly be imitated by him in action, and with still more difficulty in speech. — *Timaeus*, ii. 515.

Immortal, the world made.

—— In the fullness of time, when the change was to take place, and the earth-born race had all perished, and every soul had fallen into the earth and been sown her appointed number of times, the governor of the universe let the helm go, and retired to his place of view; and then Fate and innate desire reversed the motion of the world. Then, also, all the inferior deities who share the rule of the supreme power, being informed of what was happening, let go the parts of the world of which they were severally the guardians. And the world turning round with a sudden shock, having received an opposite impulse at both ends, was shaken by a mighty earthquake, producing a new destruction of all manner of animals. After a while the tumult and confusion and earthquake ceased, and the universal creature, once more at peace, attained to a calm, and settled down into his own orderly and accustomed course, having the charge and rule of himself and of all other creatures, and remembering and executing the instructions of the Father and Creator of the world, more particularly at first, but afterwards with less exactness. The reason of the falling off was the admixture of matter in the world; this was inherent in the primal nature, which was full of disorder, until attaining to the present cosmos or order. From God, the constructor, the world indeed received every good, but from a previous state came elements of violence and injustice, which, thence derived, first of all passed into the world and were transmitted to the animals. While the world was producing animals in unison with God, the evil was small, and great the good which worked within, but in the process of separation from him, when the world was let go, at first all proceeded well enough; but, as time went on, there was more and more forgetting, and the old discord again entered in and got the better, and burst forth; and at last small was the good, and great was the admixture of the elements of evil, and there was a danger of universal ruin of the world and the things in the world. Wherefore God, the orderer of all, in his tender care, seeing that the world was in great straits, and fearing that all might be dissolved in the storm, and go to the place of chaos and infinity, again seated himself at the helm; and reversing the elements which had fallen into dissolution and disorder when left to themselves in the previous cycle, he set them in order and restored them, and made the world imperishable and immortal. — *Statesman*, iii. 557.

Immortality of fame desired by men.

—— Marvel not then at the love which all men have of their offspring; for that universal love and interest is for the sake of immortality — I was astonished at her words and said: " Is this really true, O thou wise Diotima? " And she answered with all the authority of a Sophist: " Of that, Socrates, you may be assured; think only of the ambition of men, and you will wonder at the senselessness of their ways, unless you consider how they are stirred by the love of an immortality of fame. They are ready to run risks greater far than they would have run for their children, and to spend money and undergo any amount of toil, and even to die for the sake of leaving behind them a name which shall be eternal. Do you imagine that Alcestis would have died to save Admetus, or Achilles to avenge Patroclus, or your own Codrus in order to preserve the kingdom for his sons, if they had not imagined that the memory of their virtues, which is still retained among us, would be immortal? Nay," she said, " I am persuaded that all men do all things and the better they are the more they do them, in hope of the glorious fame of immortal virtue; for they desire the immortal." — *The Symposium*, i. 500.

Immortality in time.

—— The human race naturally partakes of immortality, of which all men have the greatest desire implanted in them; for the desire of every man that he may become famous, and not lie in the grave without a name, is only the love of continuance. Now, mankind are coeval with all time, and are ever following, and will ever follow, the course of time; and so they are immortal, inasmuch as they leave children behind them, and partake of immortality in the unity of generation. And for a man voluntarily to deprive himself of this gift, as he deliberately does who will not have a wife or children, is impiety. — *Laws*, iv. 249.

Immortality of the soul. See *Soul*.

Immortality of God. See *God unchangeable*.

Impartiality not the same as equality. See *Equality not the same*, etc.

Impassiveness of the Gods. See *Gods, impassiveness of the*.

Impiety, punishment of.

—— Now, men fall into impiety from three causes, which have been already mentioned, and from each of these causes arise two sorts of impiety, in all six, requiring judicial decision, but differing greatly in their degrees of guilt. For he who does not believe in the Gods, and yet has a righteous nature, hates the wicked and dislikes and refuses to do injustice, and avoids unrighteous men, and loves the righteous. But they who, besides believing that the world is devoid of Gods, are intemperate, and have at the same time good memories and quick wits, are worse; although both of them are unbelievers, much less injury is done by the one than by the other. The one may talk loosely about the Gods and about sacrifices and oaths, and perhaps by laughing at other men he may make them like himself, if he be not punished. But the other unbeliever, who has ability, is full of stratagem and deceit — men of this class are prophets and jugglers of all kinds, and out of their ranks sometimes come tyrants, and demagogues, and generals, and hierophants of private mysteries and the ingenuities of so-called Sophists. There are many kinds of unbelievers, but two only for whom legislation is required; one the hypocritical sort, whose crime is deserving of death many times over, while the others need only bonds and admonition. — *Laws*, iv. 421.

Impure and pure soul.

—— Are we to suppose that the soul, which is invisible, in passing to the true Hades, which like her is invisible, and pure, and noble, and on her way to the good and wise God, whither, if God will, my soul is also soon to go, — that the soul, I repeat, if this be her nature and origin, is blown away and perishes immediately on quitting the body, as the many say? That can never be, my dear Simmias and Cebes. The truth rather is, that the soul which is pure at departing draws after her no bodily taint, having never voluntarily had connection with the body, which she is ever avoiding, herself gathered into herself; (for such abstraction has been the study of her life). And what does this mean but that she has been a true disciple of philosophy, and has practiced how to die cheerfully? And is not philosophy the practice of death?

Certainly.

That soul, I say, herself invisible, departs to the invisible world, — to the divine and immortal and rational; thither arriving, she is secure of bliss and is released from the error and folly of men, their fears and wild passions and all other human ills, and forever dwells, as they say of the initiated, in company with the Gods. Is not this true, Cebes?

Yes, said Cebes, beyond a doubt.

But the soul which has been polluted, and is impure at the time of her departure, and is the companion and servant of the body always, and is in love with and fascinated by the body and by the desires and pleasures of the body, until she is led to believe that the truth only exists in a bodily form, which a man may touch and see and taste and use for the purposes of his lusts, — the soul, I mean, accustomed to hate and fear and avoid the intellectual principle, which to the bodily eye is dark and invisible, and can be attained only by philosophy; do you suppose that such a soul as this will depart pure and unalloyed?

That is impossible, he replied.

She is held fast by the corporeal, which the continual association and constant care of the body have wrought in her nature.

Very true.

And this corporeal element, my friend, is heavy and weighty, and earthy, and is that element of sight by which such a soul is depressed and dragged down again into the visible world, because she is afraid of the invisible and of the world below. — *Phaedo*, i. 409.

Impure and pure, gifts of the.

—— *Ath.* What life is agreeable to God, and becoming in his followers? One only according to an old saying, that "like agrees with like, with measure measure," but things which have no measure agree neither with themselves nor with the things which have measure. Now, God is the measure of all things, in a sense far higher than any man, as they say, can ever hope to be. And he who would be dear to God must, as far as is possible, be like him and such as he is. Wherefore the temperate man is the friend of God, for he is like him; and the intemperate man is unlike him; and different from him, and unjust. And the same holds of other things, and this is the conclusion, which is also the noblest and truest of all sayings: that for the good man to offer sacrifice to the Gods, and hold converse with them by means of prayers and offerings and every kind of service, is the noblest and best of all things, and also the most conducive to a happy life, and very fit and meet. But with the bad man, the opposite of this holds; for the bad man has an impure soul, whereas the good is pure; and from one who is polluted, neither a good man nor God is right in receiving gifts. And therefore the unholy waste their much service upon the Gods, which, when offered by any holy man, is always accepted of them. — *Laws*, iv. 244.

Individual; the State more to be valued than the. See *Citizen, obligation of the.*

Individual, the State greater than the.

—— Justice, which is the subject of our inquiry, is, as you know, sometimes spoken of as the virtue of an individual, and sometimes as the virtue of a State.

True, he replied.

And is not a State larger than an individual?

It is.

Then in the larger the quantity of justice will be larger and more easily discernible. I propose, therefore, that we inquire into the nature of justice and injustice as appearing in the State first, and secondly in the individual, proceeding from the greater to the lesser and comparing them.

That, he said, is an excellent proposal.

And suppose we imagine the State as in a process of creation, and then we shall see the justice and injustice of the State in process of creation also.

Very likely.

When the State is completed there may be a hope that the object of our search will be more easily discovered.

Yes, more easily.

And shall we make the attempt? I said; although I cannot promise you that the task will be a light one. Reflect, therefore.

I have reflected, said Adeimantus, and am anxious that you should proceed.

A State, I said, arises, as I conceive, out of the needs of mankind; no one is self-sufficing, but all of us have many wants. Can any other origin of a State be imagined?

There can be no other.

Then, as we have many wants, and many persons are needed to supply them, one takes a helper for one purpose and another for another: and when these helpers and partners are gathered together in one habitation, the body of inhabitants is termed a State.

True, he said.

And they exchange with one another, and one gives, and another receives, under the idea that the exchange will be for their good.

Very true.

Then, I said, let us begin and create a State; and yet the true creator is necessity, who is the mother of our invention. — *The Republic*, ii. 190.

Individuality and unity.

―― *Pro.* Do you mean when a person says that I, Protarchus, am by nature one and also many, dividing the single " me " in many " me's," which he distinguishes and opposes as great and small, light and heavy, and in ten thousand other ways?

Soc. Those, Protarchus, are the common and acknowledged paradoxes about the one and many, which I may say that everybody has by this time agreed to dismiss as childish and obvious and detrimental to the true course of thought; and no more favor is shown to that other puzzle, in which a person proves the members and parts of anything to be divided, and then confessing that they are all one, says laughingly in disproof of his own words, — why, here is a miracle, the one is many and infinite, and the many are only one.

Pro. But what, Socrates, are those other marvels which, as you imply, have not yet become common and acknowledged, relating to the same principle?

Soc. When, my boy, the one does not belong to the class of things that are born and perish, as in the instances which we were giving, for in those cases, and when unity is of this concrete nature, there is, as I was saying, a universal consent that no refutation is needed; but when the assertion is made that man is one, or ox is one, or beauty one, or the good one, then the interest which attaches to these and similar unities, and the attempt which is made to divide them, — gives birth to a controversy.

Pro. Of what nature?

Soc. In the first place, as to whether these unities have a real existence; and then how each individual unity, being always the same, and incapable either of generation or of destruction, but retaining a permanent individuality, can be conceived either as dispersed and multiplied in the infinity of the world of generation, or as still entire and yet derived from itself, which latter

would seem to be the greatest impossibility of all, for how can one and the same thing be at the same time in one and in many things? These, Protarchus, are the real difficulties, and this is the one and many to which they relate; they are the source of great perplexity if ill decided, and the right determination of them is very helpful. — *Philebus*, iii. 149.
Indivisible essence. See *Essence*.
Inequality and Equality. See *Equality*.
Infinite and finite. See *Finite*.
Inheritances and heirships.

—— I would not have any one fond of heaping up riches for the sake of his children, in order that he may leave them as rich as possible. For the possession of great wealth is of no use, either to them or to the State. The condition of youth which is free from flattery, and at the same time not in need of the necessaries of life, is the best and most harmonious of all, being in accord and agreement with our nature, and making life to be most entirely free from sorrow. Let parents, then, bequeath to their children, not riches, but the spirit of reverence. We, indeed, fancy that they will inherit reverence from us, if we rebuke them when they show a want of reverence. But this quality is not really imparted to them by the present style of admonition, which only tells them that the young ought always to be reverential. A sensible legislator will rather exhort the elders to reverence the younger, and above all to take heed that no young man sees or hears him doing or saying anything base; for where old men have no shame, there young men will most certainly be devoid of reverence. — *Laws*, iv. 254.
Iniquity, concealment of. See *Concealment*.
Injustice.

—— Consider further, most foolish Socrates, that the just is always a loser in comparison with the unjust. First of all, in private contracts: wherever the unjust is the partner of the just you will find the unjust man has always more and the just less. Next, in their dealings with the State: when there is an income-tax, the just man will pay more and the unjust less on the same amount of income; and when there is anything to be received the one gains nothing and the other much. Observe also that when they come into office, there is the just man neglecting his affairs and perhaps suffering other losses, but he will not compensate himself out of the public purse because he is just: moreover he is hated by his friends and acquaintance for refusing to serve them in unlawful ways. Now all this is reversed in the case of the unjust man. I am speaking, as before, of injustice on a large scale in which the advantage of the unjust is most apparent, and my meaning will be most clearly seen if we turn to that highest form of injustice in which the criminal is the happiest of men, as the sufferers or those who refuse to do injustice are the most miserable—I mean tyranny, which by fraud and force takes away the property of others, not retail but wholesale; comprehending in one, things sacred as well as profane, private and public; for any one of which acts of wrong, if he were detected perpetrating them singly, he would be punished and incur great dishonor; since they who are guilty of any of these crimes in single instances are called robbers of temples, and man-stealers and burglars and swindlers and thieves. But when a man besides taking away the money of the citizens has made slaves of them, then, instead of these dishonorable names, he is called happy and blessed, not only by the citizens but by all who hear of his having achieved the consummation of injustice. For injustice is censured because the censurers are afraid of suffering, and not from any fear which they have of doing injustice. And thus, as I have shown, Socrates, injustice, when on a sufficient scale, has more strength and freedom and mastery than justice; and, as I said at first, justice is the interest of the stronger, whereas injustice is a man's own profit and interest. — *The Republic*, ii. 165.

Injustice, doing and suffering.

—— *Pol.* At any rate you will allow that he who is unjustly put to death is wretched, and to be pitied?

Soc. Not so much, Polus, as he who kills him, and not so much as he who is justly killed.

Pol. How can that be, Socrates?

Soc. That may very well be, inasmuch as doing injustice is the greatest of evils.

Pol. But is that the greatest? Is not suffering injustice a greater evil?

Soc. Certainly not.

Pol. Then would you rather suffer than do injustice?

Soc. I should not like either, but if I must choose between them, I would rather suffer than do. — *Gorgias*, iii. 55.

Injustice, penalty of.

—— *Soc.* The unrighteous man, or the sayer and doer of unholy things, had far better not yield to the illusion that his roguery is clever; for men glory in their shame — they fancy that they hear others saying of them, "These are not mere good-for-nothing persons, burdens of the earth, but such as men should be who mean to dwell safely in a State." Let us tell them that they are all the more truly what they do not know that they are; for they do not know the penalty of injustice, which above all things they ought to know — not stripes and death, as they suppose, which evil-doers often escape, but a penalty which cannot be escaped.

Theod. What is that?

Soc. There are two patterns eternally set before them in nature: the one blessed and divine, the other godless and wretched; and they do not see, in their utter folly and infatuation, that they are growing like the one and unlike the other, by reason of their evil deeds; and the penalty is, that they lead a life answering to the pattern which they resemble. And if we tell them that unless they depart from their cunning, the place of innocence will not receive them after death; and that here on earth they will live ever in the likeness of their own evil selves, and with evil friends — when they hear this, they in their superior cunning will seem to be listening to fools.

Theod. Very true, Socrates. — *Theaetetus,* iii. 379.

Injustice and envy. See *Envy.*

Injustice, what is called.

—— I can define to you clearly, and without ambiguity, what I mean by the just and unjust, according to my notion of them: When anger and fear, and pleasure and pain, and jealousies and desires, tyrannize over the soul, whether they do any harm or not — I call them all injustice. But when the opinion of the best, whatever States or individuals may suppose that to be, has dominion in the soul and orders the life of every man, even if it be sometimes mistaken, yet what is done in accordance therewith, and the principle in individuals which obeys this rule, and is best for the whole life of man, is to be called just; although the action, done in error, is thought by the multitude to be involuntary injustice. — *Laws,* iv. 377.

Injustice. See *Wrong-doing.*

Inner voice, the.

—— *Soc.* This is the voice which I seem to hear murmuring in my ears, like the sound of the flute in the ears of the mystic; that voice, I say, is humming in my ears, and prevents me from hearing any other. And I know that anything more which you may say will be vain. Yet speak, if you have anything to say.

Cr. I have nothing to say, Socrates.

Soc. Leave me then to follow whithersoever God leads. — *Crito,* i. 359.

Inner life, harmony of the. See *Harmony of the inner man.*
Innovations, jests no bar to..

—— I should rather expect, I said, that several of our proposals, if they are carried out, being unusual, may appear ridiculous.

No doubt of it.

Yes, and the most ridiculous thing of all will be the sight of women naked in the palaestra, exercising with the men, especially when they get old ; they certainly will not be a vision of beauty any more than the wrinkled old men, who have anything but an agreeable appearance when they take to gymnastics ; this, however, does not deter them.

Yes, indeed, he said : according to present notions the proposal would appear ridiculous.

But then, I said, as we have determined to speak our minds, we must not fear the jests of the wits which will be directed against this sort of innovation ; how they will talk of women's attainments in music as well as in gymnastic, and above all about their wearing armor and riding upon horseback !

Very true, he replied.

Yet having begun, we must go on and attack the difficulty ; at the same time begging of these gentlemen for once in their life to be serious. Not long ago, as we shall remind them, the Greeks were of the opinion, which is still generally received among the barbarians, that the sight of a naked man was ridiculous and improper; and when first the Cretans and then the Lacedaemonians introduced naked exercises, the wits of that day might have ridiculed them equally.

No doubt.

But when experience showed that to let all things be uncovered was far better than to cover them up, and the ludicrous effect to the outward eye vanished before the approval of reason, then the man was seen to be a fool who laughs or directs the shafts of his ridicule at any other sight but that of folly and vice, or seriously inclines to measure the beautiful by any other standard but that of the good.

Very true, he replied. — *The Republic,* ii. 276.

Innovations forbidden in Egypt.

—— *Cle.* And what are the laws about music and dancing?

Ath. You will wonder when I tell you : Long ago they appeared to have recognized the very principle of which we are now speaking — that their young citizens must be habituated to forms and strains of virtue. These they fixed and exhibited the patterns of them in their temples ; and no painter or artist is allowed to innovate upon them, or to leave the traditional forms and invent new ones. To this day, no alteration is allowed either in these arts, or in music at all. And you will find that their works of art are painted or moulded in the same forms which they had ten thousand years ago; this is literally true and no exaggeration, — their ancient paintings and sculptures are not a whit better or worse than the work of to-day, but are made with just the same skill.

Cle. How extraordinary !

Ath. I should rather say, how wise and worthy of a great legislator ! I know that other things in Egypt are not so good. But what I am telling you about music is true and deserving of consideration, because showing that a lawgiver may institute melodies which have a natural truth and correctness without any fear of failure. To do this, however, must be the work of God, or of a divine person; in Egypt they have a tradition that their ancient chants are the composition of the Goddess Isis. And therefore, as I was saying, if a person can only find in any way the natural melodies, he might confidently embody them in a fixed and legal form. For the love of novelty which arises out of pleasure in the new, and weariness of the old, has not strength enough to vitiate the consecrated song and dance, under the plea that they have become antiquated. At any rate they are far from being antiquated in Egypt. — *Laws*, iv. 186.

Inordinate ambition.

—— My love, Alcibiades, which I hardly like to confess, would long ago have passed away, as I flatter myself, if I saw you loving your good things, or thinking that you ought to live in the enjoyment of them. But I know that you entertain other thoughts ; and I will prove to you that I have always had my eye on you by declaring them. Suppose that at this moment some God came to you and said : O Alcibiades, will you live as you are, or die in an instant if you are forbidden to make any further acquisition ? — I verily believe that you would choose death. And I will tell you the hope in which you are at present living : Before many days have elapsed, you think that you will come before the Athenian assembly, and will try to prove to them that you are more worthy of honor than Pericles, or any other man that ever lived, and having proved this, you will have the greatest power in the State ; and when you have got the greatest power among us, you will go on to other Hellenic states, and not only to Hellenes, but to all the barbarians who inhabit the same continent with us. And if the God were then to say to you again: Here in Europe is to be your seat of empire, and you must not cross over into Asia or meddle with Asiatic affairs, I do not believe that you would choose to live upon these terms ; but the world, as I may say, must be filled with your power and name — no man less than Cyrus and Xerxes is of any account with you. — *Alcibiades I.* iv. 516.

Inquiry, the spirit of.

—— *Soc.* Some things I have said of which I am not altogether confident. But that we shall be better and braver and less helpless if we think that we ought to inquire, than we should have been if we indulged in the idle fancy that there was no knowing and no use in searching after what we do not know : — that is a theme upon which I am ready to fight, in word and deed, to the utmost of my power.

Men. That again, Socrates, appears to me to be well said. *Meno*, i. 262.

Inquiry forbidden as ruinous to Arts. See *Arts, inquiry ruinous to.*

Insane, two kinds of the.

—— *Soc.* There were two kinds of madness ; one produced by human infirmity, the other by a divine release from the ordinary ways of men.

Phaedr. True.

Soc. The divine madness was subdivided into four kinds, prophetic, initiatory, poetic, erotic, having four Gods presiding over them ; the first was the inspiration of Apollo, the second that of Dionysus, the third that of the Muses, the fourth that of Aphrodite and Eros. In the description of the last kind of madness, which was also the best, being a sort of figure of love, we introduced a tolerably credible and possibly true, though partly erring myth, which was also a hymn in honor of Eros, who is your lord and also mine, Phaedrus, and the guardian of fair children, and to him we sung the hymn in measured and solemn strain. — *Phaedrus*, i. 570.

Inspiration of the poet. See *Divine power*.
Inspiration of the Statesman. See *Statesman, called divine*.
Instability of youth. See *Changeableness*.
Instinctive divining of truth.
—— *Soc.* They say that what the school of Philebus calls pleasures are all of them only avoidances of pain.
Pro. And would you, Socrates, have us agree with them?
Soc. Why, no, I would rather use them as a sort of diviners, who are enabled to divine the truth, not by any rules of art, but by an instinctive repugnance and extreme detestation which a noble nature has of the power of pleasure, in which they think that there is nothing sound, and whose seductive influence is declared by them to be witchcraft, and not pleasure. This is the use which you may make of them; you shall consider the various grounds of their dislike, and then you shall hear from me what I deem to be true pleasures; and when the nature of pleasures has been examined from both points of view, we will bring her up for judgment.
Pro. True. — *Philebus*, iii. 183.
Intelligence and knowledge.
—— When reason, which works with equal truth both in the circle of the diverse and of the same, — in the sphere of the self-moved in voiceless silence moving, — when reason, I say, is hovering around the sensible world, and the circle of the diverse also moving truly imparts the imitations of sense to the whole soul, then arise fixed and true opinions and beliefs. But when reason is dwelling in the rational, and the circle of the same moving smoothly indicates this, then intelligence and knowledge are of necessity perfected. And if any one affirms that in which these are found to be other than the soul, he will say the very opposite of the truth. — *Timaeus*, ii. 530.
Intelligence, pleasures of the.
—— But since experience and wisdom and reason are the judges, the inference of course is, that the truest pleasures are those which are approved by the lover of wisdom and reason. And so we arrive at the result, that the pleasure of the intelligent part of the soul is the pleasantest of the three, and that he of us in whom this is the ruling principle has the pleasantest life?
Unquestionably, he said, the wise man speaks with authority when he approves of his own life. — *The Republic*, ii. 413.

Intemperance and temperance.

—— *Soc.* I wish, my good friend, that you would tell me, once for all, whom you affirm to be the better and superior, and in what they are better?

Cal. I have already told you that I mean those who are wise and courageous in the administration of a State; they ought to be the rulers of their States, and justice consists in their having more than their subjects.

Soc. But whether rulers or subjects, will they or will they not have more than themselves, my friend?

Cal. How do you mean?

Soc. I mean that every man is his own ruler; but perhaps you think that there is no necessity for him to rule himself; he is only required to rule others?

Cal. What do you mean by his "ruling over himself"?

Soc. A simple thing enough; just what is commonly said, that a man should be temperate and master of himself, and ruler of his own pleasures and passions.

Cal. What innocence! you mean those fools, — the temperate?

Soc. Certainly: any one may know that to be my meaning.

Cal. Quite so, Socrates; and they are really fools — for how can a man be happy who is the servant of anything? On the contrary, I plainly assert, that he who would truly live ought to allow his desires to wax to the uttermost, and not to chastise them; but when they have grown to their greatest he should have courage and intelligence to minister to them and to satisfy all his longings. And this I affirm to be natural justice and nobility. To this the many cannot attain, and they blame the strong man, because they are ashamed of their own weakness, which they desire to conceal, and hence they say that intemperance is base. As I was saying before, they enslave the nobler natures, and being unable to satisfy their pleasures, they praise temperance and justice out of cowardice. For if a man had been originally the son of a king, or had a nature capable of acquiring an empire or a tyranny or exclusive power, what could be more truly base or evil than temperance — to a man like him, I say, who might freely be enjoying every good, and has no one to hinder him, and yet has admitted custom and reason and the opinion of other men to be lord over him? — must not he be in a miserable plight whom the reputation of justice and temperance hinders ·from giving more to his friends than to his enemies, even though he be a ruler in his city? Nay, Socrates, for you profess to be a votary of the truth, and the truth is that luxury and intemperance and license, if they are duly supported, are happiness and virtue; all the rest is a mere bauble, custom contrary to nature, fond inventions of men nothing worth. — *Gorgias*, iii. 80.

Intemperate and temperate life. See *Temperate*, etc.

Intermediate state of pleasure and pain.

—— *Soc.* Let me make a further observation; the argument appears to me to imply that there is a kind of life which consists in these affections.

Pro. Of what affections, and of what kind of life, are you speaking?

Soc. I am speaking of emptiness and replenishment, and all that relates to the preservation and destruction of living beings, and of the alternations of pain and joy which accompany them in their transitions.

Pro. True.

Soc. And what would you say of the kind of life which is intermediate between them?

Pro. What do you mean by "intermediate?"

Soc. I mean when a person is in actual suffering and yet remembers the pleasures which, if they would only come, would relieve him; but as yet he has them not. May we not say of him that he is in an intermediate state?

Pro. Certainly.

Soc. Would you say that he was in pain or in pleasure?

Pro. Nay I should say that he has two pains; in his body there is the actual experience of pain, and in his soul longing and expectation.

Soc. What do you mean, Protarchus, by the two pains? May not a man who is empty have at one time a sure hope of being filled, and at other times be quite in despair?

Pro. Very true.

Soc. And has he not the pleasure of memory when he is hoping to be filled, and yet in that he is empty is he not at the same time in pain?

Pro. Certainly.

Soc. Then man and the other animals have at one time both pleasure and pain?

Pro. I suppose so. — *Philebus*, iii. 172.

Intoxication. See *Drunkenness.*

Inventors, not good judges.

—— O most ingenious Theuth, he who has the gift of invention is not always the best judge of the utility or inutility of his own inventions to the users of them. And in this instance a paternal love of your own child has led you to say what is not the fact; for this invention of yours will create forgetfulness in the learners' souls, because they will not use their memories; they will trust to the external written characters and not remember of themselves. You have found a specific, not for memory but for reminiscence, and you give your disciples only the pretense of wisdom; they will be hearers of many things and will have learned nothing; they will appear to be omniscient and will generally know nothing; they will be tiresome company, having the show of wisdom without the reality. — *Phaedrus,* i. 580.

Iolaus. See *Heracles.*

Irritability of musicians.

—— Did you never observe, I said, the effect on the mind of exclusive devotion to gymnastic, or the opposite effect of an exclusive devotion to music?

In what way shown? he said.

In producing a temper of hardness and ferocity, or again of softness and effeminacy, I replied.

Yes, he said, I am quite aware that your mere athlete becomes too much of a savage, and that the musician is melted and softened beyond what is good for him. . . . .

And, when a man allows music to play and pour over his soul through the funnel of his ears, those sweet and soft and melancholy airs of which we were just now speaking, and his whole life is passed in warbling and the delights of song; in the first stage of the process the passion or spirit which is in him is tempered like iron, and made useful, instead of brittle and useless. But, if he carries on the softening process, in the next stage he begins to melt and waste, until he has wasted away his spirit and cut out the sinews of his soul; and he makes a feeble warrior.

Very true.

If the element of spirit is naturally weak in him this is soon accomplished, but if he have a good deal, then the power of music weakening the spirit renders him excitable; he soon flames up, and is speedily extinguished; instead of having

spirit he becomes irritable and violent and very discontented.
— *The Republic*, ii. 235.

Jest, imitation a form of. See *Imitation*.
Jests, no bar to innovations. See *Innovations*.
Judge, the virtuous.

—— But with the judge the case is different; he governs mind by mind, and he ought not therefore to have been reared among vicious minds, and to have associated with them from youth upwards, in order that, having gone through the whole calendar of crime, he may quickly infer the crimes of others, like their diseases, from the knowledge of himself; but the honorable mind which is to form a healthy judgment ought rather to have had no experience or contamination of evil habits when young. And this is the reason why in youth good men often appear to be simple, and are easily practiced upon by the evil, because they have no examples of what evil is in their own souls.

Yes, he said, that very often happens with them.

Therefore, I said, the judge should not be young; he should have learned to know evil, not from his own soul, but from late and long observation of the nature of evil in others; knowledge, and not his own experience, should be his guide.

Yes, he said, that is the ideal of a judge.

Yes, I replied, and he will be a good man (which is my answer); for he is good whose soul is good. Whereas your cunning and suspicious character, who has committed many crimes, and fancies himself to be a master in wickedness, when he is among men who are like himself, is wonderful in his precautions against others, because he judges of them by himself; but when he gets into the company of men of virtue, who have the experience of age, he appears to be a fool again, owing to his unseasonable suspicion; he cannot recognize an honest man, because he has nothing in himself which will tell him what an honest man is like; at the same time, as the bad are more numerous than the good, and he meets with them oftener, he thinks himself, and others think him, rather wise than foolish.

Most true, he said.

Then the good and wise judge whom we are seeking is not this man; the other is better suited to us; for vice cannot know virtue, but a virtuous nature, educated by time, will acquire a knowledge both of virtue and vice; the virtuous, and not the vicious man, has wisdom, in my opinion.

And in mine also. — *The Republic*, ii. 233.

Judge, the reconciling.   See *Reconciling*.

Judge, the righteous.

―― *Str.* Once more let us consider the nature of the righteous judge.

Y. Soc. Very good.

Str. Does he do anything but decide the dealings of men with one another to be just or unjust in accordance with the standard which he receives from the king and legislator, — showing his own peculiar virtue only in this, that he is not perverted by gifts, or fears, or pity, or any sort of love or hatred, into deciding the suits of men with one another contrary to the appointment of the legislator?

Y. Soc. No; his office is such as you describe.

Str. Then the inference is that the power of the judge is not royal, but only the power of a guardian of the law which ministers to the royal power?

Y. Soc. True. — *Statesman*, iii. 591.

Judges, true.

―― The judges will require virtue — they must possess wisdom and also courage; for the true judge ought not to learn from the theatre, nor ought he to be panic-stricken at the clamor of the many and his own incapacity; nor again, knowing the truth, ought he through cowardice and unmanliness carelessly to deliver a lying judgment, out of the very same lips which have just appealed to the Gods before he judged. He is sitting, not as the disciple of the theatre, but, in his proper place, as their instructor, and he ought to be the enemy of all pandering to the pleasure of the spectators. — *Laws*, iv. 188.

Judges and true opinion.

―― *Soc.* When, therefore, judges are justly persuaded about matters which you can know only by seeing them, and not in any other way, and when thus judging of them from report they attain a true opinion about them, they judge without knowledge, and yet are rightly persuaded, if they have judged well.

Theaet. Certainly.

Soc. And yet, O my friend, if true opinion in law courts and knowledge are the same, the perfect judge could not have judged rightly without knowledge; and therefore I must infer that they are not the same. — *Theaetetus*, iii. 408.

Judges, three kinds of.

—— *Ath.* Now, which would be the better judge, — one who destroyed the bad, and let the good govern themselves; or one who, while allowing the good to govern, let the bad live, and made them voluntarily submit? Or, lastly, there might be a third excellent judge, who, finding the family distracted, not only did not destroy any one, but reconciled them to one another forever after, and gave them laws which they mutually observed, and was able to keep them friends.

Cle. The last would be by far the best sort of judge and legislator. — *Laws*, iv. 158.

Just man, Christ unconsciously described as the, in contrast with the unjust.

—— I say that in the perfectly unjust man we must assume the most perfect injustice; there is to be no deduction, and we must allow him, while doing the most unjust acts, to have gained the greatest reputation for justice. If he has taken a false step he must be able to retrieve himself, being one who can speak with effect, if any of his deeds come to light, and force his way where force is required, and having gifts of courage and strength, and command of money and friends. And at his side let us place the just man in his nobleness and simplicity, being, as Aeschylus says, and not seeming. There must be no seeming, for if he seem to be just he will be honored and rewarded, and then we shall not know whether he is just for the sake of justice or for the sake of honors and rewards; therefore, let him be clothed in justice only, and have no other covering; and he must be imagined in a state of life very different from that of the last. Let him be the best of men, and be esteemed to be the worst; then let us see whether his virtue is proof against infamy and its consequences. And let him continue thus to the hour of death; being just, and seeming to be unjust. Then when both have reached the uttermost extreme, the one of justice and the other of injustice, let judgment be given which of them is the happier of the two. — *The Republic*, ii. 183.

Just man, the.

—— Justice was the reality and was concerned not with the outward man, but with the inward, which is the true self and concernment of man; for the just man does not permit the several elements within him to interfere with one another, or any of them to do the work of others, but he sets in order his own inner life, and is his own master, and at peace with himself; and when he has bound together the three principles within him, which may be compared to the higher, lower, and middle notes of the scale, and the intermediate intervals — when he has bound together all these, and is no longer many, but has become one entirely temperate and perfectly adjusted nature, then he will begin to act, if he has to act, whether in a matter of property, or in the treatment of the body, or some affair of politics or private business; in all which cases he will think and call that which preserves and coöperates with this harmonious condition, just and good action, and the knowledge which presides over it wisdom; and that which at any time destroys this condition, he will call unjust action, and the opinion which presides over it ignorance.

You have said the precise truth, Socrates.

Very good; and if we were to affirm that we had discovered the just man and the just State, and the place of justice in each of them, we should not be telling a falsehood?

Most certainly not. — *The Republic*, ii. 270.

Just and wise soul, the.

—— *Str.* Do they not say that one soul is just, and another unjust, and that one soul is wise, and another foolish?

Theaet. Certainly.

Str. And that the just and wise soul becomes just and wise by the possession and presence of justice, and the opposite by the opposite?

Theaet. Yes, they do.

Str. But surely that which may be present or may be absent will be admitted by them to exist?

Theaet. Certainly.

Str. And allowing that these qualities of virtue, justice, and the like all exist, as well as the soul in which they inhere, do they affirm any of them to be visible and tangible, or are they all invisible?

Theqet. None of them surely are invisible.

Str. And would they say that they are corporeal?

Theaet. They would distinguish; the soul would be said by them to have a body; but as to the other qualities of justice, wisdom, and the like, about which you asked, they would not venture either to deny their existence, or to maintain that they were all corporeal. — *Sophist*, iii. 484.

Just judge. See *Judge, righteous.*

—— *Ath.* The view which identifies the pleasant and the just and the good and the noble has an excellent moral and religious tendency. And the opposite view is most at variance with the designs of the legislator, and, in his opinion, infamous; for no one, if he can help, will be persuaded to do that which gives him more pain than pleasure. But as distant prospects are apt to be dimly seen, especially in childhood, the legislator will try to purge away the darkness and exhibit the truth; he will persuade the citizens, in some way or other, by customs and praises and words, that just and unjust are opposed to one another as shadow and light, and that, seen from the point of view of a man's own evil and injustice, the unjust appears pleasant and the just unpleasant; but that, seen from the just man's point of view, the very opposite is the appearance which they wear.— *Laws,* iv. 192.

Justice resembling holiness. See *Holiness.*
Justice among thieves. See *Honor among,* etc.
Justice and temperance in the State.

—— Two virtues remain to be discovered in the State, — first, temperance, and then justice, which is the great object of our search.

Very true.

Now, can we find justice without troubling ourselves about temperance?

I do not know how that can be accomplished, he said, nor do I desire that justice should be brought to light and temperance lost sight of; and therefore I wish that you would do me the favor of considering temperance first.

Certainly, I replied, I cannot be wrong in granting you a favor.

Then do as I ask, he said.

Yes, I replied, I will; — and as far as I can at present see, the virtue of temperance has more of the nature of symphony and harmony than the preceding.

How so? he asked.

Temperance, I replied, is the ordering or controlling of certain pleasures and desires; this is implied in the saying of "a man being his own master;" and there are other traces of the same notion.

No doubt, he said.— *The Republic,* ii. 255.

Justice conducing to the excellence of the State. See *State, what most conduces*, etc.

Justice, what is it.

—— I said, when we first began, ages ago, there was justice tumbling about our feet, and we, fools that we were, failed to see her, like people who go about looking for what they have in their hands: and that was the way with us; we looked away into the far distance, and this I suspect was the reason why we never saw her.

What do you mean?

I mean to say that we, having been long speaking and hearing of her, failed to recognize her.

I get impatient at the length of your exordium.

Well, then, tell me, I said, whether I am right or not; you remember the original principle of which we spoke at the foundation of the State, that every man, as we often insisted, should practice one thing only, that being the thing to which his nature was most perfectly adapted; now justice is this principle or a part of it.

Yes, we often said that one man should do one thing only.

Further, we affirmed that justice was doing one's own business, and not being a busybody; we said so again and again, and many others have said the same.

Yes, we said so.

Then this doing in a certain way one's own business may be assumed to be justice. Do you know why?

I do not, and should like to be told.

Because I think that this alone remains in the State when the other virtues of temperance and courage and wisdom are abstracted; and this is the ultimate cause and condition of the existence of all of them, and while remaining in them is also their preservative; and we were saying that if the three were discovered by us, justice would be the fourth or remaining one.

That follows of necessity. — *The Republic*, ii. 258.

Justice, approximate.

—— Let me begin by reminding you that we found our way hither in the search after justice and injustice.

True, he replied; but what of this?

I was only going to ask whether, if we have discovered them, we are to require that the just man should in nothing fail of absolute justice; or may we be satisfied with an approximation, and the attainment of a higher degree of justice than is to be found in other men? The approximation will be enough.

And we inquired into the nature of absolute justice and into the character of the perfectly just, and the possibility of his existence, and into injustice and the perfectly unjust, only that we might have an ideal. We were to look at them in order that we might judge of our own happiness and unhappiness according to the standard which they exhibited and the degree in which we resembled them, not with any view of showing that they could exist in fact.

True, he said. — *The Republic*, ii. 299.

Justice, natural.

—— *Soc.* Tell me what you and Pindar mean by natural justice: do you not mean that the superior should take the property of the inferior by force; that the better should rule the worse, the noble have more than the mean? Am I not right in my recollection?

Cal. Yes; that is what I was saying, and what I still maintain.

Soc. And do you mean by the better the same as the superior? for I could not make out what you were saying at the time — whether you meant by the superior the stronger, and that the weaker must obey the stronger, as you seemed to imply when you said that great cities attack small ones in accordance with natural right, because they are superior and stronger, as though the superior and stronger and better were the same; or whether the better may be also the inferior and weaker, and the superior the worse, or whether better is to be defined in the same way as superior: — this is the point which I want to have clearly explained. Are the superior and better and stronger the same or different?

Cal. Well; I say unequivocally that they are the same. — *Gorgias*, iii. 76.

Justice and Virtue, rewards of.

—— We have fulfilled our obligations to the argument, putting aside the rewards and glories of justice, such as you were saying that Homer and Hesiod introduced; and justice in her own nature has been shown to be best for the soul in her nature: let her do what is just, whether she have the ring of Gyges or not, and besides the ring of Gyges, the helmet of Hades.

Very true.

And now, Glaucon, there will be no harm in further enumerating, how many and how great are the rewards which justice and the other virtues procure to the soul from Gods and men, both in life and after death.

Certainly not, he said.

Will you repay me, then, what you borrowed in the argument?

What did I borrow?

The assumption that the just man should appear unjust and the unjust just: for you were of opinion that even if the true state of the case could not possibly escape the eyes of Gods and men, still this admission ought to be made for the sake of the argument, in order that pure justice might be weighed against pure injustice. Do you remember?

You would have reason to complain of me if I had forgotten.

Then, as the cause is decided, I demand on behalf of justice that the glory which she receives from Gods and men be also allowed to her by you; having been shown to have reality, and not to deceive those who truly possess her, she may now have appearance restored to her, and thus obtain the other crown of victory which is hers also.

The demand, he said, is just. — *The Republic*, ii. 444.

Justice, Courts of, establishment of. See *Courts*, etc.

King, the, a Priest.

—— *Str.* There are also priests who, as the law declares, know how to give the Gods gifts from men in the form of sacrifices, which are acceptable to them, and to ask for us a return of blessings from them. Now both these are branches of the servile or ministerial art.

Y. Soc. Yes, clearly.

Str. And here I think that we seem to be getting on the right track; for the priest and the diviner also are full of pride and prerogative — this is due to the greatness of their employments; and in Egypt, the king himself is not allowed to reign, unless he have priestly powers; and if he should be of another class, and has thrust himself in, he must get enrolled in the priesthood. In many parts of Hellas, the duty of offering the most solemn propitiatory sacrifices is assigned to the highest magistracies, and here, at Athens, the most solemn and national of the ancient sacrifices are supposed to be celebrated by the King Archon of the year. — *Statesman*, iii. 576.

King and tyrant distinguished.

—— *Str.* When an individual truly possessing knowledge rules, his name will surely be the same — he will be called a king; and thus the five names of governments, as they are now reckoned, become one.

Y. Soc. That is true.

Str. And when an individual ruler governs neither by law nor by custom, but following in the steps of the true man of science, pretends that he can only act for the best by violating the laws, while in reality appetite and ignorance direct the imitation, may not such an one be called a tyrant?

Y. Soc. Certainly.

Str. And this we believe to be the origin of the tyrant and the king, of oligarchies, and aristocracies, and democracies; because men are offended at the one monarch, and can never be made to believe that any one can be worthy of such authority, or can unite the will and the power in the spirit of virtue and knowledge to do justly and holily to all; they fancy that he will be a despot who will wrong and harm and slay whom he pleases of us; for if there could be such a despot as we describe, they would acknowledge that we ought to be too glad to have him, and that he alone would be the happy ruler of a true and perfect State.

Y. Soc. Certainly. — *Statesman*, iii. 587.

Kingly art, the.

—— *Soc.* At last we came to the kingly art, and inquired whether that gave and caused happiness, and then we got into a labyrinth, and when we thought we were at the end, came out again at the beginning, having still to seek as much as ever.

Cri. How did that happen, Socrates?

Soc. I will tell you; the kingly art was identified by us with the political.

Cri. Well, and what came of that?

Soc. To this royal or political art all the arts, including that of the general, seemed to render up the supremacy, as to the only one which knew how to use that which they created. Here obviously was the very art which we were seeking — the art which is the source of good government, and which may be described, in the language of Aeschylus, as alone sitting at the helm of the vessel of state, piloting and governing all things, and utilizing them.

Cri. And were you not right, Socrates?

Soc. You shall judge, Crito, if you are willing to hear what followed; for we resumed the inquiry, and a question of this sort was asked: Does this kingly art, having this supreme authority, do anything for us?- To be sure, was the answer. And would not you, Crito, say the same?

Cri. Yes, I should.

Soc. And what would you say that the kingly art does? If medicine were supposed to have supreme authority over the subordinate arts, and I were to ask you a similar question about that, you would say that it produces health?

Cri. I should.

Soc. And what of your own art of husbandry, supposing that to have supreme authority over the subject arts — what does that.do? Does it not supply us with the fruits of the earth?

Cri. Yes.

Soc. And what does the kingly art do when invested with supreme power? Perhaps you may not be ready with an answer?

Cri. Indeed I am not, Socrates.

Soc. No more were we, Crito. But at any rate you know that if this is the art which we were seeking, it ought to be useful.

Cri. Certainly. — *Euthydemus*, i. 194.

Kings. See *Rulers, Legislators.*
Kings, Dorian, their ruin. See *Dorian.*
Kissing of the hero by all. See *Heroic men.*
Knowledge, on buying.

—— Is not a Sophist, Hippocrates, one who deals wholesale or retail in the food of the soul? To me that appears to be the sort of man.

And what, Socrates, is the food of the soul?

Surely, I said, knowledge is the food of the soul; and we must take care, my friend, that the Sophist does not deceive us when he praises what he sells, like the dealers, wholesale or retail, who sell the food of the body; for they praise indiscriminately all their goods, without knowing what are really beneficial or hurtful: neither do their customers know, with the exception of any trainer or physician who may happen to buy of them. In like manner those who carry about the wares of knowledge, and make the round of the cities, and sell or retail them to any customer who is in want of them, praise them all alike; though I should not wonder, O my friend, if many of them were really ignorant of their effect upon the soul; and their customers equally ignorant, unless he who buys of them happens to be a physician of the soul. If, therefore, you have understanding of what is good and evil, you may safely buy knowledge of Protagoras or of any one; but if not, then, O my friend, pause, and do not hazard your dearest interests at a game of chance. For there is far greater peril in buying knowledge than in buying meat and drink: the one you purchase of the wholesale or retail dealer, and carry them away in other vessels, and before you receive them into the body as food, you may deposit them at home and call in any experienced friend who knows what is good to be eaten or drunken, and what not, and how much and when; and hence the danger of purchasing them is not so great. But when you buy the wares of knowledge you cannot carry them away in another vessel; they have been sold to you, and you must take them into the soul and go your way, either greatly harmed or greatly benefited by the lesson; and therefore we should deliberate and take counsel with our elders; for we are still young — too young to determine such a matter. — *Protagoras*, i. 114.

Knowledge, certain, Science necessary to. See *Science*.

Knowledge and opinion.

—— We seem to have discovered that the many things which are esteemed beautiful or good by the multitude, are tossing about in some region which is half-way between pure being and pure non-being.

We have.

Yes; and we had before agreed that anything of this kind which we might find was to be described as matter of opinion, and not as matter of knowledge; being the intermediate flux which is caught and detained by the intermediate faculty.

Granted.

Then those who see the many beautiful, and who yet neither see, nor can be taught to see, absolute beauty; who see the many just, and not absolute justice, and the like, — such persons may be said to have opinion but not knowledge?

That is certain.

But those who see the absolute and eternal and immutable may be said to know, and not to have opinion only?

Neither can that be denied.

The one love and embrace the subjects of knowledge, the other those of opinion? The latter are the same, as I dare say you will remember, who listened to sweet sounds and gazed upon fair colors, but would not tolerate the existence of absolute beauty.

Yes, I remember.

Shall we then be guilty of any impropriety in calling them lovers of opinion rather than lovers of wisdom, and will they be very angry with us for thus describing them?

I shall tell them that they ought not to be angry at a description of themselves which is true.

But those who love the truth of each thing are to be called lovers of wisdom and not lovers of opinion?

Assuredly. — *The Republic*, ii. 308.

Knowledge, the highest, the idea of good. See *Good, the idea of*, etc.

Knowledge and **Intellect**. See *Intellect*, etc.

Knowledge, pleasures of.

—— *Soc.* To these may be added the pleasures of knowledge, if they appear to us to have no hunger of knowledge or pains of hunger attaching to them.

Pro. And they have not.

Soc. Well, but are there not pains of forgetfulness, if a man is full of knowledge and his knowledge is lost?

Pro. They are not natural or necessary, but there may be times of reflection, when he feels grief at the loss of his knowledge.

Soc. Yes, my friend, but at present we are enumerating only the natural perceptions, and have nothing to do with reflections.

Pro. In that case you are right in saying that the loss of knowledge is not attended with pain.

Soc. These pleasures of knowledge, then, are unmixed with pain; and they are not the pleasures of the many but of a very few. — *Philebus*, iii. 191.

Knowledge, the truest.

—— I am sure that all men who have a grain of intelligence will admit that the knowledge which has to do with being and reality, and sameness and unchangeableness, is by far the truest of all. — *Philebus*, iii. 198.

Knowledge, superhuman.

—— *Soc.* Let us suppose a man who understands justice, and

has reason as well as understanding about the true nature of this and of all other things.

Pro. Let that be supposed.

Soc. Will such an one have enough of knowledge if he is acquainted only with the divine circle and sphere, and knows nothing of our human spheres and circles, and with a like ignorance uses these or any other figures or rules in the building of a house?

Pro. The knowledge which is only superhuman, Socrates, is ridiculous in man.

Soc. What do you mean? Do you mean that you are to throw into the cup and mingle the impure and uncertain art which uses the false rule and the false circle?

Pro. Yes, that must be done, if any of us is ever to find his way home. — *Philebus,* iii. 203.

Knowledge, absolute in God. See *Absolute.*
Knowledge, definition needed for. See *Definition.*

Lacedaemon, government of, doubtful. See *Government of Sparta,* etc.

Landmarks, removal of.

——— Let us first of all, then, have a class of laws which shall be called the laws of husbandmen. And let the first of them be the law of Zeus, the God of boundaries. Let no one shift the boundary line either of a fellow-citizen who is a neighbor, or, if he dwells at the extremity of the land, of any stranger who is contiguous to him, considering that this is truly " to move the immovable," and every one should be more willing to move the largest rock, which is not a landmark, than the least stone which is the sworn arbiter of friendship and hatred between neighbors; for Zeus, the God of kindred, is the witness of the citizen and Zeus, the God of strangers, of the stranger, and when aroused, terrible is their wrath. He who obeys the law will never know the fatal consequences of disobedience, but he who despises the law shall be liable to a double penalty, the first coming from the Gods, and the second from the law. For let no one voluntarily remove the boundaries of his neighbor's land, and if any one does, let him who will, inform the landowners, and let them bring him into court, and if he be convicted of redividing the land by stealth or by force, let the court determine what he ought to suffer or pay. In the next place, many small injuries done by neighbors to one another through their multiplication, may cause a weight of enmity, and make neighborhood a very disagreeable and bitter thing. Wherefore a man ought to be very careful of committing any offense against his neighbor, and especially of encroaching on his neighbor's land; for any man may easily do harm, but not every man can do good to another. He who encroaches on his neighbor's land, and transgresses his boundaries, shall make good the damage, and, to cure him of his impudence and also of his meanness, he shall pay a double penalty to the injured party. — *Laws*, iv. 357.

Laughter condemned.

—— Neither ought our guardians to be given to laughter. For a fit of laughter which has been indulged to excess almost always produces a violent reaction.

So I believe.

Then persons of worth, even if only mortal, must not be represented as overcome by laughter, and still less must such a representation of the Gods be allowed.

Still less of the Gods, as you say, he replied.

Then we shall not suffer such an expression to be used about the Gods as that in which Homer describes how —

"Inextinguishable laughter arose among the blessed Gods, when they saw Hephaestus bustling about the mansion."

On your views, we must not admit them.

On my views, if you like to father them on me; that we must not admit them is certain. — *The Republic*, ii. 211.

Laughter at self-conceit.

—— *Soc.* The vain conceits of our friends about their beauty, wisdom, wealth, of which we made three divisions, are ridiculous if they are weak, and detestable when they are powerful: May we not say, as I was saying before, that our friends who are in this state of mind, when harmless to others, are simply ridiculous?

Pro. They are ridiculous.

Soc. And do we not acknowledge this ignorance of theirs to be a misfortune?

Pro. Certainly.

Soc. And do we feel pain or pleasure in laughing at it?

Pro. Clearly we feel pleasure.

Soc. And was not envy the source of this pleasure which we feel at the misfortunes of friends?

Pro. Certainly.

Soc. Then the argument shows that when we laugh at the folly of our friends, pleasure, in mingling with envy, mingles with pain, for envy has been acknowledged by us to be mental pain, and laughter is pleasant, and we envy and laugh at the same instant. — *Philebus,* iii. 189.

Law, preamble to, distinguished from the matter of. See *Preamble,* etc.

Laws, makers of.

—— Even if a man has good parts, still, if he carries philosophy into later life, he is necessarily ignorant of all those things which a gentleman and a person of honor ought to know; for he is inexperienced in the laws of the State, and in the language which ought to be used in the dealings of man with man, whether private or public, and altogether ignorant of the pleasures and desires of mankind and of human character in general. And people of this sort, when they betake themselves to politics or business, are as ridiculous as I imagine the politicians to be, when they make their appearance in the arena of philosophy. For, as Euripides says, —

"Every man shines in that and pursues that and devotes the greatest portion of the day to that in which he thinks himself to excel most."

And anything in which he is inferior he avoids and depreciates, and praises the opposite from partiality to himself, and because he thinks that he will thus praise himself. — *Gorgias,* iii. 73.

Laws answering to virtue.

—— *Cle.* What ought we to say, then?

Ath. What truth and what justice require of us, if I am not mistaken, when speaking in behalf of divine excellence; that the legislator when making his laws, had in view not a part only, and this the lowest part of virtue, but all virtue, and that he devised classes of laws answering to the kinds of virtue; not in the way in which modern inventors of laws make the classes, for they only investigate and offer laws of which the want is being felt, and one man has a class of laws about inheritances in part or sole, another about assault; others about ten thousand other matters of a similar nature. But we say that the right way of inquiry is to proceed as we have now done, and I admired the spirit of your exposition; for you are quite right in beginning with virtue, and saying that this was the aim of the giver of the law, but I thought that you went wrong when you added that he referred all to a part, and a most inferior part of virtue, and my subsequent observations had a bearing on this. — *Laws,* iv. 161.

Laws and music. See *Music, different kinds of.*

Laws, three classes of.

—— *Ath.* The general division of laws according to their importance into a first, a second, and a third class, we who are lovers of laws may make ourselves.

Meg. Very good.

Ath. We maintain, then, that a State which would be safe and happy, as far as the nature of man allows, must and ought to distribute honor and dishonor in the right way. And the right way is to place the goods of the soul first and highest in the scale, always assuming temperance as a condition of them; and in the second place, the goods of the body; and in the third place, those of money and property. And if any legislator or State departs from this rule by giving money the place of honor, or in any way preferring that which is really last, may we not say, that he or the State is doing an unholy and unpatriotic thing?

Meg. Yes; let that be plainly asserted. — *Laws,* iv. 226.

Laws annulled by unsuitable officers.

—— *Ath.* In the government of a State there are two parts: First, the number of the magistrates, and the mode of appointing them; and secondly, when they have been appointed, laws will have to be provided for each of them, in nature and number suitable to them. But before electing the magistrates, let us stop a little and say a word in season.

Cle. What have you got to say?

Ath. This is what I have to say; every one can see, that although the work of legislation is a most important matter, yet if a well ordered city superadd to good laws unsuitable officers, there will be no use in having the good laws; not only are they ridiculous and useless, but the greatest political injury and evil accrues from them.

Cle. Of course. — *Laws,* iv. 273.

Laws not received when first imposed.

—— *Ath.* I had in my mind the free and easy manner in which we are ordaining that the inexperienced colonists shall receive our laws. Now a man need not be very wise, Cleinias, in order to see that no one can easily receive laws at their first imposition. But if we could anyhow wait until those who have been imbued with them from childhood, and have been nurtured in them, and become habituated to them, take their part in the public elections; I say, if this could be accomplished, and rightly accomplished by any way or contrivance, — then, I think that there would be very little danger, at the end of the time, of a State thus trained not being permanent. — *Laws*, iv. 274.

Laws against sensual love.

—— Was I not just now saying that I had a way to make men use natural love and abstain from unnatural, not intentionally destroying the seeds of human increase, or sowing them in stony places, in which they will take no root; and that I would command them to abstain, too, from any female field of increase in which that which is sown is not likely to grow? Now, if a law to this effect could only be made perpetual, and gain an authority such as already prevents intercourse of parents and children — such a law extending to other sensual desires, and conquering them, would be the source of ten thousand blessings. For, in the first place, moderation is the appointment of nature, and deters men from all frenzy and madness of love, and from all adulteries and immoderate use of meats and drinks, and makes them good friends to their own wives. And innumerable other benefits would result if such a law could only be enforced. I can imagine some lusty youth who is standing by, and who, on hearing this enactment, declares in scurrilous terms, that we are making foolish and impossible laws, and fills the world with his outcry. Therefore I said that I knew a way of enacting and perpetuating such a law, which was very easy in one respect, but in another most difficult. There is no difficulty in seeing that such a law is possible, and in what way; for as I was saying, the ordinance once consecrated would master the soul of every man, and terrify him into obedience. But matters have now come to such a pass that the enactment of the law seems to be impossible and never likely to take place just as the continuance of an entire state in the practice of common meals is also deemed impossible. And although this latter is partly disproven by the fact of their existence among you, still even in your cities the common meals of women would be regarded as unnatural and impossible. I was thinking of the rebelliousness of the human heart when I said that the permanent ·establishment of these things is very difficult. — *Laws*, iv. 354.

Laws, necessity for.

—— Mankind must have laws and conform to them, or their

life would be as bad as that of the most savage beast. And the reason of this is, that no man's nature is able to know what is best for the social state of man; or knowing, always able to do what is best. In the first place, there is a difficulty in apprehending that the true art of politics is concerned, not with private but with public good; for public good binds together States, but private only distracts them, — nor do men always see that the gain is greater both to the individual and the State, when the State and not the individual is first considered. In the second place, even if a person know as a matter of science that this is the truth, but is possessed of absolute and irresponsible power, he will never be able to abide in this principle or to persist in regarding the public good as primary in the State, and the private good as secondary. Human nature will be always drawing him into avarice and selfishness, avoiding pain and pursuing pleasure without any reason, and will bring these to the front, obscuring the juster and better; and so working darkness in his soul will at last fill with evils both him and the whole city. For if a man were born so divinely gifted that he could naturally apprehend the truth he would have no need of laws to rule over him; for there is no law or order which is above knowledge, nor can mind, without impiety, be deemed the subject or slave of any man, but rather the lord of all. I speak of mind, true and free and in harmony with nature. But then there is no such mind anywhere, or at least not much; and therefore we must choose law and order, which are the second best. — *Laws*, iv. 388.

Laws framed for whom.

—— Laws are partly framed for the sake of good men, in order to instruct them how they may live on friendly terms with one another, and partly for the sake of those who refuse to be instructed, whose spirit cannot be subdued, or softened, or hindered from plunging into evil. These are the persons who cause the word to be spoken which I am about to utter; for them the legislator legislates of necessity, and in the hope that there may be no need of his laws. — *Laws*, iv. 394.

Lawyer, the, a slavish man. See *Freedom of Philosophy*.

Lawyers — and courts of law. See *Courts*, etc.

Lawyers not teachers.

—— *Soc.* The trail soon comes to an end, for a whole profession is against us.

Theaet. How is that, and what profession do you mean?

Soc. The profession of the great wise ones who are called orators and lawyers; for these persuade men by their art and do not teach them, but make them think whatever they like. Do you imagine that there are any teachers in the world so clever as to be able to convey to others the truth about acts of robbery or violence, of which they were not eye-witnesses, while a little water is flowing?

Theaet. Certainly not, they can only persuade them.

Soc. And would you not say that persuading them is making them have an opinion?

Theaet. To be sure.

Soc. When, therefore, judges are justly persuaded about matters which you can know only by seeing them, and not in any other way, and when thus judging of them from report they attain a true opinion about them, they judge without knowledge, and yet are rightly persuaded, if they have judged well.

Theaet. Certainly.

Soc. And yet, O my friend, if true opinion in law courts and knowledge are the same, the perfect judge could not have judged rightly without knowledge ; and therefore I must infer that they are not the same. — *Theaetetus*, iii. 407.

Lawyers, as advocates corrupting the State. See *State, corrupting the*, etc.

Learning, the word as used.

—— Imagine then that you have gone through the first part of the sophistical ritual, which, as Prodicus says, begins with initiation into the correct use of terms. The two strange gentlemen wanted to explain to you, as you do not know, that the word. "to learn" has two meanings, and is used, first, in the sense of acquiring knowledge of some matter of which you previously have no knowledge, and also, when you have the knowledge, in the sense of reviewing this same matter done or spoken by the light of this knowledge; this last is generally called "knowing" rather than "learning;" but the word "learning" is also used, and you did not see that the term is employed of two opposite sorts of men, of those who know, and of those who do not know, as they explained. — *Euthydemus*, i. 180.

Learning, a process of recollection.

—— The soul, then, as being immortal, and having been born again many times, and having seen all things that there are, whether in this world or in the world below, has knowledge of them all; and it is no wonder that she should be able to call to remembrance all that she ever knew about virtue, and about everything; for as all nature is akin, and the soul has learned all things, there is no difficulty in her eliciting, or as men say learning, all out of a single recollection, if a man is strenuous and does not faint; for all inquiry and all learning is but recollection. — *Meno*, i. 255.

Learning, the lover of, must be truthful.

—— Let us assume that philosophical minds always love knowledge of a sort which shows them the eternal nature in which is no varying from generation and corruption.

Agreed.

And further, I said, let us admit that they are lovers of all true being; there is no part, whether greater or less, or more or less honorable, which they are willing to renounce; as we said before of the lover and the man of ambition.

True.

There is another quality which they will also need if they are to be what we were saying.

What quality?

Truthfulness; they will never intentionally receive falsehood, which is their detestation, and they will love the truth.

Yes, he said, that may be affirmed of them.

"May be," my friend, I replied, is not the word; say rather, "must be affirmed;" for he whose nature is amorous of anything cannot help loving all that belongs or is akin to the object of his affections.

Right, he said.

And is there anything more akin to wisdom than truth?

How can there be?

Or can the same nature be a lover of wisdom and a lover of falsehood?

Never.

The true lover of learning, then, must from his earliest youth, as far as in him lies, desire all truth. — *The Republic*, ii. 311.

Learning and belief.

—— *Soc.* Let me raise this question; you would say that there is such a thing as "having learned?"

Gor. Yes.

Soc. And there is also "having believed?"

Gor. Yes.

Soc. And is the "having learned" the same as "having believed," and are learning and belief the same things?

Gor. In my judgment, Socrates, they are not the same.

Soc. And your judgment is right, as you may ascertain in this way: if a person were to say to you, " Is there, Gorgias, a false belief as well as a true?" you would reply, if I am not mistaken, that there is.

Gor. Yes.

Soc. Well, but is there a false knowledge as well as a true?

Gor. No.

Soc. No, indeed; and this again proves that knowledge and belief differ.

Gor. That is true.

Soc. And yet those who have learned as well as those who have believed are persuaded?

Gor. That is so.

Soc. Shall we then assume two sorts of persuasion, — one which is the source of belief without knowledge, as the other is of knowledge?

Gor. By all means.

Soc. And which sort of persuasion does rhetoric create in courts of law and other assemblies about the just and unjust, the sort of persuasion which gives belief without knowledge, or that which gives knowledge?

Gor. Clearly, Socrates, that which only gives belief.

Soc. Then rhetoric, as would appear, is the artificer of a persuasion which creates belief about the just and unjust, but gives no instruction about them?

Gor. True. — *Gorgias*, iii. 39.

Learning, facility in.

—— Which, I said, is better — facility in learning, or difficulty in learning?·

Facility.

Yes, I said; and facility in learning is learning quickly, and difficulty in learning is learning quietly and slowly?

True.

And is it not better to teach one another quickly and energetically, rather than quietly and slowly?

Yes.

And to call to mind, and to remember, quickly and readily — that is also better than to remember quietly and slowly?

Yes.

And is not shrewdness a quickness or cleverness of the soul, and not a quietness?

True.

And is it not best to understand what is said, whether at the writing-master's or the music-master's, or anywhere else, not as quietly as possible, but as quickly as possible?

Yes.

And when the soul inquires, and in deliberations, not the quietest, as I imagine, and he who with difficulty deliberates and discovers, is thought worthy of praise, but he who does this most easily and quickly?

That is true, he said.

And in all that concerns either body or soul, swiftness and activity are clearly better than slowness and quietness?

That, he said, is the inference. — *Charmides*, i. 14.

Legacies of wealth to children an evil. See *Children, riches an evil left to.*

Legislation, the true aim of.

—— *Soc.* Whatever name he gives to the thing, he would allow that the good or expedient is the aim of legislation, and that the State as far as possible imposes all laws with a view to the greatest expediency; can legislation have any other aim?

Theod. Certainly not.

Soc. But is the aim attained always? may not mistakes often happen?

Theod. Yes, I think that there are mistakes.

Soc. The possibility of error will be more distinctly recognized, if we put the question in reference to the whole class under which the good or expedient falls. That whole class has to do with the future, and laws are passed under the idea that they will be useful in after time; which, in other words, is the future.

Theod. Very true. — *Theaetetus*, iii. 380.

Legislation cannot be particular.

—— *Str.* Let us consider, further, that the legislator who has to preside over the herd, and to enforce justice in their dealings with one another, will not be able, in enacting for the general good, to provide exactly what is suitable for each particular case.

Y. Soc. He cannot be expected to do this.

Str. He will lay down laws in a general form for the majority, roughly meeting the cases of individuals; and some of them he will deliver in writing, and others will be unwritten ; and these last will be traditional customs of the country.

Y. Soc. That will be right.

Str. Yes, that will be right; for how can he sit at every man's side all through his life, and prescribe for him the exact particulars of his duty? Who, Socrates, would be sufficient for such a task? No one who really had the royal science, if he had been able to do this, would have imposed upon himself the restriction of having a written code of laws. — *Statesman,* iii. 580.

Legislation, comprehensive. See *Laws answering to virtue.*

Legislation, the beginning of.

—— *Ath.* There is another thing which would probably happen.

Cle. What is that?

Ath. When these larger habitations grew up out of the lesser original ones, each of the lesser ones would survive in the larger ; every family would be under the rule of the eldest, and, owing to their separation from one another, would have peculiar customs in things divine and human, which they would have received from their several parents who had educated them ; and these customs would incline them to order, when the parents had the element of order in them ; and to courage, when they had the element of courage in them. And they would naturally stamp upon their children, and upon their children's children, their own institutions; and, as we are saying, they would find their way into the larger society, having already their own peculiar laws.

Cle. Certainly.

Ath. And every man surely likes his own laws best, and the laws of others not so well.

Cle. True.

Ath. Then now we seem to have stumbled upon the beginnings of legislation ?

Cle. Exactly.

Ath. The next step will be that these persons, who meet together, must choose some arbiters, who will inspect the laws of all of them, and will publicly present such of them as they approve to the chiefs who lead the tribes, and are in a manner their kings, and will give them the choice of them. These will themselves be called legislators, and will appoint the magistrates, framing some sort of aristocracy, or perhaps monarchy, out of the dynasties or lordships, and in this altered state of the government they will live.

Cle. Yes, they would be appointed in the order which you mention. — *Laws,* iv. 210.

Legislation, chance in.

—— *Ath.* I was going to say that man never legislates, but that accidents of all sorts legislate for us in all sorts of ways. The violence of war and the hard necessity of poverty are constantly overturning governments and changing laws. And the power of disease has often caused innovations in the State, when there have been pestilences, and bad seasons continuing during many years. Any one who sees all this, naturally rushes to the conclusion of which I was speaking, that no mortal legislates in anything, but that in human affairs chance is almost everything. — *Laws,* iv. 236.

Legislation, force and persuasion in. See *Persuasion.*

—— Legislators never appear to have considered that whereas they have two instruments which they might use in legislation, — persuasion and force, in so far as a rude and uneducated multitude are capable of being affected by them, they use one only ; for they do not mingle persuasion with antagonism, but employ force pure and simple. — *Laws,* iv. 249.

Legislative ignorance destroying States. See *Ignorance,* etc.

Legislative purification.

—— Take, for example, the purification of a city — there are many kinds of purification, some easier and others more difficult ; and some of them, and the best and most difficult of them, the legislator, if he be also a despot, may be able to effect ; but he who without a despotism sets up a new government and laws, even if he attempt the mildest of purgations, may think himself happy if he can complete his work. When best the purification is painful, like similar cures in medicine, involving righteous punishment and inflicting death or exile in the last resort. For in this way we commonly dispose of great sinners who are incurable, and are the greatest injury of the whole State. But the milder form of purification is as follows: When men who have nothing, and are in want of food, show a disposition to follow their leaders in an attack on the property of the rich — these, who are the natural plague of the State, are sent away by the legislator in a friendly spirit as far as he is able ; and this dismissal of them is euphemistically termed a colony And every legislator should contrive to do this at once. Our present case, however, is peculiar. For there is no need to devise any colony or purifying separation under the circumstances in which we are placed. But, as when many streams flow together from springs and mountain torrents into a single lake, we ought to attend and take care that the confluence of water should be perfectly clear; and in order to effect this, should pump and draw off and divert impurities, so in every political arrangement there may be trouble and danger. But, seeing that we are discoursing and not acting, let our selection be supposed to be completed, and the desired purity attained. Touching evil men, who want to join and be citizens of our State, we will not allow them to come until we have tested them by persuasion and time; but the good we will to the utmost of our ability receive as friends with open arms. — *Laws*, iv. 260.

Legislator, Homer not a.

—— I think that we must put a question to Homer; not about medicine, or any of the arts to which his poems only incidentally refer; we are not going to ask him, or any other poet, whether he has cured patients like Asclepius, or left behind him a school of medicine such as the Asclepiads were, or whether he only talks about medicine and other arts at secondhand, but we have a right to know respecting military tactics, politics, education, which are the chiefest and noblest subjects of his poems, and we may fairly ask him about them. " Friend Homer," then we say, " if you are only in the second remove from truth in what you say of virtue, and not in the third — not an image-maker or imitator — and if you are able to discern what pursuits make men better or worse in private or public life, tell us what State was ever better governed by your help? The good order of Lacedaemon is due to Lycurgus, and many other cities great and small have been similarly benefited by others; but who says that you have been a good legislator to them and have done them any good? Italy and Sicily can tell of Charondas, and there is Solon who is renowned among us; but what city has anything to say about you?" Is there any city which he might name?

I think not, said Glaucon; not even the Homeridae themselves pretend that he was a legislator.

Well, but is there any war on record which was carried on successfully by him, or aided by his counsels, when he was alive?

There is not.

Or is there any invention of his applicable to the arts, or to human life, such as Thales the Milesian, or Anacharsis the Scythian, and other ingenious men have made, which is attributed to him?

There is nothing at all of the kind.

But, if Homer never did any public service, was he privately a guide or teacher of any? Had he in his life-time friends and associates who loved him, and handed down to posterity an Homeric way of life, as Pythagoras was beloved and his successors, who at this day call their way of life by his name, and do appear to have a certain distinction above other men?

Nothing of the kind is recorded of him. For surely, Socrates, Creophylus, the companion of Homer, that child of flesh, whose name always makes us laugh, might be more justly ridiculed for his want of education, if, as is said, Homer was greatly neglected by him and others in his own day when he was alive?

Yes, I replied, that is the tradition. But can you imagine, Glaucon, that if Homer had really been able to educate and improve mankind, if he had possessed knowledge and not been a mere imitator — can you imagine, I say, that he would not have had many followers, and been honored and loved by them? Protagoras of Abdera, and Prodicus of Ceos, and a host of others, have only to suggest to their contemporaries that they will never be able to manage either their own house or their State unless they are made by them presidents of education; and for this wisdom of theirs they are so much beloved that their companions all but carry them about on their heads. And are we to believe that the contemporaries of Homer, or again of Hesiod, would have allowed either of them to beg their way as rhapsodists, if they had really been able to improve mankind? Would they not have been as unwilling to part with them as with gold, and have compelled them to stay at home with them? Or, if the master would not stay, then the disciples would have followed him about everywhere until they had got education enough?

Yes, Socrates, that, I think, is quite true. — *The Republic*, ii. 430.

Legislator, compared to a physician. See *Rulers, compared to*, etc.

—— *Str.* Let us put to ourselves the case of a physician, or trainer, who is about to go into a far country, and is expecting to be a long time away from his patients; he leaves written instructions for the patients or pupils, under the idea that they will not be remembered unless they are written down.

Y. Soc. True.

Str. But what would you say, if he came back sooner than he intended, and, owing to an unexpected change of the winds or other celestial influences, some other remedies happened to be better for them, — would he not venture to suggest those other remedies, although differing from his former prescription? Would he persist in observing the original law, neither himself giving any new commandments, nor the patient daring to do otherwise than was prescribed, under the idea that this course only was healthy and medicinal, all others noxious and heterodox? Viewed in the light of science and true art, would not all such regulations be utterly ridiculous?

Y. Soc. Quite true.

Str. And if he who gave laws, written or unwritten, determining what was good or bad, honorable or dishonorable, just or unjust to the tribes of men who herd in their several cities, and are governed in accordance with them; if, I say, the wise legislator were suddenly to come again, or another like to him, is he to be prohibited from changing them; 'would not this prohibition be in reality quite as ridiculous as the other?

Y. Soc. Certainly. — *Statesman*, iii. 581.

Legislators not always to obey their constituency. See *Constituency*.

Leveling of anarchy. See *Anarchy*.

Liberal education, a sign of. See *Education, sign of a*, etc.

Liberty allowed the lover.

—— Consider, how great is the encouragement which all the world gives to the lover; neither is he supposed to be doing anything dishonorable; but if he succeeds he is praised, and if he fail he is blamed. And in the pursuit of his love the custom of mankind allows him to do many strange things, which philosophy would bitterly censure if they were done from any motive of interest, or wish for office or power. He may pray, and entreat, and supplicate, and swear, and be a servant of servants, and lie on a mat at the door; in any other case friends and enemies would be equally ready to prevent him, but now there is no friend who will be ashamed of him and admonish him, and no enemy will charge him with meanness or flattery; the actions of a lover have a grace which ennobles them; and custom has decided that they are highly commendable and that there is no loss of character in them ; and what is strangest of all he only may swear and forswear himself (this is what the world says), and the Gods will forgive his transgression, for there is no such thing as a lover's oath. Such is the entire liberty which Gods and men have allowed the lover, according to the custom which prevails in our part of the world. — *The Symposium*, i. 477.

Liberty, popular. See *Democracy*.
Liberty and license. See *Anarchy*.
License, spirit of.

—— Damon tells me, and I can quite believe him; he says that when modes of music change, the fundamental laws of the State always change with them.

Yes, said Adeimantus ; and you may add my suffrage to Damon's and your own.

Then, I said, our guardians must lay the foundations of their fortress in music?

Yes, he said ; and the license of which you speak very easily creeps in.

Yes, I replied, in the form of amusement; and at first sight appears harmless.

Why, yes, he said, and there is no harm ; were it not that little by little, the spirit of license, finding a home, penetrates into manners and customs ; whence, issuing with greater force, it invades agreements between man and man, and from agreements goes on to laws and constitutions, in utter recklessness, and ends, Socrates, by an overthrow of all things, private as well as public.

Is that true ? I said.

That is my belief, he replied.

Then, as I was saying, our youth should be educated in a stricter rule from the first, for if education becomes lawless, and the youths themselves become lawless, they can never grow up into well-conducted and meritorious citizens.

Very true, he said. — *The Republic*, ii. 248.

License, freedom growing to. See *Freedom growing to*, etc.
Lie, a, when committed. See *Fiction*.
Lie, God cannot utter a. See *Deception*.
Lies for the good of the State.

—— Truth should be highly valued ; if, as we were saying, a lie is useless to the Gods, and useful only as a medicine to men, then the use of such medicines will have to be restricted to physicians; private individuals have no business with them.

Clearly not, he said.

Then if any persons are to have the privilege of lying, either at home or abroad, they will be the rulers of the State; they may be allowed to lie for the public good. But nobody else is to meddle with anything of the kind; and for a private man to lie in return to the rulers is to be deemed a more heinous fault than for a patient or the pupil of a gymnasium not to speak the truth about his own bodily illnesses to the physician or trainer, or for a sailor not to tell the captain truly how matters are going on in a ship.

Most true, he said.

If, then, the ruler catches anybody beside himself lying in the State, —

" Any of the craftsmen, whether he be priest or physician or carpenter,"

he will punish him for introducing a practice which is equally subversive of ship or State.

Yes, he said, if our theory is carried into execution. — *The Republic*, ii. 211.

Life a valued good.

—— *Soc.* If, acting under the advice of men who have no understanding, we destroy that which is improved by health and deteriorated by disease — would life be worth having? And that which has been destroyed is the body?

Cr. Yes.

Soc. Could we live, having an evil and corrupted body?

Cr. Certainly not.

Soc. And will life be worth having, if that higher part of man be destroyed, which is improved by justice and deteriorated by injustice? Do we suppose that principle, whatever it may be in man, which has to do with justice and injustice, to be inferior to the body?

Cr. Certainly not.

Soc. More honored, then?

Cr. Far more honored.

Soc. Then, my friend, we must not regard what the many say of us: but what he, the one man who has understanding of just and unjust, will say, and what the truth will say. And therefore you begin in error when you advise that we should regard the opinion of the many about just and unjust, good and evil, honorable and dishonorable. Well, some one will say, "But the many can kill us."

Cr. Yes, Socrates; that will clearly be the answer.

Soc. That is true: but still I find with surprise that the old argument is, as I conceive, unshaken as ever. And I should like to know whether I may say the same of another proposition — that not life, but a good life, is to be chiefly valued?

Cr. Yes, that also remains.

Soc. And a good life is equivalent to a just and honorable one — that holds also?

Cr. Yes, that holds. — *Crito*, i. 352.

Life of the body, the soul the. See *Soul giving life*.
Life and death not to be considered in questions of duty. See *Death and life*, etc.
Life, when unendurable.

—— In my judgment, Socrates, the question has now become ridiculous. If, when the bodily constitution is gone, life is no longer endurable, though pampered with all kinds of meats and drinks, and having all wealth and all power, shall we be told that, when the very essence of the vital principle is undermined and corrupted, even though a man be allowed to do whatever he pleases, life is still worth having to him, if he be forbidden to escape from vice and injustice, or attain justice and virtue, seeing that we now know the true nature of each?

Yes, I said, the question is, as you say, ridiculous. Still, as we are near the spot at which we may see the truth with our own eyes, let us not faint by the way. — *The Republic*, ii. 272.

Life a fearful thing.

—— *Soc.* There is a noble freedom, Callicles, in your way of approaching the argument; for what you say is what the rest of the world think, but are unwilling to say. And I must beg of you to persevere that the true rule of human life may become manifest. Tell me, then: you say, do you not, that in the rightly developed man the passions ought not to be controlled, but that we should let them grow to the utmost and somehow or other satisfy them, and that this is virtue?

Cal. Yes; that is what I say.

Soc. Then those who want nothing are not truly said to be happy?

Cal. No, indeed, for then stones and dead men would be the happiest of all.

Soc. But surely according to you life is an awful thing ; and I think that Euripides may have been right in saying, —

" Who knows if life be not death and death life; "

for I think that we are very likely dead ; and I have heard a wise man say that at this very moment we *are* dead, and that the body (σῶμα) is a tomb (σῆμα), and that the part of the soul which is the seat of the desires is liable to be blown and tossed about. — *Gorgias*, iii. 81.

Life, protracted, not to be desired.

—— O my friend ! I want you to see that the noble and the good may possibly be something different from saving and being saved, and that he who is truly a man ought not to care about living a certain time : he knows, as women say, that we must all die, and therefore he is not fond of life ; he leaves all that with God, and considers in what way he can best spend his appointed term. — *Gorgias*, iii. 104.

Life, spontaneous.

—— *Str.* It is evident, Socrates, that there was no such thing in the then order of nature as the procreation of animals from one another ; what we have heard of as the earth-born race was the one which existed in that second cycle — they sprang out of the ground in which they were sown ; and of this tradition, which is nowadays often unduly discredited, our ancestors, who came into being immediately after the end of the last period and at the beginning of this, are the heralds to us. For mark how consistent the sequel of the tale is ; after the return of age to youth, follows the return of the dead, who are lying in the earth, to life ; the wheel of their existence has been turned back, and they come together and rise and live in the opposite order, unless God has carried any of them away to some other lot. Such is the tradition of the so-called earth-born men and so of necessity they came into being. — *Statesman*, iii. 555.

Life, goods of. See *Goods*, etc.

Life, progression of. See *Progression*, etc.

Life, reason the rule of.

—— May we not regard every living being as a puppet of the Gods, either their plaything only, or created with a purpose which of the two we cannot certainly know ? But this we know, that these affections in us are like cords and strings, which pull us different and opposite ways, and to opposite actions; and herein lies the difference between virtue and vice. According to the argument there is one among these cords which every man ought to grasp and never let go, but to pull with it against all the rest; and this is the sacred and golden cord of reason, called by us the common law of the State; there are others which are hard and of iron, but this is soft because golden; and there are several other kinds. Now we ought always to coöperate with the lead of the best, which is law. For inasmuch as reason is beautiful and gentle, and not violent, her rule must needs have ministers in order to help the golden principle in vanquishing the other principles. And thus the moral tale about our being puppets will not be lost, and the meaning of the expression "superior or inferior to a man's self" will become clearer; as also that in this matter of pulling the strings of the puppet, cities as well as individuals should live according to reason; which the individual attains in himself, and the city receives from some God, or from the legislator and makes it her law in her dealings with herself and with other States. In this way virtue and vice will be more clearly distinguished by us. And when they have become clearer, education and other institutions will in like manner become clearer; and in particular that question of convivial entertainment, which may seem, perhaps, to have been a very trifling matter, and to have taken a great many more words than were necessary. — *Laws*, iv. 175.

Life, the nobler.

—— Enough has now been said of divine matters, both as touching the practices which men ought to follow, and the several characters which they ought to cultivate. But of human things we have not as yet spoken, and we must; for to men we are discoursing and not to Gods. Pleasures and pains and desires are a part of human nature, and on them every mortal being must of necessity hang and depend with the most eager interest. And therefore we must praise the noblest life, not only as the fairest in appearance, but if a man will only taste, and not as in the days of youth run away to another, he will find that this nobler life surpasses also in the very thing which we all of us desire, — I mean in having the greatest pleasure and the least pain during the whole of life. And this will be plain, and will be quickly and clearly seen, if a man has a true taste of them. But what is a true taste? That we have to learn from the argument, — the point being what is according to nature, and what is not according to nature. One life must be compared with another; the more pleasurable with the more painful, after this manner: We desire to have pleasure, but we neither desire nor choose pain; and the neutral state we are ready to take in exchange, not for pleasure, but for pain; and we also choose less pain and greater pleasure, but less pleasure and greater pain we do not choose; and an equal balance of either we cannot venture to assert that we should desire. And all these differ or do not differ severally in number and magnitude and intensity and equality, and in the opposites of these when regarded as objects of choice, in relation to the will. And such being the necessary order of things, we choose that life in which there are many great and intense elements of pleasure and pain, and in which the pleasures are in excess, and do not choose that in which the opposites exceed; nor, again, do we choose that in which the elements of either are small and few and feeble, and the pains exceed. And when, as I said before, there is a balance of pleasure and pain in life, this is to be regarded by us as the balanced life; while other lives are preferred by us because they exceed in what we like, or are rejected by us because they exceed in what we dislike. All the lives of men may be regarded by us as bound up in these, and we must also consider what sort of lives we by nature choose. And if we wish for any others, I say that we choose them only through some ignorance and inexperience of the lives which actually exist.

Now, what lives are they, and how many in which, having searched out and beheld the objects of will and desire and their opposites, and making of them a law, choosing, I say, the dear and the pleasant and the best and noblest, a man may live in the happiest way possible? Let us say that the temperate life is one kind of life, and the rational another, and the courageous another, and the healthful another; and to these four let us oppose four other lives, — the foolish, the cowardly, the intemperate, the diseased. He who knows the temperate life will describe it as in all things gentle, having gentle pains and gentle pleasures, and placid desires and loves not insane; whereas the intemperate life is impetuous in all things, and has violent pains and pleasures, and vehement and stinging desires, and loves utterly insane; and in the temperate life the pleasures exceed the pains, but in the intemperate life the pains exceed the pleasures in greatness and number and intensity.

Hence one of the two lives is naturally and necessarily more pleasant and the other more painful, and he who would live pleasantly cannot possibly choose to live intemperately. — *Laws*, iv. 258.

Likeness of the world. See *Animal*, etc.

Likeness-making.

—— *Str.* I think that I can discern two divisions of the imitative art, but I am not as yet able to see in which of them the desired form is to be found.

Theaet. Will you tell me first what are the two divisions of which you are speaking?

Str. One is the art of likeness-making; generally a likeness is made by producing a copy which is executed according to the proportions of the original, similar in length and breadth and depth, and also having colors answering to the several parts.

Theaet. But is not this always the case in imitation?

Str. Not always; in works either of sculpture or of painting, which are of any magnitude, there is a certain degree of deception; for if the true proportions were given, the upper part, which is farther off, would appear to be out of proportion in comparison with the lower, which is nearer; and so our artists give up the truth in their images and make only the proportions which appear to be beautiful, disregarding the real ones.

Theaet. Quite true.

Str. And that which being other is also like, may we not fairly call a likeness or image?

Theaet. Yes.

Str. And may we not, as I did just now, call that part of the imitative art which is concerned with making such images the art of likeness-making?

Theaet. Let that be the name.

Str. And what shall we call that resemblance of the beautiful, which is due to the unfavorable position of the spectator, but if a person had the power of seeing the great works of which I was speaking as they truly are, would appear not even like that to which it professes to be like? May we not call this an appearance, since it appears only and is not really like?

Theaet. Certainly.

Str. There is a great deal of this in painting, and in all imitation?

Theaet. Of course.

Str. And may we not fairly call the sort of art which produces an appearance and not an image, phantastic art?

Theaet. That is very fair.

Str. Then there are two kinds of image-making — the art of making likenesses and phantastic, or the art of making appearances?

Theaet. True.— *Sophist,* iii. 470.

Limit and cause in the universe.

——— *Soc.* Should we not be wise in maintaining that there is in the universe a mighty infinite and an adequate limit of which we have often spoken, as well as a cause of no mean power, which orders and arranges years and seasons and months, and may be justly called wisdom and mind?

Pro. Most justly.

Soc. And wisdom and mind cannot exist without soul?

Pro. Certainly not.

Soc. And in the divine nature of Zeus would you not say that there is the soul and mind of a king, because there is in him the power of the cause? And other Gods have other noble attributes, whereby they love severally to be called.

Pro. Very true.

Soc. Do not then suppose that these words are rashly spoken by us, O Protarchus, for they are in harmony with the testimony of those who said of old time that mind rules the universe.

Pro. True. — *Philebus,* iii. 166.

Limitation of law and order. See *Order and Law.*

Little things, God attends to.

——— *Ath.* Let us not deem God inferior to human workmen, who, in proportion to their skill, finish and perfect their works, small as well as great, by one and the same art; or that God, the wisest of beings, who is willing and able to extend his care to all things, like a lazy good-for-nothing, wants a holiday, and takes no thought of smaller and easier matters, but of the greater only. — *Laws,* iv. 415.

Love the eldest of the Gods and the source of the greatest benefits.

——— Phaedrus began by affirming that Love is a mighty God, and wonderful among Gods and men, but especially wonderful in his birth. For that he is the eldest of the Gods is an honor to him; and a proof of this is, that of his parents there is no memorial; neither poet nor prose-writer has ever affirmed that he had any. As Hesiod says: —.

> "First Chaos came, and then broad-bosomed Earth,
> The everlasting seat of all that is,
> And Love."

In other words, after Chaos, the Earth and Love, these two came into being. Also Parmenides sings of the generation of the Gods: —

> "First in the train of Gods, he fashioned Love."

And Acusilaus agrees with Hesiod. Thus numerous are the witnesses which acknowledge Love to be the eldest of the Gods. And not only is he the eldest, he is also the source of the greatest benefits to us. For I know not any greater blessing to a young man beginning life than a virtuous lover, or to the lover than a beloved youth. For the principle which ought to be the guide of men who would nobly live — that principle, I say, neither kindred, nor honor, nor wealth, nor any other motive is able to implant so well as love. Of what am I speaking? Of the sense of honor and dishonor, without which neither States nor individuals ever do any good or great work. — *The Symposium*, i. 473.

Love, courage increased by. See *Courage*.

Love, honor and dishonor in.

—— There is dishonor in yielding to the evil, or in an evil manner; but there is honor in yielding to the good, or in an honorable manner. Evil is the vulgar lover who loves the body rather than the soul, and who is inconstant because he is a lover of the inconstant; and therefore when the bloom of youth which he was desiring is over, he takes wing and flies away, in spite of all his words and promises; whereas the love of the noble mind, which is one with the unchanging, is life-long. The custom of our country would have them both proven well and truly, and would have us yield to the one sort of lover and avoid the other, and therefore encourages some to pursue and others to fly; testing both the lover and the beloved in contests and trials, which will show to which of the two classes they respectively belong. — *The Symposium*, i. 478.

Love, virtue the basis of.

—— There remains, then, only one way of honorable attachment which custom allows in the beloved, and this is the way of virtue ; for as we admitted that any service which the lover does to him is not to be accounted flattery or dishonor, so the beloved has also one way of voluntary service which is not dishonorable, and this is virtuous service.

For we have a custom, and according to our custom, any one who does service to another under the idea that he will be improved by him either in wisdom, or in some other particular of virtue — such a voluntary service, I say, is not regarded as a dishonor, and is not open to the charge of flattery. And these two customs, one the love of youth, and the other the practice of philosophy and virtue in general, ought to meet in one, and then the beloved may honorably indulge the lover. For when the lover and beloved come together, having each of them a law, and the lover thinks that he is right in doing any service which he can to his gracious loving one ; and the other that he is right in showing any kindness which he can to him who is making him wise and good ; the one capable of communicating wisdom and virtue, the other seeking to acquire them with a view to education and wisdom ; when the two laws of love are fulfilled and meet in one — then, and then only, may the beloved yield with honor to the lover. Nor when love is of this disinterested sort is there any disgrace in being deceived, but in every other case there is equal disgrace in being or not being deceived. For he who is gracious to his lover under the impression that he is rich, and is disappointed of his gains because he turns out to be poor, is disgraced all the same ; for he has done his best to show that he would turn himself to any one's base uses for the sake of money, and this is not honorable. But on the same principle he who lives for the sake of virtue, and in the hope that he will be improved by his lover's company, shows himself to be virtuous, even though the object of his affection be proved to be a villain, and to have no virtue ; and if he is deceived he has committed a noble error. For he has proved that for his part he will do anything for anybody for the sake of virtue and improvement, than which there can be nothing nobler. Thus noble in every case is the acceptance of another for the sake of virtue. This is that love which is the love of the heavenly goddess, and is heavenly, and of great price to individuals and cities, making the lover and the beloved alike eager in the work of their own improvement. But all other loves are the offspring of the other who is a common goddess. — *The Symposium*, i. 478.

Love, double in all things.

—— Eryximachus spoke as follows: Seeing that Pausanias made a fair beginning, and but a lame ending, I must endeavor to supply his deficiency. I think that he has rightly distinguished two kinds of love. But my art further informs me that a double love is to be found in all animals and plants, and I may say in all that is; and is not merely an affection of the soul of man towards the fair, or towards anything; that, I say, is a view of the subject which I seem to have gathered from my own art of medicine, which shows me how great and wonderful and universal is the deity of love whose empire extends over all that is, divine as well as human. And from medicine I will begin that I may do honor to my art. For there are in the human body two loves, which are confessedly different and unlike, and being unlike, have loves and desires which are unlike; and the desire of the healthy is one, and the desire of the diseased is another; and, as Pausanias says, to indulge good men is honorable and bad men dishonorable; and so too in the body the good and healthy elements are to be indulged, and the bad elements and the elements of desire are not to be indulged, but discouraged. And this is what the physician has to do, and in this the art of medicine consists: for medicine may be regarded generally as the knowledge of the loves and desires of the body, and how to satisfy them or not; and the good physician is he who is able to separate fair love from foul, or to convert one into the other; and he who knows how to eradicate and how to implant love, whichever is required, and can reconcile the most hostile elements in the constitution, and make them friends, is a skillful practitioner. — *The Symposium*, i. 480.

Love, divination as to. See *Divination*.

Love, the youngest.

—— I would rather praise the God first, and then speak of his gifts; this is always the right way of praising everything. May I say without impiety or offense, that of all the blessed Gods he is the blessedest because he is the fairest and best? And he is the fairest, because, in the first place, Phaedrus, he is the youngest, and of his youth he is himself the witness, fleeing out of the way of age, who is swift enough surely, swifter than most of us like: love hates him and will not come near him, but youth and love live and move together, — like to like, as the proverb says. There are many things which Phaedrus said about Love in which I agree with him: but I cannot agree that

he is older than Iapetus and Kronos — that is not the truth; as I maintain, he is the youngest of the Gods, and youthful ever. The ancient things of which Hesiod and Parmenides speak, if they were done at all, were done of Necessity and not of Love; had Love been in those days, there would have been no chaining or mutilation of the Gods, or other violence, but peace and sweetness, as there is now in heaven, since the rule of Love began. — *The Symposium,* i. 488.
Love, tenderness and flexibility of.

——— Love is young and also tender; he ought to have a poet like Homer to describe his tenderness, as Homer says of Ate, that she is a goddess and tender: —

"Her feet are tender, for she sets her steps
Not on the ground but on the heads of men:"

which is an excellent proof of her tenderness, because she walks not upon the hard but upon the soft. Let us adduce a similar proof of the tenderness of Love; for he walks not upon the earth, nor yet upon the skulls of men, which are not so very soft, but in the hearts and souls of men: in them he walks and dwells and has his home. Not in every soul without exception, for where there is hardness he departs, where there is softness there he dwells; and nestling always with his feet and in all manner of ways in the softest of soft places, how can he be other than the softest of all things? And therefore he is the tenderest as well as the youngest, and also he is of flexile form; for if he were hard and without flexure he could not enfold all things, or wind his way into and out of every soul of man undiscovered. And a proof of his flexibility and symmetry of form is his grace, which is universally admitted to be in an especial manner the attribute of Love; ungrace and love are always at war with one another. The fairness of his complexion is revealed by his habitation among the flowers; for he dwells not amid bloomless or fading beauties, whether of body or soul or aught else, but in the place of flowers and scents, there he sits and abides. Enough of his beauty, — of which, however, there is more to tell. But I must now speak of his virtue: his greatest glory is that he can neither do nor suffer wrong to or from any God or any man; for he suffers not by force if he suffers; force comes not near him, neither does he act by force. For all men in all things serve him of their own free-will, and where there is voluntary agreement, there, as the laws which are the lords of the city say, is justice. And not only is he just but exceedingly temperate, for Temperance is the acknowledged ruler of the pleasures and desires, and no pleasure ever masters Love; he is their master and they are his servants; and if he conquers them he must be temperate indeed. As to courage, even the God of War is no match for him; he is the captive and Love is the lord, for love, the love of Aphrodite, masters him, as the tale runs; and the master is stronger than the servant. And if he conquers the bravest of all others he must be himself the bravest. Of his courage and justice and temperance I have spoken; but I have yet to speak of his wisdom, and I must try to do my best, according to the measure of my ability. For in the first place he is a poet (and here, like Eryximachus, I magnify my art), and he is also the source of poesy in others, which he could not be if he were not himself a poet. And at the touch of him every one becomes a poet, even though he had no music in him before; this also is a proof that Love is a good poet and accomplished in all the fine arts; for no one can give to another that which he has not himself, or teach that of which he has no knowledge. Who will deny that the creation of the animals is his doing? Are they not all the works of his wisdom, born and begotten of him? And as to the artists, do we not know that he only of them whom love inspires has the light of fame? — he whom love touches not walks in darkness. — *The Symposium*, i. 488.

Love a spiritual power.

———— " What then is Love?" I asked; "Is he mortal?" "No." "What then?" "As in the former instance, he is neither mortal nor immortal, but in a mean between the two." "What is he then, Diotima?" "He is a great spirit (δαίμων), and like all spirits he is intermediate between the divine and the mortal." "And what," I said, "is his power?" "He interprets," she replied, "between Gods and men, conveying to the Gods the prayers and sacrifices of men, and to men the commands and replies of the Gods; he is the mediator who spans the chasm which divides them, and in him all is bound together, and through him the arts of the prophet and the priest, their sacrifices and mysteries and charms, and all prophecy and incantation, find their way. For God mingles not with man; but through Love all the intercourse and speech of God with man, whether awake or asleep, is carried on. The wisdom which understands this is spiritual; all other wisdom, such as that of arts or handicrafts, is mean and vulgar. Now these

spirits or intermediate powers are many and diverse, and one of them is Love." — *The Symposium*, i. 495.[1]
Love escaped from in age. See *Age*.
Love sensual, laws against, impossible. See *Laws against sensual love*.
Love, a madness. See *Madness*.
Loves, the two.

—— The old tale has to be repeated of fair and heavenly love — the love of Urania the fair and heavenly muse, and of the duty of accepting the temperate, and those who are as yet intemperate only that they may become temperate, and of preserving their love; and again, of the vulgar Polyhymnia, who must be used with circumspection that the pleasure may not generate licentiousness; just as in my own art it is a great matter to regulate the desires of the epicure that he may gratify his tastes without the attendant evil of disease. The conclusion is, that in music, in medicine, in all other things human as well as divine, both loves ought to be noted as far as may be, for they are both present. — *The Symposium*, i. 481.
Lover, liberty allowed the. See *Liberty allowed*.
Lover, madness of the. See *Madness of the prophet*.
Lover, wise and unwise, the.

—— O Hippothales, thou son of Hieronymus! do not say that you are, or that you are not in love; the confession is too late; for I see not only that you are in love, but that you are already far gone in your love. Simple and foolish as I am, the Gods have given me the power of understanding this sort of affections.

At this he blushed more and more.

Ctesippus said: I like to see you blushing, Hippothales, and hesitating to tell Socrates the name; when, if he were with you but for a very short time, he would be plagued to death by hearing of nothing else. Indeed, Socrates, he has literally deafened us, and stopped our ears with the praises of Lysis; and if he is a little intoxicated, there is every likelihood that we may have our sleep murdered with a cry of Lysis. His performances in prose are bad enough, but nothing at all in comparison with his verse; and when he drenches us with his poems and other compositions, that is really too bad; and what is even worse, is his manner of singing them to his love; this he does in a voice which is truly appalling, and we cannot

[1] In order to appreciate the full beauty and force of Plato's discourse upon Love, his "Symposium" should be read throughout. Only a few passages could here be given.

help hearing him; and now he has a question put to him by you, and lo! he is blushing.

Who is Lysis? I said: I suppose that he must be young, for the name does not recall any one to me.

Why, he said, his father being a very well-known man, he retains his patronymic, and is not as yet commonly called by his own name; but, although you do not know his name, I am sure that you must know his face, for that is quite enough to distinguish him.

But tell me whose son he is, I said.

He is the eldest son of Democrates, of the deme of Aexonè.

Ah, Hippothales, I said; what a noble and really perfect love you have found! I wish that you would favor me with the exhibition which you have been making to the rest of the company, and then I shall be able to judge whether you know what a lover ought to say about his love, either to the youth himself, or to others.

Nay, Socrates, he said; you surely do not attach any weight to what he is saying.

Do you mean, I said, that you disown the love of the person whom he says that you love?

No; but I deny that I make verses or address compositions to him.

He is not in his right mind, said Ctesippus; he is talking nonsense, and is stark mad.

O Hippothales, I said, if you have ever made any verses or songs in honor of your favorite, I do not want to hear them; but I want to know the purport of them, that I may be able to judge of your mode of approaching your fair one.

Ctesippus will be able to tell you, he said; for if, as he avers, I talk to him of nothing else, he must have a very accurate knowledge and recollection of that.

Yes, indeed, said Ctesippus; I know only too well; and very ridiculous the tale is: for although he is a lover, and very devotedly in love, he has nothing particular to talk about to his beloved which a child might not say. Now is not that ridiculous? He can only speak of the wealth of Democrates, which the whole city celebrates, and grandfather Lysis, and the other ancestors of the youth, and their stud of horses, and their victory at the Pythian games, and at the Isthmus, and at Nemea with four horses and single horses; and these he sings and says, and greater twaddle still. For the day before yesterday he made a poem in which he described how Heracles, who was a connection of the family, was entertained by an ancestor of Lysis as his relation; this ancestor was himself the son of Zeus and the daughter of the founder of the deme. And these are the sort of old wives' tales which he sings and recites to us, and we are obliged to listen to him.

When I heard this, I said: O ridiculous Hippothales! how can you be making and singing hymns in honor of yourself before you have won?

But my songs and verses, he said, are not in honor of myself, Socrates.

You think not, I said.

But what are they, then? he replied.

Most assuredly, I said, those songs are all in your own honor; for if you win your beautiful love, your discourses and songs will be a glory to you, and may be truly regarded as hymns of praise composed in honor of you who have conquered and won such a love; but if he slips away from you, the more you have praised him, the more ridiculous you will look at having lost this fairest and best of blessings; and this is the reason why the wise lover does not praise his beloved until he has won him, because he is afraid of accidents. There is also another danger; the fair, when any one praises or magnifies them, are filled with the spirit of pride and vainglory. Is not that true?

Yes, he said.

And the more vain-glorious they are, the more difficult is the capture of them?

I believe that.

What should you say of a hunter who frightened away his prey, and made the capture of the animals which he is hunting more difficult?

He would be a bad hunter, that is clear.

Yes; and if, instead of soothing them, he were to infuriate them with words and songs, that would show a great want of wit: do you not agree with me?

Yes.

And now reflect, Hippothales, and see whether you are not guilty of all these errors in writing poetry. For I can hardly suppose that you will affirm a man to be a good poet who injures himself by his poetry.

Assuredly not, he said: I should be a fool if I said that;

and this makes me desirous, Socrates, of taking you into my counsels, and I shall be glad of any further advice which you may have to offer. Will you tell me by what words or actions I may become endeared to my love?

That is not easy to determine, I said; but if you will bring your love to me, and will let me talk with him, I may perhaps be able to show you how to converse with him, instead of singing and reciting in the fashion of which you are accused. — *Lysis*, i. 42.

Lovers universal.

—— I dare say that you remember, and therefore I need not remind you, that a lover, if he is worthy of the name, ought to show his love, not to some one part of that which he loves, but to the whole.

I believe that I must ask you to explain, for I really do not understand.

Another, I replied, might fairly answer thus; but a man of pleasure like you ought to know that all who are in the flower of their youth do somehow or other raise a pang or emotion in a lover's breast, and are thought by him to be worthy of his affectionate regards. Is not this a way which you have with the fair: one has a snub nose, and you praise his pleasant face, another's beak, as you say, has a royal look; while he who is neither snub or hooked has the grace of regularity: the dark visage is manly, the fair are angels: and as to the sweet, "honey pale," as they are called, what is the very name but the invention of a lover who uses these pet names, and is not averse to paleness on the cheek of youth? In a word, there is no excuse which you will not make, and nothing which you will not say, in order to preserve for your use every flower that has the bloom of youth.

If you are determined to make me an authority in matters of love, for the sake of the argument, I assent. — *The Republic*, ii. 302.

Loyalty to the State. See *Obligation, individual*.

Madness, two kinds of.

—— *Soc.* I said, "love is a madness."

Phaedr. Yes.

Soc. And there were two kinds of madness; one produced by human infirmity, the other by a divine release from the ordinary ways of men.

Phaedr. True.

Soc. The divine madness was subdivided into four kinds, prophetic, initiatory, poetic, erotic, having four Gods presiding over them; the first was the inspiration of Apollo, the second that of Dionysus, the third that of the Muses, the fourth that of Aphroditè and Eros. In the description of the last kind of madness, which was also the best, being a figure of love, we introduced a tolerably credible and possibly true, though partly erring myth, which was also a hymn in honor of Eros, who is your lord and also mine, Phaedrus, and the guardian of fair children, and to him we sung the hymn in measured and solemn strain. — *Phaedrus*, i. 570.

Madness of the prophet, poet, and lover.

—— That was a lie in which I said that the beloved ought to accept the non-lover and reject the lover, because the one is sane, and the other mad. For that might have been truly said if madness were simply an evil; but there is also a madness which is the special gift of Heaven, and the source of the chiefest blessings among men. For prophecy is a madness, and the prophetess at Delphi and the priestesses at Dodona, when out of their senses have conferred great benefits on Hellas, both in public and private life, but when in their senses few or none. And I might also tell you how the Sibyl and other persons, who have had the gift of prophecy, have told the future of many an one and guided them aright; but that is obvious, and would be tedious.

There will be more reason in appealing to the ancient inventors of names, who, if they had thought madness a disgrace or dishonor, would never have called prophecy (μαντική), which is the noblest of arts, by the very same name as madness, (μανική) thus inseparably connecting them; but they must have thought that there was an inspired madness which was no disgrace; for the two words, μαντική and μανική, are really the same, and the letter τ is only a modern and tasteless insertion. And this is confirmed by the name which they gave to the rational investigation of futurity, whether made by the help of birds or of other signs; this because supplying from the reasoning faculty insight (νοῦς) and information (ἱστορία) to human thought (οἴησις), they originally termed οἰονοιστική, but the word has been lately altered and made sonorous by the modern introduction of the letter Omega (οἰονοιστική and οἰωνιστική), and in proportion as prophecy (μαντική) is higher and more perfect than divination both in name and reality, in the same proportion as the ancients testify, is madness superior to a sane mind (σωφροσύνη), for the one is only of human, but the other of divine origin. Again, where plagues and mightiest woes have bred in a race, owing to some ancient wrath, there madness enters with holy prayers and rites, and by inspired utterances finds a way of deliverance for those who are in need; and he who has part in this gift, and is truly possessed and duly out of his mind, is by the use of purifications and mysteries made whole and exempt from evil, future as well as present, and has a release from the calamity which afflicts him. There is also a third kind of madness, which is a possession of the Muses; which enters into a delicate and virgin soul, and there inspiring frenzy, awakens lyrical and all other numbers; with these adorning the myriad actions of ancient heroes for the instruction of posterity. But he who, having no touch of the Muses' madness in his soul, comes to the door and thinks that he will get into the temple by the help of art — he, I say, and his poetry are not admitted; the sane man is nowhere at all when he enters into rivalry with the madman.

I might tell of many other noble deeds which have sprung from inspired madness. And therefore let no one frighten or flutter us by saying that temperate love is preferable to mad love, but let him further show, if he would carry off the palm, that love is not sent by the Gods for any good to lover or beloved. And we, on our part, will prove in answer to him that the madness of love is the greatest of Heaven's blessings, and the proof shall be one which the wise will receive, and the witling disbelieve. —*Phaedrus*, i. 549.

Magistrates and rulers, — qualities and choice of. See *Rulers*.

—— *Ath.* Let us observe what will happen in the constitution of our intended State. In the first place, you will acknowledge that those who are duly appointed to magisterial power, and their families, should severally give satisfactory proof of what they are, from their youth upward until the time of their election ; in the next place, those who are to elect should be trained in habits of law, and be well educated, that they may have a right judgment, and may be able to select or reject men whom they approve or disapprove, as they are worthy of either. But how can we imagine that those who are brought together for the first time, and are strangers to one another, and also uneducated, can avoid making mistakes in the choice of magistrates?

Cle. Impossible. — *Laws*, iv. 273.

Man, absolute unity not in.

—— In the life of the same individual there is succession and not absolute unity ; a man is called the same ; and yet in the short interval which elapses between youth and age, and in which every animal is said to have life and identity, he is undergoing a perpetual process of loss and reparation — hair, flesh, bones, blood, and the whole body are always changing. Which is true not only of the body, but also of the soul, whose habits, tempers, opinions, desires, pleasures, pains, fears, never remain the same in any one of us, but are always coming and going. And equally true of knowledge, which is still more surprising — for not only do the sciences in general come and go, so that in respect to them we are never the same ; but each of them individually experiences a like change. — *The Symposium*, i. 500.

Man, transformation of.

—— He who lived well during his appointed time was to return to the star which was his habitation, and there he would have a blessed and suitable existence. But if he failed in attaining this, in the second generation he would pass into a woman, and should he not desist from evil in that condition, he would be changed into some brute who resembled him in his evil ways, and would not cease from his toils and transformations until he followed the original principle of sameness and likeness within him, and overcame, by the help of reason, the later accretions of turbulent and irrational elements composed of fire and air and water and earth, and returned to the form of his first and better nature. Having given all these laws to his creatures, that he might be guiltless of their future evil, the creator sowed some of them in the earth, and some in the moon, and some in the other stars which are the vessels of time ; and when he had sown them he committed to the younger Gods the fashioning of their mortal bodies, and desired them to furnish what was still lacking to the human soul, and make all the suitable additions, and rule and pilot the mortal animal in the best and wisest manner which they could, and avert from him all but self-inflicted evils. — *Timaeus*, ii. 535.

Man, his soul truly his own.

—— Listen, all ye who have just now heard the laws about Gods, and about our dear forefathers : Of all the things which a man has, next to the Gods his soul is the most divine and most truly his own. — *Laws*, iv. 252.

Many — opinion of the. See *Opinion*.
Many, the Science of Government not attained by the. See *Government not attained*.
Marathon, the men and battle of.

—— Darius had a quarrel against us and the Eretrians, because, as he said, we had conspired against Sardis, and he sent 500,000 men in transports and vessels of war, and 300 ships, and Datis as commander, telling him to bring the Eretrians and Athenians to the king, if he wished to keep his head on his shoulders. They sailed against the Eretrians, who were reputed to be amongst the noblest and most warlike of the Hellenes of that day, and they were numerous, but he conquered them all in three days; and when he had conquered them, in order that no one might escape, he searched the whole country after this manner: his soldiers, coming to the borders of Eretria and spreading from sea to sea, joined hands and passed through the whole country, in order that they might be able to tell the king that no one had escaped them. And from Eretria they went to Marathon, expecting to bind the Athenians in the same yoke of necessity in which they had bound the Eretrians. Having effected one half of their purpose, they were in the act of attempting the other, and none of the Hellenes dared to assist either the Eretrians or the Athenians, except the Lacedaemonians, and they only came the day after the battle; but the rest were panic-stricken and remained quiet, happy that they had escaped for a time. He who has present to him that conflict, will know what manner of men they were who received the onset of the barbarians at Marathon, and chastened the pride of the whole of Asia, and by the victory which they gained over the barbarians first taught other men that the power of the Persians was not invincible, but that hosts of men and the multitude of riches alike yield to virtue. And I assert that those men are the fathers not only of ourselves, but of our liberties and of the liberties of all who are on the continent, for that was the action to which the Hellenes looked back when they ventured to fight for their own safety in the battles which followed: they became disciples of the men of Marathon. To them, therefore, I assign in my speech the first place, and the second to those who fought and conquered in the sea fights at Salamis and Artemisium, for of them, too, one might have many things to say; of the assaults which they endured by sea and land,

and how they repelled them. But I will mention only that act of theirs which appears to me to be the noblest, and which was next in order of succession to Marathon, for the men of Marathon only showed the Hellenes that it was possible to ward off the barbarians by land, the many by the few; but there was no proof that they could be defeated by ships, and at sea the Persians retained the reputation of being invincible in numbers and wealth and skill and strength. This is the glory of the men who fought at sea, that they dispelled the second fear which had hitherto possessed the Hellenes, and so made the fear of numbers, whether of men or ships, to cease among them. This was the effect, and thus the soldiers of Marathon and the sailors of Salamis became the schoolmasters of Hellas; the one teaching and habituating the Hellenes not to fear the barbarians at sea, and the others not to fear them by land. — *Menexenus*, iv. 570.

Marriage, law of. See *Immortality in time.*

Marriage approved and regulated.

—— O my son, he who is born of good parents ought to make such a marriage as wise men would approve. Now they would advise you neither to avoid a poor marriage, nor specially to desire a rich one; but if other things are equal, always to honor inferiors, and with them to form connections; this will be for the benefit of the city and of the families which are united; for the equable and symmetrical tends infinitely more to virtue than the unmixed. And he who is conscious of being too headstrong, and carried away more than is fitting in all his actions, ought to desire to become the relation of orderly parents; and he who is of the opposite temper ought to seek the opposite alliance. Let there be one word concerning all marriages: Every man shall follow, not after the marriage which is most pleasing to himself, but after that which is most beneficial to the State. For somehow every one is by nature prone to that which is likest to himself, and in this way the whole city becomes unequal in property and in disposition; and hence there arise in most States results which we least desire to happen. Now, to add to the law an express provision, not only that the rich man shall not marry into the rich family, nor the powerful into the family of the powerful, but that the slower natures shall be compelled to enter into marriage with the quicker, and the quicker with the slower, may awaken anger as well as laughter in the minds of many; for there is a difficulty in perceiving that the city ought to be well mingled like a cup, in which the maddening wine is hot and fiery; but when chastened by a soberer God, receives a fair admixture and becomes an excellent and temperate drink. Yet in marriage no one is able to see the necessity of this. Wherefore also the law must leave such matters, and try to charm the spirits of men into believing the equability of their children's disposition of more importance than equality in excessive fortune when they marry; and him who is too desirous of forming a rich marriage they should endeavor to turn aside by reproaches, not, however, by any compulsion of written law. Let this then be our exhortation concerning marriage, not forgetting what was said before — that man should cling to immortality — and leave behind him posterity who shall be servants of the God in his place. All this and yet more may truly be said about the duty of marrying in the way of prelude. — *Laws*, iv. 294.

Masses swayed by rulers. See *Rulers swaying*, etc.
Melody and figure, beauty of. See *Figure*.
Memory and forgetfulness. See *Forgetfulness*.
Memory, waxen tablet of.

—— *Soc.* I would have you imagine, then, that there exists in the mind of man a block of wax, which is of different sizes in different men; harder, moister, and having more or less of purity in one than another, and in some of an intermediate quality.

Theaet. I see.

Soc. Let us say that this tablet is a gift of Memory, the mother of the Muses; and that when we wish to remember anything which we have seen, or heard, or thought in our own minds, we hold the wax to the perceptions and thoughts, and in that receive the impression of them as from the seal of a ring; and that we remember and know what is imprinted as long as the image lasts; but when the image is effaced, or cannot be taken, then we forget and do not know. — *Theaetetus*, iii. 396.

Men, compulsory care of. See *Compulsory*.
Mental and bodily habit.

—— *Soc.* And is not the bodily habit spoiled by rest and idleness, but preserved for a long time by motion and exercise?

Theaet. True.

Soc. And what of the mental habit? Is not the soul in-

formed, and improved, and preserved by thought and attention, which are motions; but when at rest, which in the soul means only want of thought and attention, is uninformed, and speedily forgets whatever she has learned?
Theaet. True. — *Theaetetus,* iii. 353.
Metallic symbols of races.

—— In the succeeding generation rulers will be appointed who have lost the guardian power of testing the metal of your different races, which, like Hesiod's, are of gold, and silver, and brass, and iron. And so iron will be mingled with silver, and brass with gold, and hence there will arise inequality and irregularity, which always and in all places are causes of enmity and war. Such is the origin of discord, wherever arising; and this is the answer of the Muses to us.

Yes, and we may assume that they answer truly.

Why, yes, I said, of course they answer truly; the Muses cannot do otherwise.

And what do the Muses say next?

When discord arose, then the two races were drawn different ways: the iron and brass fell to acquiring money and land and houses and gold and silver; but the gold and silver races, having the true riches in their own nature, inclined towards virtue and the ancient order of things. There was a battle between them, and at last they agreed to distribute their land and houses among individual owners: and they enslaved their friends and maintainers, whom they had formerly protected in the condition of freemen, and made of them subjects and servants; and they themselves were engaged in fighting and keeping watch against them. — *The Republic,* ii. 374.
Might makes right. See *Natural justice.*
Military art, youths instructed in.

—— *Lys.* What say you of the matter of which we were beginning to speak — the art of fighting in armor? Is that a practice in which the lads may be advantageously instructed?

Soc. I will endeavor to advise you, Lysimachus, as far as I can in this matter, and also in every way will comply with your wishes; but as I am younger and not so experienced, I think that I ought certainly to hear first what my elders have to say, and to learn of them, and if I have anything to add, then I may venture to give my opinion to them as well as to you. Suppose, Nicias, that one of you speaks first.

Nic. I have no objection, Socrates; and my opinion is that the acquirement of this art is in many ways useful to young men. There is an advantage in their being employed during their leisure hours in a way which tends to improve their bodily constitution, and not in the way in which young men are too apt to be employed. No gymnastics could be better or harder exercise; and this, and the art of riding, are of all arts most befitting to a freeman; for they only who are thus trained in the use of arms are the athletes of our military profession, trained in that on which the conflict turns. Moreover, in actual battle, when you have to fight in a line with a number of others, this sort of acquirement will be of some use; and will be of the greatest, when the ranks are broken and you have to fight singly; either in pursuit, when you are attacking some one who is defending himself, or in flight, when you have to defend yourself against an assailant. Certainly he who possessed the art could not meet with any harm at the hands of a single person, or perhaps of several; and in any case he would have a great advantage. Further, this sort of skill inclines a man to other noble lessons; for every man who has learned how to fight in arms will desire to learn the proper arrangement of an army, which is the sequel of the lesson; and when he has learned this, and his ambition is once fired, he will go on to learn the complete art of the general. There is no difficulty in seeing that the knowledge and practice of other military arts will be useful and valuable to a man; and this lesson may be the beginning of them. Let me add a further advantage, which is by no means a slight one, — that this science will make any man a great deal more valiant and self-possessed in the field. And I will not disdain to mention, what to some may appear to be a small matter, that he will make a better appearance at the right time; that is to say, at the time when his appearance will strike terror into his enemies. My opinion then, Lysimachus, is, as I say, that the youths should be instructed in this art, and for the reasons which I have given. — *Laches*, i. 74.

Mind, a cause.

———. I heard some one who had a book of Anaxagoras, as he said, out of which he read that mind was the disposer and cause of all, and I was quite delighted at this notion, which appeared admirable, and I said to myself: If mind is the disposer, mind will dispose all for the best, and put each particular in the best place; and I argued that if any one desired to find out the cause of the generation or destruction or existence of anything, he must find out what state of being or suffering or doing was best for that thing, and therefore a man had only to consider the best for himself and others, and then he would also know the worse, for that the same science comprised both. And I rejoiced to think that I had found in Anaxagoras a teacher of the causes of existence such as I desired, and I imagined that he would tell me first whether the earth is flat or round ; and then he would further explain the cause and the necessity of this, and would teach me the nature of the best and show that this was best ; and if he said that the earth was in the centre, he would explain that this position was the best, and I should be satisfied with the explanation given, and not want any other sort of cause. And I thought that I would then go on and ask him about the sun and moon and stars, and that he would explain to me their comparative swiftness, and their returnings and various states, active and passive, and how all of them were for the best. For I could not imagine that when he spoke of mind as the disposer of them, he would give any other account of their being as they are, except that this was best; and I thought that when he had explained to me in detail the cause of each and the cause of all, he would go on to explain to me what was best for each and what was best for all. I had hopes which I would not have sold for much, and I seized the books and read them as fast as I could in my eagerness to know the better and the worse.

What hopes I had formed, and how grievously was I disappointed! As I proceeded, I found my philosopher altogether forsaking mind or any other principle of order, but having recourse to air, and ether, and water, and other eccentricities. — *Phaedo*, i. 426.

Mind, disorders of the.

——— The disorders of the soul which originate in the body are as follows : We must acknowledge disease of the mind to be a want of intelligence; and of this there are two kinds; to wit, madness and ignorance; and whatever affection gives rise to either of them may be called disease. Excessive pains and pleasures are justly to be regarded as the greatest diseases of the soul, for a man who is in great joy or in great pain, in his irrational eagerness to attain the one and to avoid the other, is not truly able to see or to hear anything ; but he is mad, and is at the same time quite incapable of any participation in reason. He who has the seed about the spinal marrow too plentiful and overflowing, like a tree overladen with fruit, has many throes, and also obtains many pleasures in his desires and their gratifications, and is for the most part of his life mad, because his pleasures and pains are so very great; his soul is rendered foolish and disordered by his body; and he is regarded not as one diseased, but as one who is voluntarily bad, which is a bad mistake. For the truth is that the intemperance of love for the most part grows into a disease of the soul, owing to the moisture and fluidity which is produced in one of the elements, by the loose consistency of the bones. And in general, all that which is termed the intemperance of pleasure is unjustly charged upon those who do wrong, as if they did wrong voluntarily. For no man is voluntarily bad; but the bad become bad by reason of an ill disposition of the body and bad education, things which to every man are an involuntary evil; and in like manner the soul is often hurt by bodily pain. For where the sharp and briny phlegm and other bitter and bilious humors wander over the body, and find no exit or escape, but are compressed within and mingle their own vapors with the motions of the soul, and are blended with them, they produce an infinite variety of diseases in all sorts of degrees, and being carried to the three places of the soul on which any of them may severally chance to alight, they create infinite varieties of trouble and melancholy, of tempers rash and cowardly, and also of forgetfulness and stupidity. Further, when to this evil constitution of body evil forms of government are added, and evil discourses are uttered in private as well as in public, and no sort of instruction is given in youth which may heal these ills, here is another source of evil; and so the bad becomes bad, through two things which are wholly out of their power. In such cases the planters are to blame rather than the plants, the educators rather than the educated. Still we should endeavor as far as we can by education, and studies, and learning, to avoid vice and attain virtue. — *Timaeus*, ii. 577.

Mind, the life of.

—— *Pro.* And what is this life of mind?

Soc. I want to know whether any one of us would consent to live, having wisdom and mind and knowledge and memory of all things, but having no fraction of a sense of pleasure or pain, and wholly unaffected by these and the like feelings?

Pro. Neither life, Socrates, appears eligible to me, nor is likely, as I should imagine, to be chosen by any one else.

Soc. What would you say, Protarchus, to both of these in one, or to one that was made out of the union of the two?

Pro. Out of the union, that is, of pleasure with mind and wisdom?

Soc. Yes. — *Philebus,* iii. 156.

Mind, good in the. See *Good, in the mind,* etc.

Mind, depth and greatness of, reverenced.

—— I have a kind of reverence; not so much for Melissus and the others, who say that "all is one and at rest," as for the great leader himself, Parmenides, venerable and awful, as in Homeric language he may be called; him I should be ashamed to approach in a spirit unworthy of him. I met him when he was an old man, and I was a mere youth, and he appeared to me to have a glorious depth of mind. — *Theaetetus,* iii. 387.

Mind, movement of.

—— *Ath.* And what is the definition of that which is named "soul?" Can we conceive of any other than that which has been already given — the motion which is self-moved?

Cle. You mean to say that the essence which is defined as the self-moved is identical with that which we call soul?

Ath. Yes; and if this is true, do we still maintain that there is anything wanting in the proof that the soul is the first origin and moving power of all that is, or has been, or will be, and their contraries, when she has been clearly shown to be the source of change and motion in all things?

Cle. Certainly not; the soul as being the source of motion, has been most satisfactorily shown to be the oldest of all things.

Ath. And is not that motion which takes place in another, or by reason of another, but never has any self-moving power at all, being in truth the change of an inanimate body, to be reckoned in the second degree, or in any lower degree which you may prefer?

Cle. Very true.

Ath. Then we are right, and speak the most perfect and absolute truth, when we say that the soul is prior to the body, and that the body is second and comes afterwards, and is born to obey the soul which is the ruler?

Cle. Nothing can be more true. — *Laws,* iv. 408.

Minority, the government of the. See *Few*.
Minos, and naval warfare.

—— I was saying that the imitation of enemies was a bad thing; and I was thinking of a case in which a maritime people are harassed by enemies, as the Athenians were by Minos (I do not speak from any desire to recall past grievances); but he, as we know, was a great naval potentate, who compelled the inhabitants of Attica to pay him a cruel tribute; and in those days they had no ships of war as they now have, nor was the country filled with ship timber, and therefore they could not readily build them. Hence neither could they learn how to imitate their enemy at sea, or become sailors themselves, and in this way directly repel their enemies. Better for them to have lost many times over the seven youths, than that heavy-armed and stationary troops should have been turned into sailors, and accustomed to leap quickly on shore, and again to hurry back to their ships; or should have fancied that there was no disgrace in not awaiting the attack of an enemy and dying boldly; and that there were good reasons, and plenty of them, for a man throwing away his arms, and betaking himself to flight; which is not dishonorable as people say, at certain times. This is the language of naval warfare, and is anything but worthy of extraordinary praise. For we should not teach bad habits, least of all to the best part of the citizens. You may learn the evil of such a practice from Homer, by whom Odysseus is introduced, rebuking Agamemnon, because he desires to draw down the ships to the sea at a time when the Achaeans are hard pressed by the Trojans: he gets angry with him, and says:—

" Who, at a time when the battle is in full cry, biddest to drag the well-oared ships into the sea, that the prayers of the Trojans may be accomplished yet more, and high ruin fall upon us? For the Achaeans will not maintain the battle, when the ships are drawn into the sea, but they will look behind and will cease from strife; in that the counsel which you give will prove injurious."

You see that he quite knew triremes on the sea, in the neighborhood of fighting men, to be an evil; lions might be trained in that way to fly from a herd of deer. Moreover, naval powers which owe their safety to ships, do not honor that sort of warlike excellence which is most deserving of honor. For he who owes his safety to the pilot, and the captain, and the oarsman, and all sorts of rather good-for-nothing persons, cannot rightly give honor to whom honor is due. — *Laws*, iv. 233.

Mirth-giver to be rewarded.

—— *Ath.* May not the true use of music and choral festivities be described as follows: we rejoice when we think that we prosper, and again we think that we prosper when we rejoice?

Cle. Exactly.

Ath. And when rejoicing is our good fortune we are unable to be still?

.*Cle.* True.

Ath. Our young men break forth into dancing and singing, and we who are their elders deem that we are fulfilling our part in life when we look on at them. Having lost the agility of youth, we delight in their sports and merry-making: because we love to think of our former selves, and gladly institute contests for those who are able to awaken in us the memory of what we once were.

Cle. Very true.

Ath. People say that we ought to regard him as the wisest of men, and the winner of the palm, who gives us the greatest amount of pleasure and mirth. For when mirth is to be the order of the day, he ought to be honored most, and, as I was saying, bear the palm, who gives most mirth to the greatest number. Now I want to know whether this is a true way of speaking or of acting?

Cle. Possibly. — *Laws*, iv. 187.

Misanthropists and Misologists.

—— Let us take care that we avoid a danger.

And what is that? I said.

The danger of becoming misologists, he replied, which is one of the very worst things that can happen to us. For as there are misanthropists or haters of men, there are also misologists or haters of ideas, and both spring from the same cause, which is ignorance of the world. Misanthropy springs out of the too great confidence of inexperience; you trust a man and think him altogether true and sound and faithful, and then in a little while he turns out to be false and knavish; and then another and another, and when this has happened several times to a man, especially within the circle of his own most trusted friends, as he would deem them, and he has often quarreled with them, he at last hates all men, and believes that no one has any good in him at all. I dare say that you must have observed this.

Yes, I said.

And is not the feeling discreditable? Such an one having to deal with other men, had clearly no experience of them; for experience would have taught him the true state of the case, that few are the good and few the evil, and that the great majority are in the interval between them. — *Phaedo*, i. 418.

Miserly men and oligarchies.

―――― His fear has taught him to knock ambition and passion headforemost from his bosom's throne: humbled by poverty he takes to money-making, and by mean and miserly savings and hard work gets a fortune together. Is not this man likely to seat the concupiscent and covetous elements on that vacant throne? They will play the great king within him, and he will array them with tiara and collar and scimitar.

Most true, he replied.

And when he has made the reason and spirit sit on the ground obediently on either side, and taught them to know their place, he compels the one to think only of the method by which lesser sums may be converted into larger ones, and schools the other into the worship and admiration of riches and rich men; and to be ambitious only of wealth and of the means which lead to this.

Of all conversions, he said, there is none so speedy or so sure as when the ambitious youth changes into the avaricious one.

And the avaricious, I said, is the oligarchical youth?

Yes, he said; at any rate the individual out of whom he came is like the State out of which oligarchy came.

Let us then consider whether there is any likeness between them.

Very good.

First, then, they resemble one another in the value which they set upon wealth?

Certainly.

Also in their penurious, laborious character; the individual only satisfies his necessary appetites, and confines his expenditure to them; his other desires he subdues, under the idea that there is no use in them?

True.

He is a shabby fellow, I said, who saves something out of everything and makes a purse for himself; and this is the sort of man whom the vulgar applaud. Is he not like the State which he represents?

That would be my view of him, he replied; at any rate, money is highly valued by him as well as by the State.

Why, he is not a man of cultivation, I said. . . .

The man, then, will be at war with himself; he will be two men, and not one; but, in general, his better desires will be found to prevail over his inferior ones.

True.

For these reasons such an one will be more decent than many are; yet the true virtue of a unanimous and harmonious soul will be far out of his reach.

I should expect so.

And surely, the miser individually will be an ignoble competitor in a State for any prize of victory, or other object of honorable ambition; he is so afraid of awakening his expensive appetites and inviting them to help and join in the struggle; in true oligarchical fashion he fights with a small part only of his resources, and the result commonly is that he loses the prize and saves his money.

Very true.

Can we any longer doubt, then, that the miser and money-maker answers to the oligarchical State? There can be no doubt. — *Republic*, ii. 381.

Yes, I said; and men of this stamp will be covetous of money, like those who live in oligarchies; they will have a fierce secret longing after gold and silver, which they will hoard in dark places, having magazines and treasures of their own for the deposit and concealment of them; also castles which are just nests for their eggs, and in which they will spend large sums on their wives, or on any others whom they please.

That is most true, he said.

And they are miserly because they have no means of openly acquiring the money which they prize; they will spend that which is another man's in their lust; stealing their pleasures and running away like children from the law, their father: they have been schooled not by gentle influences but by force; caring nothing about the Muse, the companion of reason and philosophy, and honoring gymnastic before music.

Undoubtedly, he said, the form of government which you describe is a mixture of good and evil. — *The Republic*, ii. 375.

Misery of the unjust.

—— *Soc.* The matters at issue between us are not trifling; to know or not to know happiness and misery — that is the sum of them. And what knowledge can be nobler than this? or what ignorance more disgraceful than this? And therefore I will begin by asking you whether you do not think that a man who is unjust and doing injustice can be happy, seeing that you think Archelaus unjust and yet happy? Am I not right in supposing that to be your meaning?

Pol. Quite right.

Soc. And I say that this is an impossibility, and here is one point about which we are at issue: very good. But do you mean to say also that if he meets with retribution and punishment he will still be happy?

Pol. Certainly not; in that case he will be most miserable.

Soc. On the other hand, if the unjust be not punished, then, according to you, he will be happy?

Pol. Yes.

Soc. But in my opinion, Polus, the unjust or doer of unjust actions is miserable in any case, — more miserable, however, if he be not punished and does not meet with retribution, and less miserable if he be punished and meets with retribution, at the hands of God and men. — *Gorgias*, iii. 59.

Mixtures of pleasures and pains, of body and of soul. See *Body and soul*, etc.

Modesty and temperance.

—— Then once more, Charmides, I said, fix your attention, and look within; consider the effect which temperance has upon yourself, and the nature of that which has the effect. Think over all this, and, like a brave youth, tell me — What is temperance.

After a moment's pause, in which he made a real manly effort to think, he said: My opinion is, Socrates, that temperance makes a man ashamed or modest, and that temperance is the same as modesty.

Very good I said; and did you not admit, just now, that temperance is noble.

Yes, certainly, he said.

And the temperate are also good?

Yes.

And can that be good which does not make men good?

Certainly not.

And you would infer that temperance is not only noble, but also good?

That is my opinion.

Well, I said; and surely you would agree with Homer when he says,

" Modesty is not good for a needy man " ?

Yes, he said ; I agree to that.

Then I suppose that modesty is and is not good?

That is plain.

But temperance, whose presence makes men only good, and not bad, is always good ?

That appears to me to be as you say.

And the inference is, that temperance cannot be modesty — if temperance is a good, and if modesty is as much an evil as a good?

All that, Socrates, appears to me to be true. — *Charmides*, i. 15.

Modesty promoted by refutation   See *Purification*.
Modesty and self-conceit.   See *Self-conceit*.
Modesty, excess of.   See *Courage untempered*, etc.
Money not to be valued above friendship.   See *Friendship*.
Money, making of.   See *Miserly men*.
Money, a ruler in the State.

—— What manner of government do you term oligarchy ?

A government resting on a valuation of property, in which the rich have power and the poor are deprived of power.

I understand, he replied.

Ought I not to describe, first of all, how the change from timocracy to oligarchy arises ?

Yes.

Well, I said, no eyes are required in order to see how the one passes into the other.

How ?

The accumulation of gold in the treasury of private individuals is the ruin of timocracy ; they invent illegal modes of expenditure, but what do they or their wives care about the law ?

Very true.

And then one seeing another prepares to rival him, and thus the whole body of the citizens acquires a similar character.

Likely enough.

After that they get on in trade, and the more they think of making a fortune, the less they think of virtue ; for when riches and virtue are placed together in the scales of the balance, the one always rises as the other falls.

True.

And in proportion as riches and rich men are honored in the State, virtue and the virtuous are dishonored.

Clearly.

And what is honored is cultivated, and that which has no honor is neglected.

That is the case.

And so at last, instead of loving contention and glory, men become lovers of trade and money, and they honor and reverence the rich man, and make a ruler of him, and dishonor the poor man.

They do so.

Whereupon they proceed to make a law which fixes a sum of money as the qualification of citizenship; the money is more or less accordingly as the oligarchy is more or less exclusive; and any one whose property is below the amount fixed is not allowed to share in the government; which changes in the constitution they effect by force of arms, if intimidation has not already done their work.

Very true. — *The Republic*, ii. 377.

Money, enslaving power of. See *Enslaving*, etc.

Money not to have the place of power in the State.

—— *Ath.* We maintain, then, that a State which would be safe and happy, as far as the nature of man allows, must and ought to distribute honor and dishonor in the right way. And the right way is to place the goods of the soul first and highest in the scale, always assuming temperance as a condition of them; and in the second place, the goods of the body; and in the third place, those of money and property. And if any legislator or State departs from this rule by giving money the place of honor, or in any way preferring that which is really last, may we not say, that he or the State is doing an unholy and unpatriotic thing?

Meg. Yes; let that be plainly asserted. — *Laws*, iv. 226.

Money. See *Wealth, Riches, Property, Possession*.

Money-sting of business men. See *Business men*.

Monsters, filial. See *Filial*, etc.

Mother, ambitious. See *Woman*, etc.

Motherhood of country.

—— Their ancestors were not strangers, nor are these their

descendants sojourners only, whose fathers have come from another country; but they are the children of the soil, dwelling and living in their own land. And the country which brought them up is not like other countries, a step-mother to her children, but their own true mother; she bore them and nourished them and received them, and in her bosom they now repose. It is meet and right, therefore, that we should begin by praising the land which is their mother, and that will be a way of praising their noble birth.

The country is worthy to be praised, not only by us, but by all mankind; first, and above all, as being dear to the Gods. This is proved by the strife and contention of the Gods respecting her. And ought not that country which the Gods praise to be praised by all mankind? The second praise which may be fairly claimed by her, is that at the time when the whole earth was sending forth and creating diverse animals, tame and wild, she our mother was free and pure from savage monsters, and out of all animals selected and brought forth man, who is superior to the rest in understanding, and alone has justice and religion. And a great proof that she was the mother of us and of our ancestors, is that she provided the means of support for her offspring. For as a woman proves her motherhood by giving milk to her young ones (and she who has no fountain of milk is not a mother), so did this our land prove that she was going to be the mother of men, for in those days she alone and first of all brought forth wheat and barley for human food, which is the best and noblest sustenance for man, whom she regarded as her true offspring. And these are truer proofs of motherhood in a country than in a woman, for the woman in her conception and generation is but the imitation of the earth, and not the earth of the woman. And of the fruit of the earth she gave a plenteous supply, not only to her offspring, but to others also; and after that she made the olive to spring up to be a boon to her children, and to help them in their toils. And when she had herself nursed them and brought them up to manhood, she gave them Gods to be their rulers and teachers, whose names are well known, and need not now be repeated. They are the Gods who first ordered our lives, and gave us arts to supply our daily needs, and taught us the possession and use of arms for the guardianship of the country. — *Menexenus*, iv. 568.

Motion and rest of things. See *Rest*.

Multitude, the Science of Government not attained by the. See *Government, Science of*.

Music, enervating power of. See *Irritability*.
Music, most celebrated.

—— Music is more celebrated than any other kind of imitation, and therefore requires the greatest care of them all. For if a man makes a mistake here, he may do himself the greatest injury by welcoming evil dispositions, and the mistake may be very difficult to discern, because the poets are artists very inferior in character to the Muses themselves, who would never fall into the monstrous error of assigning to the words of men the gestures and songs of women; nor combine the melodies and gestures of freemen with the rhythms of slaves and men of the baser sort; or, beginning with the rhythms and gestures of freemen, assign to them a melody or words which are of an opposite character; nor would they mix up the voices and sounds of animals and of men and instruments, and every other sort of noise, as if they were all one. But human poets are fond of introducing this sort of inconsistent mixture, and thus make themselves ridiculous in the eyes of those who, as Orpheus says, "are ripe for pleasure." The experienced see all this confusion, and yet the poets go on and make still further havoc by separating the rhythm and the figure of the dance from the melody, setting words to metre without music, and also separating the melody and rhythm from the words, using the lyre or the flute alone. For when there are no words, it is very difficult to recognize the meaning of the harmony and rhythm, or to see that any worthy object is imitated by them. And we must acknowledge that all this sort of thing, which aims only at swiftness and smoothness and a brutish noise, and uses the flute and the lyre not as the mere accompaniments of the dance and song. is exceedingly rude and coarse. The use of either, when unaccompanied by the others, leads to every sort of irregularity and trickery. — *Laws*, iv. 199.

Music, different kinds of.

—— *Ath.* Let us speak of the laws about music; that is to say, such music as then existed; in order that we may trace the growth of the excess of freedom from the beginning; for music was early divided among us into certain kinds and manners. One sort consisted of prayers to the Gods, which were called hymns; and there was another and opposite sort called lamentations, and another termed paeans, and another called dithyrambs; of which latter the subject, if I am not mistaken, was the birth of Dionysus. And they used the actual word "**laws,**" or νόμοι, meaning "song," only adding such and such an instrument, of the harp for example, when they wanted to denote a particular strain. All these and others were duly distinguished, nor were they allowed to intermingle one sort of music with another. And the authority which determined and gave judgment, and punished the disobedient, was not expressed in a hiss, nor in the most unmusical "sweet voices" of the multitude, as in our days; nor in applause and clappings of the hands. But the directors of public instruction insisted that the spectators should listen in silence to the end; and boys and their tutors, and the multitude in general, were kept quiet by the touch of the wand. Such was the good order which the multitude were willing to observe; they would not have dared to give judgment by noisy cries. And then, as time went on, the poets themselves introduced the reign of ignorance and misrule. They were men of genius, but they had no knowledge of what is just and lawful in music; raging like Bacchanals and possessed with inordinate delights — mingling lamentations with hymns, and paeans with dithyrambs; imitating the sounds of the flute on the lyre, and making one general confusion; ignorantly affirming that music has no truth, and, whether good or bad, can only be judged of rightly by the pleasure of the hearer. And by composing such licentious poems, and adding to them words as licentious, they have inspired the multitude with lawlessness and boldness, and made them fancy that they can judge for themselves about melody and song. And in this way, the theatres from being mute have become vocal, as though they had understanding of good and bad in music and poetry; and instead of an aristocracy, an evil sort of theatrocracy has grown up. — *Laws*, iv. 229.

Musical training.

—— Musical training is a more potent instrument than any other, because rhythm and harmony find their way into the secret places of the soul, on which they mightily fasten, imparting grace and making the soul graceful of him who is rightly educated, or ungraceful of him who is ill-educated; and also because he who has received this true education of the inner being will most shrewdly perceive omissions or faults in art and nature, and with a true taste, while he praises and rejoices over and receives into his soul the good, and becomes noble and good, he will justly blame and hate the bad, now in the days of his youth, even before he is able to know the reason why; and when reason comes he will recognize and salute her as a friend with whom his education has made him long familiar. — *The Republic*, ii. 225.

Musician, the true.

—— When I hear a man discoursing of virtue, or of any sort of wisdom, who is a true man and worthy of his theme, I am delighted beyond measure; and I compare the man and his words, and note the harmony and correspondence of them. And such an one I deem to be the true musician, attuned to a fairer harmony than that of the lyre, or any pleasant instrument of music; for truly he has in his own life a harmony of words and deeds arranged, not in the Ionian, or in the Phrygian mode, nor yet in the Lydian, but in the true Hellenic mode, which is the Dorian, and no other. Such an one makes me merry with the sound of his voice; and when I hear him I am thought to be a lover of discourse; so eager am I in drinking in his words. But a man whose actions do not agree with his words is an annoyance to me; and the better he speaks the more I hate him, and then I seem to be a hater of discourse. — *Laches*, i. 81.

Musician, becoming soft. See *Irritability*.

National peace, degenerating.

—— The orderly class are always ready to lead a peaceful life, and do their own business; this is their way of living with all men at home, and they are equally ready to keep the peace with foreign States. And on account of this fondness of theirs for peace, which is often out of season where their influence prevails, they become by degrees unwarlike, and bring up their young men to be like themselves; they are at the command of others; and hence in a few years they and their children and the whole city often pass imperceptibly from the condition of freemen into that of slaves. — *Statesman*, iii. 594.

Nations. See *States destroyed*, etc.

Nature, counterparts and antagonisms in. See *Antagonisms*, etc.

Nature, reversal of the order of.

—— *Str.* The life of all animals first came to a stand, and the mortal nature ceased to be or look older, and was then reversed and grew young and delicate; the white locks of the aged darkened again, and the cheeks of the bearded man became smooth, and he was restored to his original youth; the bodies of the young grew finer and smaller, continually by day and night returning and becoming assimilated to the nature of a newly-born child in mind as well as body; in the succeeding stage they wasted away and wholly disappeared. And the bodies of those who had died by violence quickly passed through the like changes, and in a few days were no more seen. — *Statesman*, iii. 555.

Nature and chance.

—— *Ath.* They say that the greatest and fairest things are done by nature and chance, and the lesser by art, which receives from nature all the greater and primeval creations, and fashions them in detail; and these lesser works are generally termed artificial.

Cle. What do you and they mean?

Ath. You will understand their meaning better, if I take the elements as an example; they mean to say that fire and water, and earth and air, all exist by nature and chance, and not by art; and that as to the bodies which come next in order, — earth, and sun, and moon, and stars, — they are created by the help of these absolutely inanimate existences, and that they are severally moved by chance and some inherent influence according to certain affinities of hot with cold, or of dry with moist, or of soft with hard, and other chance admixtures of opposites which have united of necessity, and that on this manner the whole heaven has been created, and all that is in the heaven, including animals and all plants, and that all the seasons come from these elements, not by the action of mind, as they say, or of any God, or from art, but as I was saying, by nature and chance only; and that art sprang up after these and out of them, mortal and of mortal birth, and produced in play certain images and very partial imitations of the truth, having an affinity to one another, such as music and painting create and their companion arts. And there are other arts which have a serious purpose, and these coöperate with nature, such, for example, as medicine, and husbandry, and gymnastic. And they say that politics coöperate with nature, but in a less degree, and have more of art; also that legislation is entirely a work of art, and is based on assumptions which are not true.

Cle. How do you mean?

Ath. In the first place, my dear friend, they would say that the Gods exist neither by nature nor by art, but only by the laws of States, which are different in different places, according to the agreement of those who make them; and that the honorable is one thing by nature and another thing by law, and that the principles of justice have no existence at all in nature, but that mankind are always disputing about them and altering them; and that the alterations which are made by art and by law have no basis in nature, but are of authority for the moment and at the time at which they are made: these, my friends, are the sayings of wise men, poets and prose writers, which find a way into the minds of youth. They are told by them that the highest right is might, and in this way the young fall into impieties, under the idea that the Gods are not such as the law bids them imagine them; and hence arise contentions — the philosophers inviting them to lead a true life according to nature, which is to live in real dominion over others, and not in legal subjection to them. — *Laws*, iv. 400.

Natural gifts. See *Talents*, etc. .
Natural justice. See *Justice, natural*.
Natural appetite. See *Appetites*.
Naval warfare and potentate. See *Minos*.
Noble and just, the.

—— To him who maintains that it is profitable for the human creature to be unjust, and unprofitable to be just, let us reply, that if he be right, it is profitable for this creature to feast the multitudinous monster and strengthen the lion and the lion-like qualities and to starve and weaken the man; who is consequently at the mercy of either of the other two, and he is not to attempt to familiarize or harmonize them with one another: he ought rather to suffer them to fight and bite and devour one another.

Certainly, he said; that is what the approver of injustice says.

- To him the supporter of justice makes answer that he ought rather to aim in all he says and does at strengthening the man within him, in order that he may be able to govern the many-headed monster. Like a good husbandman he should be watching and tending the gentle shoots, and preventing the wild ones from growing; making a treaty with the lion-heart, and in common care of them all uniting the several parts with one another and with himself.

Yes, he said, that is quite what the maintainer of justice will say.

And from every point of view, whether of pleasure, honor,

or advantage, the approver of justice is right and speaks the truth, and the disapprover is wrong, and false, and ignorant?

Yes, from every point of view. — *The Republic*, ii. 420.

Noble, man, the rich.

—— From what point of view then, and on what ground, shall a man be profited by injustice or intemperance or other baseness, even though he acquire money or power?

From no point of view at all.

What shall he profit, if his injustice be undetected? for he who is undetected only gets worse, whereas he who is detected and punished has the brutal part of his nature silenced and humanized ; the gentler element in him is liberated, and his whole soul is perfected and ennobled by the acquirement of justice and temperance and wisdom, more than the body ever is by receiving gifts of beauty, strength, and health, in proportion as the soul is more honorable than the body.

Certainly, he said.

On this higher end, then, the man of understanding will concentrate the energies of his life. And in the first place, he will honor studies which impress these qualities on his soul, and will disregard others?

Clearly, he said.

In the next place, he will regulate his bodily habit, and so far will he be from yielding to brutal and irrational pleasures, that he will regard even health as quite a secondary matter ; his first object will be not that he may be fair or strong or well, unless he is likely thereby to gain temperance, but he will be always desirous of preserving the harmony of the body for the sake of the concord of the soul?

Certainly he will, he replied, if he has true music in him.

And there is a principle of order and harmony in the acquisition of wealth ; this also he will observe, and will not allow himself to be dazzled by the opinion of the world, and heap up riches to his own infinite harm?

I think not, he said.

He will look at the city which is within him, and take care to avoid any change of his own institutions, such as might arise either from superfluity or from want ; and with a view to this only he will gain or spend in so far as he is able?

Very true.

And, for the same reason, he will accept such honors as he deems likely to make him a better man ; but those which are likely to disorder his constitution, whether private or public honors, he will avoid?

Then, if that is his motive, he will not be a politician?

By the dog of Egypt, he will! in the city which is his own, though in the land of his birth perhaps not, unless by some providential accident. — *The Republic*, ii. 422.

Noble, no rhetorician is.

—— *Soc.* I am contented with the admission that rhetoric is of two sorts; one, which is mere flattery, and disgraceful declamation; the other, which is noble and aims at the training and improvement of the souls of the citizens, and strives to say what is best, whether welcome or unwelcome, to the audience; but have you ever known such a rhetoric; or if you have, and can point out any rhetorician who is of this stamp, will you tell me who he is?

Cal. But, indeed, I am afraid that I cannot tell you of any such among the orators who are at present living.

Soc. Well, then, can you mention any one of a former generation, who may be said to have improved the Athenians, who found them worse and made them better, from the day that he began to make speeches? for, indeed, I do not know of such a man.

Cal. What! did you never hear that Themistocles was a good man, and Cimon and Miltiades and Pericles, who is just lately dead, and whom you heard yourself?

Soc. Yes, Callicles, they were good men, if, as you said at first, true virtue consists only in the satisfaction of our own desires and those of others; but if not, and if, as we were afterwards compelled to acknowledge, the satisfaction of some desires makes us better and of others worse, and we ought to gratify the one and not the other, and there is an art in distinguishing them — can you tell me of any of these statesmen who did distinguish them.

Cal. No, indeed, I cannot. — *Gorgias*, iii. 94.

Nobler life. See *Life, the nobler*.

Novelty, the love of. See *Innovations*.

Novelty, the world jealous of.

—— *Euth.* I understand, Socrates; he means to attack you about the familiar sign which occasionally, as you say, comes to you. He thinks that you are a neologian, and he is going to have you up before the court for this. He knows that such a charge is readily received by the world. I can tell you that, for when I myself speak in the assembly about divine things, and foretell the future to them, they laugh at me as a madman; and yet every word that I say is true. But they are jealous of all of us. I suppose that we must be brave and not mind them.

Soc. Their laughter, friend Euthyphro, is not a matter of much consequence. For a man may be thought wise; but the Athenians, I suspect, do not trouble themselves about him until he begins to impart his wisdom to others; and then for some reason or other, perhaps, as you say, from jealousy, they are angry. — *Euthyphro*, i. 286.

Numbers no argument.

—— *Soc.* O Polus, I am not a public man, and only last year, when my tribe were serving as Prytanes, and the lot fell upon me and I was made a senator, and had to take the votes, there was a laugh at me, because I was unable to take them. And as I failed then, you must not ask me to count the suffrages of the company now; but if, as I was saying, you have no better argument than numbers, let me have a turn, and do you make trial of the sort of proof which, as I think, ought to be given; for I shall produce one witness only of the truth of my words, and he is the person with whom I am arguing; his suffrage I know how to take; but with the many I have nothing to do, and do not even address myself to them. — *Gorgias*, iii. 60.

Oaths, false.

—— Every man should regard adulteration as a particular kind of falsehood, concerning which the many are too fond of saying, that at proper times, the practice may often be right. But they leave the time and place and occasion undefined and unregulated, and from this want of definiteness in their language they do a great deal of harm to themselves and to others. Now, a legislator ought not to leave the matter undefined; he ought to prescribe some limit, either greater or less. Let this, then, be the limit prescribed: no one shall call the Gods to witness, when he says or does anything false or deceitful or dishonest, unless he would be the most hateful of mankind to them. And he is most hateful to them who takes a false oath, and never thinks of the Gods; and in the second place, he who tells a falsehood in the presence of his superiors. Now, better men are the superiors of worse men, and in general elders are the superiors of the young; wherefore, also, parents are the superiors of their children, and men of women and children, and rulers of their subjects ; for all men ought to reverence any one who is in any position of authority, and especially those who are in State offices. And this is the reason why I have spoken of these matters. For every one who is guilty of adulteration in the agora tells a falsehood, and deceives, and when he invokes the Gods, according to the customs and cautions of the wardens of the agora, he is perjured, and has no respect either for God or man. — *Laws*, iv. 428.

Office-seeking disgraceful.

—— Of course you know that ambition and avarice are said to be and are a disgrace ?

Very true.

And for this reason money and honor have no attraction for them ; they do not wish to be directly paid for governing and so get the name of hirelings, nor by indirectly helping themselves out of the public revenues to get the name of thieves. And not being ambitious they do not care about honor ; and therefore necessity must be laid upon them, and they must be induced to serve from the fear of punishment. And this, as I imagine, is the reason why the forwardness to take office, instead of waiting to be compelled, has been thought dishonorable. Now he who refuses to rule is liable to be ruled by one who is worse than himself, than which no punishment can be greater. And the fear of this, as I conceive, induces the good to take office, not because they would, but because they cannot help; nor under the idea that they are going to have any benefit or enjoyment themselves, but as a necessity, and because they are not able to commit the task of ruling to any one who is better than themselves, or indeed as good. For the probability is that if a city were composed entirely of good men, then to avoid office would be as much an object of contention as to obtain office is at present; then we should have plain proof that the true ruler is not meant by nature to regard his own interest, but that of his subjects ; and every wise man will therefore choose rather to receive a benefit from another than to have the trouble of conferring one. — *The Republic*, ii. 169.

Office-seekers.

—— You must contrive for your future rulers another and a better life than that of a ruler, then you may have a well-ordered State ; for only in the State which offers this will they rule who are truly rich, not in silver and gold, but in virtue and wisdom, which are the true blessings of life. Whereas if they go to the administration of public affairs, poor and hungering after their own private advantage, thinking that hence they are to snatch away the good of life, order there can never be; for they will be fighting about office, and the civil and domestic broils which thus arise will be the ruin of the rulers themselves and of the whole State. — *The Republic*, ii. 347.

Oligarchy. See *Miserly men; Government, property in;* and *Money.*

Opinion, true.

—— *Soc.* If a man knew the way to Larisa, or anywhere else, and went to the place and led others thither, would he not be a right and good guide?

Men. Certainly.

Soc. And a person who had a right opinion about the way, but had never been and did not know, might be a good guide also, might he not?

Men. Certainly.

Soc. And while he has true opinion about that which the other knows, he will be just as good a guide if he thinks the truth, as if he knows the truth?

Men. Exactly.

Soc. Then true opinion is as good a guide to correct action as wisdom ; and that was the point which we omitted in our speculation about the nature of virtue, when we said that wisdom only is the guide of right action ; whereas there is also right opinion.

Men. True.

Soc. Then right opinion is not less useful than knowledge?

Men. The difference, Socrates, is only that he who has knowledge will always be right ; but he who has right opinion will sometimes be right, and sometimes not right.

Soc. What do you mean? Can he be wrong who has right opinion, as long as he has right opinion?

Men. I admit the cogency of that, and therefore, Socrates, I wonder that knowledge should be preferred to right opinion — or why they should ever differ. — *Meno*, i. 273.

Opinion, right.

—— " Is that which is not wise, ignorant? do you not see that there is a mean between wisdom and ignorance?" "And what may that be?" I said. "Right opinion," she replied; "which, as you know, being incapable of giving a reason, is not knowledge (for how can knowledge be devoid of reason? nor again, ignorance, for neither can ignorance attain the truth), but is clearly something which is a mean between ignorance and wisdom." — *The Symposium*, i. 494.

Opinion, popular, not to be heeded.

—— *Soc.* But why, my dear Crito, should we care about the opinion of the many? Good men, and they are the only persons who are worth considering, will think of these things truly as they occurred.

Cr. But you see, Socrates, that the opinion of the many must be regarded, for what is now happening shows that they can do the greatest evil to any one who has lost their good opinion.

Soc. I only wish, Crito, that they could; for then they could also do the greatest good, and that would be well. But in reality they can do neither: for they cannot either make a man wise or make him foolish; and whatever they do is the result of chance. — *Crito*, i. 348.

Opinion of the many and the wise.

—— *Soc.* In questions of just and unjust, fair and foul, good and evil, which are the subjects of our present consultation, ought we to follow the opinion of the many and to fear them; or the opinion of the one man who has understanding? ought we not to fear and reverence him more than all the rest of the world: and if we desert him shall we not destroy and injure that principle in us which may be assumed to be improved by justice and deteriorated by injustice; — there is such a principle?

Cr. Certainly there is, Socrates. . . . .

Soc. Then, my friend, we must not regard what the many say of us; but what he, the one man who has understanding of just and unjust, will say, and what the truth will say. And therefore you begin in error when you suggest that we should regard the opinion of the many about just and unjust, good and evil, honorable and dishonorable. "Well," some one will say, "but the many can kill us."

Cr. Yes, Socrates; that will clearly be the answer.

Soc. That is true: but still I find with surprise that the old argument is, as I conceive, unshaken as ever. — *Crito*, i. 352.

Opinion and knowledge. See *Knowledge*, etc.

Opinion, public, compared to a great beast.

—— Let me crave your assent, also, to a further observation.

All those mercenary individuals, whom the world calls Sophists and esteems rivals, do but teach the collective opinion of the many, which are the opinions of their assemblies ; and this is their wisdom. I might compare them to a man who should study the tempers and desires of a mighty strong beast who is fed by him — he would learn how to approach and handle him, also at what times and from what causes he is dangerous or the reverse, and what is the meaning of his several cries, and by what sounds, when another utters them, he is soothed or infuriated ; and you may suppose, further, that when, by constantly living with him, he has become perfect in all this he calls his knowledge wisdom, and makes a system or art, which he proceeds to teach, not that he has any real notion of what he is teaching, but he names this honorable and that dishonorable, or good or evil, or just or unjust, all in accordance with the tastes and tempers of the great brute, when he has learnt the meaning of his inarticulate grunts. Good he pronounces to be what pleases him, and evil what he dislikes ; and he can give no other account of them except that the just and noble are the necessary, having never himself seen, and having no power of explaining to others, the nature of either, or the immense difference between them. Would not he be a rare educator ?

Indeed, he would.

And in what respects does he who thinks that wisdom is the discernment of the tastes and pleasures of the assembled multitude, whether in painting or music, or, finally, in politics, differ from such an one ? For I suppose you will agree that he who associates with the many, and exhibits to them his poem or other work of art, or the service which he has done the State, making them his judges, except under protest, will also experience the fatal necessity of producing whatever they praise. And yet the reasons are utterly ludicrous which they give in confirmation of their notions about the honorable and good Did you ever hear any of them which were not ?

No, nor am I likely to hear.

You recognize the truth of what has been said ? Then let me ask you to consider, further, whether the world will ever be induced to believe in the existence of absolute beauty rather than of the many beautiful, or of the absolute in each kind rather than of the many in each kind ?

Certainly not.

Then the world cannot possibly be a philosopher?
Impossible.
And therefore philosophers must inevitably fall under the censure of the world?
They must. — *The Republic*, ii. 319.
Opinion, right, differences as to. See *Differences.*
Opinion, false. See *False* and *Heterodoxy.*
Opinions and beliefs, true. See *Beliefs.*
Opposites, generation of. See *Generation.*
Order and Harmony, wealth acquired according to. See *Noble rich man.*
Order and harmony in the soul. See *Harmony.*
Order and Law, limitation of.

—— *Soc.* I omit to speak of ten thousand other things, such as beauty and health and strength, and of the many beauties and high perfections of the soul; methinks, O my fair Philebus, that the goddess saw the universal wantonness and wickedness of all things, having no limit of pleasure or satiety, and she devised the limit of law and order, tormenting, as you say, Philebus, or, as I affirm, saving the soul. — *Philebus,* iii. 161.
Order of nature reversed. See *Nature,* etc.

Pain and pleasure related.

—— How singular is the thing called pleasure, and how curiously related to pain, which might be thought to be the opposite of it; for they never will come to a man together, and yet he who pursues either of them is generally compelled to take the other. Their bodies are two and yet they are joined to a single head; and I cannot help thinking that if Aesop had noticed them, he would have made a fable about God trying to reconcile their strife, and how, when he could not, he fastened their heads together; and this is the reason why when one comes the other follows, as I find in my own case, pleasure comes following after the pain in my leg which was caused by the chain. — *Phaedo,* i. 386.
Pain and pleasure simultaneous.

—— *Soc.* Do you see the inference: — that pleasure and pain are simultaneous, when you say that being thirsty, you drink? For are they not simultaneous, and do they not affect at the same time the same part, whether of the soul or the body; which of them is affected, cannot be supposed to be of any consequence? Is that true or not?

Cal. True. . . . .

Soc. I envy you, Callicles, for having been initiated in the great mysteries before you were initiated into the little. I thought that was not allowable. But to return to our argument: — does not a man cease from thirsting and from the pleasure of drinking at the same moment?

Cal. True.

Soc. And if he is hungry, or has any other desire, does he not cease from the desire and the pleasure at the same moment?

Cal. Very true.

Soc. Then he ceases from pain and pleasure at the same moment?

Cal. Yes.

Soc. But he does not cease from good and evil at the same moment, as you have admitted, — do you not still admit that?

Cal. Yes, I do; but what is the inference?

Soc. Why, my friend, the inference is that the good is not the same as the pleasant, or the evil the same as the painful, for there is a cessation of pleasure and pain at the same moment; but not of good and evil. How then can pleasure be the same as good, or pain as evil? And I would have you look at the matter in another point of view, which could hardly, I think, have been considered by you when you identified them: Are not the good.good because they have good present with them, as the beautiful are those who have beauty present with them?

Cal. Yes. — *Gorgias,* iii. 86.

Pain and pleasure, qualities of.

——— *Soc.* But there is no difficulty in seeing that pleasure and pain as well as opinion have qualities, for they are great or small, and have various degrees of intensity; as was indeed said long ago by us.

Pro. Quite true.

Soc. And if there is badness in any of them, Protarchus, then we should speak of a bad opinion or of a bad pleasure?

Pro. Quite true, Socrates.

Soc. And if there is rightness in any of them, should we not speak of a right opinion or right pleasure; and in like manner of the reverse of rightness?

Pro. Certainly.

Soc. And if the thing opined be erroneous, might we not say that the opinion is erroneous, and not rightly opined?

Pro. Certainly.

Soc. And if we see a pleasure or pain which errs in respect of the object of pleasure or pain, shall we call that right or good, or by any honorable name?

Pro. Not if the pleasure is mistaken; we could not.

Soc. And surely pleasure often appears to accompany an opinion which is not true, but false?

Pro. That is quite correct; and in that case, Socrates, we call the opinion false, but no one could call the actual pleasure false.

Soc. How eagerly, Protarchus, do you rush to the defense of pleasure!

Pro. Nay, Socrates, I only say what I hear.

Soc. And is there no difference, my friend, between that pleasure which is associated with right opinion and knowledge, and that which is often found in us associated with falsehood and ignorance?

Pro. There must be a very great difference between them.
— *Philebus*, iii. 175.

Painter, the Poet like the. See *Poet*, etc.

Painting and writing.

—— *Soc.* I cannot help feeling, Phaedrus, that writing is unfortunately like painting; for the creations of the painter have the attitude of life, and yet if you ask them a question they preserve a solemn silence. And the same may be said of speeches. You would imagine that they had intelligence, but if you want to know anything and put a question to one of them, the speaker always gives one unvarying answer. And when they have been once written down they are tumbled about anywhere among those who do and among those who do not understand them. And they have no reticences or proprieties towards different classes of persons; and, if they are unjustly assailed or abused, their parent is needed to protect his offspring, for they cannot protect or defend themselves.

Phaedr. That again is most true.

Soc. May we not imagine another kind of writing or speaking far better than this is, and having far greater power, — which is one of the same family, but lawfully begotten? Let us see what his origin is.

Phaedr. Who is he, and what do you mean about his origin?

Soc. I am speaking of an intelligent writing which is graven in the soul of him who has learned, and can defend itself, and knows when to speak and when to be silent.

Phaedr. You mean the word of knowledge which has a living soul, and of which the written word is properly no more than an image?

Soc. Yes, of course that is what I mean. — *Phaedrus,* i. 581.

Painting, imitation. See *Imitation,* etc.
Painting, deception in. See *Likeness of the world.*
Parents, what the children owe to the. See *Children,* etc.

—— *Ath.* Neither God, nor a man who has understanding, will ever advise any one to neglect his parents. To a discourse concerning the honor and dishonor of parents, a prelude such as the following, about the service of the Gods, will be a suitable introduction:—There are ancient customs about the Gods which are universal, and they are of two kinds; some of the Gods we see with our eyes and honor them, of others we honor the images; raising statues of them which we adore; and though they be lifeless, yet we imagine that the living Gods have a good will and gratitude to us on this account. Now, if a man has a father or mother, or their father or mother treasured up in his house stricken in years, let him consider that no statue can be more potent to grant his requests than they are, who are sitting at his hearth, if only he knows how to show true service to them.

Cle. And what do you call the true mode of service?

Ath. I will tell you, O my friend, for such things are worth listening to.

Cle. Proceed.

Ath. Oedipus, as tradition says, when dishonored by his sons, invoked on them the fulfillment of those curses from the God which every one declares to have been heard and ratified by the Gods; and Amyntor in his wrath invoked curses on his son Phoenix, and Theseus upon Hippolytus, and innumerable others have also called down wrath upon their children, which is a plain proof that the Gods listen to the imprecations of parents; for the curses of a parent are, as they ought to be, mighty against his children as no others are. And shall we suppose that the prayers of a father or mother who is specially dishonored by his or her children, are heard by the Gods in accordance with nature; and that if a man is honored by them, and in the gladness of his heart earnestly entreats the Gods in his prayers to do them good, he is not equally heard, and that they do not minister to his request? If not, they would be very unjust ministers of good, and that we affirm to be contrary to their nature.

Cle. Certainly.

Ath. May we not think, as I was saying just now, that we can possesss no image which is more honored by the Gods, than that of a father or grandfather, or of a mother stricken in years? whom when a man honors, the heart of the God rejoices, and he is ready to answer their prayers. And, truly, the figure of an ancestor is a wonderful thing, far higher than that of a lifeless image. For when they are honored by us, they join in our prayers, and when they are dishonored, they utter imprecations against us; but lifeless objects do neither. And, therefore, if a man makes a right use of his father and grandfather and other aged relations, he will have the best of all images which can procure him the favor of the Gods.

Cle. Excellent.

Ath. Every man of understanding fears and respects the prayers of his parents, knowing well that many times and to many persons they have been accomplished. Now, these things being thus ordered by nature, good men think that they are the gainers by having aged parents living, to the end of their life, or if they depart early, they are deeply lamented by them; and to the bad they are very terrible. Wherefore let every man honor with every sort of lawful honor, his own parents agreeably to what has now been said. — *Laws,* iv. 442.

Parents, brave sons of brave. See *State, heroes,* etc.
Parental sorrow to be lightly borne. See *Sorrow.*
Parricides.

—— But what if the people go into a passion, and aver that a grown-up son ought not to be supported by his father, but that the father should be supported by the son? He did not bring him into the world in order that when he was grown up he himself should be the servant of his own servants, and should support him and his rabble of slaves and companions; but that, having such a protector, he might be emancipated from the government of the rich and aristocratic, as they are termed. And so he bids him and his companions depart, just as any other father might drive out of the house a riotous son and his party of revelers.

By heaven, he said, then the parent will discover what a monster he has been fostering in his bosom; and when he wants to drive him out, he will find that he is weak and his son strong.

Why, you do not mean to say that the tyrant will use violence? What! beat his father if he opposes him?

Yes, he will; and he will begin by taking away his arms. Then he is a parricide, and a cruel, unnatural son to an aged parent whom he ought to cherish; and this is real tyranny, about which there is no mistake; as the saying is, the people who would escape the smoke which is the slavery of freemen, has fallen into the fire which is the tyranny of slaves. Thus liberty, getting out of all order and reason, passes into the harshest and bitterest form of slavery.— *The Republic*, ii. 398.

Parties, political.

—— *Ath.* Consider, then, to whom our State is to be intrusted. For there is a thing which has occurred times without number in States —

Cle. What?

Ath. That when there has been a contest for power, and the conquerors have monopolized the government, and have refused all share to the defeated party and their descendants, they have lived watching one another, in perpetual fear that some one will come into power who has a recollection of former wrongs, and will rise up against them. Now, according to our view, such governments are not polities at all, nor are laws right which are passed for the good of particular classes and not for the good of the whole State. States which have such laws are not polities but parties, and their notion of justice is simply unmeaning. I say this, because I am going to assert that we must not intrust the government in your State to any one because he is rich, or because he possesses any advantage, such as strength, or stature, or again birth; but he who is most obedient to the laws of the State, he shall win the palm; and to him who is victorious in the first degree, shall be given the highest office and chief ministry of the Gods; and the second to him who bears the second palm; and in a similar ratio shall all the other offices be assigned to their holders. And when I call the rulers servants or ministers of the law, I give them this name not for the sake of novelty, but because I certainly believe that upon their service or ministry depends the well or ill-being of the State. For that State in which the law is subject and has no authority, I perceive to be on the highway to ruin; but I see that the State in which the law is above the rulers, and the rulers are the inferiors of the law, has salvation, and every blessing which the Gods can confer. — *Laws*, iv. 242.

Passion, incorrupt, the end of reason.

—— You remember that passion or spirit appeared at first sight to be a kind of desire, but now we should say the contrary; for in the conflict of the soul, spirit is arrayed on the side of the rational principle.

Most assuredly.

But a further question arises: Is spirit different from reason also, or only a kind of reason; in which latter case, instead of three principles in the soul, there will be only two, the rational and the concupiscent; or rather, as the State was composed of three classes, traders, auxiliaries, counselors, so may there not be in the individual soul a third element which is passion or spirit, and when not corrupted by education, is the auxiliary of reason?

Yes, he said, there must be a third. — *The Republic*, ii. 267.

Patients and doctors. See *Doctors*.

Patriarchal State.

—— *Ath.* They could hardly have wanted lawgivers as yet; nothing of that sort was likely to have existed in their days, for they had no letters at this early stage; they lived by habit and the customs of their forefathers, as they are called.

Cle. Probably.

Ath. But there was already existing a form of government which, if I am not mistaken, is generally termed a lordship, and this still remains in many places, both among Hellenes and barbarians, and is the government which is declared by Homer to have prevailed among the Cyclopes:—

"They have neither councils nor judgments, but they dwell in hollow rocks on the tops of high mountains, and every one is the judge of his wife and children, and they do not trouble themselves about one another."

Cle. That must be a charming poet of yours; I have read some other verses of his, which are very clever; but I do not know much of him, for foreign poets are not much read among the Cretans.

Meg. But they are in Lacedaemon, and he appears to be the prince of them all; the manner of life, however, which he describes is not Spartan, but rather Ionian, and he seems quite to confirm what you are saying, carrying back the ancient state of mankind by the help of tradition, to barbarism.

Ath. Yes; and we may accept his witness to the fact that there was a time when primitive societies had this form.

Cle. Very true.

Ath. And did not such States spring out of single habitations and families who were scattered and thinned in the devastations; and the eldest of them was their ruler, because with them government originated in the authority of a father and a mother, whom, like a flock of birds, they followed, forming one troop under the patriarchal rule and sovereignty of their parents, which of all sovereignties is the most just?

Cle. Very true. — *Laws*, iv. 209.

Patriotism. See *Individual, the State greater*, etc.
Patroclus and Achilles. See *Achilles*.
Paupers and criminals co-existing. See *Criminals*.
Peace in view of death. See *Calmness*.
Peace, national. See *National*.
People swayed by rulers. See *Rulers, swaying*, etc.
Persian princes, how cared for.

—— After the birth of the royal child, he is tended, not by a good-for-nothing woman-nurse, but by the best of the royal eunuchs, who are charged with the care of him, and especially with the fashioning and formation of his limbs, in order that he may be as shapely as possible; which being their calling, they are held in great honor. And when the young prince is seven years old he is put upon a horse and taken to the riding-masters and begins to go out hunting. And at fourteen years of age he is handed over to the royal schoolmasters, as they are termed; these are four chosen men, reputed to be the best among the Persians of a certain age; and one of them is the wisest, another the justest, a third the most temperate, and a fourth the most valiant. The first instructs him in the magianism of Zoroaster the son of Oromasus, which is the worship of the Gods, and teaches him also the duties of his royal office; the second, who is the justest, teaches him always to speak the truth; the third, or most temperate, forbids him to allow any pleasure to be lord over him, that he may be accustomed to be a freeman and king indeed, — lord of himself first, and not a slave; the most valiant makes him bold and fearless, telling him that if he fears he is to deem himself a slave. — *Alcibiades I.* iv. 538.

Persian State, freedom in the. See *Freedom in the*, etc.
Persuasion better than force. See *Legislation*.

—— In the days of old the Gods had the whole earth distributed among them by allotment; there was no quarreling;

and you cannot suppose that the Gods did not know what was proper for each of them to have; or, knowing this, that they would seek to procure for themselves by contention that which more properly belonged to others. Each of them by just apportionment obtained what they wanted, and peopled their own districts; and when they had peopled them they tended us human beings who belonged to them as shepherds tend their flocks, excepting only that they did not use blows or bodily force, as shepherds do, but governed us like pilots from the stern of the vessel, which is an easy way of guiding animals, holding our souls by the rudder of persuasion, according to their own pleasure; thus did they guide all mortal creatures. — *Critias*, ii. 595.

Persuasion the crown of rhetoric.

—— *Soc.* What is that which, as you say, is the greatest good of man, and of which you are the creator? Answer us.

Gor. That good, Socrates, which is truly the greatest, being that which gives to men freedom in their own persons, and to rulers the power of ruling over others in their several States.

Soc. And what would you consider this to be?

Gor. What is there greater than the word which persuades the judges in the courts, or the senators in the council, or the citizens in the assembly, or at any other political meeting? — if you have the power of uttering this word, you will have the physician your slave, and the trainer your slave, and the money-maker of whom you talk will be found to gather treasures, not for himself, but for you who are able to speak and persuade the multitude.

Soc. Now I think, Gorgias, that you have very accurately explained what you conceive to be the art of rhetoric; and you mean to say, if I am not mistaken, that rhetoric is the artificer of persuasion, having this and no other business, and that this is her crown and end. Do you know any other effect of rhetoric over and above that of producing persuasion?

Gor. No: the definition seems to me very fair, Socrates; for persuasion is the crown of rhetoric. — *Gorgias*, iii. 37.

Persuasion the greatest art.

—— *Pro.* I have often heard Gorgias maintain, Socrates, that the art of persuasion far surpassed every other; this, as he says, is by far the best of them all, for to it all things submit, not by compulsion, but of their own free will. — *Philebus* iii. 198.

Persuasion, the art of.

—— *Str.* But the art of the lawyer, of the popular orator, and the art of conversation may be called in one word the art of persuasion.

Theaet. True.

Str. And of persuasion, there may be said to be two kinds?

Theaet. What are they?

Str. One is private, and the other public. . . . .

But that sort of hireling whose conversation is pleasing and who baits his hook with pleasure and only exacts his maintenance as the price of his flattery, we should all, if I am not mistaken, describe as possessing an art of sweetening, or making things pleasant. — *Sophist,* iii. 456.

Philosopher willing to die. See *Boldness.*

—— I must try to make more successful defense before you than I did before the judges. For I am quite ready to acknowledge, Simmias and Cebes, that I ought to be grieved at death, if I were not persuaded that I am going to other Gods who are wise and good (of this I am as certain as I can be of anything of the sort), and to men departed (though I am not so certain of this last) who are better than those whom I leave behind; and therefore I do not grieve as I might have done, for I have good hope that there is yet something remaining for the dead, and as has been said of old, some far better thing for the good than for the evil. . . . .

And now I will make answer to you, O my judges, and show that he who has lived as a true philosopher has reason to be of good cheer when he is about to die, and that after death he may hope to receive the greatest good in the other world. And how this may be, Simmias and Cebes, I will endeavor to explain. For I deem that the true disciple of philosophy is likely to be misunderstood by other men; they do not perceive that he is ever pursuing death and dying; and if this is true, why, having had the desire of death all his life long, should he repine at the arrival of that which he has been always pursuing and desiring?

Simmias laughed and said: Though not in a laughing humor, I swear that I cannot help laughing, when I think what the wicked world will say when they hear this. They will say that it is delightfully true, and our people at home will agree with them in saying that the life which philosophers desire is in reality death, and that they have found them out to be deserving of the death which they desire.

And they are right, Simmias, in saying so, with the exception of the words "they have found them out;" for they have not found out what is the nature of that death which the true philosopher desires, or how he deserves or desires death. But let us leave them and have a word with ourselves: Do we believe that there is such a thing as death?

To be sure, replied Simmias.

And is this anything but the separation of soul and body? And being dead is the completion of the separation when the soul exists in herself, and is parted from the body and the body is parted from the soul — that is death?

Exactly: that and nothing else, he replied. — *Phaedo*, i. 389.

Philosopher, curiosity does not make a. See *Curiosity*.
Philosopher characterized.

—— *Soc.* Then, as this is your wish, I will describe the leaders; for there is no use in talking about the inferior sort. In the first place, the lords of philosophy have never, from their youth upwards, known their way to the Agora, or the dicastery, or the council, or any other political assembly; they neither see nor hear the laws or votes of the State written or recited; the eagerness of political societies in the attainment of offices, — clubs, and banquets, and revels, and singing-maidens, do not enter even into their dreams. Whether any event has turned out well or ill in the city, what disgrace may have descended to any one from his ancestors, male or female, are matters of which the philosopher no more knows than he can tell, as they say, how many pints are contained in the ocean. Neither is he conscious of his ignorance. For he does not hold aloof in order that he may gain a reputation; but the truth is, that the outer form of him only is in the city; his mind, disdaining the littlenesses and nothingnesses of human things, is "flying all abroad," as Pindar says, measuring with line and rule the things which are under and on the earth and above the heaven, interrogating the whole nature of each and all, but not condescending to anything which is within reach.

Theod. What do you mean, Socrates?

Soc. I will illustrate my meaning, Theodorus, by the jest which the clever, witty Thracian handmaid made about Thales, when he fell into a well as he was looking up at the stars.

She said, that he was so eager to know what was going on in heaven, that he could not see what was before his feet. This is a jest which is equally applicable to all philosophers. For the philosopher is wholly unacquainted with his next door neighbor; he is ignorant, not only of what he is doing, but he hardly knows whether he is a man or an animal; he is searching into the essence of man, and busy in inquiring what belongs to such a nature to do or suffer different from any other; I think that you understand me, Theodorus?

Theod. I do, and what you say is true.

Soc. And thus, my friend, on every occasion, private as well as public, as I said at first, when he appears in a law-court, or in any place in which he has to speak of things which are at his feet and before his eyes, he is the jest, not only of Thracian handmaids but of the general herd, tumbling into wells and every sort of disaster through his inexperience. His awkwardness is fearful, and gives the impression of imbecility. When he is reviled, he has nothing personal to say in answer to the civilities of his adversaries, for he knows no scandals of any one, and they do not interest him; and therefore he is laughed at for his sheepishness; and when others are being praised and glorified, in the simplicity of his heart he cannot help laughing openly and unfeignedly; and this again makes him look like a fool. When he hears a tyrant or king eulogized, he fancies that he is listening to the praises of some keeper of cattle,—a swineherd, or shepherd, or cowherd, who is congratulated on the quantity of milk which he squeezes from them; and he remarks that the creature whom they tend, and out of whom they squeeze the wealth is of a less tractable and more insidious nature. Then, again, he observes that the great man is of necessity as ill-mannered and uneducated as any shepherd,—for he has no leisure, and he is surrounded by a wall, which is his mountain-pen. Hearing of enormous landed proprietors of ten thousand acres and more, our philosopher deems this to be a trifle, because he has been accustomed to think of the whole earth; and when they sing the praises of family, and say that some one is a gentleman because he has had seven generations of wealthy ancestors, he thinks that their sentiments only betray a dull and narrow vision in those who utter them, and who are not educated enough to look at the whole, nor to consider that every man has had thousands and thousands of progenitors, and among them have been rich and poor, kings and slaves, Hellenes and barbarians, many times over. And when the people pride themselves on having a pedigree of twenty-five ancestors, which goes back to Heracles, the son of Amphitryon, he cannot understand their poverty of ideas. Why they are unable to calculate that Amphitryon had a twenty-fifth ancestor, who might have been anybody, and was such as fortune made him, and he had a fiftieth, and so on? He amuses himself with the notion that they cannot count, and thinks that a little arithmetic would have got rid of their senseless vanity. Now, in all these cases our philosopher is derided by the vulgar, partly because he is thought to despise them, and also because he is ignorant of what is before him, and always at a loss.

Theod. That is very true, Socrates.

Soc. But, O my friend, when he draws the other into upper air and gets him out of his pleas and rejoinders into the contemplation of justice and injustice in their own nature and in their difference from one another and from all other things; or from the commonplaces about the happiness of kings to the consideration of government, and of human happiness and misery in general — what they are, and how a man is to attain the one and avoid the other — when that narrow, keen, little legal mind is called to account about all this, he gives the philosopher his revenge: for dizzied by the height at which he is hanging, whence he looks into space, which is a strange experience to him, he being dismayed and lost, and stammering out broken words, is laughed at, not by Thracian handmaidens or any other uneducated persons, for they have no eye for the situation, but by every man who has not been brought up as a slave. Such are the two characters, Theodorus: the one of the freeman called by you useless, when he has to perform some menial office, such as packing up a bag, or flavoring a sauce, or fawning speech; the other, of the man who is able to do all this kind of service smartly and neatly, but knows not how to wear his cloak like a gentleman; still less with the music of discourse can he hymn the true life which is lived by immortals or men blessed of heaven. — *Theaetetus*, iii. 376.

Philosopher and Sophist.

—— *Str.* The art of dialectic would be attributed by you only to the philosopher pure and true?

Theaet. Who but he can be worthy?

Str. This is the region in which we shall always discover

the philosopher, both now and hereafter; like the Sophist, he is not easily discovered, but for a different reason.

Theaet. For what reason?

Str. Because the Sophist runs away into the darkness of not-being, in which he has learned by habit to feel about, and cannot be discovered himself because of the darkness of the place. Is not that true?

Theaet. Quite so.

Str. And the philosopher, always holding converse through reason with the idea of being, is also dark from excess of light; for the eyes of the soul of the multitude are unable to endure the vision of the divine.

Theaet. Yes; that is quite as true as the other.

Str. Well, the philosopher may hereafter be more fully considered by us, if we are disposed; but the Sophist plainly must not be allowed to escape until we have had a good look at him.

Theaet. Very good. — *Sophist* iii. 492.

Philosophers and Statesmen, border-ground between.

―― *Soc.* What manner of man was he who came up to you and censured philosophy; was he an orator who himself practices in the courts, or an instructor of orators, who makes the speeches with which they do battle?

Cri. He was certainly not an orator, and I doubt whether he had ever been into court; but they say that he knows the business, and is a clever man, and composes wonderful speeches.

Soc. Now I understand, Crito; he is one of an amphibious class, whom I was on the point of mentioning — one of those whom Prodicus describes as on the border-ground between philosophers and statesmen — they think that they are the wisest of all men, and that they are generally esteemed the wisest; nothing but the rivalry of the philosophers stands in their way; and they are of the opinion that if they can prove the philosophers to be good for nothing, no one will dispute their title to the palm of wisdom, for that they are themselves really the wisest, although they are apt to be mauled by Euthydemus and his friend, when they get hold of them in conversation. This opinion which they entertain of their own wisdom is very natural; for they have a certain amount of philosophy, and a certain amount of political wisdom; there is reason in what they say, for they argue that they have just enough of both, while they keep out of the way of all risks and conflicts and reap the fruits of their wisdom. — *Euthydemus,* i. 211.

Philosopher, despising bodily pleasures. See *Bodily pleasure*.
Philosophers, dizzy.

—— I have not a bad notion which came into my head only this moment: I believe that the primeval givers of names were undoubtedly like too many of our modern philosophers, who, in their search after the nature of things, are always getting dizzy from going round and round and then they imagine that the world is going round and round and moving anyhow; and this appearance, which arises out of their own internal condition, they suppose to be a reality of nature; they think that there is nothing stable or permanent, but only flux and motion, and that all is full of every sort of motion and change. — *Cratylus*, i. 650.

Philosophic nature, rare.

—— Neither is there any reason why I should again set in array the philosopher's virtues, as you will doubtless remember that courage, magnanimity, apprehension, memory, were his natural gifts. And you objected that, although no one could deny what I then said, still, if you leave words and look at facts, the persons who are thus described are some of them manifestly useless, and the greater number wholly depraved; we were then led to inquire into the grounds of these accusations, and we had arrived at the point of asking why are the many bad, which question of necessity brought us back to the examination and definition of the true philosopher.

Exactly.

And now we have to consider the corruptions of the philosophical nature, why so many are spoiled and so few escape spoiling — I am speaking of those whom you call useless but not wicked; and after that we will consider the imitators of philosophy, what manner of natures are they who aspire after a profession which is above them and of which they are unworthy, and then, by their manifold inconsistencies, bring upon philosophy, and upon all philosophers, that universal reprobation of which we speak.

What are these corruptions, he said?

I will see if I can explain them to you, I said. Every one will admit that a nature having in perfection all the qualities which make a philosopher, is a plant that rarely grows among men — there are not many of them.

They are very rare. — *The Republic*, ii. 317.

Philosophy to be followed.

—— *Soc.* Do you then be reasonable, Crito, and do not mind whether the teachers of philosophy are good or bad, but think only of Philosophy herself. Try and examine her well and truly, and if she be evil seek to turn away all men from her, and not your sons only; but if she be what I believe that she is, then follow her and serve her, you and your house, as the saying is, and be of good cheer. — *Euthydemus,* i. 212.

Philosophy delivering the soul.

—— He who is a philosopher or lover of learning, and is entirely pure at departing, is alone permitted to attain to the divine nature. And this is the reason, Simmias and Cebes, why the true votaries of philosophy abstain from all fleshly lusts, and endure and refuse to give themselves up to them, — not because they fear poverty or the ruin of their families, like the lovers of money, and the world in general; nor like the lovers of power and honor, because they dread the dishonor or disgrace of evil deeds.

No, Socrates, that would not become them, said Cebes.

No indeed, he replied; and therefore they who have a care of their own souls, and do not merely live moulding and fashioning the body, say farewell to all this; they will not walk in the ways of the blind: and when Philosophy offers them purification and release from evil, they feel that they ought not to resist her influence, and whither she leads they turn and follow. — *Phaedo,* i. 411.

Philosophy in early youth.

—— At present, I said, even those who study philosophy in early youth, or in the intervals of money-making and housekeeping, do but make an approach to the most difficult branch of the subject, and then take themselves off (I am speaking of those who have the most training, and by the most difficult branch I mean dialectic); and in after-life they perhaps go to a discussion which is held by others, and to which they are invited, and this they deem a great matter, as the study of philosophy is not regarded by them as their proper business: then, as years advance, in most cases their light is quenched more truly than Heracleitus' sun, for they never rise again.

But what ought to be their course?

Just the opposite. In childhood and youth their study, and what philosophy they learn, should be suited to their tender age: let their bodies be taken care of during the period of growth, to be hereafter the servants of philosophy; as the man advances to mature intelligence he should increase the gymnastics of the soul; but when the strength of our citizens fails, and is past civil and military duties, then let them range at will and have no other serious employment, as we intend them to live happily here, and, this life ended, to have a similar happiness in another. — *The Republic*, ii. 325.

Philosophy in the State.

—— When persons who are unworthy of education approach philosophy and make an alliance with her who is in a rank above them, what sort of ideas and opinions are likely to be generated? Will they not be sophisms captivating to the ear, yet having nothing in them genuine or worthy of or akin to true wisdom?

No doubt, he said.

Then there is a very small remnant, Adeimantus, I said, of worthy disciples of philosophy: perchance some noble nature, brought up under good influences, and detained by exile in her service who in the absence of temptation remains devoted to her; or some lofty soul born in a mean city, the politics of which he contemns or neglects; and perhaps there may be a few who, having a gift for philosophy, leave other arts, which they justly despise, and come to her; and peradventure there are some who are restrained by our friend Theages' bridle (for Theages, you know, has had everything to draw him away; but his ill-health keeps him from politics). My own case of the internal sign is indeed hardly worth mentioning, as very rarely, if ever, has such a monitor been vouchsafed to any one else. . Those who belong to this small class have tasted how sweet and blessed a possession philosophy is, and have also seen and been satisfied of the madness of the multitude, and known that there is no one who ever acts honestly in the administration of States, nor any helper who defends the cause of the just by whose aid he may be saved. Such a defender may be compared to a man who has fallen among wild beasts; he would not join in the wickedness of his fellows, but neither would he be able alone to resist all their fierce natures, and therefore he would be of no use to the State or to his friends, and would have to throw away his life before he had done any good to himself or others. When he reflects upon all this, he holds his peace, and does his own business. He is like one who retires under the shelter of a wall in the storm of dust and sleet which the driving wind hurries along; and when he sees the rest of mankind full of wickedness, he is content if only he can live his own life and be pure from evil or unrighteousness, and depart in peace and good will, with bright hopes.

Yes, he said, and he will have done a great work before he departs.

A great work,— yes; but not the greatest, unless he find a State suitable to him; for in a State which is suitable to him he will have a larger growth, and be the saviour of his country as well as of himself.

Enough, then, of the causes why philosophy is in such an evil name; how unjustly, has been explained : and now is there anything more which you wish to say?

Nothing more on that subject, he replied; but I should like to know which of the governments now existing is in your opinion the one adapted to her.

Not any of them, I said; and that is the very accusation which I bring against them: not one of them is worthy of the philosophic nature; and hence that nature is warped and deformed; as the exotic seed which is sown in a foreign land becomes denaturalized, and is vanquished and degenerates into the nature stock, even so this growth of philosophy, instead of persisting, receives another character. But if philosophy ever finds in the State that perfection which she herself is, then will be seen that she is in truth divine, and that all other things, whether natures of men or institutions, are but human; and now, I know, that you are going to ask what that State is.

No, he said; there you are wrong, for I was going to ask another question — whether it is the State of which we are the founders and inventors, or some other?

Yes, I replied, ours in most respects; but you may remember our saying before that some living authority would always be required in the State, whose idea of the constitution would be the same which guided you originally when laying down the laws.

That was said, he replied.

Yes, but imperfectly said; you frightened us with objections, which certainly showed that the discussion would be long and difficult; and even what remains is the reverse of easy.

What is that?

The question how the study of philosophy may be so ordered as to be consistent with the preservation of the State; for all great things are attended with risk: as the saying is, "Hard is the good."

Still, he said, let the point be cleared up, and the inquiry will then be complete.

I shall not be hindered, I said, by any want of will, but, if at all, by a want of power: of my zeal you shall have ocular demonstration; and please to remark in what I am about to say how courageously and unhesitatingly I affirm that a State ought not to have philosophy studied after the present fashion. — *The Republic*, ii. 323.

Philosophy, too much, is ruinous.

—— Philosophy, Socrates, if pursued in moderation and at the proper age, is an elegant accomplishment, but too much philosophy is the ruin of human life. Even if a man has good parts, still, if he carries philosophy into later life, he is necessarily ignorant of all those things which a gentleman and a person of honor ought to know; for he is ignorant of the laws of the State, and of the language which ought to be used in the dealings of man with man, whether private or public, and altogether ignorant of the pleasures and desires of mankind and of human character in general. And people of this sort, when they betake themselves to politics or business, are as ridiculous as I imagine the politicians to be, when they make their appearance in the arena of philosophy. For, as Euripides says, —

"Every man shines in that and pursues that, and devotes the greatest portion of the day to that in which he thinks himself to excel most,"

and anything in which he is inferior, he avoids and depreciates and praises the opposite from partiality to himself, and because he thinks that he will thus praise himself. The true principle is to unite them. Philosophy, as a part of education, is an excellent thing, and there is no disgrace to a man while he is young in pursuing such a study; but when he is more advanced in years, then the thing becomes ridiculous, and I feel towards philosophers as I do towards those who lisp and imitate children. For when I love to see a little child, who is not of an age to speak plainly, lisping at his play; there is an appearance of grace and freedom in his utterance, which is natural to his childish years. And when I hear some small creature carefully articulating its words, I am offended; the sound is disagreeable, and has to my ears the twang of slavery. But when I see a man lisping as if he were a child, that appears to me ridiculous and unmanly and worthy of stripes. And I have the same feeling about students of philosophy; when I see a youth so engaged, that I consider to be quite in character, and becoming a man of a liberal education, and him who neglects philosophy I regard as an inferior man, who will never aspire to anything great or noble. But if I see him continuing the study in later life, and not leaving off, I think that he ought to be beaten, Socrates; for, as I was saying, such an one, even though he have good natural parts, becomes effeminate. — *Gorgias*, iii. 73.

Philosophy, freedom of. See *Freedom of Philosophy*.
Physical force inferior to persuasion. See *Legislation* and *Persuasion*.
Physician, the false and the true.

—— Neither will he be able to distinguish the pretender in medicine from the true physician, nor between any other true and false professor of knowledge. Let us consider the matter in this way: If the wise man or any other man wants to distinguish the true physician from the false, what is he to do? He will not talk to him about medicine; and that, as we were saying, is the only thing which the physician understands.

True.

And on the other hand, knows nothing of science, for this has been assumed to be the province of wisdom.

True.

And further, since medicine is science, we must infer that he does not know anything of medicine.

Exactly.

The wise man will indeed know that the physician has some kind of science or knowledge; but when he wants to discover the nature of this he will ask, What is the subject-matter? For each science is distinguished, not as science, but by the nature of the subject. Is not that true?

Yes; that is quite true.

And medicine is distinguished from other sciences as having the subject-matter of health and disease?

Yes.

And he who would inquire into the nature of medicine must pursue the inquiry into health and disease, and not into what is extraneous?

True.

And he who judges rightly will judge of the physician as a physician in what relates to these?

He will.

He will consider whether what he says is true, and whether what he does is right in relation to these? — *Charmides*, i. 27.

Physician for the State. See *State, physician for the*, etc.

Physician, legislator compared to a. See *Legislator*.

Physician, tried by boys.

—— I shall be tried just as a physician would be tried in a court of little boys at the indictment of the cook. What would he reply in such a case, if some one were to accuse him, saying, " O my boys, many evil things has this man done to you: he is the death of you, especially of the younger ones among you, cutting and burning and starving and suffocating you, until you know not what to do; he gives you the bitterest potions, and compels you to hunger and thirst. How unlike the variety of meats and sweets on which I feasted you!" What do you suppose that the physician would reply when he found himself in such a predicament? If he told the truth he could only say, " All this, my boys, I did with a view to health," and then would there not just be a clamor among a jury like that? How they would cry out! — *Gorgias*, iii. 113.

Physicians and patients. See *Doctors*, etc.

Physicians and cookery. See *Cookery*.

Piety, conceptions of. See *Holiness*, etc.

Pleasant, just and good. See *Just judge*.

Pleasure as related to pain. See *Pain*.

Pleasure and pain, qualities of. See *Pain, qualities of*, etc.

Pleasure to be desired.

—— *Soc.* Let us next assume that in the soul herself, there is an antecedent hope of pleasure which is sweet and consoling, and an expectation of pain, fearful and anxious.

Pro. Yes; this is another class of pleasures and pains, which is of the soul only, and is produced by expectation without the body.

Soc. Right; and I think that the examination of these two kinds, unalloyed as I suppose them to be, and not compounds of pleasure and pain, will most clearly show whether the whole class of pleasure is to be desired, or whether this quality of entire desirableness is not rather to be attributed to another of the classes which have been mentioned; and whether pleasure and pain, like heat and cold, and other things of this kind, are not sometimes to be desired and sometimes not to be desired, as being not in themselves good, but sometimes and in some instances admitting of the nature of good.

Pro. You say most truly that this is the track which the investigation should follow. — *Philebus*, iii. 168.

Pleasure, victory over.

—— *Ath.* Have we not heard of Iccus of Tarentum, who, with a view to the Olympic and other contests, in his zeal for his art, and also because he was of a manly and temperate constitution, never had any connection with a woman or a youth during the whole time of his training? And the same is said of Crison and Astylus and Diopompus and many others, and yet, Cleinias, they were far worse educated in their minds than your and my fellow-citizens, and in their bodies far more lusty.

Cle. No doubt this fact has been often affirmed positively by the ancients of these athletes.

Ath. And shall they be willing to abstain from what is ordinarily deemed a pleasure for the sake of a victory in wrestling, running, and the like; and our young men be incapable of a similar endurance for the sake of a much nobler victory, which is the noblest of all, as from their youth upwards we will tell them, charming them, as we hope, into the belief of this, by tales in prose and verse?

Cle. Of what victory are you speaking?

Ath. Of the victory over pleasure, which if they win they will live happily, or if conquered the reverse of happily. And, further, will not the fear of impiety enable them to master that which other inferior people have mastered?

Cle. I dare say. — *Laws*, iv. 355.

Pleasures of the body. See *Bodily*, etc.
Pleasures of the intelligent. See *Intelligence*.
Pleasures and pains mixed and unmixed. See *Body and Soul*.
Pleasures, true.

—— *Pro.* Which are the true pleasures, Socrates, and what is the right conception of them?

Soc. True pleasures are those which are given by beauty of color and form, and most of those which arise from smells; those of sound, again, and in general those of which the want is painless and unconscious, and the gratification afforded by them palpable to sense, and pleasant and unalloyed with pain. — *Philebus*, iii. 190.

Pleasures of Knowledge. See *Knowledge*.
Pleasures as hindrances.

—— *Soc.* Do you wish to have the greatest and most vehement pleasures for your companions in addition to the true ones?

Why, Socrates, they will say, how can we? seeing that they are the source of ten thousand hindrances to us; they trouble the souls of men, which are our habitation, with their madness; they prevent us from coming to the birth, and are commonly the ruin of our children when they do come to the birth, causing them to be forgotten and unheeded; but the other true and pure pleasures, of which you spoke, know to be of our kindred, and the pleasures which accompany health and temperance, and are in a manner the handmaidens and inseparable attendants of virtue as of a God, — mingle these and not the others; there would be great want of sense in any one who desires to see the fair and untroubled stream, and to find in the admixture what is the highest good in man and in the universe, and to divine what is the true form of good — there would be great want of sense in his allowing the pleasures, which are always in the company of folly and vice, to mingle with mind in the cup: Is not this a very rational and suitable reply, which mind has made, both on her own behalf, as well as on that of memory and true opinion, to the question which has been asked of us?

Pro. Most certainly. — *Philebus,* iii. 204.

Pleasures, harmless. See *Amusements.*

Poetry, imitative. See *Imitative.*

Poetry expelled from the State.

—— Poetry feeds and waters the passions instead of drying them up; she lets them rule instead of ruling them as they ought to be ruled, with a view to the happiness and virtue of mankind.

I cannot deny it.

Therefore, Glaucon, I said, whenever you meet with any of the eulogists of Homer declaring that he has been the educator of Hellas, and that he is profitable for the management and administration of human things, and that you should take him up and get to know him and regulate your whole life according to him, we may love and honor the intentions of these excellent people, as far as their lights extend; and we are ready to acknowledge that Homer is the greatest of poets and first of tragedy writers; but we must remain firm in our conviction that hymns to the Gods and praises of famous men are the only poetry which ought to be admitted into our State. For if you go beyond this and allow the honeyed muse to enter, either in epic or lyric verse, not law and the reason of mankind, which by common consent has ever been deemed the best, but pleasure and pain will be the rulers in our State.

That is most true, he said.

Let this, then, be our excuse for expelling poetry, that the argument constrained us ; but let us also make an apology to her, lest she impute to us any harshness or want of politeness. We will tell her, that there is an ancient quarrel between philosophy and poetry; of which there are many proofs, such as the saying of " the yelping hound howling at her lord," or of one " mighty in the vain talk of fools;" and " the mob of sages circumventing Zeus," and the " subtle thinkers who are beggars after all ; " and there are ten thousand other signs of ancient enmity between them. Notwithstanding this, let us assure our sweet friend, and the sister arts of imitation, that if she will only prove her title to existence in a well-ordered State we shall be delighted to receive her, knowing that we ourselves also are very susceptible of her charms ; but we may not on that account betray the truth. I dare say, Glaucon, that you are as much charmed by her as I am, especially when you see her in the garb of Homer ?

Yes, indeed, I am greatly charmed.

Shall I propose, then, that she be allowed to return from exile, on this condition — that she is to make a defense of herself in lyrical or some other metre ?

Certainly.

And to those of her defenders who are lovers of poetry and yet not poets I think that we may grant a further privilege ; they shall be allowed to speak in prose on her behalf : let them show not only that she is pleasant but also useful to States and to human life, and we will gladly listen, for if this can be proved we shall surely be the gainers, that is to say, if there is a use in poetry as well as a delight ?

Certainly, he said, we shall be the gainers.

If her defense fails, then, my dear friend, though much against our will, we must give her up, after the manner of lovers who abstain when they think that their love is not good for them ; for we too are inspired by that love of poetry which the education of noble States has implanted in us, and therefore we would have her appear at her best and truest ; but so long as she is unable to make good her defense, even though our ears may listen, this argument of ours will be like a charm to us, and into the childish love which the many have of her we shall take care not to fall again, for we see that poetry, being such as she is, is not to be pursued in earnest or regarded seriously as attaining to the truth ; and he who listens to her will be on his guard against her seductions, fearing for the safety of the city which is within him, and he will attend to our words. — *The Republic*, ii. 438.

Poets, poor.

—— Ctesippus said: I like to see you blushing, Hippothales, and hesitating to tell Socrates the name ; when, if he were with you but for a very short time, he would be plagued to death by hearing of nothing else. Indeed, Socrates, he has literally deafened us, and stopped our ears with the praises of Lysis ; and if he is a little intoxicated, there is every likelihood that we may have our sleep murdered with a cry of Lysis. His performances in prose are bad enough, but nothing at all in comparison with his verse ; and when he drenches us with his poems and other compositions, that is really too bad ; and what is even worse, is his manner of singing them to his love ; this he does in a voice which is truly appalling, and we cannot help hearing him ; and now he has a question put to him by you, and lo ! he is blushing. — *Lysis*, i. 42.

Poets our guides.

—— Let us proceed no further in this direction (for the road seems to be getting troublesome), but take the other in which the poets will be our guide ; for they are to us in a manner the fathers and authors of wisdom, and they speak of friends in no light or trivial manner, but God himself, as they say, makes them and draws them to one another ; and this they express, if I am not mistaken, in the following words : —

" God is ever drawing like towards like, and making them acquainted."

I dare say that you have heard those words.

Yes, he said ; I have. — *Lysis*, i. 53.

Poets, madness of the. See *Madness of the prophet*, etc.

Poets like painters.

—— Must we not infer that all the poets, beginning with Homer, are only imitators ; they copy images of virtue and the like, but the truth they never reach ? The poet is like a painter who, as has already been observed, will make a likeness of a cobbler though he understands nothing of cobbling ; and his picture is good enough for those who know no more than he does, and judge only by colors and figures. Also the poet lays over his words and expressions certain colors taken from the several arts, himself understanding their nature only enough to imitate them; and other people who are as ignorant as he is, and judge only from his words, imagine that if he speaks of cobbling, or of military tactics, or of anything else, in metre and harmony and rhythm he speaks very well — such is the sweet influence which melody and rhythm by nature have. And I think that you must know, for you have often seen what a poor appearance the tales of poets make when stripped of the colors which music puts upon them, and recited in prose?

Yes, he said.

They are like faces which were never really beautiful, but only blooming; and now the bloom of youth has passed away from them?

Exactly. — *The Republic*, ii. 431.

Poets, the talk about the.

—— The talk about the poets seems to me like a commonplace entertainment to which a vulgar company have recourse; who, because they are not able to converse or amuse one another, while they are drinking, with the sound of their own voices and conversation by reason of their stupidity, raise the price of flute-girls in the market, hiring for a great sum the voice of a flute instead of their own breath, to be the medium of intercourse among them: but where the company are real gentlemen and men of education, you will see no flute-girls, nor dancing-girls, nor harp-girls; and they have no nonsense or games, but are contented with one another's conversation, of which their own voices are the medium, and which they carry on by turns and in an orderly manner, even though they are very liberal in their potations. And a company like this of ours, and men such as we profess to be, do not require the help of another's voice, or of the poets whom you cannot interrogate about the meaning of what they are saying; people who cite them declaring, some that the poet has one meaning, and others that he has another; and the point which is in dispute can never be decided. This sort of entertainment they decline, and prefer to talk with one another, and put one another to the proof in conversation. — *Protagoras*, i. 147.

Poets, tragic, promoters of tyranny.

—— The tragic poets being wise men will forgive us and others who have the perfect form of government, if we object to having them in our State, because they are the eulogists of tyranny.

Yes, he said, those who have the wit will doubtless forgive us.

But still, I said, they go about to other cities and attract mobs, and hire voices fair and loud and persuasive, and draw the cities over to tyrannies and democracies.

Very true.

Moreover, they are paid for this and receive honor — the greatest honor from tyrants, and the next greatest from democracies; but the higher they ascend our constitution hill, the more their reputation fails, and seems unable from shortness of breath to proceed farther.

True. — *The Republic*, ii. 398.

Poets destroyed by popular demands.

—— *Ath.* The true legislator will persuade, and, if he cannot persuade, will compel the poet to express as he ought, by fair and noble words, in his rhythms, the figures, and in his melodies, the music of temperate, and brave, and in every way good men.

Cle. And do you really imagine, Stranger, that this is the way in which poets generally compose in States at the present day? As far as I can observe there is nothing of the sort, except among us and among the Lacedaemonians, as you now tell me; in other places novelties are always being introduced in dancing and in music, generally not under the authority of any law, but at the instigation of lawless pleasures; and these pleasures are so far from being the same, as you describe the Egyptian to be, or having the same principles, that they are never the same. — *Laws*, iv. 189.

Political bond.

—— When the foundation of politics is in the letter only, and in custom, and knowledge is divorced from action, can we wonder, Socrates, at the miseries that there are, and always will be, in States? Any other art, built on such a foundation, would be utterly undermined, — there can be no doubt of that. Ought we not rather to wonder at the strength of the political bond? For States have endured all this, time out of mind, and yet some of them still remain and are not overthrown, though many of them, like ships foundering at sea, are perishing and have perished, and will hereafter perish, through the incapacity of their pilots and crews, who have the worst sort of ignorance of the highest truths — I mean to say, that they are wholly unacquainted with politics, of which, above all other sciences, they believe themselves to have acquired the most perfect knowledge. — *Statesman*, iii. 588.

Political parties. See *Parties.*
Politicians as philosophers. See *Laws, makers of.*
Politicians not Statesmen.

—— *Str.* But who are these elected kings and priests who now come into view with a crowd of retainers, as the former class disappears and the scene changes?
Y. Soc. Whom do you mean?
Str. How strangely they look!
Y. Soc. Why strangely?
Str. A minute ago I thought that they were all sorts of animals; for many of them are like lions and centaurs, and many more like satyrs and the weak and versatile sort of animals, — Protean shapes ever changing their form and nature; and now, Socrates, I begin to see who they are.
Y. Soc. Who are they? You seem to be gazing on some strange vision.
Str. Yes; every one looks strange when you do not know him; and at first sight, coming suddenly upon him, I did not recognize the politician and his troop.
Y. Soc. Who is he?
Str. The chief of Sophists and most accomplished of wizards, who must at any cost be separated from the true king or Statesman, if we are ever to see daylight in the present inquiry.
Y. Soc. That certainly is not a hope to be lightly renounced.
— *Statesman,* iii. 576.

Popular liberty. See *Democracy.*
Popular opinion. See *Opinion, public.*
Popular influence on Poetry. See *Poetry,* etc.
Possessing and having. See *Having.*
Poverty and wealth equally deteriorating. See *Wealth.*
Poverty and riches in Age.

—— They think that old age sits lightly upon you, not because of your happy disposition, but because you are rich, and wealth is well known to be a great comforter.

That is true, he replied; they do not believe me: and there is something in what they say; not, however, so much as they imagine. I might answer them as Themistocles answered the Seriphian who was abusing him and saying that he was famous, not for his own merits but because he was an Athenian; " If you had been an Athenian and I a Seriphian, neither of us would have been famous." And to those who are not rich and **are impatient of old age,** the same reply may be made; for neither can a good poor man lightly bear age, nor can a bad rich man ever be at peace with himself. — *The Republic*, ii. 150.

Praise and esteem distinguished. See *Esteem*.

Prayer with every enterprise.

—— *Soc.* I see that I shall receive in my turn a perfect and splendid feast of reason. And now, Timaeus, you, I suppose, are to follow, first offering up a prayer to the Gods according to custom.

Tim. All men, Socrates, who have any degree of right feeling, at the beginning of every enterprise, whether small or great, always call upon God. And we, too, who are going to discourse of the nature of the universe, how created or how existing without creation, if we be not altogether out of our wits, must invoke and pray the Gods and goddesses that we may say all things in a manner pleasing to them and likewise consistent with ourselves. Let this, then, be our invocation of the Gods, to which I add an exhortation of myself that I may set forth this high argument in the manner which will be most intelligible to you, and will most accord with my own intent. — *Timaeus*, ii. 523.

Preamble to law, distinguished from the matter.

—— All this time, from early dawn until noon, we have been talking about laws in this charming retreat : now we are going to promulgate our laws, and what has preceded was only the prelude of them. Why do I mention this ? For this reason : Because all discourses and vocal exercises have preludes and overtures, which are a sort of artistic beginnings, intended to help the strain which is to be performed ; lyric measures and every other sort of music have preludes framed with wonderful care. But of the truer and higher strain of law and politics, no one has ever yet uttered any prelude, or composed or published any, as though there was no such thing in nature. Whereas our present discussion seems to me to imply that there is — these double laws, of which we were speaking, are not exactly double, but they are in two parts, the law and the prelude of the law. The arbitrary command, which was compared to the commands of the physicians, whom we described as of the meaner sort, was the law pure and simple ; and that which preceded, and was described by our friend as hortatory only, was, in fact, an exhortation, and is analogous to the preamble of a discourse. For I imagine that all this language of conciliation, which the legislator has been uttering in the preface of the law, was intended to create good-will in the person whom he addressed, in order that, by reason of this good-will, he might more intelligently receive his command, that is to say, the law. And therefore, in my way of speaking, this is more rightly described as the preamble than as the matter of the law. —*Laws*, iv. 250.

Presentiment of death in Socrates.

—— *Soc.* Do not repeat the old story — that he who likes will kill me and get my money; for then I shall have to repeat the old answer that he will be a bad man and will kill the good, and that the money will be of use to him; but that he will wrongly use that which he wrongly took, and if wrongly, basely, and if basely, hurtfully.

Cal. How confident you are, Socrates, that you will never come to harm! you seem to think that you are living in another country, and can never be brought into a court of justice, as you very likely may be brought by some miserable and mean person.

Soc. Then I must indeed be a fool, Callicles, if I do not know that in the Athenian State any man may suffer anything. And if I am brought to trial and incur the dangers of which you speak, he will be a villain who brings me to trial — of that I am very sure, for no good man would accuse the innocent. Nor shall I be surprised if I am put to death. Shall I tell you why I anticipate this?

Cal. By all means.

Soc. I think that I am the only or almost the only Athenian living who practices the true art of politics; I am the only politician of my time. Now, seeing that when I speak I speak not with any view of pleasing, and that I look to what is best and not to what is most pleasant, having no mind to use those arts and graces which you recommend, I shall have nothing to say in the justice court. . . . . . For I shall not be able to rehearse to the people the pleasures which I have procured for them, and which, although I am not disposed to envy either the procurers or the enjoyers of them, are deemed by them to be benefits and advantages. And if any one says that I corrupt young men, and perplex their minds, or that I speak evil of old men, and use bitter words towards them, whether in private or public, it is useless for me to reply, as I truly might: "All this I do for the sake of justice, and with a view to your interest, my judges, and of that only." And therefore there is no saying what may happen to me.

Cal. And do you think, Socrates, that a man, who is thus defenseless, is in a good position?

Soc. Yes, Callicles, if he have that defense which you have often admitted that he should have; if he be his own defense, and have never said or done anything wrong, either in respect of Gods or men; for that has often been acknowledged by us to be the best sort of defense. And if any one could convict me of inability to defend myself or others after this sort, I should blush for shame, whether I was convicted before many, or before a few, or by myself alone; and if I died for want of ability to do so, that would indeed grieve me. But if I died because I have no powers of flattery or rhetoric, I am very sure that you would not find me repining at death. For no man but an utter fool and coward is afraid of death itself, but he is afraid of doing wrong. For to go to the world below, having one's soul full of injustice, is the last and worst of all evils. — *Gorgias*, iii. 112.

Pride, personal.

—— *Soc.* I dare say that you may be surprised to find, O son of Cleinias, that I, who am your first lover, not having spoken to you for many years, when the rest of the world were wearying you with their attentions, am the last of your lovers who still speaks to you. The reason was, that I was hindered from speaking to you by a power — not human but divine, the nature of which I will some day explain to you; that impediment has been now removed, and I present myself before you, hoping that the hindrance will not again occur. Meanwhile, I have observed that your pride has been too much for the pride of your admirers; they were very numerous, but they have all run away, overpowered by your superior force of character; not one of them remains. And I want you to understand the reason why you have overpowered them. You imagine that you have no need of any other man at all, as you have great possessions and abundance of all things, beginning with the body, and ending with the soul. In the first place, you think that you are the fairest and tallest of the citizens, and this every one who has eyes sees to be true; in the second place, that you are among the noblest of them, highly connected both on the father's and the mother's side, and sprung from one of the most distinguished families in your own State, which is the greatest in Hellas, and having many friends and kinsmen of the best sort, who can assist you when in need; and there is one potent relative, who is more to you than all the rest, Pericles, the son of Xanthippus, whom your father left guardian of you and your brother, and who cannot only do as he pleases in this city, but in all Hellas, and among many and mighty barbarous nations. Moreover, you are rich; but I must say that you value yourself least of all upon your possessions. And all these things have lifted you up, and you have overcome your lovers, and they have acknowledged that you were too much for them. Have you not remarked their absence? And now I know that you wonder why I have not gone away like the rest of them, and what can be my motive in remaining. — *Alcibiades I.* iv. 515.

Priest, the, a King. See *King*, etc.
Primeval race, without procreation. See *Spontaneous life.*
Primitive Society. See *Patriarchal State.*
Prime of life, the age of begetting.

——— What is the prime of life? May not that be defined as a period of about twenty years in a woman's life, and thirty in a man's.

Which years do you mean to include?

A woman, I said, may begin to bear children to the State at twenty years of age, and continue to bear until forty; a man may begin at five-and-twenty, when he has passed the point at which the pulse of life beats quickest, and continue to beget children until he be fifty-five.

Certainly, he said, both in men and women that is the prime of physical as well as of intellectual vigor.

Any one above or below the prescribed ages who takes part in the public hymeneals shall be said to have done an unholy and unrighteous thing; the child of which he is the father, if it steals into life, will have been conceived under other auspices than those of sacrifice and prayers, which at each hymeneal priestesses and priests and the whole city will offer, that the new generation may be better and more useful than their good and useful parents : whereas his child will be the offspring of darkness and strange lust. — *The Republic*, ii. 286.

Principle and reason to be our guides.

——— *Soc.* Dear Crito, your zeal is invaluable, if a right one; but if wrong, the greater the zeal the greater the danger; and therefore we ought to consider whether I shall, or shall not do as you say. For I am and always have been one of those natures who must be guided by reason, whatever the reason may be which upon reflection appears to me to be the best; and now that this fortune has come upon me, I cannot put away the conclusion at which I had arrived: the principles which I have hitherto honored and revered I still honor, and unless we can at once find other and better principles, I am certain not to agree with you; no, not even if the power of the multitude could inflict many more imprisonments, confiscations, deaths, frightening us like children with hobgoblin terrors. — *Crito*, i. 350.

Procreation, primeval race without. See *Spontaneous life*.
Production, three kinds of.

—— *Str.* In the first place, there are two kinds of creation.
Theaet. What are they?
Str. One of them is human and the other divine.
Theaet. I do not follow.
Str. Every power, as you may remember our saying originally, which is the cause of things afterwards existing which did not exist before, was defined by us as creative.
Theaet. I remember.
Str. Looking, now, at the world and all the animals and plants which grow upon the earth from seeds and roots, and at inanimate substances which form within the earth, fusile or non-fusile, shall we say that they come into existence — not having existed previously — by the creation of God, or shall we agree with vulgar opinion about them?
Theaet. What is that?
Str. The opinion that nature brings them into being from some spontaneous and unintelligent cause. Shall we say this, or that they come from God, and are created by divine reason and knowledge?
Theaet. I dare say that, owing to my youth, I may often waver in my view, but when I look at you and see that you incline to refer them to God, at present I defer to your authority.
Str. Nobly said, Theaetetus, and if I thought that you were one of those who would hereafter change your mind, I would have gently argued with you, and forced you to assent; but as I perceive that you will come of yourself and without any argument of man to that belief which, as you say, attracts you, I will leave time to do the rest. Let me suppose, then, that things which are made by nature are the work of divine art, and that things which are made by man out of these are works of human

art. And so there are two kinds of making and production, the one human and the other divine. — *Sophist*, iii. 506.

Progression of human life.

—— What is implied in the word "recollection," but the departure of knowledge, which is ever being forgotten and is renewed and preserved by recollection and appears to be the same although in reality new, according to that law of succession by which all mortal things are preserved, not absolutely the same but by substitution, the old worn-out mortality leaving another new and similar existence behind — unlike the divine which is always the same and not another? And in this way, Socrates, the mortal body, or mortal anything, partakes of immortality; but the immortal in another way. Marvel not then at the love which all men have of their offspring; for that universal love and interest is for the sake of immortality. — *The Symposium*, i. 500.

Property in Government. See *Government*.

Prophet, madness of the. See *Madness of the*, etc.

Protector become a tyrant.

—— The people have always some champion whom they nurse into greatness.

Yes, that is their way.

This and no other is the root from which a tyrant springs; when he first appears above ground he is a protector.

Yes, that is quite clear.

How then does a protector begin to change into a tyrant?

Clearly when he does what the man is said to do in the tale of the Arcadian temple of Lycaean Zeus.

What tale?

The tale is that he who has tasted the entrails of a single human victim minced up with the entrails of other victims is destined to become a wolf. Did you never hear that?

Oh, yes.

And the protector of the people is like him; having a mob entirely at his disposal, he is not restrained from shedding the blood of kinsmen; by the favorite method of false accusation he brings them into court and murders them, making the life of man to disappear, and with unholy tongue and lips tasting the blood of his fellow citizens; some of whom he kills and others he banishes, at the same time proclaiming abolition of debts and partition of lands: and after this, what can be his destiny but either to perish at the hands of his enemies, or from being a man to become a wolf — that is a tyrant?

Inevitably.

This, I said, is he who begins to make a party against the rich.

The same.

And then he is driven out, and comes back, in spite of his enemies, a tyrant full grown.

That is clear.

And if they are unable to drive him out, or get him condemned to death by public opinion, they form the design of putting him out of the way secretly.

Yes, he said, their usual way.

Then comes the famous request of a body-guard, which is made by all those who have got thus far in their career, " Let not the people's friend," as they say, " be lost to them."

Exactly.

The people readily assent; all their fears are for him — they have no fear for themselves.

Very true.

And when a man who is wealthy and is also accused of being an enemy of the people sees this, then, my friend, as the oracle said to Croesus, —

" By pebbly Hermas' shore he flees and rests not, and is not ashamed to be a coward."

And quite right too, said he, for, if he were, he would never be ashamed again.

But if he is caught he dies.

Of course.

And he, the protector of whom we spoke, is not fallen in his might, but himself the overthrower of many, is to be seen standing up in the chariot of State with the reins in his hand, no longer protector, but tyrant absolute. — *The Republic*, ii. 394.

Prudence and temperance.

—— *Cle.* I suppose, Megillus, that this companion virtue of which the Stranger speaks must be temperance?

Ath. Yes, Cleinias, temperance in the vulgar sense, not that which in the exaggerated language of some philosophers is demonstrated to be prudence, but that which is the natural gift of children and animals, and makes some of them live continently and others incontinently, but when isolated was, as we said, hardly worth reckoning in the catalogue of goods. I think that you must understand my meaning?

Cle. Certainly. — *Laws*, iv. 237.

Public opinion compared to a great beast. See *Opinion, public*, etc.

Public works, construction of.

—— *Soc.* Well, then, if you and I, Callicles, were engaged in the administration of political affairs, and were advising one another about some public work, such as walls, docks, or temples of the largest size, ought we not to examine ourselves, first, as to whether we know or do not know the art of building, and who taught us? — would not that be necessary, Callicles?

Cal. True.

Soc. In the second place, we should have to consider whether we had ever constructed any private house, either of our own or for our friends, and whether this building was a success or not; and if upon consideration we found that we had had good and eminent masters, and had been successful in building, not only with their assistance, but without them, by our own unaided skill, — in that case prudence would not dissuade us from proceeding to the construction of public works. But if we had no master to show, and only a number of worthless buildings or none at all, then, surely, it would be ridiculous in us to attempt public works, or to advise one another to undertake them. Is not this true?

Cal. Certainly. — *Gorgias*, iii. 105.

Public men, criminality of. See *Criminality*, etc.

Pugnacity, a motive to authorship. See *Authorship*.

Punishment, effect of, on evil-doers.

—— If you will think, Socrates, of the effect which punishment has on evil-doers, you will see at once that in the opinion of mankind virtue may be acquired; no one punishes the evil-doer under the notion, or for the reason, that he has done wrong, — only the unreasonable fury of a beast acts in that way. But he who desires to inflict rational punishment does not retaliate for a past wrong, which cannot be undone; he has regard to the future, and is desirous that the man who is punished, and he who sees him punished, may be deterred from doing wrong again. He clearly punishes for the sake of prevention, thereby implying that virtue is capable of being taught. This is the notion of all who retaliate upon others either privately or publicly. And the Athenians, too, your own citizens, like other men, retaliate on all whom they regard as evil-doers; which argues them to be of the number of those who think that virtue may be acquired and taught. — *Protagoras*, i 124.

Punishment, office of twofold. See *Injustice.*

—— Now the proper office of punishment is twofold; he who is rightly punished ought either to become better and profit by it, or he ought to be made an example to his fellows, that they may see what he suffers, and fear and become better. Those who are improved, when they are punished by Gods and men, are those whose sins are curable; and they are improved, as in this world so also in another, by pain and suffering; for there is no other way in which they can be delivered from their evil. But they who have been guilty of the worst crimes, and are incurable by reason of their crimes, are made examples; for, as they are incurable, the time has passed at which they can receive any benefit themselves. But others get good when they behold them forever enduring the most terrible and painful and fearful sufferings as the penalty of their sins; there they are, hanging up as examples, in the prison-house of the world below, a spectacle and a warning to all unrighteous men who come thither. — *Gorgias,* iii. 116.

Punishment of souls, the. See *Soul after death.*

Pure and impure soul. See *Impure.*

Purifications.

—— *Str.* As to the question which you were asking about the name which was to comprehend all these arts of purification, whether of animate or inanimate substances, the spirit of dialectic is in no wise particular about fine words, if she may be only allowed to have a general name for all other purifications, binding them up together and separating them off from the purification of the soul or intellect. For this is the purification at which she wants to arrive, and this we should understand to be her aim.

Theaet. Yes, I understand; and I agree that there are two sorts of purification, and that one of them is concerned with the soul, and that there is another which is concerned with the body. — *Sophist,* iii. 461.

Purification by refutation.

—— *Str.* There is the time-honored mode which our fathers commonly practiced towards their sons, and which is still adopted by many — either of roughly reproving their errors, or of gently advising them, which may be called by the general term of admonition.

Theaet. True.

Str. But whereas some appear to have arrived at the conclusion that all ignorance is involuntary, and that no one who thinks himself wise is willing to learn any of those things, in which he is conscious of his own cleverness, and that the admonitory sort of instruction gives much trouble and does little good —

Theaet. There they are quite right.

Str. Accordingly, they set to work to eradicate the spirit of conceit in another way.

Theaet. In what way.

Str. They cross-examine a man as to what he is saying, when he thinks that he is saying something and is saying nothing; he is easily convicted of inconsistency in his opinions; these they collect, and placing them side by side, show that they contradict one another about the same things, in relation to the same things, and in the same respect. He seeing this is angry with himself, and grows gentle towards others, and thus is entirely delivered from great prejudices and harsh notions, in a way which is most entertaining to hear, and produces the most lasting good effect on the person who is the subject of the operation. For as the physician considers that the body will receive no benefit from taking food until the internal obstacles have been removed, so the instructor of the soul is conscious that his patient will receive no benefit from the applications of knowledge until he is refuted, and from refutation learns modesty; he must be purged of his prejudices, and think that he knows only what he knows, and no more.

Theaet. That is certainly the best and most temperate state.

Str. For all these reasons, Theaetetus, we must admit that refutation is the greatest and chiefest of purifications, and he who has not been refuted, though he be the great King himself, is in the highest degree impure; he is uninstructed and deformed in those things in which he who would be truly blessed ought to be pure and fair.

Theaet. Very true. — *Sophist*, iii. 464.

Purification, legislative. See *Legislative*, etc.

Purification, Colonization a means of.

—— Another piece of good fortune must not be forgotten, which, as we were saying, the Heraclid colony had, and which is also ours, — that we have escaped division of land and the abolition of debts; for these are always a source of dangerous contention, and a city which is driven to legislation upon such matters can neither allow the old ways to continue, nor yet venture to alter them. We must have recourse to prayers, as men say, and hope that a slight change may be cautiously effected in a length of time. And such a change can be accomplished by those who have abundance of land, and having also many debtors, are willing, in a kindly spirit, to share with those who are in want, sometimes remitting and sometimes giving, holding fast in a path of moderation, and deeming poverty to be the increase of a man's desires and not the diminution of his property. For this is the chiefest foundation of a State, and upon this lasting basis may be erected afterwards whatever political order is suitable under the circumstances; but if the change be based upon an unsound principle, the political superstructure which is added will hardly succeed. That is a danger, which, as I am saying, is escaped by us, and yet we had better say how we, if we had not escaped, might have escaped; and we may venture now to assert that no other way of escape, whether narrow or broad, can be devised but a just contentment: upon this rock our city shall be built: for there ought to be no disputes among citizens about property. If there are quarrels of long standing among them, no legislator of any degree of sense will proceed a step in the arrangement of the State until they are settled. But that they to whom God has given, as he has to us, to be the founders of a new State free from enmity — that they should create themselves enmities, by reason of their mode of dividing lands and houses, would be superhuman folly and wickedness. — *Laws*, iv. 261.

Quarreling unholy.

—— Neither, if we mean our future guardians to regard the habit of quarreling as dishonorable, should anything be said of the wars in heaven, and of the plots and fightings of the Gods against one another, which are quite untrue. Far be it from us to tell them of the battles of the giants, and embroider them on garments; or of all the innumerable other quarrels of Gods and heroes with their friends and relations. If they would only believe us we would tell them that quarreling is unholy, and that never up to this time has there been any quarrel between citizens; this is what old men and old women should begin by telling children, and the same when they grow up. — *The Republic*, ii. 201.

Quietness, temperance is.

—— In order, then, that I may form a conjecture whether you

have temperance abiding in you or not, tell me, I said, what, in your opinion, is Temperance?

At first he hesitated, and was very unwilling to answer: then he said that he thought temperance was doing things orderly and quietly, such things for example as walking in the streets, and talking, or anything else of that nature. In a word, he said, I should answer that, in my opinion, temperance is quietness.

Are you right, Charmides? I said. No doubt some would affirm that the quiet are the temperate; but let us see whether there is any meaning in this; and first tell me whether you would not acknowledge temperance to be of the class of the honorable and good?

Yes. — *Charmides*, i. 13.

Race, community of. See *Colonization*.
Races, metallic symbols of. See *Metallic*.
Real, shadows seeming. See *Shadows*, etc.
Real being. See *Being*.
Reason and principle, our guides. See *Principle*.
Reason, incorrupt passion the rod of. See *Passion*.
Reason, steps of. See *Hypotheses*.
Reason in the sphere of sense. See *Intellect* and *Knowledge*.
Reason the rule of life. See *Life*, etc.
Recollection, learning a process of. See *Learning*.
Reconciling judge.

—— *Ath.* Now, which would be the better judge, one who destroyed the bad, and required the good to govern themselves; or one who, while allowing the good to govern, let the bad live, and made them voluntarily submit? Or, lastly, there might be a third excellent judge, who, finding the family distracted, not only did not destroy any one, but reconciled them to one another forever after, and gave them laws which they mutually observed, and was able to keep them friends.

Cle. The last would be by far the best sort of judge and legislator. — *Laws*, iv. 158.

Reflecting and unchanging, the soul.

—— Were we not saying long ago that the soul when using the body as an instrument of perception, that is to say, when using the sense of sight or hearing or some other sense (for the meaning of perceiving through the body is perceiving through the senses), — were we not saying that the soul too is then dragged by the body into the region of the changeable, and wanders and is confused; the world spins round her, and she is like a drunkard when possessed by change?

Very true.

But when returning into herself she reflects; then she passes into the other world, the abode of purity, and eternity, and immortality, and unchangeableness, which are her kindred, and with them she ever lives, when she is by herself and is not let or hindered; then she ceases from her erring ways, and being in communion with the unchanging is unchanging. And this state of the soul is called wisdom?

That is well and truly said, Socrates, he replied.

And to which class is the soul more nearly alike and akin, as far as may be inferred from this argument, as well as from the preceding one?

I think, Socrates, that, in the opinion of every one who follows the argument, the soul will be infinitely more like the unchangeable, — even the most stupid person will not deny that.

And the body is more like the changing?

Yes. — *Phaedo*, i. 407.

Reflection, not sensation, the source of knowledge. See *Sensation*.

Refutation a common good.

—— You are only doing what you denied that you were doing just now, trying to refute me, instead of pursuing the argument.

And what if I am? How can you think that I have any other motive in refuting you but what I should have in examining into myself? which motive would be just a fear of my unconsciously fancying that I knew something of which I was ignorant. And at this moment I pursue the argument chiefly for my own sake, and perhaps in some degree also for the sake of my other friends. For is not the discovery of things as they truly are a common good to all mankind?

Yes, certainly, Socrates, he said.

Then, I said, be cheerful, sweet sir, and give your opinion in answer to the question which I asked, without minding whether Critias or Socrates is the person refuted; attend only to the argument, and see what will come of the refutation.

I think that you are right, he replied; and I will do as you say. — *Charmides*, i. 22.

Refutation, a purification. See *Purification*.

Remembrance and burial of the dead. See *Burial*, etc.

Respiration and inspiration.

—— Let us further consider the phenomena of respiration, and inquire what are the real causes of it. They are as follows:— Seeing that there is no such thing as a vacuum into which any of those things which are moved can enter, and the breath is carried from us into the external air, the next point is, as will be clear to every one, that it does not go into a vacant space, but pushes its neighbor out of its place, and that which is thrust out again thrusts out its neighbor; and in this way everything of necessity at last comes round to that place from whence the breath came forth, and enters in there, and follows with the breath, and fills up the place; and this goes on like the circular motion of a wheel, because there can be no such thing as a vacuum. Wherefore also the breast and the lungs, which emit the breath, are again filled up by the air which surrounds the body and which enters in through the pores of the flesh and comes round in a circle; and, again, the air which is sent away and passes out through the body forces the breath within to find a way round through the passage of the mouth and the nostrils. Now, the origin of this may be supposed to be as follows:— Every animal has his inward parts about the blood and the veins as warm as possible; he has within him a fountain of fire, which we compare to the texture of a net of fire extended through the centre of the body, while the outer parts are composed of air. Now, we must admit that heat naturally precedes outward to its own place and to its kindred element; and as there are two exits for the heat, the one through the body outwards, and the other through the mouth and nostrils, when it moves towards the one, it drives round the other air, and that which is driven round falls into the fire and is warmed, and that which goes forth is cooled. But when the condition of the heat changes, and the particles at the other exit grow warmer, the hotter air inclining in that direction and carried towards its native element, fire, pushes round the other; and thus, by action and reaction, there being this circular agitation and alternation produced by the two, — by this double cause, I say, inspiration and expiration are produced. — *Timaeus,* ii. 570.

Rest and motion of things.

—— Some one says to me, "O Stranger, are all things in rest and nothing in motion, or is the exact opposite of this true, or are some things in motion and others at rest?" To this I shall reply that some are in motion and others at rest. "And do not things which move, move in place, and are not the things which are at rest, at. rest in a place?" Certainly. "And some move or rest in one place and some in more places than one?" You mean to say, we shall rejoin, that those things which rest at the centre move in the same place, as when the circumference goes round and the circle is said to be at rest? "Yes." And we observe that, in the revolution, the motion which carries round the larger and the lesser circle at the same time is proportionally distributed to greater and smaller, and is greater and smaller in a certain proportion. Here is a wonder which might be thought an impossibility, that the same motion should impart swiftness and slowness in due proportion to larger and lesser circles. Very true. "And when you speak of bodies moving in many places, you seem to me to mean those which move from one place to another, and sometimes have one centre of motion and sometimes several in the course of their revolutions; and sometimes impinging upon each other they come against bodies which are at rest, and are divided by them, or meeting other bodies which are coming violently from an opposite direction unite with them and interpenetrate them." — *Laws*, iv. 405.

Retribution for the erring. See *Punishment*, etc.
Retribution for injustice. See *Injustice*, etc.
Reverence, youthful, for the aged. See *Mind*, etc., *reverenced*.
Rewards, glorious.

—— The Olympic victor I said, is deemed happy in receiving a part only of the happiness which is the lot of our citizens, who have won a more glorious victory and have a more complete maintenance at the public cost. For the victory which they have won is the salvation of the whole State; and the crown with which they and their children are crowned is the fullness of all that life needs; they receive rewards from the hands of their country while living, and after death have an honorable burial.

Yes, he said, they are are indeed glorious rewards. — *The Republic*, ii. 292.

Rhadamanthus, the decision of.

—— The so-called decision of Rhadamanthus is worthy of all admiration. He knew that the men of his own time believed and had no doubt that there were Gods, which was a reasonable belief in those days, because most men were the sons of

Gods, and according to tradition he was one himself. He appears to have thought that he ought to commit judgment to no man, but to the Gods only, and in this way suits were simply and speedily decided by him. For he made the two parties at issue take an oath respecting the points in dispute, and so got rid of the matter speedily and safely. But now that a certain portion of mankind do not believe at·all in the existence of the Gods, and others imagine that they have no care of us, and the opinion of most men and of the worst men is that in return for a small sacrifice and flattering words they will aid them in abstracting a great deal of money, and deliver them from divers and great penalties, the way of Rhadamanthus is no longer suited to the needs of justice, for as the opinions of men about the Gods are changed, the laws should also be changed. — *Laws*, iv. 458.

Rhapsode, the profession of a. See *Homer*.
Rhetoric and dialecticians.

—— *Soc.* I am a great lover of these processes of division and generalization; they help me to speak and think. And if I find any man who is able to see a One and Many in nature, him I follow, and walk in his steps as if he were a God. And those who have this art, I have hitherto been in the habit of calling dialecticians; but God knows whether the name is right or not. And I should like to know what name you would give to your or Lysias' disciples, and whether this may not be that famous art of rhetoric which Thrasymachus and others practice? Skillful speakers they are, and impart their skill to any who will consent to worship them as kings and to bring them gifts.

Phaedr. Yes, they are royal men; but their art is not the same with the art of those whom you call, and rightly, in my opinion, dialecticians. — *Phaedrus*, i. 571.

Rhetoric, flattery in. See *Flattery*.
Rhetoric, persuasion the crown of. See *Persuasion*.
Rhetoric, the art of discourse.

—— *Soc.* Why if you call rhetoric the art which treats of discourse, and all the other arts treat of discourse, do you not call them arts of rhetoric?

Gor. Because, Socrates, the knowledge of the other arts has only to do with some sort of external action, as of the hand; but there is no such action of the hand in rhetoric which operates and is perfected through the medium of discourse. And therefore I am justified, as I maintain, in saying that rhetoric treats of discourse.

Soc. I do not know whether I entirely understand you, but I dare say that I shall soon find out: please to answer me a question : you would allow that there are arts?

Gor. Yes.

Soc. And in some of the arts a great deal is done and nothing or very little said; in painting, or statuary, or many other arts, the work may proceed in silence ; and these are the arts with which, as I suppose you would say, rhetoric has no concern ?

Gor. You perfectly conceive my meaning, Socrates.

Soc. And there are other arts which work wholly by words, and require either no action or very little, as, for example, the arts of arithmetic, of calculation, of geometry, and of playing draughts ; in some of which words are nearly coextensive with things : but the greater number of them are dependent wholly on words for their efficacy and power: and I take your meaning to be that rhetoric is an art of this better sort?

Gor. Exactly. — *Gorgias*, iii. 35.

Rhetoric an experience, process, or habit.

—— *Pol.* I will ask; and do you answer me, Socrates, the same question which Gorgias, as you suppose, is unable to answer : What is rhetoric?

Soc. Do you mean what sort of an art ?

Pol. Yes.

Soc. Not an art at all, in my opinion, if I am to tell you the truth, Polus.

Pol. Then what, in your opinion, is rhetoric?

Soc. A thing of which, I was lately reading in a book of of yours, you say that you have made an art.

Pol. What thing ?

Soc. I should say a sort of experience.

Pol. Does rhetoric seem to you to be an experience?

Soc. That is my view, if that is yours.

Pol. An experience in what ?

Soc. An experience in producing a sort of delight and gratification.

Pol. And if able to gratify others, must not rhetoric be a fine thing ?

Soc. What are you saying, Polus ? Why do you ask me whether rhetoric is a fine thing or not, when I have not as yet told you what rhetoric is ?

Pol. Why, did you not tell me that rhetoric was a sort of experience ?

Soc. As you are so fond of gratifying others, will you gratify me in a small particular?
Pol. I will.
Soc. Will you ask me, what sort of an art is cookery?
Pol. What sort of an art is cookery?
Soc. Not an art at all, Polus.
Pol. What then?
Soc. I should say an experience.
Pol. In what? I wish that you would tell me.
Soc An experience in producing a sort of delight and gratification, Polus.
Pol. Then are cookery and rhetoric the same?
Soc. No, they are only different parts of the same profession.
Pol. And what is that?
Soc. I am afraid that the truth may seem discourteous; I should not like Gorgias to imagine that I am ridiculing his profession, and therefore I hesitate to answer. For whether or no this is that art of rhetoric which Gorgias practices I really do not know: from what he was just now saying, nothing appeared of what he thought of his art, but the rhetoric which I mean is a part of a not very creditable whole. — *Gorgias*, iii. 47.

Rhetorician, the skillful.

—— *Soc.* Until a man knows the truth of the several particulars of which he is writing or speaking, and is able to define them as they are, and having defined them again to divide them until they can be no longer divided, and until in like manner he is able to discern the nature of the soul and discover the different modes of discourse which are adapted to different natures, and to arrange and dispose them in such a way that the simple form of speech may be addressed to the simpler nature, and the complex and composite to the complex nature — until he has accomplished all this, he will be unable to handle arguments according to rules of art, as far as their nature allows them to be subjected to art, either for the purpose of teaching or persuading; that is the view which is implied in the whole preceding argument.

Phaedr. Yes, that was our view, certainly.

Soc. Secondly, as to the justice of the censure which was passed on speaking or writing discourses — did not our previous argument show —?

Phaedr. Show what?

Soc. That whether Lysias or any other writer that ever was or will be, whether private man or statesman, tries his hand at authorship in making laws, and fancies that there is a great certainty and clearness in his performance, the fact of his writing as he does is only a disgrace to him, whatever men may say. For entire ignorance about the nature of justice and injustice, and good and evil, and the inability to distinguish the dream from the reality, cannot in truth be otherwise than disgraceful to him, even though he have the applause of the whole world.

Phaedr. Certainly.

Soc. But he who thinks that in the written word there is necessarily much which is not serious, and that neither poetry nor prose, spoken or written, are of any great value — if, like the compositions of the rhapsodes, they are only recited in order to be believed, and not with any view to criticism or instruction; and who thinks that even the best of them are but a reminiscence of what we know, and that only in principles of justice and goodness and nobility taught and communicated orally and written in the soul, which is the true way of writing, is there clearness and perfection and seriousness; and that such principles are like legitimate offspring; being, in the first place, that which the man finds in his own bosom; secondly, the brethren and descendants and relations of his idea which have been duly implanted in the souls of others; and who cares for them and no others — this is the right sort of man; and you and I, Phaedrus, would pray that we may become like him.

Phaedr. That is most assuredly my desire and prayer.

Soc. And now the play is played out; and of rhetoric enough. — *Phaedrus*, i. 582.

Rhetorician to make good use of his art.

—— *Gor.* I like your way of leading us on, Socrates, and I will endeavor to reveal to you the whole nature of rhetoric. You must have heard, I think, that the docks and the walls of the Athenians and the plan of the harbor were devised in accordance with the counsels, partly of Themistocles and partly of Pericles and not at the suggestion of the builders.

Soc. Certainly, Gorgias, that is the tradition about Themistocles, and I myself heard the speech of Pericles when he advised us about the middle wall.

Gor. And you will observe, Socrates, that when a decision has to be given in such matters the rhetoricians are the advisers; they are the men who win their point.

Soc. I had that in my admiring mind, Gorgias, when I asked what is the nature of rhetoric, which always appears to me, when I look at the matter in this way, to be a marvel of greatness.

Gor. A marvel indeed, Socrates, if you only knew how rhetoric comprehends and holds under her sway all the inferior arts. Let me offer you a striking example of this. On several occasions I have been with my brother Herodicus or some other physician to see one of his patients, who would not allow the physician to give him medicine, or apply the knife or hot iron to him; and I have persuaded him to do for me what he would not do for the physician just by the use of rhetoric. And I say that if a rhetorician and a physician were to go to any city, and there had to argue in the Ecclesia or any other assembly as to which should be elected, the physician would have no chance; but he who could speak would be chosen if he wished, and in a contest with a man of any other profession the rhetorician more than any one would have the power of getting himself chosen, for he can speak more persuasively to the multitude that any of them, and on any subject. Such is the power and quality of rhetoric, Socrates. And yet rhetoric ought to be used like any other competitive art, not against everybody, — the rhetorician ought not to abuse his strength any more than a pugilist or pancratiast or other master of fence; because he has powers which are more than a match either for enemy or friend, he ought not therefore to strike, stab, or slay his friends. And suppose a man who has been trained in the palaestra and is a skillful boxer, and in the fullness of his strength he goes and strikes his father or mother or one of his familiars or friends, that is no reason why the trainer or master of fence should be held in detestation or banished, — surely not. For they taught this art for a good purpose, as an art to be used against enemies and evil-doers, in self-defense, not in aggression, and others have perverted their instructions, making a bad use of their strength and skill. But not on this account are the teachers bad, neither is the art in fault or bad in itself; I should rather say that those who make a bad use of the art are to blame. And the same holds good of rhetoric; for the rhetorician can speak against all men and on any subject, and in general he can persuade the multitude of anything better than any other man, but he ought not on that account to defraud the physician or any other artist of his reputation merely because he has the power; he ought to use rhetoric fairly, as he would also use his athletic powers. And if after having become a rhetorician he makes a bad use of his strength and skill, his instructor surely ought not on that account to be held in detestation or banished. For he was intended by his teacher to make a good use of his instructions, and he abuses them. And therefore he is the person who ought to be held in detestation, banished, and put to death, and not his instructor. — *Gorgias*, iii. 41.

Rhetoricians, two sorts of.

—— *Soc.* Do the rhetoricians appear to you always to aim at what is best in their speeches, and to desire only the greatest improvement of the citizens, or are they too bent upon giving them pleasure, forgetting the public good in the thought of their own interest, playing with the people as with children, and trying to amuse them, but never considering whether they are better or worse for this?

Cal. I must distinguish. There are some who have a real care of the public in what they say, while others are such as you describe.

Soc. I am contented with the admission that rhetoric is of two sorts; one which is mere flattery and disgraceful declamation; the other, which is noble and aims at the training and improvement of the souls of the citizens, and strives to say what is best, whether welcome or unwelcome, to the audience; but have you ever known such a rhetoric; or if you have, and can point out any rhetorician who is of this stamp, will you tell me who he is?

Cal. But, indeed, I am afraid that I cannot tell you of any such among the orators who are at present living.

Soc. Well, then, can you mention any one of a former generation, who may be said to have improved the Athenians, who found them worse and made them better, from the day that he began to make speeches? for, indeed, I do not know of such a man. — *Gorgias*, iii. 94.

Rhetoricians, none noble. See *Noble*, etc.

Rhythm, the order of motion.

—— *Ath.* I was speaking at the commencement of our discourse, as you will remember, of the fiery nature of young creatures; I said that they were unable to keep quiet either in limb or voice, and that they called out and jumped about in a disorderly manner; and that no other animal attained to any perception of order, but man only. Now the order of motion is called rhythm, and the order of the voice, in which high and low are duly mingled, is called harmony; and both together are termed choric song. And I said that the Gods had pity on us, and gave us Apollo and the Muses to be our playfellows and leaders in the dance; and Dionysus, as I dare say that you will remember, was the third.

Cle. I quite remember. — *Laws,* iv. 194.

Rich man, bad company.

—— May I ask, Cephalus, whether you inherited or acquired the greater part of your wealth?

Acquired! Socrates; do you want to know how much I acquired? In the art of making money I have been midway between my father and grandfather; for my grandfather, whose name like my own was Cephalus, doubled and trebled the value of his inheritance, but my father Lysanias reduced the property below what I now have; and I shall be satisfied if I leave my sons a little more than I received.

That was why I asked you the question, I said, because I saw that you were indifferent about money, which is a characteristic rather of those who have inherited their fortunes than of those who have acquired them; for the latter have a second love of money as a creation of their own, resembling the affection of authors for their own poems, or of parents for their children, besides that natural love of money for the sake of use and enjoyment which is common to them and all men. And hence they are very bad company, for they talk about nothing but the praises of wealth.

That is true, he said.

Yes, that is very true, I said; but may I ask another question? — What do you consider to be the greatest blessing which you have reaped from wealth? — *The Republic,* ii. 150.

Rich man, the true and noble. See *Noble,* etc.
Riches in government. See *Money a ruler.*
Riches and poverty in age. See *Poverty.*
Riches an evil left to children. See *Children.*
Ridicule no test of truth.

—— But then, I said, as we have determined to speak our minds, we must not fear the jests of the wits which will be directed against this sort of innovation; how they will talk of women's attainments in music as well as in gymnastic, and above all about their wearing armor and riding upon horseback!

Very true, he replied.

Yet having begun, we must go on and attack the difficulty; at the same time begging of these gentlemen for once in their life to be serious. Not long ago, as we shall remind them, the Greeks were of the opinion, which is still generally received among the barbarians, that the sight of a naked man was ridiculous and improper; and when first the Cretans and then the Lacedaemonians introduced naked exercises, the wits of that day might have ridiculed them equally.

No doubt.

But when experience showed that to let all things be uncovered was far better than to cover them up, and the ludicrous effect to the outward eye vanished before the approval of reason, then the man was seen to be a fool who laughs or directs the shafts of his ridicule at any other sight but that of folly and vice, or seriously inclines to measure the beautiful by any other standard but that of the good.

Very true, he replied.

First, then, whether the question is to be put in jest or in earnest, let us ask about the nature of woman; Is she capable of sharing either wholly or partially, in the actions of men or not at all? And is the art of war one of those arts in which she can or cannot share? That will be the best way of commencing the inquiry, and will probably lead to the fairest conclusion.

That will be best. — *The Republic*, ii. 276.

Ridicule at self-conceit. See *Laughter*.
Right and duty *versus* life and death. See *Death and life*.
Right, ridicule no test of. See *Ridicule*.
Right determined by might. See *Might*.
Right and wrong determined by the State.

—— *Soc.* Again, in politics, while affirming that right and wrong, honorable and disgraceful, holy and unholy, are in reality to each State such as the State thinks and makes lawful, and that in determining these matters no individual or State is wiser than another, still the followers of Protagoras will not deny that in determining the sphere of expediency one counselor is better than another, and one State wiser than another;

they will scarcely venture to maintain, that what a city deems expedient will always be really expedient. But in the other case, I mean when they speak of justice and injustice, piety and impiety, they are confident that these have no natural or essential basis — the truth is that which is agreed on at the time of agreement, and as long as the agreement lasts; and this is the philosophy of many who do not altogether go along with Protagoras. — *Thaeatetus*, iii. 374.

Right opinion, differences as to. See *Differences*, etc.
Righteous judge. See *Judge*, etc.
Round world. See *Earth, rotundity of the*.
Rulers swaying the people.

—— Your own Agathocles pretended to be a musician, but was really an eminent Sophist; also Pythocleides and Cean; and there were many others; and all of them, as I was saying, adopted these arts as veils or disguises because they were afraid of the envy of the multitude. But that is not my way, for I do not believe that they effected their purpose, which was to deceive the government, who were not blinded by them; and as to the people, they have no understanding, and only repeat what their rulers are pleased to tell them. — *Protagoras*, i. 117.

Rulers in the State, who should be.

—— Now then, I said, I go to meet that which I liken to the greatest of the waves, yet shall the word be spoken, even though the overflowing of the laughing wave shall drown me in laughter and dishonor; and do you attend to me.

Proceed.

I said: Until, then, philosophers are kings, or the kings and princes of this world have the spirit and power of philosophy, and political greatness and wisdom meet in one, and those commoner natures who follow either to the exclusion of the other are compelled to stand aside, cities will never cease from ill — no, nor the human race, as I believe — and then only will our State have a possibility of life and behold the light of day: this was the thought, my dear Glaucon, which I was wanting to utter, if it had not seemed too extravagant; for to be convinced that in no other State can there be private or public happiness is indeed a hard thing.

Socrates, what do you mean? I would have you consider that the word which you have spoken is one at which numerous persons, and very respectable persons too, pulling off their coats in a moment and seizing any weapon that comes to hand, will run at you might and main, intending to do heaven knows what; and if you don't prepare an answer, and put yourself in motion, you will be "pared by their fine wits," and no mistake.

You got me into the scrape, I said.

And I was quite right; however, I will do all I can to get you out; but I can only give you wishes and exhortations, and also, perhaps, I may be able to fit answers to your questions better than another — that is all. And now having such an auxiliary, you must do your best to show the unbelievers that you are right.

I ought to try, I said, since you offer me such valuable assistance. And I think that, if there is to be a chance of our escaping, we must define who these philosophers are who, as we say, are to rule in the State; then we shall be able to defend ourselves: there will be discovered to be some natures who ought to rule and to study philosophy; and others who are not born to be philosophers, and are meant to be followers rather than leaders. — *The Republic*, ii. 301.

Rulers, who and what they must be.

—— The women and children are done with but there remains the further question of the rulers, which I must now investigate from the beginning. We were saying, as you will remember, that they were to be lovers of their country, tried by the test of pleasures and pains, and neither in labors, nor fears, nor any other change of circumstances were to lose their patriotism; he was to be rejected who failed but he who always came forth pure, like gold tried in the refiner's fire, was to be made a ruler, and to receive honors and rewards in life and after death. That was the sort of thing which was being said, and then the argument turned aside and veiled her face; not liking to stir the question which has now arisen.

I perfectly remember, he said.

Yes, my friend, I said. and I then shrank from hazarding the bold word; but now let me dare to say, — that the perfect guardian must be a philosopher.

Yes, he said, let that be proclaimed.

And do not suppose that there will be many of them, — for the gifts which we said were essential rarely grow together; they are mostly found in shreds and patches.

What do you mean? he said.

You are aware, I replied, that persons who have quick intelligence, memory, sagacity, shrewdness, and similar gifts, are not often of a nature which is willing at the same time to live orderly and in a peaceful and settled manner ; and this is equally true of the high-spirited and magnanimous ; they are driven any way by their impetuosity, and all solid principle goes out of them.

Very true, he said.

On the other hand, those steadfast, immovable natures which in a battle are impregnable to fear and can better be depended on are equally immovable when there is anything to be learned ; they seem to be in a torpid state, and are apt to yawn and go to sleep over any intellectual toil.

Quite true.

And yet we were saying that both qualities were necessary in those to whom the higher education is to be imparted, and who are to share in any office or command.

Certainly, he said.

And will they be a class which is rarely found ?

Yes, indeed.

Then the aspirant must not only be tested in those labors and dangers and pleasures which we mentioned before ; and there is another kind of probation which we did not mention, he must be exercised also in many kinds of knowledge, to see whether the soul will be able to endure the highest of all, or will faint under them, as many do amid the toils of the games.

Yes, he said, you are quite right in testing them. — *The Republic*, ii. 330.

Rulers compared to gold and silver.

—— I have only told you half. Citizens, we shall say to them in our tale, you are brothers, yet God has framed you differently. Some of you have the power of command, and these he has composed of gold, wherefore also they have the greatest honor ; others of silver, to be auxiliaries ; others again who are to be husbandmen and craftsmen he has made of brass and iron ; and the species will generally be preserved in the children. But as you are of the same original family, a golden parent will sometimes have a silver son, or a silver parent a golden son. And God proclaims to the rulers, as a first principle, that before all they should watch over their offspring, and see what elements mingle in their nature ; for if the son of a golden or silver parent has an admixture of brass and iron, then nature orders a transposition of ranks, and the eye of the ruler must not be pitiful towards his child because he has to descend in the scale and become a husbandman or artisan, just as there may be others sprung from the artisan class who are raised to honor, and become guardians and auxiliaries. For an oracle says that when a man of brass or iron guards the State, it will then be destroyed. — *The Republic*, ii. 240.

Rulers must be characterized by truth and virtue.

—— Inasmuch as philosophers only are able to grasp the eternal and unchangeable, and those who wander in the region of the many and variable are not philosophers, I must ask you which of the two kinds should be the rulers of our State?

And how can we truly answer that question? he said.

Ask yourself, I replied, which of the two are better able to guard the laws and institutions of our State; and let them be our guardians.

Very good.

Neither, I said, can there be any question that the guardian who is to keep anything should have eyes rather than no eyes?

There can be no question of that.

And are not those who are truly and indeed without the knowledge of the true being of each thing, and have in their souls no clear pattern, and are unable as with a painter's eye to look at the very truth and to that original to repair, and having perfect vision of the other world to order the laws about beauty, goodness, justice in this, if not already ordered and to guard and preserve the order of them — are they not, I say, simply blind?

Assuredly, he replied, that is very much their condition.

And shall they be our guardians when there are others who, besides being their equals in experience and not inferior to them in any particular of virtue, have also the knowledge of the truth?

There can be no reason, he said, for rejecting those who have this great and preëminent quality, if they do not fail in any other respect.

Suppose then, I said, that we determine how far they can unite this and the other excellences.

By all means.

In the first place, as we began by observing, the nature of

the philosopher was to be ascertained; about which, if we are agreed, then, if I am not mistaken, we shall also be agreed that such an union of qualities is possible, and that those in whom they are united, and those only, should be rulers in the State. — *The Republic*, ii. 310.

Rulers compared to pilots and physicians.

—— *Str.* I must again have recourse to my favorite images; through them, and them alone, can I describe kings and rulers.

Y. Soc. What images?

Str. The noble pilot and the wise physician, who "is worth many another man;" in the similitude of these let us endeavor to discover some image of the king.

Y. Soc. What sort of an image?

Str. Well, such as this: every man will reflect that he suffers strange things at their hands; the physician saves any whom he wishes to save, and many whom he wishes to injure he injures — cutting or burning them, and at the same time requiring them to bring him payments, which are a sort of tribute, of which a very small part is spent upon the sick man, and the greater part is consumed by him and his domestics; and the finale is, that he receives money from the relations of the sick man or from some enemy of his, and puts him out of the way. And the captains of ships are guilty of numberless evil deeds of the same kind; they play false and leave you ashore when the hour of sailing arrives, or they wreck their vessels and cast away freight and lives; not to speak of other rogueries. Now suppose that we, bearing all this in mind, were to determine, after consideration, that neither of these arts shall any longer be allowed to exercise absolute control either over freemen or over slaves, but that we will summon an assembly either of all the people, or of the rich only, and that anybody who likes, whatever may be his calling, or even if he have no calling, may offer an opinion either about ships or about diseases; whether as to the manner in which physic or surgical instruments are to be applied to the patient, or about the vessels and the nautical instruments which are required in navigation, and how to meet the dangers of winds and waves which are incidental to the voyage — how to behave when encountering pirates; and what is to be done with the old-fashioned galleys, if they have to fight with others of a similar build: and that, whatever shall be decreed by the multitude on these points, upon the advice of persons skilled or unskilled, shall be written down on triangular tablets and columns, or embalmed unwritten as national customs; and that in all future time vessels shall be navigated and remedies administered to the patient after this fashion.

Y. Soc. What a strange notion!

Str. Suppose, further, that the admirals and physicians are appointed annually, either out of the rich, or out of the whole people, and that they are elected by lot, and that after their election they navigate vessels and heal the sick according to the written rules.

Y. Soc. Worse and worse.

Str. But hear what follows: when the year of office has expired, the admiral or physician has to come before a court of review, in which the judges are either selected from the wealthy classes or chosen by lot out of the whole people; and anybody who pleases may accuse them, and he will lay to their charge, that during the past year they have not navigated their vessels or healed their patients, according to the letter of the law or according to the ancient customs of their ancestors; and if either of them is condemned, there must be persons to fix what he is to suffer or pay.

Y. Soc. He who is willing to take a command under such conditions, deserves to suffer any penalty. — *Statesman*, iii. 583.

Rulers and warriors, gentleness of. See *Gentleness*.

Rulers, qualities of. See *Magistrates*.

Salvation of human life. See *Human life*, etc.

Science of time.

—— *Soc.* And now let me see whether you agree with Laches and myself in a third point.

Nic. What is that?

Soc. I will tell you. He and I have a notion that there is not one knowledge or science of the past, another of the present, a third of what will be and will be best in the future; but that of all three there is one science only: for example, there is one science of medicine which is concerned with the inspection of health equally in all times, present, past, and future; and of husbandry in like manner, which is concerned with the productions of the earth in all times. As to the general's art, yourselves will be my witnesses, that the general has to think of the future as well as the present; and he considers that he is not to be the servant of the soothsayer, but his master, because he knows better what is happening or is likely to happen in war: and accordingly the law places the soothsayer under the general, and not the general under the soothsayer. Am I not correct, Laches?

La. Quite correct.

Soc. And do you, Nicias, also acknowledge that the same science has understanding of the same things, whether future, present, or past?

Nic. Yes, indeed, Socrates; that is my opinion. — *Laches,* i. 92.

Science *versus* sense.

—— You, I replied, have in your mind a sublime conception of how we know the things above. And I dare say that if a person were to throw his head back and study the fretted ceiling, you would still think that his mind was the percipient and not his eyes. And you are very likely right and I may be a simpleton, but in my opinion, that knowledge only which is of being and of the unseen can make the soul look upwards and whether a man gapes at the heavens or blinks on the ground, seeking to learn some particular of sense, I would deny that he can learn, for nothing of that sort is matter of science; his soul is looking, not upwards, but downwards, whether his way to knowledge is by water or by land, in whichever element he may lie on his back and float. — *The Republic,* ii. 357.

Science, certain knowledge necessary to.

—— I must add that the power of dialectic alone can reveal this, and only to one who is a disciple of the previous sciences.

Of that assertion you may be as certain as of the last.

And certainly no one, will argue that there is any other method or way of comprehending all true existence; for the arts in general are concerned with the wants or opinions of men, or are cultivated for the sake of production and construction or for the care of such productions and constructions; and as to the mathematical arts which, as we were saying, have some apprehension of true being — geometry and the like — they only dream about being, and never can they behold the waking reality so long as they leave the hypotheses which they use unexamined and are unable to give an account of them. For when a man knows not his own first principle, and when the conclusion and intermediate steps are also constructed out of he knows not what, how can he imagine that such a conventional statement will ever become science?

Impossible, he said.

Then dialectic, and dialectic alone, goes directly to the first principle, and is the only science which does away with hypotheses in order to make certain of them; the eye of the soul, which is literally buried in an outlandish slough, is by her taught to look upwards; and she uses as handmaids, in the work of conversion, the sciences which we have been discussing. Custom terms them sciences, but they ought to have some other name, implying greater clearness than opinion and less clearness than science: and this, in our previous sketch, was called understanding. But there is no use in our disputing about names when we have realities of such importance to consider.

No, he said; any name will do which expresses the thought clearly. — *The Republic*, ii. 361.

Science of government, wherein resident. See *Government, science of*.

Science, political, not attained by the many. See *Government, science of*.

Science, political, refining of.

—— *Str.* There are, however, natures more nearly akin to the king, and more difficult to discern; the examination of them may be compared to the process of refining gold.

Y. Soc. What is your meaning?

Str. The workmen begin by sifting away the earth and stones and the like; they then draw off in the fire, which is the only way of abstracting them, the more precious elements of copper, silver, or other metallic substance, which have an affinity to gold; these are at last refined away by the use of tests, and the gold is left quite pure.

Y. Soc. Yes, that is the way in which these things are said to be done.

Str. In like manner, all alien and uncongenial matter has been separated from political science; and what is precious and of a kindred nature has been left; there remain the nobler arts of the general and the judge, and the higher sort of oratory, which is an ally of the royal art, and persuades men to do justice, and assists in guiding the helm of States. What way can be found of taking them away, leaving him whom we seek alone and unalloyed?

Y. Soc. That is clearly what has to be attempted. — *Statesman*, iii. 589.

Sculpture, deception in. See *Likeness-making.*
Sea, evil influence of the, on cities. See *Cities.*
Seen and **unseen.**

—— What would you say of the many beautiful — whether men or horses or garments or any other things which may be called equal or beautiful, — are they all unchanging and the same always, or quite the reverse? May they not rather be described as almost always changing and hardly ever the same, either with themselves or with one another?

The latter, replied Cebes; they are always in a state of change.

And these you can touch and see and perceive with the senses, but the unchanging things you can only perceive with the mind — they are invisible and are not seen?

That is very true, he said.

Well then, Socrates, let us suppose that there are two sorts of existences, one seen, the other unseen.

Let us suppose them.

The seen is the changing, and the unseen is the unchanging?

That may be also supposed.

And, further, is not one part of us body, and the rest of us soul?

To be sure.

And to which class may we say that the body is more alike and akin?

Clearly to the seen: no one can doubt that.

And is the soul seen or not seen?

Not by man, Socrates.

And what we mean by "seen" and "not seen" is that which is or is not visible to the eye of man?

Yes, to the eye of man.

And what do we say of the soul? is that seen or not seen?

Not seen.

Unseen then?

Yes.

Then the soul is more like to the unseen, and the body to the seen?

That is most certain, Socrates.[1] — *Phaedo,* i. 407.

Self-assertion of Hippias.

—— *Eud.* I am sure that Hippias will have no objection to answer anything that you ask him; tell me, Hippias, if Socrates asks you a question, will you answer him?

[1] For the further discussion of this point, see *Reflecting,* etc.

Hippias. Indeed, Eudicus, I should be strangely inconsistent if I refused to answer Socrates, when at each Olympic festival, as I went up from my house at Elis to the temple of Olympia, where all the Hellenes were assembled, I continually professed my willingness to perform any of the exhibitions which I had prepared, and to answer any questions which any one had to ask.

Soc. Truly, Hippias you are a happy man if at every Olympic festival you have such an encouraging opinion of your own powers when you go up to the temple. I doubt whether any muscular hero would be as fearless and confident in offering his body to the combat at Olympia, as you are in offering your mind.

Hip. And with good reason, Socrates; for since the day when I first entered the lists at Olympia I never found any one who was my superior in anything.

Soc. What an ornament, Hippias, will the reputation of your wisdom be to the city of Elis and to your parents! But to return: what do you say of Odysseus and Achilles? Which of the two is the better of them? and in what particular does either surpass the other? For when you were exhibiting and company was in the room, though I could not follow you, I did not like to ask what you meant, because there were other people present, and I was afraid that the question might interrupt your exhibition. — *Lesser Hippias,* iv. 493.

Self-conceit of youth.

—— At length they seize upon the citadel of the young man's soul, which they perceive to be void of all fair accomplishments and pursuits and of every true word, which are the best guardians and sentinels in the minds of men who are dear to the Gods.

None better.

False and boastful words and conceits mount upwards instead of them, and occupy the vacant post.

They are sure to do so.

And so the young man returns into the country of the lotus-eaters and takes up his abode there in the face of all men; and if any help be sent by his friends to the oligarchical part of him the same vain conceits shut the gate of the king's fastness; they will not allow the new allies to pass. And if private individuals, venerable for their age, come and parley, they do not receive them; there is a battle and they win; then modesty which they call silliness, is ignominiously thrust into exile by them. They affirm temperance to be unmanliness and her also they contemptuously eject; and they pretend that moderation and orderly expenditure are vulgarity and meanness, and by the help of a rabble of evil appetites they drain them beyond the border. . . . . Neither does he receive or let pass into the fortress any true word of advice, if any one says to him that some pleasures are the satisfactions of good and noble desires, and others of evil desires, and that he ought to use and honor some, and curtail and reduce others, whenever this is repeated to him he shakes his head and says that they are all alike and that one is as honorable as another. — *The Republic*, ii. 388.

Self-conceit, laughter at. See *Laughter*, etc.
Self-conceit purged out by refutation. See *Purification*, etc.
Self-control. See *Intemperance* and *Self-mastery*.
Self-deception.

—— *Crat.* You are right, Socrates, in saying that I have attended to these matters, and possibly I might even turn you into a disciple. But I fear that the converse is more probable and I already find myself moved to say to you what Achilles in the " Prayers " says to Ajax, —

"Illustrious Ajax, son of Telamon, king of men,
You appear to have spoken in all things much to my mind."

And you, Socrates, appear to me to be an oracle, and to give answers much to my mind, whether you are inspired by Euthyphro, or whether some Muse may have long been an inhabitant of your breast, unconsciously to yourself.

Soc. Excellent Cratylus, I have long been wondering at my own wisdom; I cannot trust myself. And I think that I ought to stop and ask myself what am I saying, for there is nothing worse than self-deception — when the deceiver is always at] home and always with you — that is indeed terrible, and therefore I ought often to retrace my steps and endeavor to " look before me and behind me " in the words of the aforesaid Homer. — *Cratylus*, i. 667.

Self-elevation. See *Elevation*, etc.
Self-gratification. See *Intemperance*.
Self-ignorance.

—— *Soc.* Are there not three ways in which ignorance of self may be shown?

Pro. What are they?

Soc. In the first place, about money: the ignorant may fancy himself richer than he is.

Pro. Yes, that is a very common error.

Soc. And still more often he will fancy that he is taller or fairer than he is, or that he has some other advantage of person which he has not really.

Pro. Certainly.

Soc. And yet surely by far the greatest number err about the goods of the mind; they imagine that they are a great deal better than they are.

Pro. Yes, that is by far the commonest delusion.

Soc. And of all the virtues, is not wisdom the one which the mass of mankind are always claiming, and which most arouses in them a spirit of contention and lying conceit of wisdom?

Pro. Certainly.

Soc. And may not all this be truly called an evil condition?

Pro. Very evil.

Soc. But we must pursue the division a step further, Protarchus, if we would find the singular mixture of pleasure and pain; — pain is envy of the playful sort.

Pro. How can we make the further division which you suggest?

Soc. All who are silly enough to entertain this lying conceit of themselves may be divided, like the rest of mankind, into two classes — one of them having power and might; and the other the reverse.

Pro. Certainly.

Soc. Let this, then, be the principle of division; those of them who are weak and unable to revenge themselves, when they are laughed at, may be truly called ridiculous, but those who can defend themselves may be more truly described as strong and formidable, for ignorance in the powerful is hateful and horrible, because hurtful to others both in reality and in fiction, but powerless ignorance may be reckoned, and in truth is, ridiculous. — *Philebus*, iii. 188.

Self-knowledge and temperance.

—— But, Socrates, he said, I will withdraw my previous admissions, rather than admit that a man can be temperate or wise, who does not know himself; and I am not ashamed to confess that I was in error. For self-knowledge would certainly be maintained by me to be the very essence of knowledge, and in this I agree with him who dedicated the inscription, "Know thyself!" at Delphi. That word, if I am not mistaken, is put there as a sort of salutation which the God addresses to those who enter the temple; as much as to say that the ordinary salutation of "Hail!" is not right, and that the exhortation "Be temperate!" would be a far better way of saluting one another. The notion of him who dedicated the inscription was, as I believe, that the God speaks to those who enter his temple not as men speak; but, when a worshiper enters, the first word which he hears is "Be temperate!" This, however, like a prophet he expresses in a sort of riddle, for "Know thyself!" and "Be temperate!" are the same, as I maintain, and as the writing implies [σωφρόνει, γνῶθι σεαυτόν], and yet they may be easily misunderstood; and succeeding sages who added "Never too much," or, "Give a pledge, and evil is nigh at hand," would appear to have misunderstood them; for they imagined that "Know thyself!" was a piece of advice which the God gave, and not his salutation of the worshipers at their first coming in; and they wrote their inscription under the idea that they would give equally useful pieces of advice. Shall I tell you, Socrates, why I say all this? My object is to leave the previous discussion (in which I know not whether you or I are more right, but, at any rate, no clear result was attained), and to raise a new one in which I will attempt to prove, if you deny, that temperance is self-knowledge.

Yes, I said, Critias; but you come to me as though I professed to know about the questions which I ask, and as though I could, if only I would, agree with you. Whereas the fact is that I inquire with you into the truth 'of that which is advanced from time to time, just because I do not know; and when I have inquired, I will say whether I agree with you or not. Please then to allow me time to reflect.

Reflect, he said.

I am reflecting, I replied, and discover that temperance, or wisdom, if implying a knowledge of anything, must be a science, and a science of something.

Yes, he said, the science of itself. — *Charmides,* i. 20.

Self-mastery. See *Intemperance.*

—— There is something ridiculous in the expression "master of himself;" for the master is also the slave and the slave the master; and in all these modes of speaking the same person is denoted.

Certainly.

The meaning is, I believe, that the human soul has a better principle, and has also a worse principle; and when the better principle controls the worse, then a man is said to be master of himself; and this is a term of praise: but when, owing to evil education or association, the better principle, which is less, is overcome by the worse principle, which is greater; in this case he is blamed and is called the slave of self and unprincipled.

Yes, there is reason in that.

And now, I said, look at our newly-created State, and there you will find one of these two conditions realized; for the State, as you will acknowledge, may be justly called master of self, if the words "temperance" and "self-mastery" truly express the rule of the better over the worse. — *The Republic*, ii. 256.

Self-motion.

—— *Ath.* When one thing moves another, and that another, will there be any primary changing element? Can there be, considering that what changes first will always have been changed by another? There cannot. And when the self-moved changes other, and that again other, and thus, thousands upon tens of thousands of bodies are set in motion, must not the beginning of all this motion be the change of the self-moving principle?

Cle. Very true, and I quite agree.

Ath. Or, to put the question in another way: If, as most of these philosophers have the audacity to affirm, all things were at rest in one mass, which of the above-mentioned principles of motion would first spring up among them?

Cle. Clearly the self-moving; for there could be no change in them arising out of any external cause, if there had been no previous change in themselves.

Ath. Then we must say that self-motion being the origin and beginning of motion, as well among things at rest as among things in motion, is the eldest and mightiest principle of change, and that which is changed by another and yet moves other is second.

Cle. Quite true. — *Laws*, iv. 407.

Self-moving power of the soul.

—— The soul is immortal, for that is immortal which is ever in motion; but that which moves another and is moved by another, in ceasing to move ceases also to live. Therefore, only that which is self-moving, never leaving self, never ceases to move, and is the fountain and beginning of motion to all that moves besides. Now, the beginning is unbegotten, for that which is begotten has a beginning; but the beginning itself has no beginning, for if a beginning were begotten of something, that something would not be a beginning. But that which is unbegotten must also be indestructible; for if beginning were destroyed, there could be no beginning out of anything, or anything out of a beginning; and all things must have a beginning. And therefore the self-moving is the beginning of motion; and this can neither be destroyed nor begotten, else the whole heavens and all creation would collapse and stand still, and never again have motion or birth. But if the self-moving is immortal, he who affirms that self-motion is the very idea and essence of the soul will not be put to confusion. For the body which is moved from without is soulless; but that which is moved from within has a soul, for such is the nature of the soul. But if the soul be truly affirmed to be the self-moving, then must she also be without beginning, and immortal. — *Phaedrus*, i. 550.

Self-praise, ill manners.

—— Charmides blushed, and the blush heightened his beauty, for modesty is becoming in youth; he then said very ingenuously, that he really could not at once answer, either yes, or no, to the question which I had asked : For, said he, if I affirm that I am not temperate, that would be a strange thing for me to say of myself, and also I should give the lie to Critias, and many others, who think that I am temperate, as he tells you : but, on the other hand, if I say that I am, I shall have to praise myself, which would be ill manners; and therefore I have no answer to make to you. — *Charmides*, i. 12.

Self-ruling. See *Intemperance*, etc., and *Self-mastery*.
Self-sacrifice of Achilles. See *Achilles*.
Self-slavery. See *Self-mastery*.
Self-taught men.

—— *La.* Socrates ; did you never observe that some persons, who have had no teachers, are more skillful than those who have, in some things ?

Soc. Yes, Laches, I have observed that ; but you would not be very willing to trust them if they only professed to be masters of their art, unless they could show some proof of their skill or excellence in one or more works.

La. That is true.— *Laches,* i. 78.

Self-wise disputers. See *Disputers.*

Sensation, not a sufficient source of knowledge.

—— *Soc.* The simple sensations which reach the soul through the body are given at birth to men and animals by nature, but their reflections on these and on their relations to being and use, are slowly and hardly gained, if they are ever gained, by education and long experience.

Theaet. Assuredly.

Soc. And can a man attain truth who fails of attaining being?

Theaet. Impossible.

Soc. And can he who misses the truth of anything, have a knowledge of that thing?

Theaet. He cannot.

Soc. Then knowledge does not consist in impressions of sense, but in reasoning about them; in that only, and not in the mere impression, truth and being can be attained?

Theaet. Clearly. — *Theaetetus,* iii. 390.

Sense, bodily, a bar to truth. See *Bodily pleasures,* etc.

Sense *versus* science. See *Science,* etc.

Sense, reason in the sphere of. See *Intellect and knowledge.*

Sense, soul at first without.

—— By reason of all these affections, the soul when inclosed in a mortal body is at first without intelligence; but when the stream of growth and nutriment flows in with diminished speed, and the courses of the soul attaining a calm go their own way and become steadier as time advances, then the revolutions of the several circles return to their natural figure, and call the same and the other by their right names, and make the possessor of them a rational being. And if these combine in him with any true nurture or education, he attains the fullness and health of the perfect man, and escapes the worst disease of all; but if he neglects education he walks lame while alive to the end of his journey, and returns imperfect and good for nothing to the world below. — *Timaeus,* ii. 536.

Senses, the source of knowledge.

—— Must we not allow, that when I or any one, looking at any object, observes that the thing which he sees aims at being some other thing, but falls short of, and cannot be that other, — he who makes this observation must have had a previous knowledge of that to which the other, although similar, was inferior?

Certainly.

And has not this been our own case in the matter of equals and of absolute equality?

Precisely.

Then we must have known equality previously to the time when we first saw the material equals, and reflected that all these apparent equals strive to attain absolute equality, but fall short of it?

That is true.

And we recognize also that this absolute equality has only been known, and can only be known, through the medium of sight or touch, or of some other of the senses, which are alike in this respect?

Yes, Socrates, as far as the argument is concerned, one of them is the same as the other.

And from the senses then is derived the knowledge that all sensible things aim at an absolute equality of which they fall short — is not that true?

Yes.

Then before we began to see or hear or perceive in any way, we must have had a knowledge of absolute equality, or we could not have referred to that standard the equals which are derived from the senses? — for to that they all aspire, and of that they fall short?

That, Socrates, is certainly to be inferred from the previous statements. — *Phaedo*, i. 402.

Sensible images, some truths have not. See *Images*.
Sensual and earthly. See *Earthly*, etc.
Sensual love, laws against, impossible. See *Laws against sensual love*.
Sensuality and gluttony. See *Gluttony*, etc.
Shades and images, the dead are our. See *Dead*.
Shadows seeming real.

—— Let me show you in a figure, how far our nature is enlightened or unenlightened: — Behold! human beings living in an underground den, which has a mouth open towards the light and reaching all along the den; they have been here from their childhood, and have their legs and necks chained so that they cannot move, and can only see before them; for the chains are arranged in such a manner as to prevent them from turning round their heads. Above and behind them the light of a fire is blazing at a distance, and between the fire and the prisoners there is a raised way; and you will see, if you look, a low wall built along the way, like the screen which marionette players have in front of them, over which they show the puppets.

I see.

And do you see, I said, men passing along the wall some apparently talking and others silent, carrying vessels and statues, and figures of animals, made of wood and stone and various materials, and which appear over the wall?

You have shown me a strange image, and they are strange prisoners.

Like ourselves, I replied; and they see only their own shadows, or the shadows of one another, which the fire throws on the opposite wall of the cave?

True, he said; how could they see anything but the shadows if they were never allowed to move their heads?

And of the objects which are being carried in like manner they would only see the shadows?

Yes, he said.

And if they were able to talk with one another, would they not suppose that they were naming what was actually before them?

Very true.

And suppose, further, that the prison had an echo which came from the other side, would they not be sure to fancy that the voice which they heard was that of a passing shadow?

No question, he replied.

Beyond question, I said, the truth would be to them just nothing but the shadows of the images.

That is certain.

And now look again, and see how they are released and cured of their folly. At first, when any one of them is liberated and compelled suddenly to turn his neck round and go up and look at the light, he will suffer sharp pains; the glare will distress him, and he will be unable to see the realities of which in his former state he had seen the shadows; and then imagine some one saying to him, that what he saw before was an illusion, but that now he is approaching real being and has a truer sight and vision of more real things, — what will be his reply? And you may further imagine that his instructor is pointing to the objects as they pass and requiring him to name them, — will he not be in a difficulty; Will he not fancy that the shadows which he formerly saw are truer than the objects which are now shown to him?

Far truer.

And if he is compelled to look at the light, will he not have a pain in his eyes which will make him turn away to take refuge in the objects of vision which he can see, and which he will conceive to be in reality clearer than the things which are now being shown to him?

True, he said.

And suppose once more, that he is reluctantly dragged up a steep and rugged ascent, and held fast until he is forced into the presence of the sun himself, do you not think that he will be pained and irritated, and when he approaches the light he will have his eyes dazzled, and will not be able to see any of the realities which are now affirmed to be the truth?

Not all in a moment, he said.

He will require to grow accustomed to the sight of the upper world. And first he will see the shadows best, next the reflections of men and other objects in the water, and then the objects themselves; then he will gaze upon the light of the moon and the stars; and he will see the sky and the stars by night, better than the sun, or the light of the sun, by day?

Certainly.

And at last he will be able to see the sun, and not mere reflections of him in the water, but he will see him as he is in his own proper place, and not in another; and he will contemplate his nature.

Certainly.

And after this he will reason that the sun is he who gives the seasons and the years, and is the guardian of all that is in the visible world, and in a certain way the cause of all things which he and his fellows have been accustomed to behold?

Clearly, he said, he would come to the other first and to this afterwards.

And when he remembered his old habitation, and the wisdom of the den and his fellow-prisoners, do you not suppose that he would felicitate himself on the change, and pity them?

Certainly, he would.

And if they were in the habit of conferring honors on those who were quickest to observe and remember and foretell which of the shadows when they moved, went before, and which followed after, and which were together, do you think that he would care for such honors and glories, or envy the possessors of them? Would he not say with Homer, —

"Better to be a poor man, and have a poor master,"

and endure anything, rather than to think and live after their manner?

Yes, he said, I think that he would rather suffer anything than live after their manner.

Imagine once more, I said, such an one coming suddenly out of the sun to be replaced in his old situation, would he not be certain to have his eyes full of darkness?

To be sure, he said.

And if there were a contest, and he had to compete in measuring the shadows with the prisoners who had never moved out of the den, while his sight was still weak, and before his eyes are steady (and the time which would be needed to acquire this new habit of sight might be very considerable), would he not be ridiculous? Men would say of him that up he went and down he came without his eyes; and that there was no use in even thinking of ascending; and if any one tried to loose another and lead him up to the light, let them only catch the offender in the act, and they would put him to death.

No question, he said. — *The Republic*, ii. 341.

Shams or simulations. See *Cookery*.
Simplicity of good men. See *Good men*.
Sin, God not the author of. See *Evil*, etc.
Sleep, quiet and unquiet.

—— I do not think that we have adequately determined the nature and number of the appetites, and until this is accomplished the inquiry will always be perplexed.

Well, but you may supply the omission.

Very true, I said; and observe the point which I want to understand. Certain of the unnecessary pleasures and appetites are deemed to be unlawful; every man appears to have them, but in some persons they are controlled by the laws and by reason, and the better desires prevail over them, — either they are wholly banished or they are few and weak: while in the case of others they are stronger, and there are more of them.

Which appetites do you mean?

I mean those which are awake when the reasoning and human and ruling power is asleep; when the wild beast in our nature, gorged with meat or drink, starts up and leaps about and seeks to go and satisfy his desires, there is no conceivable folly or crime, however shameless or unnatural, — not excepting incest or parricide, or the eating of forbidden food, — of which at such a time, you know, a man may not believe himself to be capable.

Most true, he said.

But when a man's pulse is healthy and temperate, and when before going to sleep he has awakened his rational powers, and fed them on noble thoughts and inquiries, collecting himself in meditation; after having indulged his appetites neither too much nor too little, but just enough to lay them to sleep, and prevent them and their enjoyments and pains from interfering with the higher principle — which he leaves in the solitude of pure abstraction, free to contemplate and aspire to the knowledge of the unknown, whether in past, present, or future : when again he has allayed the passionate element, if he has a quarrel against any one — I say, when, after pacifying the two irrational principles, he rouses up the third, which is reason, before he takes his rest, then, as you know, he attains truth most nearly, and is least likely to be the sport of fanciful and lawless visions.

I quite agree. — *The Republic*, ii. 400.

Social strife, origin of. See *Metallic races*.
Society, primitive. See *Patriarchal State*.
Socrates, the death of.

—— Me, already, as the tragic poet would say, the voice of fate calls. Soon I must drink the poison ; and I think that I had better repair to the bath first, in order that the women may not have the trouble of washing my body after I am dead.

When he had done speaking, Crito said : And have you any commands for us, Socrates — anything to say about your children, or any other matter in which we can serve you?

Nothing particular, he said: only, as I have always told you, I would have you to look to yourselves ; that is a service which you may always be doing to me and mine as well as to yourselves. And you need not make professions; for if you take no thought for yourselves, and walk not according to the the precepts which I have given you, not now for the first time, the warmth of your professions will be of no avail.

We will do our best, said Crito. But in what way would you have us bury you?

In any way that you like ; only you must get hold of me, and take care that I do not walk away from you. Then he turned to us, and added with a smile : — I cannot make Crito believe that I am the same Socrates who has been talking and conducting the argument; he fancies that I am the other Socrates whom he will soon see a dead body — and he asks, How shall he bury me? And though I have spoken many words in the endeavor to show that when I have drunk the poison I shall leave you and go to the joys of the blessed, — these words of mine, with which I comforted you and myself, have had, as I perceive, no effect upon Crito. And therefore I want you to be surety for me now, as he was surety for me at the trial : but let the promise be of another sort; for he was my surety to the judges that I would remain, but you must be my surety to him that I shall not remain, but go away and depart; and then he will suffer less at my death, and not be grieved when he sees my body being burned or buried. I would not have him sorrow at my hard lot, or say at the burial, Thus we lay out Socrates, or, Thus we follow him to the grave or bury him; for false words are not only evil in themselves, but they infect the soul with evil. Be of good cheer then, my dear Crito, and say that you are burying my body only, and do with that as is usual, and as you think best.

When he had spoken these words, he arose and told us to wait until he went into the bath-chamber with Crito ; and we waited, talking and thinking of the subject of discourse, and also of the greatness of our sorrow : he was like a father of whom we were being bereaved, and we were about to pass the rest of our lives as orphans. When he had taken the bath his children were brought to him — (he had two young sons and an elder one) ; and the women of his family also came, and he talked to them and gave them a few directions in the presence of Crito ; and he then dismissed them and returned to us.

Now the hour of sunset was near, for a good deal of time had passed while he was within. When he came out, he sat down with us again after his bath, but not much was said. Soon the jailer, who was the servant of the eleven, entered and stood by him, saying: To you, Socrates, whom I know to be the noblest and gentlest and best of all who ever came to this place, I will not impute the angry feelings of other men, who rage and swear at me when, in obedience to the authorities, I bid them drink the poison — indeed I am sure that you will not be angry with me ; for others, as you are aware, and not I, are the guilty cause. And so fare you well, and try to bear lightly what must needs be; you know my errand. Then bursting into tears he turned away and went out.

Socrates looked at him and said; I return your good wishes, and will do as you bid. Then turning to us, he said, How charming the man is: since I have been in prison he has always been coming to see me, and at times he would talk to me, and was as good as could be, and now see how generously he sorrows for me. But we must do as he says, Crito ; let the cup be brought, if the poison is prepared : if not, let the attendant prepare some.

Yet, said Crito, the sun is still upon the hill-tops, and I know that many a one has taken the draught late, and after the announcement has been made to him, he has eaten and drunk, and enjoyed the society of his beloved ; do not hasten then, there is still time.

Socrates said : Yes, Crito, and they of whom you speak are right in doing thus, for they think that they will gain by the delay ; but I am right in not doing thus, for I do not think that I should gain anything by drinking the poison a little later ; I should be sparing and saving a life which is already gone : I could only laugh at myself for this. Please then to do as I say, and not to refuse me.

Crito made a sign to the servant, who was standing by; and he went out, and having been absent for some time, and returned with the jailer carrying the cup of poison. Socrates said : You, my good friend, who are experienced in these matters, shall give me directions how I am to proceed. The man answered : You have only to walk about until your legs are heavy, and then to lie down, and the poison will act, At the same time he handed the cup to Socrates, who in the easiest and gentlest manner, without the least fear or change of color or feature, looking at the man with all his eyes, Echecrates, as his manner was, took the cup and said : What do you say about making a libation out of this cup to any God? May I, or not ? The man answered : We only prepare, Socrates, just so much as we deem enough. I understand, he said : yet I may and must ask the Gods to prosper my journey from this to that other world — even so — and so be it according to my prayer. Then holding the cup to his lips, quite readily and cheerfully he drank off the poison. And hitherto most of us had been able to control our sorrow; but now when we saw him drinking, and saw too that he had finished the draught, we could no longer forbear, and in spite of myself my own tears were flowing fast; so that I covered my face and wept over myself, for certainly I was not weeping over him, but at the thought of my own calamity in having lost such a friend. Nor was I the first, for Crito, when he found himself unable to restrain his tears, had got up and moved away, and I followed; and at that moment, Apollodorus, who had been weeping all the time, broke out into a loud and passionate cry which made cowards of us all. Socrates alone retained his calmness: What is this strange outcry? he said. I sent away the women mainly in order that they might not offend in this way, for I have heard that a man should die in peace. Be quiet then, and have patience. When we heard that, we were ashamed, and refrained our tears; and he walked about until, as he said, his legs began to fail, and then he lay on his back, according to the directions, and the man who gave him the poison now and then looked at his feet and legs; and after a while he pressed his foot hard and asked him if he could feel; and he said, No; and then his leg, and so upwards and upwards, and showed us that he was cold and stiff. And he felt them himself, and said: When the poison reaches the heart, that will be the end. He was beginning to grow cold about the groin, when he uncovered his face, for he had covered himself up, and said (they were his last words) — he said: Crito, I owe a cock to Asclepius; will you remember to pay the debt? The debt shall be paid, said Crito; is there anything else? There was no answer to this question; but in a minute or two a movement was heard, and the attendants uncovered him; his eyes were set, and Crito closed his eyes and mouth.

Such was the end, Echecrates, of our friend, whom I may truly call the wisest, and justest, and best of all the men whom I have ever known. — *Phaedo*, i. 444.

Socrates, presentiment of death in. See *Presentiment*, etc.
Soldiers and Rulers. See *Gentleness*.
Solitude of the lost soul.

—— For after death, as they say, the genius of each individual, to whom he belonged in life, leads him to a certain place in which the dead are gathered together, whence after judgment they must go into the world below, following the guide, who is appointed to conduct them from this world to the other: and when they have there received their due and remained their time, another guide brings them back again after many revolutions of ages. Now this journey to the other world is not, as Aeschylus says in the Telephus, a single and straight path, — no guide would be wanted for that, and no one could miss a single path; but there are many partings of the road, and windings, as I must infer from the rites and sacrifices which are offered to the Gods below in places where three ways meet on earth. The wise and orderly soul follows in the path, and knows what is happening; but the soul which desires the body, and which, as I was relating before, has long been fluttering about the lifeless frame and the world of sight, is, after many struggles and many sufferings, hardly and with violence carried away by her attendant genius, and when she arrives at the place where the other souls are gathered, if she be impure and have done impure deeds, or been concerned in foul murders or other crimes which are the brothers of these, and the works of brothers in crime, — from that soul every one flees and turns away; no one will be her companion, no one her guide, but alone she wanders in extremity of evil until certain times are fulfilled, and when they are fulfilled, she is borne irresistibly to her own fitting habitation; as every pure and just soul which has passed through life in the company and under the guidance of the Gods has also her own proper home. — *Phaedo*, i. 438.

Song and harmony, choral. See *Choral*, etc.
Sons, unfilial. See *Parricides*.
Sons, brave, of brave fathers. See *State, heroes*, etc.
Sons of good fathers, why they turn out ill. See *Fathers*, etc.
Sophist and Philosopher. See *Philosopher and Sophist*.
Sophist summarized.

—— *Str.* And who is the maker of the longer speeches? Is he the statesman or the public orator?
Theaet. The latter.
Str. And what shall we call the other? Is he the philosopher or the Sophist?
Theaet. The philosopher he cannot be, for upon our view he is ignorant; but since he is an imitator of the wise he will have a name which is formed by an adaptation of the word σοφός. What shall we name him? I am pretty sure that I cannot be mistaken in terming him the true and very Sophist.
Str. Shall we bind up his name as we did before, making a chain from one end to the other?
Theaet. By all means.

Str. He, then, who traces the pedigree of his art as follows: He who, belonging to the conscious or dissembling section of the art of making contradictions, is an imitator of appearance, and has divided off from the art of image-making, which is a branch of phantastic, that further division of creative art, the juggling of words, a creation human, and not divine — any one who affirms the real Sophist to be of this blood and lineage will say the very truth.

Theaet. Undoubtedly. — *Sophist,* iii. 510.

Sophists, are they corrupters?

—— Do you really think, as people are fond of saying, that our youth are corrupted by the Sophists, or that private teachers of the art corrupt them in any degree worth speaking of? Are not the public who say these things the greatest of all Sophists? And do they not educate to perfection alike young and old, men and women, and fashion them after their own hearts? . . . .

To that I quite assent, he replied.

Then let me crave your assent also to a further observation.

What are you going to say?

Why, that all those mercenary individuals, whom the world calls Sophists and esteems rivals, do but teach the collective opinion of the many, which are the opinions of their assemblies; and this is their wisdom. I might compare them to a man who should study the tempers and desires of a mighty strong beast who is fed by him — he would learn how to approach and handle him, also at what times and from what causes he is dangerous or the reverse, and what is the meaning of his several cries, and by what sounds, when another utters them, he is soothed or infuriated; and you may suppose, further, that when, by constantly living with him, he has become perfect in all this he calls his knowledge wisdom, and he makes a system or art, which he proceeds to teach, not that he has any real notion of what he is teaching, but he names this honorable and that dishonorable, or good or evil, or just or unjust, all in accordance with the tastes and tempers of the great brute, when he has learnt the meaning of his inarticulate grunts. Good he pronounces to be what pleases him, and evil what he dislikes; and he can give no other account of them except that the just and noble are the necessary, having never himself seen, and having no power of explaining to others, the nature of either, or the immense difference between them. Would not he be a rare educator?

Indeed, he would.

And in what respects does he who thinks that wisdom is the discernment of the tastes and pleasures of the assembled multitude, whether in painting or music, or, finally, in politics, differ from such an one? For I suppose you will agree that he who associates with the many, and exhibits to them his poem or other work of art or the service which he has done the State, making them his judges, except under protest, will also experience the fatal necessity of producing whatever they praise. And yet the reasons are utterly ludicrous which they give in confirmation of their notions about the honorable and good. Did you ever hear any of them which were not?

No, nor am I likely to hear. — *The Republic*, ii. 318.

Sorrow, manifestations of.

—— Reflect: — our principle is that the good man will not consider death terrible to a good man.

Yes, that is our principle.

And therefore he will not sorrow for his departed friend as though he had suffered anything terrible?

He will not.

Such an one, as we further maintain, is enough for himself and his own happiness, and therefore is least in need of other men.

True, he said.

And for this reason the loss of a son or brother, or the deprivation of fortune, is to him of all men least terrible.

Assuredly.

And therefore he will be least likely to lament, and will bear with the greatest equanimity any misfortune of this sort which may befall him.

Yes, he will feel such a misfortune far less than another.

Then we shall be right in getting rid of the lamentations of famous men, and making them over to women (and not even to women who are good for anything), or to men of a baser sort, that those who are being educated by us to be the defenders of their country may scorn to do the like.

That will be very right.

Then we will once more entreat Homer and the other poets not to depict Achilles, who is the son of a goddess, as first lying on his side, then on his back, and then on his face; then starting up and sailing in a frenzy along the shores of the barren sea, now taking the dusky ashes in both his hands and pouring them over his head, or bewailing and sorrowing in the various modes which Homer has delineated. Nor should he describe Priam, the kinsman of the Gods, as praying and beseeching,

"Rolling in the dirt, calling each man loudly by his name."

Still more earnestly will we beg of him not to introduce the Gods lamenting and saying, —

"Alas! my misery! alas! that I bore the bravest to my sorrow."

— *The Republic*, ii. 210.

Sorrow, parental, to be lightly borne.

—— Some of us have fathers and mothers still living, and we would urge them, if, as is likely, we shall die, to bear the calamity as lightly as possible, and not to condole with one another; for they have sorrows enough, and will not need any one to stimulate them. While we gently heal their wounds, let us remind them that the Gods have heard the chief part of their prayers; for they prayed, not that their children might live forever, but that they might be famous and brave. And this which is the greatest good they have attained. A mortal man cannot expect to have everything in his own life turning out according to his will; and they, if they bear their misfortunes bravely, will be truly deemed brave fathers of the brave. But if they give way to their sorrows, either they will be suspected of not being our parents, or we of not being such as our panegyrists declare. Let not either of the two alternatives happen, but rather let them be our chief and true panegyrists, who show in their lives that they are true men, and had men for their sons. The ancient saying, "never too much," appears to be, and really is, well said. For he whose happiness rests with himself, if possible, wholly, and if not, as far as is possible, — who is not hanging in suspense on other men, or changing with the vicissitude of their fortune, — has his life ordered for the best. He is the temperate and valiant and wise; and when his riches come and go, when his children are given and taken away, he will remember the proverb, "Neither rejoicing overmuch nor grieving overmuch," for he relies upon himself. And such we would have our parents to be — that is our word and wish, and as such we now offer ourselves, neither lamenting overmuch, nor fearing overmuch, if we are to die at this instant. And we entreat our fathers and mothers to retain these feelings throughout their future life, and to be assured that they will not please us by sorrowing and lamenting over us. But, if the dead have any knowledge of the living, they will displease us most by making themselves miserable and by taking their misfortunes to heart, and they will please us best if they bear their loss lightly and temperately. For our life will have the noblest end which is vouchsafed to man, and should be glorified rather than lamented. And if they will direct their minds to the care and nurture of our wives and children, they will soonest forget their misfortunes, and live more honorably and uprightly, and in a way that is more agreeable to us. — *Menexenus*, iv. 579.

Sorrow, suppressed.

—— Were we not saying that a good man, when he loses his son or anything else which is most dear to him, will bear the loss with more equanimity than another?

Yes.

But will he have no sorrow, or shall we say that, although he cannot help sorrowing, he will moderate his sorrow?

Yes, he said, the latter is the truer statement.

Tell me: will he be more likely to struggle and hold out against his sorrow, when he is seen by his equals, or when he is by himself alone.

He will be more likely to hold out when he is in company.

But when he is left alone he will not mind saying or doing many things which he would be ashamed of any one hearing or seeing?

True.

There is a principle of law and reason in him which bids him resist, while passion urges him to indulge his sorrow?

True. — *The Republic*, ii. 435.

Sorrow, patience under.

—— The law would say that to be patient under suffering is best, and that we should not give way to impatience, as there is no knowing whether such things are good or evil; and nothing is gained by impatience; also, because no human thing is of serious importance, and grief stands in the way of that which at the moment is most required.

What is most required? he asked.

That we should take counsel about the past, and when the dice have been thrown, order our affairs accordingly by the advice of reason, not, like children who have had a fall, keeping hold of the part struck and wasting time in setting up a howl, when we should be accustoming the soul forthwith to apply a remedy, raising up that which is sickly and fallen, banishing the cry of sorrow by a real cure.

Yes, he said, there is no better way of meeting the attacks of fortune.

Yes, I said; and the higher principle is ready to follow this suggestion of reason?

Clearly.

And the other principle which inclines us to recollection of our troubles and to lamentation, and can never have enough of them, we may call irrational, indolent, and cowardly?

Indeed, we may. — *The Republic*, ii. 436.

Soul, immortality of the. See *Self-moving power of the soul*.

——— *Soc.* I have heard from certain wise men and women who spoke of things divine that —

Men. What did they say?

Soc. They spoke of a glorious truth, as I conceive.

Men. What was that? and who were they?

Soc. Some of them were priests and priestesses, who had studied how they might be able to give a reason of their profession; there have been poets also, such as the poet Pindar and other inspired men. And what they say is — mark, now and see whether their words are true — they say that the soul of man is immortal, and at one time has an end, which is termed dying, and at another time is born again, but is never destroyed. And the moral is, that a man ought to live always in perfect holiness. For in the ninth year Persephone sends the souls of those from whom she has received the penalty of ancient crime back again into the light of this world, and these are they who become noble kings and mighty men and great in wisdom, and are called saintly heroes in after ages. The soul, then, as being immortal, and having been born again many times, and having seen all things that there are, whether in this world or in the world below, has knowledge of them all; and it is no wonder that she should be able to call to remembrance all that she ever knew about virtue, and about everything; for as all nature is akin, and the soul has learned all things, there is no difficulty in her eliciting, or as men say learning, all out of a single recollection, if a man is strenuous and does not faint; for all inquiry and all learning is but recollection. — *Meno*, i. 255.

Are you not aware, I said, that the soul is immortal and imperishable?

He looked at me in astonishment, and said: No, by heaven; surely you are not prepared to affirm that?

Yes, I said, I ought to be, and you too, for there is no difficulty.

I see a great difficulty; but I should like to hear you state this argument of which you make so light.

Listen, then.

I am attending.

You speak of good and of evil?

Yes, he replied.

Would you agree with me in thinking that the corrupting and destroying element is the evil, and the saving and improving element the good?

Yes.

And you admit that everything has a good and also an evil; as ophthalmia is the evil of the eyes, and disease of the whole body; as mildew is of corn, and rot of timber, or rust of iron and steel: in everything, or in almost everything, there is an inherent evil and disease?

Yes, he said.

And anything which is infected by any of these evils is made evil, and at last wholly dissolves and dies?

True.

The vice and evil which is inherent in each is the destruction of each; and if this does not destroy them there is nothing else that will, for good certainly will not destroy them, nor, again, that which is neither good nor evil.

Certainly not.

If, then, we find any nature which having this inherent corruption cannot be dissolved or destroyed, we may be certain that of such a nature there is no destruction?

That may be assumed.

Well, I said, and is there no evil which corrupts the soul?

Yes, he said, there are all the evils of which we were speaking: unrighteousness, intemperance, cowardice, ignorance.

But do any of these dissolve or destroy her? — and here do not let us fall into the error of supposing that the unjust and foolish, when they are detected, perish through their injustice, which is an evil of the soul. Take the analogy of the body: The evil of the body is a disease which wastes and reduces and annihilates the body; and all the things of which we were just now speaking come to annihilation through their own inherent evil clinging to them and destroying them. Is not this true?

Yes, he said.

Now consider the soul in the same way. Do the injustice and other evils of the soul waste and consume the soul? Do they, by inhering in her and clinging to her at last, bring her to death, and separate her from the body?

Certainly not.

And yet, I said, it is unreasonable to suppose that anything can perish from without through external affection of evil, which could not be destroyed from within by any internal corruption?

It is, he replied.

Consider, I said, Glaucon, that even the badness of food, whether staleness, decomposition, or any other kind of badness, when confined to the actual food, is not supposed to destroy the body; although if the corruption of food communicates corruption to the body, then the body also suffers from internal corruption or disease and perishes; but that the body, being one thing, can be destroyed by the badness of food, which is another thing, without any internal infection — that will never be admitted by us?

Very true.

And, on the same principle, unless some bodily evil can produce an evil of the soul, we must not suppose that the soul, which is one thing, can be dissolved by any external evil which belongs to another?

Yes, he said, there is reason in that.

Either, then, let us refute this argument, or, while this argument of ours remains unrefuted, let us never say that fever, or any other disease, or the knife put to the throat, or even the cutting up of the whole body into the minutest pieces, can destroy the soul, until the soul also is proved to become more unholy or unrighteous in consequence of these things being done to the body; but that the soul or anything else which is not destroyed by an internal evil, can be destroyed by an external one, is not to be supposed.

No one, he replied, will ever show that the souls of men become more unjust in consequence of death.

And if some one who would rather not admit the immortality of the soul boldly denies this, and says that the dying do really become more evil and unrighteous, then, if the speaker is right, I suppose that injustice, like disease, must be assumed to be fatal to the unjust, and that those who take this disorder die by the natural inherent power of destruction which evil has, and which kills them sooner or later in quite another way from that in which, at present, the wicked receive death at the hands of others as the penalty of their deeds?

Nay, he said, in that case injustice, if fatal to the unjust, will not be so very terrible to him, for he will be delivered from evil. But I rather suspect the opposite to be the truth, and that injustice which murders others keeps the murderer alive — aye, and unsleeping too; so far removed is her dwelling-place from being a house of death.

True, I said; if the inherent natural vice or evil of the soul is unable to kill or destroy her, hardly will that which is appointed to be the destruction of the body destroy a soul or anything which is not a body.

Yes, that can hardly be.

But the soul which cannot be destroyed by evil, whether inherent or external, must exist forever, and, if existing forever, must be immortal?

Certainly.

That is the conclusion, I said; and if a true conclusion, then the souls must always be the same, for if none be destroyed they will not diminish in number. Neither will they increase, for the increase of the immortal natures must come from something mortal, and all things would thus end in immortality.

Very true.

But the argument will not allow us to believe this, nor yet to believe that the soul, in her true nature, is full of variety and difference and dissimilarity.

What do you mean? he said.

The soul, I said, as is now proven, being immortal, must be the fairest of compositions, and cannot be compounded of many elements?

Certainly not. — *The Republic*, ii. 440.

Soul, change to all things having a.

—— *Ath.* All things which have a soul change, and possess in themselves a principle of change, and in changing move according to law and the order of destiny: lesser changes of nature move on level ground, but greater crimes sink into the abyss, that is to say, into Hades and other places in the world below, of which the very names terrify men, and about which they dream that they live in them absent from the body. And whenever the soul receives more of good and evil from her own energy and the strong influence of others, when she has communion with divine virtue and becomes divine, she is carried into another and better place, which is also divine and perfect in holiness; and when she has communion with evil, then she also changes the place of her life.

"For that is the justice of the Gods who inhabit heaven."

O youth or young man, who fancy that you are neglected by the Gods, know that if you become worse you shall go to the worse souls, or if better to the better, and in every succession of life and death you will do and suffer what like may fitly suffer at the hands of like. This is a divine justice, which neither you nor any other unfortunate will ever glory in escaping, and which the ordaining powers have specially ordained; take good heed of them, for a day will come when they will take heed of you. If you say, I am small and will creep into the depths of the earth, or I am high and will fly up to heaven, you are not so small or so high but that you shall pay the fitting penalty, either in the world below or in some yet more savage place still whither you shall be conveyed. — *Laws*, iv. 417.

Soul, imperishability of the.

—— What do we call that principle which does not admit of death?

The immortal, he said.

And does the soul admit of death?

No.

Then the soul is immortal?

Yes, he said.

And may we say that this is proven?

Yes, abundantly proven, Socrates, he replied.

And supposing that the odd were imperishable, must not three be imperishable?

Of course.

And if that which is cold were imperishable, when the warm principle came attacking the snow, must not the snow have retired whole and unmelted — for it could never have perished, nor could it have remained and admitted the heat?

True, he said.

Again, if the uncooling or warm principle were imperishable, the fire, when assailed by cold, would not have perished or have been extinguished, but would have gone away unaffected?

Certainly, he said.

And the same may be said of the immortal: if the immortal is also imperishable, the soul when attacked by death cannot perish; for the preceding argument shows that the soul will not admit of death, or ever be dead, any more than three or the odd number will admit of the even, or fire, or the heat in the fire, of the cold. Yet a person may say: "But although the odd will not become even at the approach of the even, why may not the odd perish and the even take the place of the odd?" Now to him who makes this objection, we cannot answer that the odd principle is imperishable; for this has not been acknowledged, but if this had been acknowledged, there would have been no difficulty in contending that at the approach of the even the odd principle and the number three took their departure; and the same argument would have held good of fire and heat and any other thing.

Very true.

And the same may be said of the immortal: if the immortal is also imperishable, then the soul will be imperishable as well as immortal; but if not, some other proof of her imperishableness will have to be given.

No other proof is needed, he said; for if the immortal, being eternal, is liable to perish, then nothing is imperishable.

Yes, replied Socrates, all men will agree that God, and the essential form of life, and the immortal in general, will never perish.[1] — *Phaedo*, i. 437.

Soul, truth attained by the.

—— What, again, shall we say of the actual acquirement of knowledge? — is the body, if invited to share in the inquiry, a hinderer or a helper? I mean to say, have sight and hearing any truth in them? Are they not, as the poets are always telling us, inaccurate witnesses? and yet, if even they are inaccurate and indistinct, what is to be said of the other senses? For you will allow that they are the best of them?

Certainly, he replied.

Then when does the soul attain truth? for in attempting to consider anything in company with the body she is obviously deceived.

Yes, that is true.

Then must not existence be revealed to her in thought, if at all?

[1] See the continuation of this discussion on p. 418.

• Yes.

And thought is best when the mind is gathered into herself, and none of these things trouble her — neither sounds nor sights nor pain nor any pleasure, — when she has as little as possible to do with the body, and has no bodily sense or feeling, but is aspiring after true being?

That is true.

And in this the philosopher dishonors the body; his soul runs away from the body and desires to be alone and by herself?

That is true. — *Phaedo*, i. 391.

Soul, philosophy delivering the. See *Philosophy delivering*, etc.
Soul degenerated by the body. See *Body affecting soul*.
Soul, solitude of the lost. See *Solitude*.
Soul, nature of the.

—— Must we not, said Socrates, ask ourselves — What is that which, as we imagine, is liable to be scattered away, and about which we fear? and what, again, is that about which we have no fear? And then we may proceed to inquire whether that which suffers dispersion is or is not of the nature of soul — our hopes and fears as to our own souls will turn upon the answer to these questions.

Very true, he said.

Now the compound or composite may be supposed to be naturally capable as of being compounded so also of being dissolved; but that which is uncompounded, and that only, must be, if anything is, indissoluble.

Yes; I should imagine so, said Cebes.

And the uncompounded may be assumed to be the same and unchanging, whereas the compound is always changing and never the same.

That I also think, he said.

Then, now, let us return to the previous discussion. Is that idea or essence, which in the dialectical process we define as essence or true existence — whether essence of equality, beauty, or anything else: are these essences, I say, liable at times to some degree of change? or are they each of them always what they are, having the same simple self-existent and unchanging forms, and not admitting of variation at all, or in any way, or at any time?

They must be always the same, Socrates, replied Cebes.[1] — *Phaedo*, i. 406.

[1] For the continuation of this discussion, see *Seen and unseen*.

Soul, reflecting and unchanging. See *Reflecting*, etc.
Soul resembling the divine. See *Divine*, etc.

—— Listen all ye who have just now heard the laws about Gods, and about our dear forefathers: — Of all the things which a man has, next to the God, his soul is the most divine and most truly his own. Now in every man there are two parts: the better and superior part, which rules, and the worse and inferior part, which serves; and the ruler is always to be preferred to the servant. Wherefore I am right in bidding every one next to the Gods, who are our masters, and those who in order follow them, to honor his own soul, which every one seems to honor, but no one honors as he ought; for honor is a divine good, and no evil thing is honorable; and he who thinks that he can honor the soul by word or gift, or any sort of compliance, without making her in any way better, seems to honor her, but honors her not at all. For example, every man, from his very boyhood, fancies that he is able to know everything, and thinks that he honors his soul by praising her, and he is very ready to let her do whatever she may like. But I mean to say that in acting thus he only injures his soul, and does not honor her; whereas, in our opinion, he ought to honor her as second only to the Gods. Again, when a man thinks that others are to be blamed, and not himself, for the errors which he has committed, and the many and great evils which befell him in consequence, and is always fancying himself to be exempt and innocent, he is under the idea that he is honoring his soul; whereas the very reverse is the fact, for he is really injuring her. And when, disregarding the word and approval of the legislator, he indulges in pleasure, then again he is far from honoring her; he only dishonors her, and fills her full of evil and remorse; or when he does not endure to the end the labors and fears and sorrows and pains which the legislator approves, but gives way before them, then, by yielding, he does not honor the soul, but by all such conduct he makes her to be dishonorable; nor when he thinks that life at any price is a good, does he honor her, but yet once more he dishonors her; for the soul having a notion that the world below is all evil, he yields to her, and does not resist and teach or convince her that, for aught she knows, the world of the Gods below, instead of being evil, may be the greatest of all goods. Again, when any one prefers beauty to virtue, what is this but the real and utter dishonor of the soul? For such a preference implies that the body is more honorable than the soul: and this is false, for there is nothing of earthly birth which is more honorable than the heavenly, and he who thinks otherwise of the soul has no idea how greatly he undervalues this wonderful possession. — *Laws*, iv. 252.

Soul, impure and pure. See *Impure*, etc.
Soul, sensual and earthly. See *Earthly*.
Soul, transmigration of the.

—— The happiest both in themselves and their place of abode are those who have practiced the civil and social virtues which are called temperance and justice, and are acquired by habit and attention without philosophy and mind.

Why are they the happiest?

Because they may be expected to pass into some gentle social nature which is like their own, such as that of bees or wasps or ants, or even back again into the form of man, and just and moderate men to spring from them.

That is not impossible. — *Phaedo*, i. 411.

Soul, self-moving. See *Self-moving*.
Soul, indestructible.

—— Seeing then that the immortal is indestructible, must not the soul, if she is immortal, be also imperishable?

Most certainly.

Then when death attacks a man, the mortal portion of him may be supposed to die, but the immortal retires at the approach of death and is preserved safe and sound?

True.

Then, Cebes, beyond question, the soul is immortal and imperishable, and our souls will truly exist in another world! — *Phaedo*, i. 437.

Soul, care for the.

—— O my friends, he said, if the soul is really immortal, what care should be taken of her, not only in respect of the portion of time which is called life, but of eternity! And the danger of neglecting her from this point of view does indeed appear to be awful. If death had only been the end of all, the wicked would have had a good bargain in dying, for they would have been happily quit not only of their body, but of their own evil together with their souls. But now, inasmuch as the soul is manifestly immortal, there is no release or salvation from evil except the attainment of the highest virtue and wisdom. For the soul when on her progress to the world below takes nothing with her but nurture and education; and these are said greatly to benefit or greatly to injure the departed, at the very beginning of his pilgrimage in the other world. — *Phaedo*, i. 437.

— Soul, at first without sense. See *Sense*.

Soul, giving life to the body.

——— *Soc.* You want me first of all to examine the natural fitness of the word ψυχή (soul), and then of the word σῶμα (body)?

Her. Yes.

Soc. If I am to say what occurs to me at the moment, I should imagine that those who first used the name ψυχή meant to express that the soul when in the body is the source of life, and gives the power of breath and revival, and when this reviving power fails then the body perishes and dies, and this, if I am not mistaken, they called psyche. But please stay a moment; I fancy that I can discover something which will be more acceptable to the disciples of Euthyphro, for I am afraid that they will scorn this explanation. What do you say to another?

Her. Let me hear.

Soc. What is that which holds and carries and gives life and motion to the entire nature of the body? What is that but the soul?

Her. Just that.

Soc. And do you not believe with Anaxagoras, that mind or soul is the ordering and containing principle of all things?

Her. Yes; I do.

Soc. Then you may well call that power φυσέχη which carries and holds nature, and this may be refined away into ψυχή.

Her. Certainly; and I think that this is a more scientific derivation.

Soc. True; and yet I cannot help laughing if I am to suppose that this is the original meaning.

Her. But what shall we say of the next word?

Soc. You mean σῶμα (the body).

Her. Yes.

Soc. That may be variously interpreted; and yet more variously if a little permutation is allowed. For some say that the body is the grave (σῆμα) of the soul, which may be thought to be buried in our present life; or again the index of the soul, because the soul indicates (σημαίνει) through the body;

probably the Orphic poets were the inventors of the name, and they were under the impression that the soul is suffering the punishment of sin, and that the body is an inclosure or prison in which the soul is incarcerated, kept (σῶμα σώζηται), as the name σῶμα implies, until the penalty is paid; according to this view, not even a letter of the word need be changed. — *Cratylus*, i. 638.

Soul, harmony of, and form. See *Harmony of*, etc.

Soul, its part in our action.

—— Once more then, O my friend, we have alighted upon an easy question — whether the soul has these three principles or not?

An easy question! Nay, rather, Socrates, the proverb holds that hard is the good.

Very true, I said; and I confess that the method which we are employing, in my judgment, seems to be altogether inadequate to the accurate solution of this question; for, the true method is another and a longer one. Still we may arrive at a solution not below the level of the previous inquiry.

May we not be satisfied with that? he said; under the circumstances, I am quite content.

I too, I replied, shall be extremely well satisfied.

Then faint not in pursuing the speculation, he said.

Can I be wrong, I said, in acknowledging that in the individual there are the same principles and habits which there are in the State? for if they did not pass from one to the other, whence did they come? Take the quality of passion or spirit; it would be ridiculous to imagine that this quality, which is characteristic of the Thracians, Scythians, and in general of the northern nations, when found in States, does not originate in the individuals who compose them; and the same may be said of the love of knowledge, which is the special characteristic of our part of the world, or the love of money, which may, with equal truth, be attributed to the Phoenicians and Egyptians.

Exactly, he said.

There is no difficulty in understanding this.

None whatever.

But the difficulty begins as soon as we raise the question whether these principles are three or one; whether, that is to say, we learn with one part of our nature, are angry with another, and with a third part desire the satisfaction of our natural appetites; or whether the whole soul comes into play in each sort of action — to determine that is the difficulty.

Yes, he said, there lies the difficulty. — *The Republic*, ii. 261.

Soul, disfiguration of the.

—— Her immortality may be proven by the previous argument and by other arguments; but to see her as she really is, not as we now behold her, marred by communion with the body and other miseries, you should look upon her with the eye of reason, in her original purity, and then her beauty would be discovered, and in her image justice would be more clearly seen, and injustice, and all the things which we have described. Thus far we have spoken the truth concerning her as she appears at present, but we must remember that we have seen her only in a condition which may be compared to that of the sea-God Glaucus, whose original image can hardly be discerned because his natural members are broken off and crushed, and in many ways damaged by the waves, and incrustations have grown over them of sea-weed and shells and stones, so that he is liker to some sea-monster than to his natural form. And the soul is in a similar condition, disfigured by ten thousand ills. But not there, Glaucon, not there must we look.

Where then?

At her love of wisdom. Let us see whom she affects, and what converse she seeks in virtue of her near kindred with the immortal and eternal and divine; also how different she would become if wholly following this superior principle, and borne by a divine impulse out of the ocean in which she now is, and disengaged from the stones and shells and things of earth and rock which in wild variety grow around her because she feeds upon earth, and is crusted over by the good things of this life as they are termed: then you would see her as she is, and know whether she have one form only or many, or what her nature is. Of her character and affections in this present life I have said enough.

True, he said. — *The Republic*, ii. 440.

Soul made prior to the body. See *Corporeal essence*.

Soul, disorders of the. See *Mind*, etc.

Soul, compared to a vessel.

—— I have heard a philosopher say that at this moment we are dead, and that the body (σῶμα) is a tomb (σῆμα) and that the part of the soul which is the seat of the desires is liable to be blown and tossed about; and some ingenious man, probably a Sicilian or an Italian, playing with the word, invented a tale in which he called the soul a vessel (πίθος), meaning a believing (πιστικὸς) vessel, and the ignorant he called the uninitiated or leaky, and the place in the souls of the uninitiated in which the desires are seated, being the intemperate and incontinent part, he compared to a vessel full of holes, because they can never be satisfied. He is not of your way of thinking, Callicles, for he declares, that of all the souls in Hades, meaning the invisible world (ἀειδὲς), these uninitiated or leaky persons are the most miserable, and that they carry water to a vessel which is full of holes in a similarly holey colander. The colander, as he declares, is the soul, and the soul which he compares to a colander is the soul of the ignorant, which is full of holes, and therefore incontinent, owing to a bad memory and want of faith. — *Gorgias*, iii. 81.

Soul, effect of harmony and order in the. See *Harmony*, etc.
Soul, health of body and. See *Body*, etc.
Soul and body, two processes of training. See *Body and soul*, etc.
Soul after death.

—— Whatever was the habit of the body during life would be distinguishable after death, either perfectly, or in a great measure and for a considerable time. And I should imagine that this is equally true of the soul, Callicles; when a man is stripped of the body, all the natural or acquired affections of the soul are laid open to view. And when they come to the judge, as those from Asia come to Rhadamanthus, he places them near him and inspects them quite impartially, not knowing whose the soul is: perhaps he may lay hands on the soul of the great king, or of some other king or potentate, who has no soundness in him, but his soul is marked with the whip, and is full of the prints and scars of perjuries, and crimes with which each action has stained him, and he is all crooked with falsehood and imposture, and has no straightness, because he has lived without truth. Him Rhadamanthus beholds, full of deformity and disproportion, which is caused by license and luxury and insolence and incontinence, and dispatches him ignominiously to his prison, and there he undergoes the punishment which he deserves. — *Gorgias*, iii. 116.

Soul, waxen heart of the.

—— *Soc.* The explanation of truth and error is as follows: when the wax in the soul of any one is deep and abundant, and smooth and perfectly tempered, then the impressions which pass through the senses and sink into the [waxen] heart of the soul, as Homer says in a parable, meaning to indicate the likeness of the soul to wax (κῆρ κηρὸς) — these, I say, being pure and clear, and having a sufficient depth of wax, are also lasting, and minds such as these easily learn and easily retain, and are not liable to confusion, but have true thoughts, for they have plenty of room, and having clear impressions of things, as we term them, quickly distribute them into their proper places on the block. And such men are called wise. Do you agree?

Theaet. Entirely.

Soc. But when the heart of any one is shaggy, as the poet who knew everything says, or muddy and of impure wax, or very soft, or very hard, then there is a corresponding defect in the mind: the soft are good at learning, but apt to forget; and the hard are the reverse; the shaggy and rugged and gritty, or those who have an admixture of earth or dung in their composition, have the impressions indistinct, as also the hard, for there is no depth in them; and the soft too are indistinct, for their impressions are easily confused and effaced. Yet greater is the indistinctness when they are all jostled together in a little soul, which has no room. These are the natures which have false opinion; for when they see or hear or think of anything, they are slow in assigning the right objects to the right impressions: in their stupidity they confuse them, and are apt to see and hear and think amiss; and such men are said to be deceived in their knowledge ·of objects, and ignorant.

Theaet. No man, Socrates, can say anything truer than that. — *Theaetetus,* iii. 400.

Soul, original and primeval.

—— *Ath.* I suppose that I must repeat the singular argument of those who manufacture the soul according to their own impious notions; they affirm that which is the first cause of the generation and destruction of all things, to be not first but last, and that which was last to be first, and hence they have fallen into error about the true nature of the Gods.

Cle. Still I do not understand you.

Ath. Nearly all of them, my friends, seem to be ignorant of the nature and power of the soul, especially in what relates to her origin : they do not know that she is among the first of bodies, and before them all, and is the chief author of their changes and transpositions. And if this is true, and if the soul is older than the body, must not the things which are of the soul's kindred be of necessity before those which appertain to the body?

Cle. Certainly.

Ath. Then thought and attention and mind and art and law will be prior to that which is hard and soft and heavy and light; and the great and primitive works and actions will be works of art; they will be the first, and after them will come nature and works of nature, which, however, is a wrong term to apply to them; these will follow, and be under the government of art and mind.

Cle. But why is the word "nature" wrong?

Ath. Because those who use the term mean to say that nature is the first creative power; but if the soul turn out to be the primeval element and not fire or air, then in the truest sense and beyond other things the soul may be said to have a natural or creative power: and this would be true if you proved that the soul is older than the body, but not otherwise.

Cle. You are quite right. — *Laws*, iv. 403.

Soul, like a book.

—— *Soc.* Well, now, I wonder whether you would agree in my explanation of this phenomenon.

Pro. What is your explanation?

Soc. I think that the soul at such times is a like a book.

Pro. How so?

Soc. Memory and perception meet, and they and their attendant feelings seem to me almost to write down words in the soul, and when the inscribing feeling writes truly, then true opinion and true propositions grow in our souls, — but when the scribe within us writes falsely the result is false.

Pro. I quite assent and agree to your statement.

Soc. I must bespeak your favor also for another artist, who is busy at the same time in the chambers of the soul.

Pro. Who is that?

Soc. The painter, who paints the images of the words which the scribe or registrar has already written down.

Pro. But when and how does he do this?

Soc. When abstracting from sight, or some other sense, the opinions which he then received or the words which he heard, he retains the image of them in his mind; that is a very common mental phenomenon.

Pro. Certainly. — *Philebus*, iii. 176.

Soul, divided, feelings of body and. See *Body and soul, mixtures of.*
Soul, envy, a pain of the. See *Envy,* etc.
Soul, the just and wise. See *Just,* etc.
Soul, definition of the. See *Mind, movement of.*
Soul, prior to the body. See also *Body and soul,* etc.

—— *Ath.* Then we are right, and speak the most perfect and absolute truth, when we say that the soul is prior to the body, and that the body is second and comes afterwards, and is born to obey the soul which is the ruler?

Cle. Nothing can be more true.

Ath. Do you remember our old admission, that if the soul was prior to the body the things of the soul were also prior to those of the body?

Cle. Certainly.

Ath. And characters and manners, and wishes and reasonings, and true opinions, and reflections, and recollections are prior to length and breadth and depth and strength of bodies, if the soul is prior to the body.

Cle. Of course.

Ath. In the next place, must we not of necessity admit that the soul is the cause of good and evil, base and honorable, just and unjust, and of all other opposites, if we suppose her to be the cause of all things?

Cle. Certainly.

Ath. And as the soul orders and inhabits all things moving every way, must we not say that she orders also the heavens?

Cle. Of course.

Ath. One soul or more? More than one — I will answer for you; at any rate, we must not suppose that there are less than two — one the author of good, and the other of evil.

Cle. Very true.

Ath. Yes, very true; the soul then directs all things in heaven, and earth, and sea by her movements, and these are described by the terms — will, consideration, attention, deliberation, opinion true and false, joy and sorrow, confidence, fear, hatred, contentment, and other primary motions akin to these; which again receive the secondary motions of corporate substances, and guide all things to growth and decay, to composition and decomposition, and to the qualities which accompany them, such as heat and cold, heaviness and lightness, hardness and softness, blackness and whiteness, bitterness and sweetness, and all those other qualities which the soul uses, herself a goddess, when truly receiving the divine mind and disciplining all things rightly to their happiness; but when the companion of folly, doing the very contrary of all this. Shall we assume this, or do we still entertain doubts?

Cle. There is no room at all for doubt.

Ath. Shall we say, then, that soul is the nature which controls heaven and earth, and the whole world? Is it the principle of wisdom and virtue, or that which has neither wisdom nor virtue? Suppose that we make answer as follows:—

Cle. How would you answer?

Ath. If, my friend, we say that the whole path of heaven, and the movement of all that is therein, is by nature akin to the movement and revolution and calculation of mind, and proceeds by kindred laws, then, as is plain, we must say that the best soul takes care of the world and guides it along the good path.

Cle. True.

Ath. But when the world moves wildly and irregularly, then the evil soul guides it.

Cle. True again. — *Laws,* iv. 408.

Soul, sun and stars without.

—— *Ath.* Are we assured that there are two things which lead men to believe in the Gods, as we have already stated?

Cle. What are they?

Ath. One is the argument about the soul, which has been already mentioned — that it is the eldest and most divine of all things, to which motion attaining generation gives perpetual existence; the other was an argument from the order of motion of the heavens, and of all things under the dominion of the mind which ordered the universe. If a man look upon the world not lightly or foolishly, there was never any one so godless who did not experience an effect opposite to that which the many imagine. For they think that those who handle these matters by the help of astronomy, and the accompanying arts of demonstration, may become godless; because they see, as far as they can see, things happening by necessity, and not by an intelligent will accomplishing good.

Cle. But what, then, is the fact?

Ath. Just the opposite of that opinion which once prevailed among men, that the sun and stars are without soul. Even in those days men wondered about them, and that which is now ascertained was then conjectured by some who had a more exact knowledge of them — that if they had been things without soul, and had no mind, they could never have moved according to such exact calculations; and even at that time some ventured to hazard the conjecture that mind was the orderer of the universe. But these same persons, again mistaking the nature of the soul, which they conceived to be younger and not older than the body, once more overturned the world, or rather, I should say, themselves, for what they saw before their eyes in heaven, all appeared to be full of stones, and earth, and many other lifeless bodies, and to these they assigned the various causes of all things. Such studies gave rise to much atheism and perplexity, and the poets took occasion to be abusive, — comparing the philosophers to she-dogs, uttering vain howlings, and saying other nonsense of the same sort. But now, as I said, the case is reversed.

Cle. How is that?

Ath. No man can be a true worshiper of the Gods who does not know these two principles — that the soul is the eldest of all things born, and is immortal and rules over all bodies; moreover, as I have now said several times, he who has not contemplated the mind of nature which is said to exist in the stars, and acquired the previous training, and seen the connection of them with music, and harmonized them all with laws and institutions, is not able to give a reason of such things as have a reason. And he who is unable to acquire this in addition to the ordinary virtues of a citizen, can hardly be a good ruler of a whole State; but he should be the subordinate of other rulers. — *Laws,* iv. 477.

Souls, punishment of. See *Soul after death.*

Speech, common, having a divine meaning.

—— His words are like the images of Silenus which open; they are ridiculous when you first hear them: he clothes himself in language that is as the skin of the wanton satyr — for his talk is of pack-asses and smiths and cobblers and curriers, and he is always repeating the same things in the same words, so that an ignorant man who did not know him might feel disposed to laugh at him; but he who opens the mask and sees what is within will find that they are the only words which have a meaning in them, and also the most divine, abounding in fair examples of virtue, and of the widest comprehension, or rather extending to the whole duty of a good and honorable man. — *The Symposium,* i. 512.

Speech and thought.

—— *Theaet.* Give me the knowledge which you would wish me to gain.

Str. Is not thought the same as speech, with this exception: thought is the unuttered conversation of the soul with herself?

Theaet. Quite true.

Str. But the stream of thought which flows through the lips and is audible is called speech.

Theaet. True.

Str. And we know that in speech there is affirmation and denial?

Theaet. Yes, that we know.

Str. When the affirmation or denial takes place silently and in the mind only, what would you call that but opinion?

Theaet. There can be no other name.

Str. And when this state of opinion is presented, not simply, but in some form of sense, ought you not to call it phantasy?

Theaet. Certainly.

Str. And seeing that language is true and false, and that thought is the conversation of the soul with herself, and opinion is the end of thinking, and phantasy or imagination is the union of sense and opinion, the inference is that these also, as they are akin to language, should have an element of false as well as true?

Theaet. Certainly. — *Sophist*, iii. 504.

Spherical form of the earth. See *Earth, rotundity of the.*

Spiritual truths, uncertainty of.

—— I dare say that you, Socrates, feel as I do, how very hard or almost impossible is the attainment of any certainty about questions such as these in the present life. And yet I should deem him a coward who did not prove what is said about them to the uttermost, or whose heart failed him before he had examined them on every side. For he should persevere until he has attained one of two things: either he should discover or be taught the truth about them; or, if this is impossible, I would have him take the best and most irrefragable of human theories, and let this be the raft upon which he sails through life — not without risk, as I admit, if he cannot find some word of God which will more surely and safely carry him. — *Phaedo*, i. 414.

Spontaneous life. See *Life*.
Starry heavens, the symbols of truth. See *Heavenly bodies*, etc.
Stars and sun, without soul. See *Soul, sun and stars*.
State, loyalty to the. See *Citizen*, etc.
State the, a parent. See *Citizen*, etc.
State, authority of the. See *Citizen*, etc.
State, right of the. See *Citizen*, etc.
State, more than the individual. See *Citizen*, etc.
State, rulers of the, who and what they must be. See *Rulers*.
State, poetry expelled from the. See *Poetry*.
State, origin of the. See *Individual*.
State, lies for the good of the. See *Lies*.
State, object of constructing the.

—— How would you answer, Socrates, said he, if a person were to say that you make your citizens miserable, and miserable of their own accord; for they are the actual owners of the city, and are none the better; whereas other men acquire lands, and build large and handsome houses, and have everything handsome about them, offering sacrifices to the Gods on their own account, and practicing hospitality; moreover, as you were saying just now, they have gold and silver, and all that is usual among the favorites of fortune; while our poor citizens are no better than mercenaries who are fixed in the city and do nothing but mount guard?

Yes, I said; and you may add that they are only fed, and not paid, in addition to their food, like other men; and therefore they cannot make a journey of pleasure, they have no money to spend on a mistress or any other luxurious fancy, which, as the world goes, is thought to be happiness; and many other accusations of the same nature might be added.

But, said he, let us suppose all that included in the charge.

You mean to ask, I said, what is to be our answer?

Yes, he replied.

If we proceed on the path along which we are already going, I said, my belief is that we shall find the answer. Even if our guardians were such as you describe, there would not be anything wonderful in their still being the happiest of men; but let that pass, for our object in the construction of the State is the greatest happiness of the whole, and not that of any one class; and in a State which is ordered with a view to the good of the whole, we think that we are most likely to find justice, and in the ill-ordered State injustice: and, having found them, we shall then be able to decide which of the two is the happier. At present we are constructing the happy State, not piecemeal, or with a view of making a few happy citizens, but as a whole; and by and by we will proceed to view the opposite kind of State. If we were painting a statue, and some one were to come and blame us for not putting the most beautiful colors on the most beautiful parts of the body — for the eyes, he would say, ought to be purple, but they are black — in that case we might fairly answer, sir, do not imagine that we ought to beautify the eyes to such a degree that they are no longer eyes; but see whether, by giving this and the other features their due, we make the whole beautiful. And so I would say now, do not compel us to assign to the guardians a sort of happiness which will make them anything but guardians; for we also should have no difficulty in clothing our husbandmen in fine linen, and setting crowns of gold on their heads, bidding them till the ground no more than they like. There would be nothing easier than to allow our potters to repose on couches, and feast by the fireside, passing round the glittering bowl, while their wheel is conveniently at hand, and working at pottery as much as they like, and no more; in this way we may make every class happy — and then as you imagine, the whole State will be happy. But do not suggest this; for, if we listen to you, the husbandman will be no longer a husbandman, the potter will cease to be a potter, and no class will have any distinct character. Now this is not of much importance where the corruption of society, and pretension to be what you are not, extends only to cobblers; but when the guardians of the laws of the government are only seemers and not real guardians, that, you will observe, is the utter ruin of the State: as, on the other hand, with them alone rests the order and happiness of a State. If we then really mean that our guardians are to be the saviours and not the destroyers of the State, and the advocate of the other view is talking of peasants at a festival, enjoying a life of revelry, rather than fulfilling the duties of citizens, we mean different things, and he is speaking of something which is not a State. And therefore we must consider whether in appointing our guardians we look to their greatest happiness, or whether this principle of happiness does not rather reside in the State as a whole. But if so, the guardians and auxiliaries, and all others equally with them, must be compelled or induced to do their own work in the best way; and then the whole State

growing up in a noble order, the several classes will only have to receive the proportion of happiness which nature assigns to them.
I think that you are quite right. — *The Republic*, ii. 243.
State, unity in the.

—— The State may increase to any size which is consistent with unity; that, I think, is the limit.

Very good, he said;

Here then, I said, is another order which will have to be conveyed to our guardians, — that our city is to be neither large nor small, but of such a size as is consistent with unity.

And surely, said he, this is not a very severe order which we impose upon them.

And the other, said I, of which we were speaking before, is lighter still, — I mean the duty of degrading the offspring of the guardians when inferior, and of elevating the offspring of the lower classes, when naturally superior, into the rank of guardians. The intention was, that, in the case of the citizens generally, we should put each individual man to the use for which nature designed him, and then every man would do his own business, and be one and not many, and the whole city would be one and not many.

Yes, he said; there will be even less difficulty in that.

These things, my good Adeimantus, are not, as might be supposed, a number of great principles, but trifles all, if care be taken, as the saying is, of the one great thing, — a thing, however, which I would rather call not great, but enough for our purpose.

What may that be? he asked.

Education, I said, and nurture. For if our citizens are well educated, and grow into sensible men, they will easily see their way through all this as well as other matters. — *The Republic*, ii. 247.

State, courage in the. See *Courage*, etc.
State, highest good in the. See *Evil*, etc.; also *Injustice*.
State, ideal philosophers to be kings in the. See *Rulers*, etc.
State, philosophy in the. See *Philosophy*, etc.
State, weakness in the.

—— Where a body is weak the addition of a touch from without may bring on illness, and sometimes even when there is no external provocation, a commotion may arise within; in the same way where there is weakness in the State there is also likely to be illness, of which the occasion may be very slight, one party introducing their democratical, the other their oligarchical allies, and the State falls sick, and is at war with herself and may be at times distracted, even when there is no external cause? — .

Yes surely.

And then democracy comes into being after the poor have conquered their opponents, slaughtering some and banishing some, while to the remainder they give an equal share of freedom and power; and this is the form of government in which the magistrates are commonly elected by lot. — *The Republic,* ii. 384.

State, physician for the.

—— *Soc.* If you and I were physicians, and were advising one another that we were competent to practice as State-physicians, should I not ask you, and would you not ask me, Well, but how about Socrates himself, has he good health? and was any one else ever known to be cured by him, whether slave or freeman? And I should make the same inquiries about you. And if we arrived at the conclusion that no one, whether citizen or stranger, man or woman, had ever been any the better for the medical skill of either of us, then, by Heaven, Callicles, what an absurdity to think that we or any human being should be so silly as to set up as a State-physician, and advise others like ourselves to do the same. without having first practiced in private, whether successfully or not, and acquired experience of the art. Is not this. as they say, to begin with the big jar when you are learning the potter's art; which is a foolish thing?

Cal. True. — *Gorgias,* iii. 105.

State, right and wrong determined by the. See *Right.*
State, education the foundation of the. See *Education,* etc.
State, divine bonds in the. See *Divine,* etc.
State, actual and ideal.

—— Let me begin by reminding you that we found our way hither in the search after justice and injustice.

True, he replied; but what of this?

I was only going to ask whether, if we have discovered them, we are to require that the just man should in nothing fail of absolute justice; or may we be satisfied with an approximation, and the attainment in him of a higher degree of justice than is to be found in other men?

The approximation will be enough.

And we inquired into the nature of absolute justice, and into the character of the perfectly just man and the possibility of his existence, and into injustice and the perfectly unjust only that we might have an ideal. We were to look at them in order that we might judge of our own happiness and unhappiness according to the standard which they exhibited and the degree in which we resembled them, not with any view of showing that they could exist in fact.

True, he said.

How would a painter be the worse painter because, after having painted with consummate art an ideal of a perfectly beautiful man, he was unable to show that any such man could ever have existed?

He would not.

Well, and were we not creating an ideal of a perfect State? To be sure.

And is our theory a worse theory because we are unable to prove the possibility of a city being ordered in the manner described?

Surely not, he replied.

That is the truth, I said. But if, at your request, I am to try and show how and under what condition the possibility is highest, I must ask you, having this in view, to repeat your former admissions.

What admissions?

I want to know whether ideas are ever realized in fact? Is not speech more than action and must not the actual, whatever a man may think, fall short of the truth? What do you say?

I agree.

Then you must not insist on my proving that the actual State will in every respect coincide with the ideal: if we are only able to discover how a city may be governed nearly as we proposed, you will admit that we have discovered the possibility which you demand; and will be contented — will not you?

Yes, I will. — *The Republic*, ii. 299.

State, a luxurious.

—— The question which you would have me consider is, not only how a State, but how a luxurious State is to be created; and possibly there is no harm in this, for in such a State we shall be more likely to see how justice and injustice grow up.

I am certainly of opinion that the true and healthy constitution of the State is the one which I have described. But if you wish to see the State in a fever I have no objection. For I suppose that many will be dissatisfied with the simpler way of life. They will be for adding sofas, and tables, and other furniture; also dainties, and perfumes, and incense, and courtesans, and cakes, not of one sort only, but in profusion and variety; we must go beyond the necessaries of which I was at first speaking, such as houses and clothes and shoes; and the arts of the painter and embroiderer will have to be set in motion, and gold and ivory and other materials of the arts will be required.

True, he said.

Then we must enlarge our borders; for the original healthy State is too small. Now will the city have to fill and swell with a multitude of callings which are not required by any natural want; such as the whole tribe of hunters and actors, of whom one large class have to do with postures and colors, another are musicians; there will be poets and their attendant train of rhapsodists, players, dancers, contractors; also makers of divers kinds of utensils, including women's ornaments. And we shall want more servants. Will not tutors be also in request, and nurses wet and dry, tirewomen and barbers, as well as confectioners and cooks; and swineherds, too, who were not needed and therefore had no place in the former edition of our State, but are needed now? They must not be forgotten: and there will be hosts of animals, if people are to eat them.

Certainly.

And living in this way we shall have much greater need of physicians than before?

Much greater.

And the country which was enough to support the original inhabitants will be too small now, and not enough?

Quite true.

Then a slice of our neighbor's land will be wanted by us for pasture and tillage, and they will want a slice of ours, if, like ourselves, they exceed the limit of necessity, and give themselves up to the unlimited accumulation of wealth?

That, Socrates, will be unavoidable.

And then we shall go to war, Glaucon,— that will be the next thing.

So we shall, he replied.

Then, without determining as yet whether war does good or

harm, thus much we may affirm, that now we have discovered war to be derived from causes which are also the causes of almost all the evils in States, private as well as public.
Undoubtedly. — *The Republic*, ii. 194.
State, what most conduces to the excellence of the.

—— Further, we affirmed that justice was doing one's own business, and not being a busybody; we said so again and again, and many others have said the same.

Yes, we said so.

Then this doing in a certain way one's own business may be assumed to be justice. Do you know why?

I do not, and should like to be told.

Because I think that this alone remains in the State when the other virtues of temperance and courage and wisdom are abstracted; and this is the ultimate cause and condition of the existence of all of them, and while remaining in them is also their preservative; and we were saying that if the three were discovered by us, justice would be the fourth or remaining one.

That follows of necessity.

Still, I said, if a question should arise as to which of these four qualities contributed most by their presence to the excellence of the State, whether the agreement of rulers and subjects, or the preservation in the soldiers of the opinion which the law ordains about the true nature of dangers, or wisdom and watchfulness in the rulers would claim the palm, or whether this which I am about to mention, and which is found in children and women, bond and free, artisan, ruler, subject, is not the one which conduces most to the excellence of the State, — this quality, I mean, of every one doing his own work, and not being a busybody, — the question would not be easily determined.

Certainly, he replied, to answer the question would not be easy.

Then the power of each individual in the State to do his own work appears to compete with the other virtues of wisdom, temperance, and courage?

Yes, he said.

And the virtue which enters into this competition is justice?
Exactly.

Look at the matter in another light. Are not the rulers in a State those to whom you would intrust the office of determining causes?

Certainly.

And they will act on the principle that individuals are neither to take what is another's, nor to be deprived of what is their own.

Yes; that will be their principle.

Which is a just principle?

Yes.

Then on this view, also, justice will be admitted to be the having and doing what is a man's own, and belongs to him?

That is true. . . . .

Let us not, I said, be over-positive as yet; but if, on trial, this conception of justice be verified in the individual as well as in the State, then there will be no longer any room for doubt; if not, there must be another inquiry. Let us, however, finish the old investigation, which we began, as you remember, under the impression that, if we could first examine justice on the larger scale, there would be less difficulty in recognizing her in the individual. That larger example appeared to be the State, and accordingly we constructed one, as good a one as we could, knowing well that in the good State justice would be surely found. Let us now apply what we discovered there to the individual, and if they agree, we are satisfied; or, if there be a difference in the individual, we will come back to the State and have another trial of the theory. The friction of the two when rubbed together may possibly strike a light in which justice will shine forth, and the vision which is then revealed we will fix in our souls.

That is reasonable; and let us do as you say. — *The Republic*, ii. 258.

State, an allegory of the.

—— I perceive, I said, that you are vastly amused at having plunged me into such a hopeless discussion; and now you shall hear the parable in order that you may judge better of the meagreness of my imagination: for the treatment which the the best men experience from their States is so grievous that no single thing on earth can be compared with them; and therefore if I would defend them I must have recourse to fiction, and make a compound of many things, like the fabulous unions of goats and stags which are found in pictures. Imagine, then, a fleet or a ship in which there is a captain who is taller and stronger than any of the crew, but he is a little deaf and has a similar infirmity in sight, and his knowledge of navigation is not much better. Now the sailors are quarreling with one another about the steering; every one is of opinion that he ought to steer, though he has never learned and cannot tell who taught him or when he learned, and will even assert that the art of navigation cannot be taught, and is ready to cut in pieces him who says the contrary. They throng about the captain, and do all that they can to make him commit the helm to them; and if he refuses them and others prevail, they kill the others or throw them overboard, and having first chained up the noble captain's senses with drink or some narcotic drug, they mutiny and take possession of the ship and make themselves at home with the stores; and thus, eating and drinking, they continue their voyage with such success as might be expected of them. Him who is their partisan and zealous in the design of getting the ship out of the captain's hands into their own, whether by force or persuasion, they compliment with the name of sailor, pilot, able seaman, and abuse the other sort of man and call him a good-for-nothing; but they have not even a notion that the true pilot must pay attention to the year and seasons and sky and stars and winds, and whatever else belongs to his art, if he intends to be really qualified for the command of a ship; while at the same time he must and will be the steerer, whether other people like or not; and they think that to combine the exercise of command with the steerer's art is impossible. Now in vessels which are thus circumstanced, and among sailors of this class, how will the true pilot be regarded? Will he not be called by the mutineers a prater, a star-gazer, a good-for-nothing?

Of course, said Adeimantus.

I do not suppose, I said, that you would care to hear the interpretation of the figure, which is an allegory of the true philosopher in his relation to the State; for you understand already.

Certainly. — *The Republic*, ii. 314.

State, well ordered, a waking reality.

—— You have again forgotten, my friend, I said, the intention of the legislator; he did not aim at making any one class in the State happy above the rest; the happiness was to be in the whole State, and he held the citizens together by persuasion and necessity, making them benefactors of the State, and therefore benefactors of one another; to this end he created them, not that they should please themselves, but they were to be his instruments in binding up the State.

True, he said, I had forgotten.

Observe, Glaucon, that there will be no injustice in compelling our philosophers to have a care and providence of others; we shall explain to them that in other States, men of their class are not obliged to share in the toils of politics: and this is reasonable, for they grow up at their own sweet will, and the government would rather not have them. Now the wild plant which owes culture to nobody, has nothing to pay for culture. But we have brought you into the world to be rulers of the hive, kings of yourselves and of the other citizens, and have educated you far better and more perfectly than they have been educated, and you are better able to share in the double duty. Wherefore each of you, when his turn comes, must go down to the general underground abode, and get the habit of seeing in the dark; for all is habit; and by accustoming yourselves you will see ten thousand times better than the dwellers in the den, and you will know what the images are, and of what they are images, because you have seen the beautiful and just and good in their truth. And thus the order of our State and of yours will be a reality, and not a dream only, as the order of States too often is; for in most of them men are fighting with one another about shadows and are distracted in the struggle for power, which in their eyes is a great good. Whereas the truth is, that the State in which the rulers are most reluctant to govern is best and most quietly governed, and the State in which they are most willing, the worst.

Quite true, he replied.

And will our pupils, when they hear this, refuse to share in turn the toils of State, when they are allowed to spend the greater part of their time with one another in the heaven of ideas?

Impossible, he answered; for they are just men, and the commands which we impose upon them are just; there can be no doubt that every one of them will take office as a stern necessity and not like our present ministers of State.[1] — *The Republic*, ii. 346.

State, the corrupting art of the advocate in the.

—— There are many noble things in human life, but to most of them attach evils which corrupt and spoil them. Is not justice noble which has been the civilizer of humanity? How then can the advocate of justice be other than noble? And

[1] For the remainder of this thought see *Office-Seekers*.

yet upon this profession which is presented under the fair name of science, has come an evil reputation. In the first place, we are told that by ingenious pleas and the help of an advocate, the law enables a man to win a particular cause, whether just or unjust; and that both the art and the power of speech which is thereby imparted are at the service of him who is willing to pay for them. Now, in our State this so-called art, whether really an art or only an experience and practice destitute of any art, ought if possible never to come into existence, or if existing among us should listen to the request of the legislator and go away into another land, and not speak contrary to justice. If the offenders obey we say no more; but if they disobey let them hear the voice of the law: If any one thinks that he will pervert the power of justice in the minds of the judges, and unseasonably litigate or advocate, let any one who likes indict him for malpractices of law and dishonest advocacy, and let him be judged in the court of select judges; and if he be convicted let the court determine whether he may be supposed to act from a love of money or from contentiousness. And if he be supposed to act from contentiousness, the court shall fix a time during which he shall not be allowed to institute or plead a cause; and if he be supposed to act as he does from love of money, in case he be a stranger he shall leave the country, and never return under penalty of death; but if he be a citizen he shall die, because he is a lover of money, however gained; and equally, if he be judged to have acted more than once from contentiousness, he shall die. — *Laws,* iv. 449.

State, the order of the.

—— *Ath.* Do we not see that the city is the trunk, and are not the younger guardians, who are chosen for their natural gifts, placed in the head of the State, having their souls all full of eyes, with which they look about the whole city? They keep watch and hand over their perceptions to the memory, and inform the elders of all that happens in the city; and those whom we compared to the mind, because they have many wise thoughts — that is to say, the old men — take counsel, and making use of the younger•men as their ministers, and advising with them, — in this way both together truly preserve the whole State — Shall this be the order of our State, or shall we have some other order? Shall we say that they are all alike the owners of the State, and not merely individuals among them, who have had the most careful training and education?

Cle. That, my good sir, is impossible.

Ath. Then we ought to proceed to some more exact training than that which has preceded. . . . .

Cle. I bow to your authority, Stranger: let us proceed in the way which you propose.

Ath. Then, as would appear, we must compel the guardians of our divine state to perceive, in the first place, what that principle is which is the same in all the four — the same, as we affirm, in courage and in temperance, and in justice and in prudence, and which being one, we call, as we ought, by the single name of virtue. To this, my friends, we will, if you please, hold fast, and not let go until we have sufficiently explained what that is to which we are to look, whether to be regarded as one or as a whole, or as both, or in whatever way. Are we likely ever to be in a virtuous condition, if we cannot tell whether virtue is many, or four, or one? Certainly, if you will take our advice, we shall in some way contrive that this principle has a place amongst us; but if you have made up your mind that we should let the matter alone, we will. — *Laws,* iv. 475.

State, heroes who have died for the.

—— Such were the actions of the men who are here interred, and of others who have died on behalf of their country; many and glorious things I have told of them, and there are yet many more and more glorious things remaining to be told, which many days and nights would not suffice to tell. Let them not be forgotten, and let every man remind their descendants that they also are soldiers who must not desert the ranks of their ancestors, or fall behind from cowardice. Even as I exhort you this day, and in all future time, and on every occasion on which I meet with any of you, I shall continue to remind and exhort you, O ye sons of heroes, that you strive to be the bravest of men. And I think that I ought now to repeat to you what your fathers desired to have said to you who are their survivors, when they went out to battle, in case anything happened to them. I will tell you what I heard them say, and what, if they had only speech, they would fain be saying, judging from what they then said. And you must imagine that you hear them saying what I now repeat to you.

Sons, the event proves that your fathers were brave men;

for we might have lived dishonorably, but have preferred to die honorably rather than bring you and your children into disgrace, and rather than dishonor our fathers and forefathers; considering that life is not life to one who is a dishonor to his race, and that to such an one neither men nor Gods are friendly, either while he is on the earth or after death in the world below. Remember our words, then, and whatever is your aim let virtue be the condition of the attainment of your aim, and know that without this all possessions and pursuits are dishonorable and evil. For neither does wealth bring honor to the owner, if he be a coward; of such an one the wealth belongs to another, and not to himself. Nor does beauty and strength of body, when dwelling in a base and cowardly man, appear comely, but the reverse of comely, making the possessor more conspicuous, and manifesting forth his cowardice. And all knowledge, when separated from justice and virtue, is seen to be cunning and not wisdom; wherefore make this your first and last and only and everlasting desire, that if possible you may exceed not only us but all your ancestors in virtue; and know that to excel you in virtue only brings us shame, but that to be excelled by you is a source of joy to us. And we shall most likely be defeated, and you will most likely be victors in the contest, if you learn so to order your lives as not to misuse or waste the reputation of your ancestors, knowing that to a man who has any self-respect, nothing is more dishonorable than to be honored, not for his own sake, but on account of the reputation of his ancestors. The honor of parents is a fair and noble treasure to their posterity, but to have the use of a treasure of wealth and honor, and to leave none to your successors, because you have neither money nor reputation of your own, is alike base and dishonorable. And if you follow our precepts you will be received by us as friends, when the hour of destiny brings you hither; but if you neglect our words and are disgraced in your lives, no one will receive you friendly. This is the message which is to be delivered to our children. — *Menexenus*, iv. 576.

State, the mother of her citizens.

—— To the State we would say: — Let her take care of our parents and sons, educating the one in principles of order, and worthily cherishing the old age of the other. But we know that she will of her own accord take care of them, and does not need exhortation from us.

These, O ye children and parents of the dead, are the words which they bid us proclaim to you, and which I do proclaim to you with the utmost good-will. And on their behalf I beseech you, the children, to imitate your fathers, and you, parents, to be of good cheer about yourselves; for we will nourish your age, and take care of you both publicly and privately in any place in which one of us may meet one of you who are the parents of the dead. And the care which the city shows you yourselves know; for she has made provision by law concerning the parents and children of those who die in war; and the highest authority is specially intrusted with the duty of watching over them above all other citizens, in order to see that there is no wrong done to them. She herself takes part in the nurture of the children, desiring as far as it is possible that their orphanhood may not be felt by them; she is a parent to them while they are children, and when they arrive at the age of manhood she sends them to their several duties, clothing them in armor; she displays to them and recalls to their minds the pursuits of their fathers, and puts into their hands the instruments of their fathers' virtues; for the sake of the omen, she would have them begin and go to rule over their own houses arrayed in the strength and arms of their fathers. And she never ceases honoring the dead every year, celebrating in public the rites which are proper to each and all; and in addition to this, holding gymnastic and equestrian festivals, and musical festivals of every sort. She is to the dead in the place of a son and heir, and to their sons in place of a father, and to their parents and elder kindred in the place of a protector — ever and always caring for them. Considering this, you ought to bear your calamity the more gently : for thus you will be most endeared to the dead and to the living, and your sorrows will heal and be healed. And now do you and all, having lamented the dead together in the usual manner, go your ways. — *Menexenus*, iv. 578.

States destroyed by ignorance. See *Ignorance*, etc.

―― *Ath.* Consider what is really the greatest ignorance. I should like to know whether you and Megillus would agree with me about this: for my opinion is —

Cle. What?

Ath. That the greatest ignorance is when a man hates that which he nevertheless thinks to be good and noble, and loves and embraces that which he knows to be unrighteous and evil.

This disagreement between the sense of pleasure and the judgment of reason in the soul is, in my opinion, the worst ignorance; and the greatest too, because affecting the great mass of the human soul; for the principle which feels pleasure and pain in the individual, is like the mass or populace in a State. And when the soul is opposed to knowledge, or opinion, or reason, which are her natural lords, that I call folly, just as in the State, when the multitude refuses to obey their rulers and the laws; or, again, in the individual, when fair reasonings have their habitation in the soul and yet do no good, but rather the reverse of good. All these cases I term the worst ignorance, whether in individuals or in States. I am not speaking, Stranger, as you will understand, of the ignorance of handicraftsmen.

Cle. Yes, my friend, we understand and agree.

Ath. Let this, then, in the first place declare and affirm that the citizen who does not know these things ought never to have any kind of authority intrusted to him; he must be stigmatized as ignorant, even though he be skillful in calculation and versed in all sorts of accomplishments, and feats of mental dexterity; and the opposite are to be called wise, even although, in the words of the proverb, they know neither how to read nor how to swim; and to them, as to men of sense, authority is to be committed. For, O my friends, how can there be the least shadow of wisdom when there is no harmony? There is none; but the noblest and greatest of harmonies may be truly said to be the greatest wisdom; and of this he is a partaker who lives according to reason; whereas he who is devoid of reason is the destroyer of his house and the opposite of the saviour of the State: he is ignorant of political wisdom. — *Laws,* iv. 218.

Statesmen, are they good teachers of virtue? See *Virtue,* etc.

—— *Any.* Have there not been many good men in this city?

Soc. Yes, certainly, Anytus: and many good statesmen also there always have been, and there are still, in the city of Athens. But the question is whether they were also good teachers of their own virtue; — not whether there are, or have been, good men, but whether virtue can be taught, is the question which we have been discussing. Now, do we mean to say that the good men of our own and of other times knew how to impart to others that virtue which they had themselves; or is this virtue incapable of being communicated or imparted by one man to another? That is the question which I and Meno have been arguing. Look at the matter in your own way. Would you not admit that Themistocles was a good man?

Any. Certainly; no man better.

Soc. And must not he then have been a good teacher, if any man ever was a good teacher, of his own virtue?

Any. Yes, certainly, — if he wanted to be that.

Soc. But would he not have wanted? He would, at any rate, have desired to make his own son a good man and a gentleman; he could not have been jealous of him, or have intentionally abstained from imparting to him his own virtue. Did you never hear that he made Cleophantus, who was his son, a famous horseman? — he would stand upright on horseback and hurl a javelin; and many other marvelous things he could do which his father had him taught; and in anything which the skill of a master could teach him he was well trained. Have you not heard from our elders of this?

Any. I have.

Soc. Then no one could say that his son showed any want of capacity?

Any. Possibly not.

Soc. But did any one, old or young, ever say in your hearing that Cleophantus, the son of Themistocles, was a wise or good man, as his father was?

Any. I have certainly never heard that.

Soc. And if virtue could have been taught, would his father Themistocles have sought to train him in minor accomplishments, and allowed him who, as you must remember, was his own son, to be no better than his neighbors in those qualities in which he himself excelled?

Any. Indeed, indeed I think not.

Soc. Here, then, is a teacher of virtue whom you admit to be among the best men of the past. — *Meno,* i. 268.

Statesmen, called divine.

—— *Soc.* Not by any wisdom, and not because they were wise, did Themistocles and those others of whom Anytus spoke govern States. And this was the reason why they were unable to make others like themselves, — because their virtue was not grounded on knowledge.

Men. That is probably true, Socrates.

Soc. But if not by knowledge, the only alternative which remains is that statesmen must have guided States by right opinion, which is in politics what divination is in religion ; for diviners and also prophets say many things truly, but they know not what they say.

Men. Very true.

Soc. And may we not, Meno, truly call those men divine who, having no understanding, yet succeed in many a grand deed and word?

Men. Certainly.

Soc. Then we shall also be right in calling those divine whom we were just now speaking of as diviners and prophets, as well as all poets. Yes, and statesmen, above all, may be said to be divine and illumined, being inspired and possessed of God, in which condition they say many grand things, not knowing what they say.

Men. Yes.

Soc. And the women too, Meno, call good men divine; and the Spartans, when they praise a good man, say " that he is a divine man."

Men. And I think, Socrates, that they are right; although very likely our friend Anytus may take offense at the word. — *Meno,* i. 275.

Statesmen and politicians distinguished. See *Politicians,* etc.

Strangers, treatment of.

—— In his relations to strangers, a man should consider that a contract is a most holy thing, and that all concerns and wrongs of strangers are more directly dependent on the protection of God, than the wrongs done to citizens ; for the stranger having no kindred and friends, is more to be pitied by Gods and men. Wherefore, also, he who is most able to assist him is most zealous in his cause; and he who is most able is the divinity and God of the stranger, who follows in the train of Zeus, the God of strangers. And for this reason, he who has a spark of caution in him, will do his best to pass through life without sinning against the stranger. And of offenses committed, whether against strangers or fellow-countrymen, that against suppliants is the greatest. For the God who witnessed to the agreement made with the suppliant, becomes in a special manner the guardian of the sufferer ; and he will certainly not suffer unavenged. — *Laws,* iv. 255.

Strength, physical, inferior to persuasion. See *Legislation* and *Persuasion.*

Style, mixed and unmixed.

—— Suppose, I answered, that a just and good man in the course of narration comes on some saying or action of another good man, — I should imagine that he will like to personate him, and will not be ashamed of this sort of imitation : he will be most ready to play the part of the good man when he is acting firmly and wisely ; in a less degree when his steps falter, owing to sickness or love, or again from intoxication or any other mishap. But when he comes to a character which is unworthy of him, he will not make a study of that; he will disdain his inferiors, and will wear their likeness, if at all, for a moment only when they are doing some good ; at other times he will be ashamed to play a part which he has never practiced, nor will he like to fashion and frame himself after the baser models ; he feels that the serious use of such an art would be beneath him, and his mind revolts at it.

That is what I should expect, he replied.

Then he will adopt a mode of narration such as we have illustrated out of Homer, that is to say, his style will be both imitative and narrative; but there will be very little of the former, and a great deal of the latter. Do you agree?

Certainly, he said ; that is the model which such a speaker must necessarily take.

But another sort of character will narrate anything, and the worse he is the more unscrupulous he will be ; nothing will be beneath him: moreover, he will be ready to imitate anything, not as a joke, but in right good earnest, and before a large audience. As I was just now saying, he will attempt to represent the roll of thunder, the rattle of wind and hail, or the creaking of wheels and pulleys, and the various sounds of flutes, pipes, trumpets, and all sorts of instruments ; also he will bark like a dog, bleat like a sheep, and crow like a cock ; his entire art will consist in imitation of voice and gesture, and there will be very little narration.

That, he said, will be his mode of speaking.

These, then, are the two kinds of style?

Yes.

And you would agree with me in saying that one of them is simple and has but slight changes ; and if the harmony and rhythm· are also chosen for their simplicity, the result is that the speaker, if he speaks correctly, is always pretty much the same in style, and keeps within the limits of a single harmony (for the changes are not great), and also keeps pretty nearly the same rhythm?

That is quite true, he said.

Whereas the other style requires all sorts of harmonies and all sorts of rhythms, if the music is to be expressive of the variety and complexity of the words?

That is also perfectly true, he replied.

And do not the two styles, or the mixture of the two, comprehend all poetry, and every form of expression in words? No one can say anything except in one or other of them, or in both together?

They include all, he said.

And shall we receive one or both of the two pure styles? or would you include the mixed?

I should prefer only to admit the pure imitator of virtue.

Yes, I said, Adeimantus; but the mixed style is also very charming: and indeed the pantomimic, which is the opposite of the one chosen by you, is the most popular style with children and their instructors, and with the world in general.

I do not deny it.

But I suppose you mean to say that such a style is unsuitable to our State, in which human nature is not twofold or manifold, for one man plays one part only?

Yes; quite unsuitable. — *The Republic*, ii. 220.

Substitution and succession in life. See *Unity*, etc., *the greatest*.
Suffering, community of. See *Evil*, etc.
Suffering evil, less than doing it. See *Injustice*.
Suffering, intermediate state between pleasure and. See *Intermediate*, etc.
✗**Sufficiency** of the good.

—— *Soc.* And is not and was not this a further point which was conceded between us —.

Pro. What was the point?

Soc. That the good differs from all other things?

Pro. In what way?

Soc. In that the being who possesses good always, everywhere, and in all things, has the most perfect sufficiency, and is never in need of anything else.

Pro. Exactly.

Soc. And did we not endeavor to make an ideal division of them into two distinct lives, so that pleasure was wholly excluded from wisdom, and wisdom in like manner had no part whatever in pleasure?

Pro. That we did.

Soc. And did we think that either of them alone would be sufficient?

Pro. Certainly not.

Soc. And if we erred in any point, then let any one who will, take up the inquiry again, and assuming memory and wisdom and knowledge and true opinion to belong to the same class, let him consider whether he would desire to possess or acquire, I will not say pleasure, however abundant or intense,. if he has no real perception that he is pleased, nor any consciousness of what he feels, nor any recollection, however momentary, of the feeling, — but would he desire to have anything at all, if these were wanting to him? And about wisdom I ask the same question; can you conceive that any one would choose to have all wisdom absolutely devoid of pleasure, rather than having a certain degree of pleasure, or all pleasure devoid of wisdom, rather than having a certain degree of wisdom?

Pro. Certainly not, Socrates; but why repeat such questions any more? — *Philebus*, iii. 201.

"**Summum Bonum**" in the State. See *Evil, the greatest*, etc., and *Good, greatest*.

Sun and **stars** without soul. See *Soul*, etc.

Superhuman knowledge. See *Knowledge*.

Suspicious character, a.

—— Your cunning and suspicious character, who has committed many crimes and fancies himself to be a master in wickedness when he is among men who are like himself, is wonderful in his precautions against others, because he judges of them by himself: but when he gets into the company of men of virtue, who have the experience of age, he appears to be a fool again, owing to his unseasonable suspicion; he cannot recognize an honest man, because he has nothing in himself
· which will tell him what an honest man is like; at the same time, as the bad are more numerous than the good, and he meets with them oftener, he thinks himself and others think him rather wise than foolish. — *The Republic*, ii. 234.

Symbols, the starry heavens are. See *Heavenly bodies*.

Symbols, metallic, of races. See *Metallic*, etc.

Talents, natural.

—— Come, now, and we will ask you a question : — when you said that one man has natural gifts and another not, was this your meaning ? — that the former will acquire a thing easily which the latter will have a difficulty in acquiring ; a little learning will lead the one to discover a great deal; whereas the other, after a great deal of learning and application, will only forget what he has learned ; or again, you may mean, that the one has a body which is a good servant to his mind, while the body of the other is at war with his mind — would these be the sort of differences which distinguish the man of capacity from the man who is wanting in capacity ?

The existence of such differences, he said, will be universally allowed. — *The Republic*, ii. 279.

Talking, idle. See *Idle*.
Taste, what is a true. See *Life, the nobler*.
Teachers, skillful and unskillful.

—— As Lysimachus and Melesias, in their anxiety to improve the minds of their sons, have asked our advice about them, we too should tell them who our teachers were, if we say that we have had any, and prove them to be men of merit and experienced trainers of the minds of youth and really our teachers. Or if any of us says that he has no teacher, but that he has works to show of his own ; then he should point out to them, what Athenians or strangers, bond or free, he is generally acknowledged to have improved. But if he can show neither teachers nor works, then he should tell them to look out for others ; and not run the risk of spoiling the children of friends, which is the most formidable accusation that can be brought against any one by those nearest to him. As for myself, Lysimachus and Melesias, I am the first to confess that I have never had a teacher ; although I have always from my earliest youth desired to have one. But I am too poor to give money to the Sophists, who are the only professors of moral improvement ; and to this day I have never been able to discover the art myself, though I should not be surprised if Nicias or Laches may have learned or discovered it ; for they are far wealthier than I am, and may therefore have learnt of others. And they are older too ; so that they have had more time to make the discovery. And I really believe that they are able to educate a man ; for unless they had been confident in their own knowledge, they would never have spoken thus decidedly of the pursuits which are advantageous or hurtful to a young man. I repose confidence in both of them; but I am surprised to find that they differ from one another. And therefore, Lysimachus, as Laches suggested that you should detain me, and not let me go until I answered, I in turn earnestly beseech and advise you to detain Laches and Nicias, and question them. I would have you say to them: Socrates avers that he has no knowledge of the matter, — he is unable to decide which of you speaks truly; neither discoverer nor student is he of anything of the kind. But you, Laches and Nicias, should either of you tell us who is the most skillful educator whom you have ever known; and whether you invented the art yourselves, or learned of another; and if you learned, who were your respective teachers, and who were their brothers in the art; and then, if you are too much occupied in politics to teach us yourselves, let us go to them, and present them with gifts, or make interest with them, or both, in the hope that they may be induced to take charge of all our families, in order that they may not grow up inferior, and disgrace their ancestors. But if you are yourselves original discoverers in that field, give us some proof of your skill. Who are they who, having been inferior persons, have become under your care good and noble? For if this is your first attempt at education, there is a danger that you may be trying the experiment not on the "vile corpus" of a Carian slave, but on your own sons, or the sons of your friend, and as the proverb says, "Break the large vessel in learning to make pots." — *Laches*, i. 78.

Teachers, lawyers not. See *Lawyers*, etc.
Temperance and modesty. See *Modesty*, etc.
Temperance and justice. See *Justice*, etc.
Temperance, harmony of. See *Harmony*, etc.
Temperate man, the.

——— Ought not the rational principle, which is wise, and has the care of the whole soul, to rule, and the passionate or spirited principle to be the subject and ally?

Certainly.

And, as we were saying, the united influence of music and gymnastic will bring them into accord, nerving and sustaining the reason with noble words and lessons, and moderating and soothing and civilizing the wildness of passion with harmony and rhythm?

Quite true, he said.

And these two, thus nurtured and educated, and having learned truly to know their own functions, will rule over the concupiscent part of every man, which is the largest and most insatiable; over this they will set a guard, lest waxing great with the fullness of bodily pleasures, as they are termed, and no longer confined to her own sphere, the concupiscent soul should attempt to enslave and rule those who are not her natural-born subjects, and overturn the whole life of man?

Very true, he said.

The two will be the defenders of the whole soul and the whole body against attacks from without; the one counseling, and the other fighting under his leader, and courageously executing his commands and counsels.

True.

And he is to be deemed courageous in whom the element of spirit holds fast in pain and in pleasure the command of reason about which he ought or ought not to fear?

Right, he replied.

And he is wise who has in him that little part which rules and gives orders; that part being supposed to have a knowledge of what is for the interest of each and all of the three other parts?

Assuredly.

And would you not say that he is temperate who has these same elements in friendly harmony, in whom the one ruling principle of reason, and the two subject ones of spirit and desire, are equally agreed that reason ought to rule, and do not rebel?

Certainly, he said, that is the true account of temperance, whether in the State or individual.— *The Republic*, ii. 268.

Temperate and intemperate life, the.

—— Let us say that the temperate life is one kind of life, and the rational another, and the courageous another, and the healthful another; and to these four let us oppose four other lives,— the foolish, the cowardly, the intemperate, the diseased. He who knows the temperate life will describe it as in all things gentle, having gentle pains and gentle pleasures, and placid desires and loves not insane; whereas the intemperate life is impetuous in all things, and has violent pains and pleasures, and vehement and stinging desires, and loves utterly insane; and in the temperate life the pleasures exceed the pains and in the intemperate life the pains exceed the pleasures in greatness and number and intensity. Hence one of the two lives is naturally and necessarily more pleasant and the other more painful, and he who would live pleasantly cannot possibly choose to live intemperately. And if this is true, the inference clearly is that no man is voluntarily intemperate; but that the whole multitude of men lack temperance in their lives, either from ignorance or from want of self-control or both. And the same holds of the diseased and healthy life; they both have pleasures and pains, but in health the pleasure exceeds the pain, and in sickness the pain exceeds the pleasure. Now, our intention in choosing the lives is not that the painful should exceed, but the life in which pain is exceeded by pleasure we determine to be the more pleasant life. And we should say that the temperate life has the elements both of pleasure and pain fewer and minuter and less concentrated than the intemperate. — *Laws*, iv. 259.

Temperate man, duty of the.

—— And will not the temperate man do what is proper, both in relation to Gods and to men; for he would not be temperate if he did not? Certainly he will do what is proper. In his relation to other men he will do what is just; and in his relation to the Gods he will do what is holy; and he who does what is just and holy cannot be other than just and holy? Very true. And he must be courageous, for the duty of a temperate man is not to follow or to avoid what he ought not, but what he ought, whether things or men or pleasures or pains, and patiently to endure when he ought; and therefore, Callicles, the temperate man being as we have described, also just and courageous and holy, cannot be other than a perfectly good man, nor can the good man do otherwise than well and perfectly whatever he does: and he who does well must of necessity be happy and blessed, and the evil man who does evil, miserable: now this latter is he whom you were applauding — the intemperate, who is the opposite of the temperate. Such is my position which I assert to be true, and if I am right then I affirm that he who desires to be happy must pursue and practice temperance and run away from intemperance as fast as his legs will carry him; he had better order his life so as not to need punishment. — *Gorgias*, iii. 98.

Thought, boldness in. See *Boldness*.
Thought and speech. See *Speech*.

Time, science of. See *Science.*
Trade, ruining virtue. See *Money, a ruler.*
Trade, men of, their money-sting. See *Business men.*
Traditional forms adhered to.

—— *Ath.* Long ago in Egypt they appear to have recognized the very principle of which we are now speaking — that their young citizens must be habituated to forms and strains of virtue. These they fixed, and exhibited the patterns of them in their temples; and no painter or artist is allowed to innovate upon them, or to leave the traditional forms and invent new ones. To this day, no alteration is allowed either in these arts, or in music at all. And you will find that their works of art are painted or moulded in the same forms which they had ten thousand years ago; this is literally true and no exaggeration, — their ancient paintings and sculptures are not a whit better or worse than the work of to-day, but are made with just the same skill.

Cle. How extraordinary!

Ath. I should rather say, how wise and worthy of a great legislator! I know that other things in Egypt are not so good. But what I am telling you about music is true and deserving of consideration, because showing that a lawgiver may institute melodies which have a natural truth and correctness without any fear of failure. To do this, however, must be the work of God, or of a divine person; in Egypt they have a tradition that their ancient chants are the composition of the Goddess Isis. And therefore, as I was saying, if a person could only find in any way the natural melodies, he might confidently embody them in a fixed and legal form. For the love of novelty which arises out of pleasure in the new, and weariness of the old, has not strength enough to vitiate the consecrated song and dance, under the plea that they have become antiquated. At any rate they are far from being antiquated in Egypt. — *Laws,* iv. 186.

Transformation of man. See *Man,* etc.
Truth, ridicule, no test of. See *Ridicule.*
Truthfulness must characterize the lover of learning. See *Learning.*
Truths, spiritual, uncertainty of. See *Spiritual,* etc.
Tyrant, produced from a protector. See *Protector.*
Tyrant and king distinguished. See *King.*

Unity in the State. See *State, unity,* etc.
Unity and individuality. See *Individuality,* etc.
Unjust, misery of the. See *Misery,* etc.

Vanity of youth. See *Self-conceit.*
Virtue, can it be taught? See *Statesmen, are they good teachers?*
—— The best and wisest of our citizens are unable to impart their political wisdom to others : as, for example, Pericles, the father of these young men, who gave them excellent instruction in all that could be learned from masters, in his own department of politics neither taught them nor gave them teachers, but they were allowed to wander at their own free-will, in a sort of hope that they would light upon virtue of their own accord. Or take another example : There was Cleinias the younger brother of our friend Alcibiades, of whom this very same Pericles was the guardian ; and he being in fact under the apprehension that Cleinias would be corrupted by Alcibiades, took him away, and placed him in the house of Ariphron to be educated ; but before six months had elapsed, Ariphron sent him back, not knowing what to do with him. And I could mention numberless other instances of persons who were good themselves, and never yet made any one else good, whether friend or stranger. Now I, Protagoras, having before me these examples, am inclined to think that virtue cannot be taught. But then, again, when I listen to your words, I am disposed to waver ; and I believe that there must be something in what you say, because I know that you have great experience, and learning, and invention. And I wish that you would, if possible, show me a little more clearly that virtue can be taught. — *Protagoras,* i. 120.
Virtue, the gift of God.
—— *Soc.* To sum up our inquiry, — the result seems to be, if we are at all right in our view, that virtue is neither natural nor acquired, but an instinct given by God to the virtuous. Nor is the instinct accompanied by reason, unless there may be supposed to be among statesmen any one who is also the educator of statesmen. And if there be such an one, he may be said to be among the living what Tiresias was among the dead, who "alone," according to Homer, "of those in the world below has understanding ; but the rest flit as shades ; " and he and his virtue in like manner will be a reality among shadows.

Men. That is excellent, Socrates.

Soc. Then, Meno, the conclusion is that virtue comes to the virtuous by the gift of God. — *Meno,* i. 276.

Virtue, the basis and bond of love. See *Love,* etc.
Virtue and justice, rewards of. See *Justice,* etc.
Virtue, not by chance, but order.

—— The virtue of each thing, whether body or soul, instrument or creature, when given to them in the best way comes to them not by chance but as the result of the order and truth and art which are imparted to them. Am I not right? I maintain that I am. And is not the virtue of each thing dependent on order or arrangement? Yes, I say. And that which makes a thing good is the proper order inhering in each thing? That is my view. And is not the soul which has an order of her own better than that which has no order of her own? Certainly. — *Gorgias,* iii. 98.

Virtue, laws answering to. See *Laws answering to,* etc.
Virtue, the law-giver's aim.

—— *Ath.* Remember, my good friend, what I said at first about the Cretan laws, that they looked to one thing only, and this, as you both agreed, was war; and I replied that such laws, in so far as they tended to promote virtue, were good: but in that they regarded a part only, and not the whole of virtue, I disapproved of them. And now I hope that you in your turn will follow and watch me if I legislate with a view to anything but virtue, or only with a view to a part of virtue. For I consider that the true law-giver, like an archer, aims only at that on which some eternal beauty is always attending, and dismisses everything else, whether wealth or any other benefit, when separated from virtue. — *Laws,* iv. 233.

Voice, inner. See *Inner.*

War, women, and children.

—— You agree then, I said, that men and women are to have a common way of life such as we have described — common education, common children; and they are to watch over the citizens in common whether abiding in the city or going out to war; they are to guard together, and to hunt together like dogs; and always and in all things women are to share with the men? And in so doing they will act for the best and will not violate, but preserve the natural relation of the sexes.

I agree with you, he replied.

The inquiry, I said, has yet to be made, whether such a community will be found possible — as among other animals so also among men — and if possible, in what way possible?

That, he said, is just the question which I was going to ask.

There is no difficulty I said, in seeing how war will be carried on by them.

How?

Why, of course they will go on expeditions together; and will take with them any of their children who are strong enough, that, like the children of artisans in general, they may look on at the work, which they will have to do when they are grown up; and besides looking on they will be able to help and be of use in war, and to wait upon their fathers and mothers. Did you never observe in the arts how the potters' boys look on and help, long before they touch the wheel?

Certainly.

And shall potters be more careful than our guardians in educating their children and giving them the opportunity of seeing and practicing their duties?

The notion would be ridiculous, he said.

There is also the effect on the parents, with whom, as with other animals, the presence of their cubs will be the greatest incentive to valor.

That is quite true, Socrates; and yet if they are defeated which may often happen in war, how great the danger is! the children will be lost as well as their parents, and the State will never recover.

True, I said; but would you never allow them to run any risk? I am far from saying that.

Well, but if they are ever to run a risk should they not run the risk when there is a chance of their improvement?

Clearly. — *The Republic*, ii. 293.

War and discord. See *Discord*.

War, geometry in. See *Geometry*.

War of Gods and giants. See *Essence*, etc.

War, two kinds of.

—— *Ath.* Come, now, and let us all join in asking this question of Tyrtaeus: O most divine poet, we will say to him, the excellent praise which you have bestowed on those who excel in war sufficiently proves that you are wise and good, and I and Megillus and Cleinias of Cnosus do, as I believe, entirely agree with you. But we should like to be quite sure that we are speaking of the same men; tell us, then, do you agree with us in thinking that there are two kinds of war; or what would you say? A far inferior man to Tyrtaeus would have no difficulty in replying quite truly, that there are two kinds of war, — one which is universally called civil war and is, as we were just now saying, of all wars the worst; the other, as we should all admit, in which we fall out with other-nations' who are of a different race, is a far milder form of warfare.

Cle. Certainly, far milder.

Ath. Well, now, when you praise and blame war in this high-flown strain, whom are you praising or blaming, and to which kind of war are you referring? I suppose that you must mean foreign war, if I am to judge from expressions of yours in which you say that you abominate those —

"Who refuse to look upon fields of blood, and will not draw near and strike at their enemies."

And we shall naturally go on to say to him, — You, Tyrtaeus, certainly appear to praise those who distinguish themselves in external and foreign war; and he must admit this.

Cle. Certainly. — *Laws,* iv. ~~160.~~ 150.

War, expeditions of.

—— Now for expeditions of war much consideration and many laws are required; the great principle of all is that no one of either sex should be without a commander; nor should the mind of any one be accustomed to do anything either in jest or earnest of his own motion, but in war and in peace he should look to and follow his leader, and in the least things be under his guidance; for example, he should stand or move, or exercise, or wash, or take his meals, or get up in the night to keep guard and deliver messages when he is bidden; and in the hour of danger he should not pursue and not retreat except by order of his superior; and in a word, not teach the soul or accustom her to know or understand how to do anything apart from others. Of all soldiers the life should be in common and together; there neither is nor ever will be a higher, or better, or more scientific principle than this for the attainment of salvation and victory in war. And from youth upwards we ought to practice this habit of commanding others, and of being commanded by others; anarchy should have no place in the life of man or of the beasts who are subject to man. I may add that all dances ought to be performed with a view to military excellence, and agility and ease should be cultivated with a similar view; and also endurance of the want of meats and drinks, and winter cold and summer heat, and hard couches; and, above all, care should be taken not to destroy the natural qualities of the head and the feet by surrounding them with extraneous coverings, and so hindering their natural growth of hair and soles. For these are the extremities, and of all the parts of the body, whether they are preserved or not is of the greatest consequence; the one is the servant of the whole body and the other the master in whom all the ruling senses are by nature set. Let the young man, when I say this, imagine that he hears the praises of the military life; and the law shall be as follows: He shall serve in war who is enrolled or appointed to some special service, and if any one wrongly absents himself, and without the leave of the generals, he shall be indicted before the military commanders for failure of service when the army comes home. — *Laws*, iv. 452.

Warriors, gentleness of. See *Gentleness*, etc.

Warfare, naval. See *Minos*.

Wars, civil, how arising.

—— When a young man who has been brought up as we are just now describing, in a vulgar and miserly way, has tasted drones' honey and has come to associate with fierce and dangerous natures who are able to provide for him all sorts of refinements and varieties of pleasure, — then, as you may imagine, the change will begin of the oligarchical principle within him into the democratical.

Inevitably.

And as in the city like was helping like, and the change was effected by an alliance from without assisting one division of the citizens, so the young man also changes by a class of desires from without assisting the unsatisfied desires within him, that which is akin and alike again helping that which is akin and alike.

Certainly.

And if there be any ally which aids the oligarchical principle within him, whether the influence of friends or kindred, advising or rebuking him, then there arises a faction and an opposite faction, and the result is a civil war.

It must be so. — *The Republic*, ii. 388.

Wealth and poverty equally deteriorating.

—— There seem to be two causes of the deterioration of the arts.

What are they?

Wealth, I said, and poverty.

How do they act?

The process is as follows: When a potter becomes rich he no longer takes the same pains with his art?

Certainly not.

He grows more and more indolent and careless?

Very true.

And the result is that he becomes a worse potter?

Yes; he greatly deteriorates.

But, on the other hand, if he has no money, and is unable to buy tools or instruments, he will not work equally well himself, nor will he teach his sons or apprentices to work equally well.

Certainly not.

Then workmen, and also their works, are apt to degenerate under the influence both of poverty and of wealth?

That is evident.

Here, then, is a discovery of new evils, I said, which the guardians will have to watch, or they will creep into the city unobserved.

What evils?

Wealth, I said, and poverty; for the one is the parent of luxury and indolence, and the other of meanness and viciousness, and both of discontent. — *The Republic*, ii. 245.

Wickedness, the road to.

—— *Ath.* I should wish the citizen to be as receptive of virtue as possible ; this will surely be the aim of the legislator in all his laws is evident.

Cle. Certainly.

Ath. What I have been proposing appears to me to have some use; for a person will listen with more gentleness and good-will to the precepts addressed to him by the legislator, when his soul is not altogether unprepared to receive them. Even a little done in the way of conciliation gains his ear, and is always worth having. For there is no great inclination or readiness on the part of mankind to be made as good, or as quickly good, as possible. The case of the many proves the wisdom of Hesiod, who says that the road to wickedness is smooth and very short, and there is no need of perspiring: —

" But before virtue the immortal Gods have placed the sweat of labor, and long and steep is the way thither, and rugged at first but when you have reached the top, then, however difficult, it becomes easy.

Cle. Yes; and he certainly speaks well. — *Laws,* iv. 246.

Wine, divers effect of.

—— *Soc.* The wine which I drink when I am in health, appears sweet and pleasant to me?

Theaet. True.

Soc. For, as has been already acknowledged, the patient and agent meet together and produce sweetness and a perception of sweetness, which are in simultaneous motion, and the perception which comes from the patient makes the tongue percipient, and the quality of sweetness which arises out of and is moving about the wine, makes the wine both to be and to appear sweet to the healthy tongue.

Theaet. Certainly; that has been already acknowledged.

Soc. But when I am sick, the wine really acts upon me as if I were another and a different person?

Theaet. Yes.

Soc. The combination of the draught of wine, and the Socrates who is sick, produces quite another result which is the sensation of bitterness in the tongue, and the motion and creation of bitterness in the wine, which becomes not bitterness but bitter; as I myself become not perception but percipient?

Theaet. True. — *Theaetetus,* iii. 360.

Wine, forbidden.

——*Ath.* I have first to add a crown to my discourse about drink.

Cle. What more would you say?

Ath. I should say that if a city seriously means to adopt this practice of drinking, under due regulation and with a view to the enforcement of temperance, and in like manner, and on the same principle, will allow of other pleasures, designing to gain the victory over them — in this way all of them may be used. But if the State makes drinking an amusement only, and whoever likes may drink whenever he likes, and with whom he likes, and add to this any other indulgences, I shall never agree or allow that this city or this man should adopt such a usage of drinking. I would go farther than the Cretans and Lacedaemonians, and am disposed rather to the law of the Carthaginians, that no one while he is on a campaign should be allowed to taste wine at all; but I would say that he should drink water during all that time, and that in the city no slave, male or female, should ever drink wine; and that no rulers should drink during their year of office, nor pilots of vessels, nor judges while on duty should taste wine at all; nor any one who is going to hold a consultation about any matter of importance, nor in the daytime at all, unless in consequence of exercise or as medicine; nor again at night, when any one, either man or woman, is minded to get children. There are numberless other cases, also, in which those who have good sense and good laws ought not to drink wine, so that if what I say is true, no city will need many vineyards. Their husbandry and their way of life in general will follow an appointed order, and their cultivation of the vine will be the most limited and moderate of their employments. And this, Stranger, shall be the crown of my discourse about wine, if you agree.

Cle. Excellent: we agree. — *Laws*, iv. 203.

Wine-drinking, a bad practice.

—— Socrates took his place on the couch and supped with the rest; and then libations were offered, and after a hymn had been sung to the God, and there had been the usual ceremonies, they were about to commence drinking when Pausanias said: And now my friends, how can we drink with least injury to ourselves? I can assure you that I feel severely the effect of yesterday's potations and must have time to recover, and I suspect that most of you are in the same predicament, for you were of the party yesterday. Consider this. He would therefore ask, How can the drinking be made easiest?

I entirely agree, said Aristophanes, that we should, by all means, avoid hard drinking, for I was myself one of those who were yesterday drowned in drink.

I think that you are right, said Eryximachus the son of Acumenus; but I should like to hear one other person speak. What are the inclinations of our host?

I am not able to drink, said Agathon.

Then, said Eryximachus, the weak heads like myself, Aristodemus, Phaedrus, and others who never can drink, are fortunate in finding that the stronger ones are not in a drinking mood. (I do not include Socrates, who is able either to drink or to abstain, and will not mind whichever we do.) Well, as none of the company seem disposed to drink much, I may be forgiven for saying, as a physician, that drinking deep is a bad practice, which I never follow if I can help, and certainly do not recommend to another, least of all to any one who still feels the effects of yesterday's carouse.

I always do what you advise, and especially what you prescribe as a physician, rejoined Phaedrus the Myrrhinusian, and the rest of the company, if they are wise, will do the same.

All agreed that drinking was not to be the order of the day. — *The Syposium*, i. 471.

Wise and just soul. See *Just*, etc.

Wisdom, as differing from other sciences.

——— I want to know what is that which is not wisdom, and of which wisdom is the science?

That is precisely the old error, Socrates, he said. You come asking in what wisdom differs from the other sciences; and then you try to discover some respect in which they are alike: but they are not, for all the other sciences are of something else, and not of themselves; wisdom alone is a science of other sciences, and of itself. And of this, as I believe, you are very well aware; and that you are only doing what you denied that you were doing just now, trying to refute me, instead of pursuing the argument.

And what if I am? How can you think that I have any other motive in refuting you but what I should have in examining into myself? which motive would be just a fear of my unconsciously fancying that I knew something of which I was ignorant. And at this moment I pursue the argument chiefly for my own sake, and perhaps in some degree also for the sake of my other friends. For is not the discovery of things as they truly are a common good to all mankind?

Yes, certainly, Socrates, he said.

Then, I said, be cheerful, sweet sir, and give your opinion in answer to the question which I asked, never minding whether Critias or Socrates is the person refuted; attend only to the argument, and see what will come of the refutation.

I think that you are right, he replied; and I will do as you say.

Tell me, then, I said, what you mean to affirm about wisdom.

I mean, he said, that wisdom is the only science which is the science of itself and of the other sciences as well.

But the science of science, I said, will also be the science of the absence of science.

Very true, he said.

Then the wise or temperate man, and he only, will know himself, and be able to examine what he knows or does not know, and see what others know, and think that they know and do really know; and what they do not know, and fancy that they know, when they do not. No other person will be able to do this. And this is the state and virtue of wisdom, or temperance, and self-knowledge, which is just knowing what a man knows, and what he does not know. That is your view?

Yes, he said. — *Charmides*, i. 21.

Wisdom, advantages of.

—— What profit, Critias, I said, is there any longer in wisdom or temperance which yet remains, if this is wisdom? If, indeed, as we were supposing at first, the wise man had been able to distinguish what he knew and did not know, and that he knew the one and did not know the other, and to recognize a similar faculty of discernment in others, there would certainly have been a great advantage in being wise, for then we should never have made a mistake, but have passed through life the unerring guides of ourselves and of those who were under us; and we should not have attempted to do what we did not know, but we should have found out those who knew, and confided in them; nor should we have allowed those who were under us to do anything which they were not likely to do well; and they would be likely to do well just that of which they had knowledge; and the house or state which was ordered or administered under the guidance of wisdom, and everything else of which wisdom was the lord, would have been well ordered; for truth guiding, and error having been expelled, in all their doings, men would have done well, and would have been happy. Was not this, Critias, what we spoke of as the great advantage of wisdom — to know what is known and what is unknown to us?

Very true, he said.

And now you perceive, I said, that no such science is to be found anywhere.

I perceive, he said.

May we assume, then, I said, that wisdom, viewed in this new light merely as a knowledge of knowledge and ignorance, has this advantage — that he who possesses such knowledge will more easily learn anything which he learns; and that everything will be clearer to him, because, in addition to the knowledge of individuals, he sees the science, and this also will better enable him to test the knowledge which others have of what he knows himself; whereas the inquirer who is without this knowledge may be supposed to have a feebler and weaker insight? Are not these, my friend, the real advantages which are to be gained from Wisdom? And are not we looking and seeking after something more than is to be found in her?

That is very likely, he said. — *Charmides*, i. 28.

Wisdom, the sway of.

—— Let us suppose that wisdom is such as we are now defining, and that she has absolute sway over us; then each action will be done according to the arts or sciences, and no one professing to be a pilot when he is not, or any physician or general, or any one else pretending to know matters of which he is ignorant, will deceive or elude us; our health will be improved; our safety at sea, and also in battle, will be assured; our coats and shoes, and all other instruments and implements will be well made, because the workmen will be good and true. Aye, and if you please, you may suppose that prophecy, which is the knowledge of the future, will be under the control of Wisdom, and that she will deter deceivers and set up the true prophet in their place as the revealer of the future. Now I quite agree that mankind, thus provided, would live and act according to knowledge, for wisdom would watch and prevent ignorance from intruding on us. But we have not as yet discovered why, because we act according to knowledge, we act well and are happy, my dear Critias.

Yet I think, he replied, that if you discard knowledge you will hardly find the crown of happiness in anything else. — *Charmides*, i. 30.

Wisdom, a means of good.

—— You perceive that in things which we know every one will trust us, — Hellenes and barbarians, men and women, — and we may do as we please about them, and no one will like to interfere with us; we shall be free, and masters of others; and these things will be really ours, for we shall be benefited by them. But in things of which we have no understanding, no one will trust us to do as seems good to us — they will hinder us as far as they can; and not only strangers, but father and mother, and the friend, if there be one, who is dearer still, will also hinder us; and we shall be subject to others; and these things will not be ours, for we shall not be benefited by them. Do you admit that?

He assented.

And shall we be friends to others? and will any others love us, in as far as we are useless to them?

Certainly not.

Neither can your father or mother love you, nor can anybody love anybody else, in as far as they are useless to them?

No.

And therefore, my boy, if you are wise, all men will be your friends and kindred, for you will be useful and good; but if you are not wise, neither father, nor mother, nor kindred, nor any one else, will be your friends. And in matters of which you have as yet no knowledge can you have any conceit of knowledge?

That is impossible, he replied.

And you, Lysis, if you require a teacher, have not as yet attained to wisdom.

True.

And therefore you are not conceited, having nothing of which to be conceited?

Indeed, Socrates, I think not. — *Lysis*, i. 48.

Wisdom makes men fortunate.

—— In what company shall we find a place for wisdom — among the goods or not?

Among the goods.

And now, I said, think whether we have left out any considerable goods.

I do not think that we have, said Cleinias.

Upon recollection, I said, indeed I am afraid that we have left out the greatest of them all.

What is that? he asked.

Fortune, Cleinias, I replied; which all, even the most foolish, admit to be the greatest of goods.

True, he said.

On second thoughts, I added, how narrowly, O son of Axiochus, have you and I escaped making a laughing-stock of ourselves to the strangers.

Why do you say that?

Why, because we have already spoken of fortune, and are but repeating ourselves.

What do you mean?

I mean that there is something ridiculous in putting fortune again forward, and saying the same thing twice over.

He asked what was the meaning of this, and I replied: Surely wisdom is good fortune; even a child may know that.

The simple-minded youth was amazed; and, observing this,

I said to him: Do you not know, Cleinias, that flute-players are most fortunate and successful in performing on the flute?
He assented.
And are not the scribes most fortunate in writing and reading letters?
Certainly.
Amid the dangers of the sea, again, are any more fortunate on the whole than wise pilots?
None, certainly.
And if you were engaged in war, in whose company would you rather take the risk — in company with a wise general, or with a foolish one?
With a wise one.
And if you were ill, whom would you rather have as a companion in a dangerous illness — a wise physician, or an ignorant one?
A wise one.
You think, I said, that to act with a wise man is more fortunate than to act with an ignorant one?
He assented.
Then wisdom always makes men fortunate: for by wisdom no man would ever err, and therefore he must act rightly and succeed, or his wisdom would be wisdom no longer.
We contrived at last somehow to agree in a general conclusion, that he who had wisdom had no need of fortune. I then recalled to his mind the previous state of the question. You remember, I said, our making the admission that we should be happy and fortunate if many good things were present with us?
He assented.
And should we be happy by reason of the presence of good things, if they profited us not, or if they profited us?
If they profited us, he said.
And would they profit us, if we only had them and did not use them? For example, if we had a great deal of food and did not eat, or a great deal of drink and did not drink, should we be profited?
Certainly not, he said. — *Euthydemus*, i. 181.
Wisdom through the touch.

—— How I wish, said Socrates, taking his place as he was desired, that wisdom could be infused by touch, out of the fuller into the emptier man, like water which is poured through wool out of a fuller vessel into an emptier one; in that case how much I should prize sitting by you! For you would have filled me full of much and beautiful wisdom, in comparison of which my own is of a very mean and questionable sort, no better than a dream; but yours is bright and only beginning, and was manifested forth in all the splendor of youth the day before yesterday, in the presence of more than thirty thousand Hellenes.

You are mocking, Socrates, said Agathon, and ere long you and I will have to settle who bears off the palm of wisdom. — *The Symposium*, i. 471.

Wise endurance. See *Courage*.
Wit, no bar to progress. See *Ridicule*, etc.
Wives, community of. See *Community*, etc.
Woman, only a lesser man.

—— Can you mention any pursuit of man in which the male sex has not all these qualities in a far higher degree than the female? Need I waste time in speaking of the art of weaving, and the management of pancakes and preserves, in which womankind does really appear to be great, and in which for her to be beaten is the most absurd of all things?

You are quite right, he replied, in maintaining the general inferiority of the female sex; at the same time many women are in many things superior to many men, though speaking generally, what you say is true.

And so, I said, my friend, in the administration of a State neither a woman as a woman, nor a man as a man has any special function, but the gifts of nature are equally diffused in both sexes; all the pursuits of men are the pursuits of women also, and in all of them a woman is only a weaker man.

Very true. — *The Republic*, ii. 280.
Woman, ambitious. See *Ambitious*, etc.
Women and war. See *War*.
Wonder is philosophic.

—— *Soc.* I see, my dear Theaetetus, that Theodorus had a true insight into your nature when he said that you were a philosopher, for wonder is the feeling of a philosopher and philosophy begins in wonder; he was not a bad genealogist who said that Iris, the messenger of heaven, is the child of Thaumas (wonder). — *Theaetetus*, iii. 356.

Words, a lie in, an imitation.

—— I do not comprehend you.

The reason is I replied, that you attribute some graud meaning to me; but I am only saying that deception, or being deceived or uninformed about realities in the highest faculty, which is the soul, and in that part of them to have and to hold the lie, is what mankind least like; — that, I say, is what they utterly detest.

There is nothing more hateful to them.

And, as I was just now remarking, this ignorance in the soul of him who is deceived may be called the true lie ; for the lie in words is only a kind of imitation and shadowy image of a previous affection of the soul, not pure unadulterated falsehood. Am I not right?

Perfectly right. — *The Republic*, ii. 205.

Words, opposition of. See *Contradiction*, etc.

World, future state of. See *Future state*, etc.

World, made immortal. See *Immortal*, etc.

Writing, and painting. See *Painting*.

Wrong-doing, disgrace of.

—— *Soc.* I certainly think that I and you and every man do really believe, that to do is a greater evil than to suffer injustice : and not to be punished than to be punished.

Pol. And I should say neither I nor any man; would you yourself, for example, suffer rather than do injustice?

Soc. Yes, and you, too; I or any man would.

Pol. Quite the reverse; neither you, nor I, nor any man.

Soc. But will you answer?

Pol. To be sure, I will ; for I am curious to hear what you are going to say.

Soc. Tell me, then, and you will know, and let us suppose that I am beginning at the beginning: — Which of the two, Polus, in your opinion, is the worst? — to do injustice or to suffer?

Pol. I should say that suffering was worst.

Soc. And which is the greater disgrace? — Answer.

Pol. To do. — *Gorgias*, iii. 61.

Wrong-doing, judgment for, to be sought.

—— *Soc.* To do wrong, then, is second only in the scale of evils ; but to do wrong and not to be punished, is first and greatest of all ?

Pol. That is true.

Soc. Well, and was not this the point in dispute, my friend? You deemed Archelaus happy, because he was a very great criminal and unpunished : I, on the other hand, maintained that he or any other who like him has done wrong and has not been punished, is and ought to be, the most miserable of all men ; and that the doer of injustice, whether Archelaus or any other, is more miserable than the sufferer ; and he who escapes punishment, more miserable than he who suffers. Was not that what I said?

Pol. Yes.

Soc. And that has been proved to be true?

Pol. Certainly.

Soc. Well, Polus, but if this is true, where is the great use of rhetoric? If we admit what has been just now said, every man ought in every way to guard himself against doing wrong, for he will thereby suffer great evil?

Pol. True.

Soc. And if he, or any one about whom he cares, does wrong, he ought of his own accord to go where he will be immediately punished; he will run to the judge, as he would to the physician, in order that the disease of injustice may not be rendered chronic and become the incurable cancer of the soul; must we not allow that, Polus, if our former admissions are to stand? and is there any other inference which is consistent with them?

Pol. To that, Socrates, there can be but one answer.

Soc. Then rhetoric is of no use to us, Polus, in helping a man to excuse his own injustice, or that of his parents or friends, or children or country ; but may be of use to any one who holds that instead of excusing he ought to accuse — himself above all, and in the next degree, his family, or any of his friends who may be doing wrong ; if he does not want to conceal, but to bring to light the iniquity, that the wrong-doer may suffer and be healed, and if he would force himself and others to stand firm, closing their eyes manfully, and letting the physician cut, as I may say, and burn them, in the hope of attaining the good and the honorable, not regarding the pain ; but if he have done things worthy of stripes, allowing himself to be scourged, or if of bonds to be bound, or if of a fine to be fined, or if of exile to be exiled, or if of death to die, and himself being the first to accuse himself, and his own relations, and using rhetoric to this end, that his and their just actions may be made manifest, and that they themselves may be delivered from injustice, which is the greatest evil. Then, Polus, rhetoric would indeed be useful. Do you say "Yes" or "No" to that?

Pol. To me, Socrates, what you are saying appears very strange, though probably in agreement with your premises.

Soc. Is not this the conclusion if the premises are not disproven?

Pol. Yes; that is true.

Soc. And from the opposite point of view of doing harm to some one, whether he be an enemy or not — I except the case in which I am myself suffering injury at the hands of another, for I must take precautions against that — but if my enemy injures a third person, then in every sort of way by word as well as deed, I should try to prevent his being punished, or appearing before the judge; and if he appears, I should contrive that he should escape, and not suffer punishment: if he has stolen a sum of money, let him keep and spend what he has stolen on him and his, regardless of religion and justice; and if he have done things worthy of death, let him not die, but rather be immortal in his wickedness; or, if this is not possible, let him at any rate be allowed to live as long as he can. — *Gorgias,* iii. 68.

Wrong-doing, responsibility and voluntariness in.

—— *Soc.* This appears to me to be the aim which a man ought to have, and towards which he ought to direct all the energies both of himself and of the State, acting so that he may have temperance and justice present with him and be happy, not suffering his lusts to be unrestrained, and in the never-ending desire to satisfy them leading a robber's life. Such an one is the friend neither of God nor man, for he is incapable of communion, and he who is incapable of communion is also incapable of friendship. And philosophers tell us, Callicles, that communion and friendship and orderliness and temperance and justice bind together heaven and earth and Gods and men, and that this universe is therefore called Cosmos or order, not disorder or misrule, my friend. But although you are a philosopher you seem to me never to have observed that geometrical equality is mighty, both among Gods and men; you think that you ought to cultivate inequality or excess, and do not care about geometry. Well, then, either the principle that the happy are made happy by the possession of justice and temperance, and the miserable miserable by the possession of vice, must be refuted, or, if it is granted, what will be the consequences? All the consequences which I drew before, Callicles, and about which you asked me whether I was in earnest when I said that a man ought to accuse himself and his son and his friend if he did anything wrong, and that to this end he should use his rhetoric — all these consequences are true. And that which you thought that Polus was led to admit out of modesty is also true, viz: that to do injustice, if more disgraceful than to suffer is in that degree worse; and the other position which according to Polus Gorgias admitted out of modesty, that he who would truly be a rhetorician ought to be just and have a knowledge of justice — has also turned out to be true. And now, let us proceed in the next place, to consider whether you are right in throwing in my teeth that I am unable to help myself or any of my friends or kinsmen, or to save them in the extremity of danger, or that I am like an outlaw to whom any one may do what he likes; he may box my ears, which was a brave saying of yours; or he may take away my goods or banish me, or even do his worst and kill me, and this, as you say, is the height of disgrace. My answer to you is one which has been already often repeated, but may as well be repeated once more. I tell you, Callicles, that to be boxed on the ears wrongfully is not the worst evil that can befall a man, nor to have my face and purse cut open, but that to smite and slay me and mine wrongfully is far more disgraceful and more evil; aye, and to despoil and enslave and pillage, or in any way at all to wrong me and mine, is far more disgraceful and evil to the doer of the wrong than to me who am the sufferer. These truths, which have been already set forth as I state them in the previous discussion, would seem now, if I may use an expression which is certainly bold, to have been fixed and riveted by us in iron and adamantine bonds; and unless you or some other still more enterprising hero shall break them, there is no possibility of denying what I say. For what I am always saying is, that I know not the truth about these things, and yet that I have never known anybody who could say anything else, any more than you can, and not be ridiculous. This has always been my position, and if this position is a true one, and if injustice is the greatest of evils to the doer of injustice, and yet there is if possible a greater than the greatest evils, in an unjust man not suffering retribution, what is that defense without which a man will be truly ridiculous? Must not the defense be one which will avert the greatest of human evils? And will not the worst of all defenses be that with which a man is unable to defend himself or his family or his friends? and next will come that which is unable to avert the next greatest evil; thirdly, that which is unable to avert the third greatest evil; and so of other evils. As is the greatness of evil so is the honor of being able to avert them in their several degrees, and the disgrace of not being able to avert them. Am I not right, Callicles?

Cal. Yes, quite right.

Soc. Seeing, then, that there are these two evils, the doing injustice and the suffering injustice, — and we affirm that to do injustice is a greater, and to suffer injustice a lesser evil, — how can a man succeed in obtaining the two advantages, the one of not doing and the other of not suffering injustice — must he have the power or only the will to obtain them? I mean whether a man will escape injustice if he has only the will to escape, or must he have provided himself with the power?

Cal. He must have provided himself with the power; that is clear.

Soc. And what do you say of doing injustice? Is the will only sufficient, and will that prevent him from doing injustice, or must he have provided himself with power and art; and if he have not studied and practiced will he be unjust still? Surely you might say, Callicles, whether you think that Polus and I were right in admitting to the conclusion that no one does wrong voluntarily, but that all do wrong against their will?

Cal. Granted, Socrates, if you will only have done. — *Gorgias*, iii. 99.

Wrong-doing. See *Injustice*.

Young men, training of.
Youth instructed in military arts. See *Military arts*.
—— You have never acquired the knowledge of the most beautiful kind of song in your military way of life, which is modeled after the camp, and is not like that of dwellers in cities; and you have your young men herding and feeding together like young colts. No one takes his own individual colt and drags him away from his fellows against his will, raging and foaming, and gives him a groom for him alone, and trains and rubs him down privately, and gives him the qualities in education which will make him not only a good soldier, but

also a governor of a state and of cities. Such an one, as we were saying at first, would be a greater warrior than he of whom Tyrtaeus sings; and he would honor courage everywhere, but always as the fourth, and not as the first part of virtue, either in individuals or States. — *Laws*, iv. 196.

Youth, philosophy in early. See *Philosophy*.

Youth to be tested by trial.

—— Therefore, as I was just now saying, we must inquire who are the best guardians of their own conviction that the interest of the State is to be the rule of all their actions. We must watch them from their youth upwards, and make them perform actions in which they are most likely to forget or to be deceived, and he who remembers and is not deceived is to be selected, and he who fails in the trial is to be rejected. That will be the way?

Yes.

And there should also be toils and pains and conflicts prescribed for them, in which they will give further proof of the same qualities.

Very right, he replied.

And then, I said, we must try them with enchantments — that is the third sort of test — and see what will be their behavior: like those who take colts amid noises and cries to see if they are of a timid nature, so must we take our youth amid terrors of some kind, and again pass them into pleasures, and try them more thoroughly than gold is tried in the fire, in order to discover whether they are armed against all enchantments, and of a noble bearing always, good guardians of themselves and of the music which they have learned, and retaining under all circumstances a rhythmical and harmonious nature, such as will be most serviceable to the man himself and to the State. And he who at every age, as boy and youth and in mature life, has come out of the trial victorious and pure, shall be appointed a ruler and guardian of the State; he shall be honored in life and death, and shall receive sepulture and other memorials of honor, the greatest that we have to give. — *The Republic*, ii. 238.

Youth, the avaricious. See *Miserly men*.

Youth, self-conceit of. See *Self-conceit*.

Youthful genius. See *Genius*, etc.

Youth and children, education of. See *Children*, etc.

—— *Ath.* Let me once more recall our doctrine of right education; which, if I am not mistaken, depends on the due regulation of convivial intercourse.

Cle. You talk rather grandly.

Ath. Pleasure and pain I maintain to be the first perceptions of children, and I say that they are the forms under which virtue and vice are originally present to them. As to wisdom and true and fixed opinions, happy is the man who acquires them, when declining in years; and he who possesses them, and the blessings which are contained in them, is a perfect man. Now, I mean by education that training which is given by suitable habits to the first instincts of virtue in children; when pleasure, and friendship, and pain, and hatred, are rightly implanted in souls not yet capable of understanding the nature of them, and who find them, after they have attained reason, to be in harmony with her. This harmony of the soul, when perfected, is virtue; but the particular training in respect of pleasure and pain, which leads you always to hate what you ought to hate, and love what you ought to love, from the beginning to the end, may be separated off; and, in my view, will be rightly called education.

Cle. I think, Stranger, that you are quite right in all that you have said and are saying about education.

Ath. I am glad to hear that you agree with me; for, indeed, the true discipline of pleasure and pain which, when rightly ordered, is a principle of education, has been often relaxed and corrupted in human life. And the Gods, pitying the toils which our race is born to undergo, have appointed holy festivals, in which men alternate rest with labor; and have given them the Muses, and Apollo the leader of the Muses, and Dionysus, as the partners in their revels, that they may improve what education they have, at the festivals of the Gods, and by their aid. I should like to know whether a common saying is true to nature or not. For what men say is that the young of all creatures cannot be quiet in their bodies or in their voices; they are always wanting to move, and cry out; at one time leaping and skipping, and overflowing with sportiveness and delight at something, and then again uttering all sorts of cries. But, whereas other animals have no perception of order or disorder in their movements, that is, of rhythm or harmony, as they are called, to us, the Gods, who, as we say, have been appointed to be our partners in the dance, have given the pleasurable sense of harmony and rhythm. . . . .

Ath. The inference at which we arrive for the third or fourth time is, that education is the constraining and directing of youth towards that right reason, which the law affirms, and which the experience of the best of our elders has agreed to be truly right. In order, then, that the soul of the child may not be habituated to feel joy and sorrow in a manner at variance with the law, and those who obey the law, but may rather follow the law and rejoice and sorrow at the same things as the aged, — in order, I say, to produce this effect, songs appear to have been invented, which are really charms, and are designed to implant the harmony of which we speak. And because the mind of the child is incapable of enduring serious training, they are called plays or songs, and are performed in play; just as when men are sick and ailing in their bodies, their attendants give them wholesome diet in pleasant meats and drinks, but unwholesome diet disagreeable in things, in order that they may learn as they ought, to like the one and to dislike the other. — *Laws,* iv. 182.

Zeal right and wrong.

—— *Soc.* Dear Crito, your zeal is invaluable, if a right one; but if wrong, the greater the zeal the greater the danger; and therefore we ought to consider whether I shall or shall not do as you say. For I am and always have been one of those natures who must be guided by reason, whatever the reason may be which upon reflection appears to me to be the best; and now that this fortune has come upon me, I cannot put away the conclusion at which I had arrived: the principles which I have hitherto honored and revered I still honor, and unless we can at once find other and better principles I am certain not to agree with you; no, not even if the power of the multitude could inflict many more imprisonments, confiscations, deaths, frightening us like children with hobgoblin terrors. — *Crito,* i. 350.

B. 19a

www.ingramcontent.com/pod-product-compliance
Lightning Source LLC
Chambersburg PA
CBHW051858300426
44117CB00006B/445